COMPLETE BOOK OF
1990
BASEBALL
CARDS

Louis Weber, C.E.O.
Publications International, Ltd.
7373 North Cicero Avenue
Lincolnwood, Illinois 60646

ISBN 0-517-01997-3

Contributing writer: Tom Owens.
Special thanks to Steve Gold/AU Sports Memorabilia, Skokie, Illinois.

Photo credits: ALLSPORT USA: John Cordes, p. 4; Stephen Dunn, pp. 10 (bottom), 12; Otto Greule Jr., p. 7; Joe Patronite, p. 10 (top); J. Rettaliata, p. 9; Bob Rosato, p. 8; Kirk Schlea, pp. 6, 13; Rick Stewart, p. 11 (top).

This edition published by Beekman House, Distributed by Crown Publishers, Inc., 225 Park Avenue South, New York, New York 10003

Beekman House

CONTENTS

Will Clark

BATTER UP!

Baseball card collecting, one of the hottest trends of the 1980s, will be an accepted tradition in the 1990s. Fans of all ages have discovered that baseball cards provide a great way to appreciate the sport of baseball.

One of the best ways to appreciate this ever-growing hobby is through the *Complete Book of 1990 Baseball Cards.* This volume is an innovative step in the hobby. To help you prepare for the upcoming season, you will have in-depth profiles for more than 600 different players who could be key performers for their 1990 teams. Each player's newest baseball cards are shown in color, giving every fan an early, low-cost preview of the best possible hobby investments.

Everyone can benefit from *Complete Book of 1990 Baseball Cards.* Even the most casual followers of baseball will want to investigate the statistics to help predict the top clubs and stars of 1990. For the first time, the minor league statistics are available for those young players who have not received enough major league experience on which to support investment strategy. Readers will find Triple-A (AAA), Double-A (AA), or Class-A (A) stats for selected players. Collectors will value the expert investment advice for each player's cards. Each profile has a rating of the best 1990 card. We've used several criteria to rate the cards, including the technical quality, aesthetics, and composition of the photo; integration of the photo into the card design; and the presentation of information on the back of the card. Hobbyists should take these factors into account when ranking the 1990 cards.

What can collectors expect from the 1990 season? For starters, more cards than ever before will be available. Score was the first company to announce an expanded set for 1990. After producing 660-card sets for its first two years as a card competitor, Score's 1990 offering will be 704 cards. The new ownership in Fleer might mean some exciting changes from past sets, which have been 660-cards. Donruss, which has issued 660-card sets in the past, may follow suit. Topps, the senior citizen on the hobby block, plans on a 792-card set. These four sets, which have been the most popular collecting and investing choices for several years, will be the primary focus of this book.

Upper Deck provided the major hobby news of the baseball card season. The company issued its first set in 1989, saying that it issues the highest of quality cards. Upper Deck cards boasted glossy fronts on heavy-duty cardboard, thicker than other card stocks. Each card back contained an additional color photo. A counterfeit-proof aspect was added to each card by way of a tiny hologram marking. The company never tried to underprice other card makers. Instead, a 15-card package had an original retail price of 89 cents. Soon, even major retailers sensed great demand and hiked package prices to $1.25 and higher.

Proceed slowly in assessing the multitude of cards produced in 1990. Sets from so many different manufacturers may sound great, but collectors unable to afford every new issue need some preliminary knowledge of which cards will be the best possible investments.

The three-dimensional Sportflics cards will return, but they haven't been accepted as a mainstream collectible yet. All of the companies previously mentioned are sure to issue supplementary sets, including autumn-released subsets of traded players and rookies. But, in most cases, these sets aren't as popular as the larger sets, partially because many "traded" sets are sold only through hobby dealers (instead of publicly, in convenience stores and other retail outlets). Also, Topps and Fleer are likely to continue production of 33- and 44-card boxed sets of superstar players. Nevertheless, players with favorable reviews in this book would be the best investments in such sets.

The booming baseball card hobby can be fun and profitable for any educated collector. In the 1960s and early '70s, collectors paid little attention to individual players. Getting "one of everyone" in complete set form was the standard goal in the hobby. Star and rookie cards weren't recognized as separate realms of collecting. Now, the hobby has exploded. Baseball cards are marketed in specialty shops and large conventions which often draw more than 10,000 collectors a day. Baseball cards are a new investment commodity, right beside stocks and bonds or gold and silver.

Jerome Walton

That's why the information in this book is so important. Anyone can become a successful collector or investor with only a little effort. With only a small budget, it's possible to build an impressive collection or investment portfolio. Remember, those high-priced star cards of today once could be bought for only a few cents.

The principle of supply and demand determines the market prices of cards for individual players. When certain cards are available to the collecting public in smaller quantities, the prices for all of those cards will increase. In 1989, Upper Deck's high-number series (from 701 to 800) was produced in midseason to reflect team personnel changes. Although these cards were issued in some foil packs, many retail outlets were still selling first-series cards and didn't bother reordering new material. Therefore, even a card of a common player from that series is worth one-third more than any of the first 700 cards.

Ordinarily, a collector has an equal chance of acquiring any card when purchasing a pack from the candy store. Although all major card companies keep their production numbers a closely guarded secret, it's assumed that equal numbers of all cards are printed. The only difference between the card of an All-Star and a benchwarmer is popularity. Therefore, the usual card supply of superstars like Don Mattingly and Will Clark can't satisfy their millions of fans. When that happens, the prices increase.

Baseball cards are sold in several types of packages. The best-known wax pack (sold in a waxy wrapper) has sold for 45 cents in the past, although a nickel price increase is predicted for the near future. Anywhere from 15 to 17 cards come in each package.

It's inaccurate to call all baseball cards "bubblegum cards," because Topps is the only manufacturer who includes gum in each pack. Fleer includes a team logo sticker in each pack, Score offers a 3-D trivia card, Donruss offers three jigsaw puzzle pieces, and Upper Deck has created a small hologram team sticker. Upper Deck and Fleer have stayed a step ahead of the competition by marketing

Rickey Henderson

of cellos. Keep each opened pack in its original order and jot down the numerical sequences. Then, by seeing the top and bottom cards on future packs, it'll be possible to estimate the middle cards in the package.

This system works best with rack packs, packages of three cellophane pockets of cards which are displayed vertically on store racks. Rack packs will reveal six cards in the pack, three top and bottom cards. Remember that different collating methods will be used for rack packs and cellos, but the code-cracking procedure works the same. Unlike wax or cello packs, it's highly unlikely that a rack pack can be tampered with and resealed. Never buy entire boxes of packs without opening a couple of test packages beforehand to see if the assortment is reasonable. Deal with dealers you know and trust when buying assortments of cards.

Buying complete sets of cards isn't so convenient when a collector wants to speculate on individual cards. A complete set will guarantee you one of every card, but no more than 200 of those individual cards will ever have any potential investment value. Sometimes, complete sets may seem easier to obtain than individual packages. For instance, large retail outlets have offered complete sets of 1989 baseball cards from many manufacturers. These complete sets were collated at the card factory. Fewer large retail markets offered smaller wax packs.

Ironically, the prices of these sets can be substantially lower than what hobby dealers demand. The 1989 Bowman set (produced by Topps) is a good example. Dealers wanted $25 to $30 for the set during the summer. Factory-collated sets began appearing in September and prices nosedived. Some retailers marked the sets down to $20. These factory sets don't always stay on the shelves long. Some desperate dealers rush to retail stores and buy out inventories in hopes of reselling them at profits.

None of the card assortments will offer any investment advantages unless a hobbyist takes calculated gambles. Study the sports pages just like a Wall Street tycoon would

their cards in tamper-proof containers. Upper Deck has a foil pack and Score uses a poly-pack. These wrappers have to be torn open, and cannot be discreetly resealed. This prevents others from tampering with the selection of cards inside and resealing the pack, as has happened with wax packs in the past.

Wax packs are sold 36 to the box. It's possible to get discounts on wax pack boxes from dealers. Also companies will use sales incentives like cards printed on wax pack boxes or special card inserts available only in selected wax packs.

Every company except Upper Deck has offered economy packs known as "cellos" (for the cellophane package wrapping). You'll get a larger number of cards for a lower per-unit price than wax packs. Collectors can get sneak peaks at cards through the see-through packaging, often getting to view the identities of both the top and bottom cards in the pack. Also, it's sometimes possible to predict the cards in the middle of packages by cracking the company's "code." Because the cards in cello packs are mechanically collated, it's possible to detect the sorting patterns after studying a couple of boxes worth

Tom Gordon

scan the stock market section of the newspaper. Follow the long-term progress of players who might be good card investments. Even players with average abilities may be great card investments if they get a lot of publicity. Managers like Whitey Herzog and Sparky Anderson were mediocre players during their careers in the 1950s. However, their older cards are popular now because of their famous second careers. Also, off-the-field news can help influence card values. Colorful sports announcers like Joe Garagiola and Bob Uecker have hotly pursued cards from their playing days in the 1950s and '60s. Look for daily clues from the media to determine who might be tomorrow's superstars.

More insight into individual players can be found in various baseball magazines. This type of publication may take deeper looks into a player's career and rank him against his contemporaries and other accomplished players from baseball's past. During the pre-season, a flood of baseball magazines will be found on newsstands. These once-a-year publications will include team-by-team scouting reports, and will try to forecast the future of many newcomers.

Don't think that an investor should monitor only the major leagues. Each year, several unknown faces will debut with many clubs. Informed hobbyists will be acquainted with each rookie's collegiate and minor league record to know what potential each young player holds. College career information and minor league stats are included for many young players in this publication.

Hobby-oriented newspapers and magazines can be helpful, too. Many collectors will guard their investment strategies, but clues to top investments can be gathered from various advertisements. After pitcher Gregg Olson was named American League Rookie of the Year, numerous collectors began seeking his cards. However, smart investors socked away Olson cards when he helped the Baltimore Orioles climb into the pennant race. When he won his award, his card prices naturally soared. Some investors made a handsome profit. Looking at both the buying and selling ads helped determine a standard market price for his cards. Some hobby papers provide regular price guides which supposedly monitor price increases in certain cards. These guides are of only limited use, however. They seldom account for regional interest in cards. Wisconsin fans, for instance, might have to pay area dealers more for cards of Milwaukee Brewer heroes Robin Yount and Paul Molitor.

Collectors and investors can obtain cards from numerous sources these days. Retail stores are obvious starting places. Hobby stores, which are popping up in large and small communities across the nation, cater strictly to the collector and will offer more options. Either a hobby store, a mail-order hobby dealer, or a dealer at a baseball card convention will sell individual cards. Expect any kind of hobby dealer to want a profit on his cards, due to his labor and other expenses. It's safe to assume that 1990 cards of nondescript players will start selling at prices of 3 to 5 cents each. (Upper Deck commons, however, will sell for 7 to 10 cents each.)

Gregg Olson

Many dealers sell their cards by mail. This is a good alternative for collectors living far away from hobby stores or conventions. The only drawback here is postage and handling costs, along with not seeing the merchandise beforehand.

When you decide what sources you'll use to obtain individual cards, it's time to make a want list. This preparation can be valuable. Make a simple list which details which cards you want to speculate on, how many cards of each player you want to invest in, and how much you want to pay. Being focused on a goal helps avoid making needless impulse buys, and your research will win you respect from dealers you meet. Giving the impression that you can't be fooled may win you a better deal with a dealer.

Think about how committed you'll be to your investments. If you find a promising player who has 1989 cards selling at 3 cents, it would be easy to invest in a couple hundred cards. However, trying to buy 200 cards of Jose Canseco might be an expensive proposition. You'll find that a few dealers will mar-

ket 1990 cards of individual players in lots of 25, 50, and 100 cards. Buying large quantities of certain players will get you better discounts.

If you've acquired a few thousand 1989 cards looking for certain players, you may have lots of trading material. When trading, consult price guides first to know current market values. Don't expect a dealer to trade you for the full estimated value of your cards. Dealers are trying to make money on every transaction, and they may give you only 25 to 50 percent of a card's worth.

Newcomers to the hobby may wonder how investors actually make money with their cards. It's easy to open a price guide and appraise your own hoard of cards for a certain value. However, getting actual money for those cards would be another matter.

The first tip smart investors pass along is not to be greedy. Suppose one of your card investments gains 10 cents in value only a week after you made your move. It's easy, but

Nolan Ryan

perhaps foolish to believe that the card will be worth a dollar more in 10 weeks. Card values change as fast as the stock market. A prolonged slump, career-ending injury or numerous personal problems may quickly erase all value that player's card has gained. Does that mean to sell your entire investment stock fast?

Not really. Such a method would become too predictable, and wouldn't bring much profit. Instead, try a saner approach. Suppose you've invested $5 in 100 nickel cards of a certain player. When you notice that his cards are worth a dime, you could sell off half your supply to regain your initial investment. Then, if your dreams come true and the card becomes a $2 item by season's end, you still have 50 cards to strike it rich with.

When selling, remember the comments about trading with dealers will apply to selling, too. In most cases, dealers have the expenses of advertising, traveling to weekend shows, or running a shop to cope with. Their usual way of covering those expenses is to make at least 50 percent on any transaction. Excep-

tions to this include pressing needs for certain cards. After any World Series, many dealers will want to build up their inventory of cards from the winning team.

Selling in the fall, directly after a World Series can be a profitable move. Everyone on a World Championship team gets added respect, which translates to higher card prices. It might be wise to sell those cards before spring, when that same team could wind up in last place. Cards of postseason award winners, such as Cy Young Award winners or Most Valuable Players, see dramatic upswings in their card values immediately after they earn their awards. Keep in mind that regional interest can benefit you when selling cards. East Coast collectors quite likely would pay much more for cards of any New York Met or Yankee player.

The only investment-worthy card in the 1980s is a Mint one. Today's picky dealers and collectors won't accept anything less. Just because the card is fresh out of a wax pack, don't think it's Mint. The hobby's grading standards (which vary in definition slightly with different collector publications) classify Mint cards as one with four square, sharp corners. All the major companies have these problems occasionally. Because millions of cards are produced yearly, the quality suffers occasionally. Cards like these, although

Tony Gwynn

unharmed by any human hands, are still considered less valuable than a pristine specimen. Rounded edges are a major danger for any card intended for resale.

Any other minor printing flaw — such as gum stains, ink streaks, or paper creases — will lower the value and grade of the card as well. Collectors expect Mint cards to have well-focused photographs, free of the any imperfections. A Mint card has a well-centered photo, so that all the borders seem equal in width. Again, this is a flaw which occurs before the card is shipped out of the factory, so collectors should be aware of this problem when buying singles.

Ordinarily, it's a relatively easy process to grade a card, if you know what you're looking for. However, when you buy a handmade assortment of cards from a dealer, don't assume the cards are all Mint. It's easy to accidentally or purposely stick a few battered cards in the middle of a Mint stack which is being sold in a plastic container. Likewise, if you're going to buy just one star card which is housed in a plastic protector, it's best to see the card up close, out of its container.

Robin Yount

Bret Saberhagen

Dealers unwilling to accommodate serious buyers don't deserve your business. Cards with even some of these minor flaws can lose more than one-third of their value instantly.

When the cards you obtained pass your scrutiny and indeed look Mint, you're ready to preserve your acquisitions. A variety of durable plastic cases are available in hobby publications or from dealers to keep those Mint cards Mint. Get a container which keeps cards tightly enclosed, so your investments don't slop around and deteriorate over time. Don't make the age-old mistakes youngsters made decades ago. Keeping cards stored loosely in a shoebox, or tightly trussed up in rubber bands can destroy cards quickly.

How do you handle the sale of a card of a future Hall of Famer? Very carefully! Some superstars will keep climbing in value forever. Unless you truly need the cash, reconsider your sale. Nolan Ryan is a sure bet for the Hall of Fame. Cards from his playing career will always be big sellers. Their values may never level off. You won't see big gains, but the gains will be consistent.

Mark Davis

"Star" cards, cards of veteran players at a crossroads in their careers, are tougher calls to make. If a player over age 30 has his first great season in his career, you may want to move quickly for a short-term profit. Try to project the long-term success of a sudden star. Was his success a one-time affair? Can he last another decade? Could he succeed with a lower-quality club? Will his lifetime stats remain memorable, or perhaps earn him a spot in the Hall of Fame? If a player's future seems shaky, sell while there is still marginal interest in his card.

A pitcher may prove the most baffling card investment. Many hurlers may have pitched up to four years in college and possibly a few more seasons in the minors before making a major league debut. Several pitchers each year are permanently sidelined by arm injuries, simply because they've been active for so long. Unlike hitters who can succeed anywhere, a great pitcher is helpless without a competent team behind him.

Another sometimes-befuddling area is with rookie cards. In the past, investors have been stuck with hundreds of cards of J.R. Richard, Mark Fidrych, or Ron Kittle, three electrifying rookies who never lived up to their initial billings. These cards, once big sellers, now are only lukewarm in popularity. Cautious investors unwilling to take modest profits missed out on any real gains. However, many rookie cards keep appreciating in value. The two most popular rookie cards in 1989 were those of Tom Gordon and Ken Griffey, Jr. Both neared the $4 mark by World Series time. Those cards could double in price if both men have successful sophomore seasons. If you've recovered your initial investment on an assortment of one player's cards with a partial sale, go ahead and be daring with the remainder. Generally, though, investors feel that tripling your investment is good enough. The final decision rests with your sense of adventure.

Don't despair, though, if one of your investments starts losing some of its appraised value. An example of this is Kevin Mitchell. His initial rookie cards appeared in 1986, when he was a New York Mets rookie. Mitchell's cards floundered when he was traded to the San Diego Padres. However, when Mitchell became the leading homer and RBI man in the majors for 1989, patient investors got a big reward. His 1986 Fleer card is now an $8 item.

If the 1989 season was any indication of things to come, the 1990 campaign should bring more excitement to all fans. Last season in the American League, the Oakland Athletics looked like a future dynasty by dominating the entire American League with more than 100 wins for the second straight year. Pitcher Dave Stewart won 20 games for his third straight season. Speedster Rickey Henderson returned to put on a dazzling postseason offensive show, in hopes that he could land a $3 million salary for 1990.

In the other division, the upstart Toronto Blue Jays won their pennant on the final weekend of the season against the favored Baltimore Orioles. Toronto's top winner earned just 13 victories, but their offense was buoyed by A.L. homer champion Fred McGriff, tops in the junior circuit with 36 round-trippers.

Over in the National League, the Chicago Cubs and San Francisco Giants gained the spotlight. Chicago battled the Cardinals into the last week of the season, while the Giants edged the Padres only a few days earlier. For the Cubs, N.L. Rookie of the Year Jerome Walton stole the show as a dependable center fielder. Mitch "Wild Thing" Williams made an impressive debut in the National League and gave the Cubs a strong stopper in the bullpen.

San Francisco was more dominant in its division. Mitchell and Will Clark both topped 100 RBI, becoming baseball's toughest one-two punch. Clark battled San Diego's Tony Gwynn for the batting title down to the final days of the season before Gwynn won the crown by just three percentage points. The Padres owned the strongest reliever in baseball in Mark Davis. Davis had a Cy Young Award-winning season, pacing both leagues with 44 saves.

The excitement of baseball only partially explains the enormous appeal of baseball cards. Ever since baseball cards made their debut in packages of cigarettes more than 100 years ago, someone somewhere has wanted to collect these unique slabs of cardboard. Since then, baseball cards have been premiums in a variety of products, ranging from breakfast cereal to hot dogs to dog food.

Perhaps collectors see a deeper-than-money value in baseball cards. These tiny squares, with dazzling photography, detailed statistics and condensed biographies, give detailed insight into a player's career. Baseball cards capture moments in time and preserve the history of the sport. Any true baseball fan, both young and old, can appreciate this.

The most important element in collecting or investing in baseball cards is enjoyment. Either activity can be a low-cost pastime. You can earn big dividends with some investments, but your losses don't have to be great if you invest wisely. So be daring, but don't forget to have fun in your hobby pursuits.

Good luck!

Kevin Mitchell

JIM ABBOTT

	W	L	ERA	G	CG	IP	H	ER	BB	SO
1989	12	12	3.92	29	4	181	190	79	74	115
Life	12	12	3.92	29	4	181	190	79	74	115

Position: Pitcher
Team: California Angels
Born: September 19, 1967 Flint, MI
Height: 6'3" **Weight:** 200 lbs.
Bats: Left **Throws:** Left
Acquired: First-round pick in 6/88
        free-agent draft

Abbott disproved the theory that young players need to spend time in the minors by moving directly from the University of Michigan to California. The Angels originally planned to start his career in 1989 with a stint in Double-A, but those plans were scrapped once he won a job in spring training. His win total made him the team's most prosperous rookie hurler since Frank Tanana debuted in 1974. Abbott pitched the USA baseball team to a gold medal in the 1988 Olympics. His complete-game effort downed Japan in the championship 5-3.

Despite his rookie success, Abbott has only one year of professional experience to his credit. Expect his 1990 cards to open at 50 cents or more, a price which seems risky for such an inexperienced hurler. Our pick for his best 1990 card is Topps.

JIM ACKER

	W	L	ERA	G	SV	IP	H	ER	BB	SO
1989	2	1	1.59	14	0	28	24	5	12	24
Life	26	34	3.96	280	6	595	609	262	229	305

Position: Pitcher
Team: Toronto Blue Jays
Born: September 24, 1958 Freer, TX
Height: 6'2" **Weight:** 212 lbs.
Bats: Right **Throws:** Right
Acquired: Traded from Braves for
        Tony Castillo and
        Francisco Cabrera, 8/89

One key trade that helped the 1989 Blue Jays to an A.L. East pennant was the acquisition of Acker. Although he spent less than a month with the Blue Jays, he became a successful set-up man for Toronto's Tom Henke. Acker's ERA was less than half of his previous best effort, a 3.23 mark with Toronto in 1985. He has bounced between the Toronto and the Atlanta organizations three times. Acker compiled a career-best record of 7-2 in 1985. The Blue Jays traded Acker to Atlanta in 1986, and although he amassed a career high of 14 saves in 1987, he had to attend the 1989 spring camp as a nonroster invitee. With his recent turnaround in Toronto, Acker should have more job security in 1990.

Wait until Acker succeeds in a full season before buying his common-priced 1990 cards. Our pick for his best 1990 card is Donruss.

JUAN AGOSTO

	W	L	ERA	G	SV	IP	H	ER	BB	SO
1989	4	5	2.93	71	1	83	81	27	32	46
Life	24	18	3.47	344	23	392	382	151	158	195

Position: Pitcher
Team: Houston Astros
Born: February 23, 1958
      Rio Piedras, Puerto Rico
Height: 6'2" **Weight:** 190 lbs.
Bats: Left **Throws:** Left
Acquired: Signed as a free agent, 4/87

Agosto's 1989 season was one of the busiest for any N.L. reliever. The Astros lefty appeared in 71 games, tying for fourth in the league. His workload wasn't as stiff as the 1988 burden he carried, however. During his first full season with Houston, he appeared in 75 games, a new Astro record. He set another team mark with ten consecutive wins, which was tops in the senior circuit. During his record-setting year, Agosto was unscored upon in 56 of his outings. He began his pro career at age 16 in the Boston organization, but was released in late 1978 with arm problems. After stints with the White Sox and Twins, Agosto became a vital part of the Astros staff.

    Normally, only cards of closers are investment-worthy, so wait on investing in Agosto's 1990 commons. Our pick for his best 1990 card is Donruss.

RICK AGUILERA

	W	L	ERA	G	CG	IP	H	ER	BB	SO
1989	3	5	3.21	11	3	75	71	27	17	57
Life	34	26	3.71	89	8	478	487	197	133	328

Position: Pitcher
Team: Minnesota Twins
Born: December 31, 1961 San Gabriel, CA
Height: 6'5" **Weight:** 200 lbs.
Bats: Right **Throws:** Right
Acquired: Traded from Mets with David
      West, Kevin Tapani, and Tim
      Drummond for Frank Viola, 8/89

Filling in for a Cy Young winner can be difficult, but Aguilera made the most of the opportunity with the 1989 Twins. He was the most experienced hurler sent from New York as part of the package for Frank Viola. With Minnesota, Aguilera registered the finest ERA (3.21) of his five-year major league career. He worked in just 11 games in 1988 because he was sidelined by right elbow surgery. In 1987, he posted a seven-game winning streak en route to a career-high 11-3 season. Aguilera went 10-7 in 1986 and sparkled in postseason play. He hurled five scoreless innings in the N.L.C.S., then gained the win in the sixth game of the World Series.

    Aguilera may become one of the Twins biggest winners, making his common-priced 1990 cards tempting investments. Our pick for his best 1990 card is Topps.

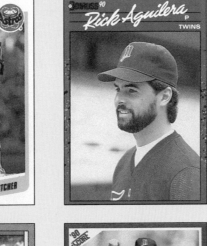
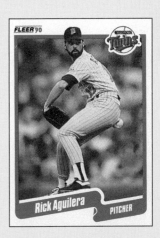

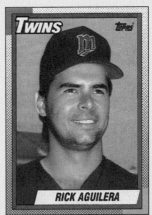

DOYLE ALEXANDER

	W	L	ERA	G	CG	IP	H	ER	BB	SO
1989	6	18	4.44	33	5	223	245	110	76	95
Life	194	174	3.76	561	98	3366	3376	1406	978	1528

Position: Pitcher
Team: Detroit Tigers
Born: September 4, 1950 Cordova, AL
Height: 6'3" **Weight:** 200 lbs.
Bats: Right **Throws:** Right
Acquired: Traded from Braves for
John Smoltz, 8/87

Alexander owned one of the American League's worst won-lost records in 1989. However, he toiled for the Tigers, a team which lost 103 times (the most in baseball). Previously, Alexander had won in double figures every year since 1984. This well-traveled veteran began his pro career in 1968, and made his big league debut with the Dodgers in 1971. Since then, his career has involved nine different stops in the majors. Of his 3,000-plus innings of work, he's been a reliever in more than 100 games. Nevertheless, Alexander is one of just six pitchers in history to own wins against all 26 teams.

Quite likely, Alexander will break the 200-win barrier in '90. Don't expect his 1990 cards to be worth more than a nickel, unless he becomes part of a World Series squad. Our pick for his best 1990 card is Donruss.

ANDY ALLANSON

	BA	G	AB	R	H	2B	3B	HR	RBI	SB
1989	.232	111	323	30	75	9	1	3	17	4
Life	.246	395	1204	121	296	33	4	12	112	20

Position: Catcher
Team: Cleveland Indians
Born: December 22, 1961 Richmond, VA
Height: 6'5" **Weight:** 225 lbs.
Bats: Right **Throws:** Right
Acquired: Second-round pick in 6/83
free-agent draft

Allanson spent his second consecutive season as the Indians starting catcher in 1989. His numbers were consistently down from his 1988 production, when he caught a league-high 133 games. His five homers and 50 RBI that season were career highs. Defensively, he topped the junior circuit in putouts, total chances, and double plays in 1988. During his 1986 rookie season, Allanson stole ten bases, the most of any Indians catcher in the last 50 years. His first major league homer was the first round-tripper of his entire professional career, ending a wait of 1,025 at-bats in the minors and the bigs. Because the Indians value his steady glove-work, Allanson should be an active member of the Tribe in 1990.

Until Allanson begins to hit forcefully, his 1990 cards will never be worth their commons prices of 3 cents or less. Our pick for his best 1990 card is Score.

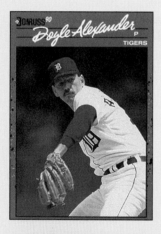
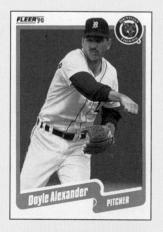
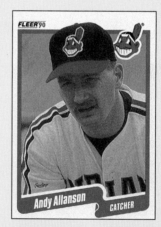

ROBERTO ALOMAR

	BA	G	AB	R	H	2B	3B	HR	RBI	SB
1989	.295	158	623	82	184	27	1	7	56	42
Life	.282	301	1168	166	329	51	7	16	97	66

Position: Second base
Team: San Diego Padres
Born: February 5, 1968
        Ponce, Puerto Rico
Height: 6'   **Weight:** 155 lbs.
Bats: Both   **Throws:** Right
Acquired: Signed as a free agent, 2/85

Alomar beat the sophomore jinx with a solid season at second base for the 1989 Padres. After a respectable rookie season in 1988, he achieved new highs in virtually every category during '89. He led the team in stolen bases (42) and tied with Tony Gwynn for top spot in games played (158) and doubles (27). Alomar's average (.295) was third among Padres regulars. His big league debut came April 22, 1988, and was highlighted by a single off Nolan Ryan in his first at-bat. Alomar's stardom seemed inevitable after 1986, when he hit a league-leading .346 at Class-A Reno.

After getting rookie cards from all sets in 1989, Alomar's 1990 offerings should be more affordable. His cards would be a good investment at any price. However, smart speculators will try to pay a dime or less per card. Our pick for his best 1990 card is Fleer.

SANDY ALOMAR

	BA	G	AB	R	H	2B	3B	HR	RBI	SB
89 AAA	.306	131	523	88	160	33	8	13	101	3
89 Major	.211	7	19	1	4	1	0	1	6	0

Position: Catcher
Team: San Diego Padres
Born: June 18, 1966   Salinas, Puerto Rico
Height: 6'5"   **Weight:** 200 lbs.
Bats: Right   **Throws:** Right
Acquired: Signed as a free agent, 10/83

The son of Padres coach Sandy Alomar and brother of Padres second baseman Roberto, Sandy Alomar Jr. is one of baseball's brightest rookies. The catcher remained stuck for a second year at Triple-A in 1989. His biggest obstacle in reaching the majors is Padres catcher Benito Santiago. In 1988, Alomar's first year at Triple-A Las Vegas, he batted .297 with 16 homers and 71 RBI, despite missing nearly a month with a knee injury. He was a starting catcher in the Triple-A All-Star game that year. He has all the assets needed to play in the majors. All Alomar needs is a starting position.

Being named the 1989 Minor League Player of the Year by *Baseball America* gives Alomar's 1990 cards more appeal. Stock up if you find his cards at 35 cents or less. Our pick for his best 1990 card is Score.

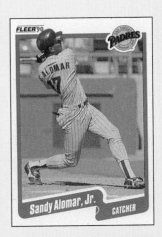

LARRY ANDERSEN

	W	L	ERA	G	SV	IP	H	ER	BB	SO
1989	4	4	1.55	60	3	87	63	15	24	85
Life	27	28	3.34	469	27	723	701	268	227	496

Position: Pitcher
Team: Houston Astros
Born: May 6, 1953 Portland, OR
Height: 6'3" **Weight:** 205 lbs.
Bats: Right **Throws:** Right
Acquired: Signed as a free agent, 5/86

Andersen registered a career-best ERA while in the Astros bullpen in 1989, tallying nearly one strikeout per inning pitched. The Astros have kept him busy during the last three seasons; he has averaged 60 appearances yearly. Houston discovered him in 1986, just two days after the Phillies released him. Signing him to a free-agent contract provided an immediate boost to the club's bullpen. Andersen started his pro career in 1971, and first reached the majors with the 1975 Indians. In 469 major league appearances, he started just one game. Andersen will play his 20th professional season in 1990.

Although Andersen's 1990 commons will not see short-term price gains, his cards are long-shot investments. When Andersen retires, he could become the next Bob Uecker. Andersen is well liked by the media for his wacky personality and humor. Our pick for his best 1990 card is Donruss.

ALLAN ANDERSON

	W	L	ERA	G	CG	IP	H	ER	BB	SO
1989	17	10	3.81	33	4	196	214	83	53	169
Life	37	25	3.73	88	8	495	539	205	130	206

Position: Pitcher
Team: Minnesota Twins
Born: January 7, 1964 Lancaster, OH
Height: 6' **Weight:** 194 lbs.
Bats: Left **Throws:** Left
Acquired: Second-round pick in 6/82
free-agent draft

When the Minnesota Twins traded pitching ace Frank Viola in mid-1989, they looked to Anderson to serve as the team's senior starter. On the surface, he seemed like an unlikely choice: although Anderson debuted with the Twins in late 1986, he hadn't spent a full season in the majors prior to 1989. However, he responded to the added pressure beautifully, leading the 1989 club in virtually every pitching category. He bested his 1988 record of 16-9, although he didn't come close to his league-leading 2.45 ERA. Anderson's 1988 accomplishment marked the first time a Twins pitcher paced the junior circuit in ERA.

With Viola gone, Anderson becomes the cornerstone of the Twins' staff. Scoop up his 1990 cards at a dime apiece. Those prices will seem paltry if Anderson is the team's next Cy Young winner. Our pick for his best 1990 card is Topps.

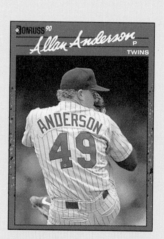

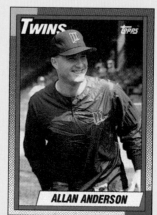

KENT ANDERSON

	BA	G	AB	R	H	2B	3B	HR	RBI	SB
88 AAA	.251	113	374	51	94	22	3	2	39	10
89 Major	.229	86	223	27	51	6	1	0	17	1

Position: Shortstop
Team: California Angels
Born: August 12, 1963 Florence, SC
Height: 6'1" **Weight:** 180 lbs.
Bats: Right **Throws:** Right
Acquired: Fourth-round pick in 6/84
　　　　　free-agent draft

When the Angels needed a solid glove to plug a leak in their infield, they called upon Anderson. He began his minor league career in 1984, so he provided California with an experienced defensive backup for shortstop Dick Schofield. Anderson, a product of the University of South Carolina, gained his major league job through a successful 1988 campaign at Triple-A Edmonton. He hit a respectable .251 (with career highs of 22 doubles and ten stolen bases) in 113 games. If Schofield's broken hand is slow to mend, Anderson will be dependable insurance for the Angels in 1990.

　　Don't invest too much in Anderson's 1990 rookie cards, which will sell from 15 to 25 cents. Keep all of his cards that you find in wax packs. If Schofield isn't healthy in 1990, Anderson may never give up the team's starting job. Our pick for his best 1990 card is Score.

ERIC ANTHONY

	BA	G	AB	R	H	2B	3B	HR	RBI	SB
89 AAA	.300	107	403	67	121	16	2	28	79	14
89 Major	.180	25	61	7	11	2	0	4	7	0

Position: Outfield
Team: Houston Astros
Born: November 8, 1967 San Diego, CA
Height: 6'2" **Weight:** 195 lbs.
Bats: Left **Throws:** Left
Acquired: 34th-round pick in 6/86
　　　　　free-agent draft

In 1989, Anthony found the ideal vehicle to prove his worth. During his first week with the Astros, he racked up a double and home run in a nationally televised game. Although he hit .156 in his first ten games, he had two homers and four RBI. Double-A Southern League managers, in a poll conducted by *Baseball America,* ranked Anthony as the league's best batting prospect in '89. Active in pro ball since 1986, he starred at Class-A Asheville in 1988, leading the league with 37 doubles and 29 homers. Power hitters always have been welcomed by the Astros; because Anthony fits that mold, he has a bright future with the club.

　　The Astros hope Anthony will become Glenn Davis's home run companion. At 20 cents, Anthony's 1990 cards should bring sure dividends. Our pick for his best 1990 card is Donruss.

KEVIN APPIER

	W	L	ERA	G	CG	IP	H	ER	BB	SO
1989	1	4	9.42	6	0	21	34	22	12	10
Life	1	4	9.42	6	0	21	34	22	12	10

Position: Pitcher
Team: Kansas City Royals
Born: December 6, 1967 Lancaster, CA
Height: 6'2" **Weight:** 180 lbs.
Bats: Right **Throws:** Right
Acquired: First-round pick in 6/87
          free-agent draft

Appier reached the top of the Royals' organization in two pro seasons. He was one of the top starters at Triple-A Omaha in 1989: He advanced to Omaha on the strength of his success in the two previous seasons. In 1988, Appier was 2-0 with a 1.83 ERA in three starts with Double-A Memphis. He spent his first 24 games in 1988 with Class-A Baseball City. His ten wins topped his Florida State League squad, while his 24 starts, 147 1/3 innings pitched, and 112 strikeouts were second. He was 5-2 in 1987 at Class-A Eugene, with 72 Ks in 77 innings. Appier has the youth and the ability to be a viable pitching prospect for future Royals teams.

Investors may want to wait for another audition from Appier before investing any money in his 1990 cards. His new issues will go for 10 to 20 cents. Our pick for his best 1990 card is Score.

LUIS AQUINO

	W	L	ERA	G	CG	IP	H	ER	BB	SO
1989	6	8	3.50	34	2	141	148	55	35	68
Life	8	9	3.58	48	7	191	195	72	55	84

Position: Pitcher
Team: Kansas City Royals
Born: May 19, 1964 Santurce, Puerto Rico
Height: 6'1" **Weight:** 175 lbs.
Bats: Right **Throws:** Right
Acquired: Traded from Blue Jays for
          Juan Beniquez, 7/87

After seven years in pro baseball, Aquino finally earned a full season on a major league roster. He spent 1989 with Kansas City, working both as a starter and reliever. While he didn't have a great record, Aquino appeared in more than 30 games for the Royals. He made his first appearance with the Royals on August 9, 1988. His first win came five days later, a six-hit shutout against the Blue Jays. Earlier that year, Aquino threw a no-hitter in Triple-A. He began his career in the Toronto organization after signing as an undrafted free agent in 1982. In 1986, Aquino was 1-1 in seven games with the Blue Jays.

After only one full major league season, Aquino is an unproven commodity. Even though his 1990 cards will be commons, they aren't worthy investments yet. Our pick for his best 1990 card is Fleer.

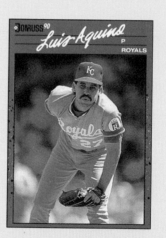

TONY ARMAS

	BA	G	AB	R	H	2B	3B	HR	RBI	SB
1989	.257	60	202	22	52	7	1	11	30	7
Life	.252	1432	5164	614	1302	204	39	251	815	25

Position: Designated hitter; outfield
Team: California Angels
Born: July 2, 1953 Anzoatequi, Venezuela
Height: 6'1" **Weight:** 220 lbs.
Bats: Right **Throws:** Right
Acquired: Signed as a free agent, 7/87

Despite nagging injuries, Armas was one of the most productive hitters on the Angels roster in 1989. Even while playing in 60 games, he was one of eight Angels to reach double figures in home runs. He collected his 800th career RBI in 1989, his 14th season in the majors. Armas broke in with Pittsburgh in 1976 (marking his only National League appearance), but he began a permanent residency in the A.L. the following season. The two-time All-Star has posted double-digit totals in homers in 11 different campaigns, with his best totals coming with the 1984 Red Sox (a league-leading 43 homers and 123 RBI).

Unfortunately, injuries and age are catching up with Armas. As he nears the end of his career, his 1990 cards won't be worth more than a nickel. Our pick for his best 1990 card is Fleer.

JACK ARMSTRONG

	W	L	ERA	G	CG	IP	H	ER	BB	SO
1989	2	3	4.71	9	0	42	40	22	21	23
Life	6	10	5.38	23	0	107	103	64	59	68

Position: Pitcher
Team: Cincinnati Reds
Born: March 7, 1965 Englewood, NJ
Height: 6'5" **Weight:** 220 lbs.
Bats: Right **Throws:** Right
Acquired: First-round pick in 6/87
  free-agent draft

Armstrong continued to live up to his billing as an eventual starting pitcher for the Reds. He got his first chance to pitch in the majors in 1987, after only 27 games of minor league experience. With the 1988 Reds, he was 4-7 in 14 appearances. One of his best starts came against Montreal on July 24, when he fanned eight. With Triple-A Nashville before his 1988 call-up, Armstrong was 5-5 with 115 strikeouts in 120 innings. His season highlight included an August 7 no-hitter versus Indianapolis. At the University of Oklahoma, he set a school record with 129 single-season strikeouts in 1987. Following a 9-3 record, Armstrong won All-Big Eight honors.

Armstrong will face a do-or-die season with Cincinnati. His mediocre showing so far should discourage investors from socking more than a nickel apiece in his 1990 issues. Our pick for his best 1990 card is Donruss.

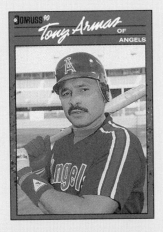
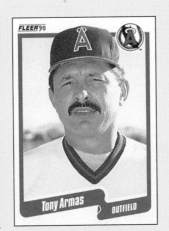

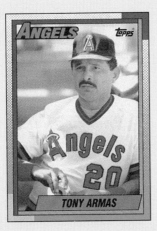

PAUL ASSENMACHER

	W	L	ERA	G	SV	IP	H	ER	BB	SO
1989	3	4	3.99	63	0	76	74	34	28	79
Life	19	15	3.56	94	14	278	265	111	110	386

Position: Pitcher
Team: Chicago Cubs
Born: December 10, 1960 Detroit, MI
Height: 6'3" **Weight:** 200 lbs.
Bats: Left **Throws:** Left
Acquired: Traded from Braves for Kelly
　　　　　Mann and Pat Gomez, 8/89

When the Cubs needed a pitcher as pennant insurance, the team acquired Assenmacher. After more than three seasons with the Braves, he became a top-notch middle reliever with Chicago. He topped the 60-appearance mark for his third time in four seasons. Assenmacher broke in with the Braves in 1986, when he went 7-3 with seven saves and a 2.50 ERA in 61 games. Atlanta signed him as an undrafted free agent in 1983, and the Braves brought him up after he posted a 6-0 mark with four saves at Double-A Greenville in 1985. Assenmacher should be a mainstay in the bullpen for the Cubs in 1990.

Middle relievers seldom earn many wins or saves, so they earn little fame. Assenmacher is no exception, which makes his common-priced 1990 cards poor investments. Our pick for his best 1990 card is Fleer.

DON AUGUST

	W	L	ERA	G	CG	IP	H	ER	BB	SO
1989	12	12	5.31	31	2	142	175	84	58	51
Life	25	19	4.19	55	8	290	312	135	106	117

Position: Pitcher
Team: Milwaukee Brewers
Born: July 3, 1963 Mission Viejo, CA
Height: 6'3" **Weight:** 190 lbs.
Bats: Right **Throws:** Right
Acquired: Traded from Astros with Mark
　　　　　Knudson for Danny Darwin, 8/86

For the second consecutive season, August had the second-most wins on the Brewers staff. In his sophomore year of 1989, he achieved his second straight double-digit win season. He was fourth in A.L. Rookie of the Year balloting in 1988, following a 13-7 campaign. He went 5-1 during his last six starts of the season. August was a first-round draft choice of the Astros in June 1984, following his appearance on the U.S. Olympic team. During his first pro year, at Double-A Columbus, he won 14 games. August won his first major league game on June 2, 1988, in relief, versus the Angels.

With two winning seasons to his credit, August could be a star of the Brewers staff. Buying his 1990 cards at 3 cents or less would be a reasonable gamble. Our pick for his best 1990 card is Score.

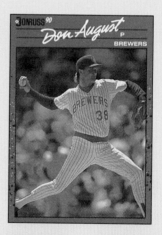

STEVE AVERY

	W	L	ERA	G	CG	IP	H	ER	BB	SO
89 AA	6	3	2.77	13	1	84	69	21	34	73
89 A	6	4	1.45	13	3	87	59	14	20	90

Position: Pitcher
Team: Atlanta Braves
Born: April 14, 1970   Trenton, MI
Height: 6'4"   **Weight:** 180 lbs.
Bats: Left   **Throws:** Left
Acquired: First-round pick in 6/88
   free-agent draft

Avery is pegged as the next pitching star for Atlanta. In just a season and a half, he has established himself as one of the best young arms in pro baseball. At Double-A Greenville in 1989, he won his first four decisions while striking out 35 in 45 innings. Avery was the third player in the nation drafted in June 1988. That year in the Appalachian League, he was 7-1 with a 1.50 ERA and 80 strikeouts in 66 innings. He had a career mark of 29-4 in high school. He chose a career with the Braves over Stanford, and Atlanta had him attend spring training before his 19th birthday. Everyone considers Avery a can't-miss prospect for the majors.

Avery's 1990 cards will start at 50 cents. Buy them fast. The price could triple if he makes the 24-man roster. Our pick for his best 1990 card is Donruss.

SCOTT BAILES

	W	L	ERA	G	SV	IP	H	ER	BB	SO
1989	5	9	4.28	34	0	113	116	54	29	47
Life	31	41	4.71	172	13	491	533	257	165	225

Position: Pitcher
Team: Cleveland Indians
Born: December 18, 1961   Chillicothe, OH
Height: 6'2"   **Weight:** 175 lbs.
Bats: Left   **Throws:** Left
Acquired: Traded from Pirates for
   John LeMaster, 5/85

Bailes shared the same dismal fate suffered by many of the 1989 Indians. His fourth big league season was his worst, as he suffered career lows in several departments. His slump was not typical of his previous three years, during which he served the Tribe both as a starter and reliever. In 1986, his first year with Cleveland when he made the jump from the Double-A directly to the majors, Bailes went 10-10 with seven saves. The lefty notched a 7-8 mark with six saves the following year. The Indians have used him in various pitching capacities, which has hampered his career statistics. Bailes still has years to prove his worth to the Indians.

Until Cleveland defines his role, Bailes won't gain much fame. His 1990 cards aren't appealing investments, even at 3 cents. Our pick for his best 1990 card is Topps.

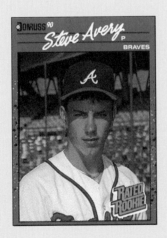

HAROLD BAINES

	BA	G	AB	R	H	2B	3B	HR	RBI	SB
1989	.309	146	505	73	156	29	1	16	72	0
Life	.288	1428	5363	679	1547	276	44	189	835	29

Position: Outfield; designated hitter
Team: Texas Rangers
Born: March 15, 1959 Easton, MD
Height: 6'2" **Weight:** 195 lbs.
Bats: Left **Throws:** Left
Acquired: Traded from White Sox with
　　　　　Fred Manrique for Wilson
　　　　　Alvarez, Scott Fletcher, and Sam
　　　　　Sosa, 7/89

A nine-and-a-half-year career with the White Sox ended for Baines when Texas obtained his services. Before he left in 1989, he earned a place in the all-time lists for several White Sox offensive categories. He became the team's all-time homer leader when he hit his 155th round-tripper at home on July 22, 1987. In 1989, Baines gave the Rangers another .300 hitter. While with the White Sox, he twice drove in 100-plus runs and hit a career-high 29 homers in 1984. If Baines can keep his knees in good shape, he can continue to contribute to the Rangers for several years.

　Baines should be active for many more years as a designated hitter. His 1990 cards will be affordable at a nickel or less, a great price for investors. Our pick for his best 1990 card is Donruss.

DOUG BAIR

	W	L	ERA	G	SV	IP	H	ER	BB	SO
1989	2	3	2.27	44	1	67	52	17	29	47
Life	56	43	4.71	562	81	883	809	354	394	670

Position: Pitcher
Team: Pittsburgh Pirates
Born: August 22, 1949 Defiance, OH
Height: 6' **Weight:** 180 lbs.
Bats: Right **Throws:** Right
Acquired: Signed as a free agent, 6/89

Bair spent his 18th professional season back with the Pirates bullpen in 1989, the same team he earned his major league debut with 13 years earlier. He gave the National Leaguers vital long and middle relief. Only fellow reliever Bill Landrum had a better ERA for the Bucs. Previously, Bair notched a career-high 28 saves with the 1978 Reds. Other teams he has served with include the A's, Cardinals, Tigers, and Phillies. Because he's been cast aside by so many major league teams recently, he decided to cover all of his professional bases. Bair was the first active major leaguer to pursue employment in the Senior Professional Baseball Association.

　Bair hasn't developed the fame or career statistics to have investment-worthy baseball cards. Avoid his common-priced 1990 issues. Our pick for his best 1990 card is Score.

DOUG BAKER

	BA	G	AB	R	H	2B	3B	HR	RBI	SB
1989	.295	43	78	17	23	5	1	0	9	0
Life	.208	133	245	38	51	11	2	0	22	3

Position: Infield
Team: Minnesota Twins
Born: April 3, 1961   Fullerton, CA
Height: 5'9"   **Weight:** 165 lbs.
Bats: Both   **Throws:** Right
Acquired: Traded from Tigers for
　　　　Julius McDougal, 2/88

Baker made a strong bid in 1989 to become the Twins utility infielder. Even though he batted just .237 at Triple-A Portland, he got substantial exposure with Minnesota, playing in 43 games. After coming into 1989 with a career batting average of .168, Baker's accomplishments seem even more remarkable. He hadn't seen so much action since his 1984 debut season with the Tigers, when he played in 43 games. Before he was signed as a ninth-round selection by the Tigers in 1982, he had a noted collegiate career. Baker was on the 1981 College World Series champion Arizona State University team.

After eight professional seasons, Baker hasn't won a starting job in the majors yet. Because of his limited pro success, his common-priced 1990 cards aren't decent investments. Our pick for his best 1990 card is Fleer.

STEVE BALBONI

	BA	G	AB	R	H	2B	3B	HR	RBI	SB
1989	.237	110	300	33	71	12	2	17	59	0
Life	.232	842	2849	327	660	121	11	164	461	1

Position: Designated hitter
Team: New York Yankees
Born: January 5, 1957   Brockton, MA
Height: 6'3"   **Weight:** 235 lbs.
Bats: Right   **Throws:** Right
Acquired: Traded from Mariners for
　　　　Dana Ridenour, 3/89

Despite only working part-time, Balboni was one of only four players to have a double-digit homer total with the 1989 Yankees. His 17 home runs tied for second on the team. The Yankees obtained Balboni to provide more bench strength because they were impressed with his 1988 comeback with the Mariners: In just 97 games, he clubbed 21 homers and 61 RBI. From 1984 through 1987, he started at first base for the Royals. In the 1985 World Series, he hit .320 in seven games. Balboni came up through the Yankees' system, making his major league debut with New York in 1981.

Balboni is a home run threat. However, due to defensive liabilities and a lack of speed, he will remain a part-timer. His 1990 cards are so-so investments, even at 3 cents. Our pick for his best 1990 card is Donruss.

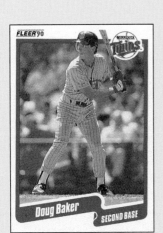

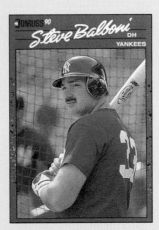

JEFF BALLARD

	W	L	ERA	G	CG	IP	H	ER	BB	SO
1989	18	8	3.43	35	4	215	240	82	57	62
Life	28	28	4.27	74	10	438	507	208	134	130

Position: Pitcher
Team: Baltimore Orioles
Born: August 13, 1963   Billings, MT
Height: 6'2" **Weight:** 198 lbs.
Bats: Left **Throws:** Left
Acquired: Seventh-round pick in
6/85 free-agent draft

With the aid of an Orioles record-setting April, Ballard became Baltimore's biggest winner in 1989. Never before had any O's pitcher gone unbeaten in the month of April, prior to Ballard's 5-0 start. Although his winning ways soon cooled, he remained the Orioles ace throughout the season. Prior to 1989, he had been anything but successful in Baltimore. Ballard's lifetime record had been 10-20 with a 5.09 ERA in his two seasons of work. His career mark in four minor league seasons was 41-18. During his collegiate career, Ballard set records for wins, innings, and strikeouts while at Stanford University.

If the Orioles remain competitive, Ballard could be a perennial 20-game winner. His 1990 cards could pay future dividends if purchased for a nickel or less. Our pick for his best 1990 card is Donruss.

SCOTT BANKHEAD

	W	L	ERA	G	CG	IP	H	ER	BB	SO
1989	14	6	3.34	33	3	210	187	78	63	140
Life	38	32	4.03	105	7	615	591	276	175	431

Position: Pitcher
Team: Seattle Mariners
Born: July 31, 1963   Raleigh, NC
Height: 5'10" **Weight:** 185 lbs.
Bats: Right **Throws:** Right
Acquired: Traded from Royals with
Steve Shields and Mike Kingery
for Danny Tartabull and
Rick Luecken, 12/86

Once the Mariners generated some offensive for Bankhead, he became a winner. He led Seattle in wins, starts, innings pitched, and strikeouts in 1989. His career-best season was a turnaround from 1988, when he began the season on the disabled list with a shoulder injury. Bankhead wound up with a 7-9 record in 21 games. He was 9-8 in 1987, his first season with Seattle. His major league debut came with the Royals in 1986, when he posted an 8-9 record. The Royals drafted Bankhead on the first round after he won five games for the 1984 U.S. Olympic team. The Mariners will look to Bankhead to be the team's ace.

Bankhead could have won 20 games with many teams in 1989, but he won't achieve stardom until the Mariners gain some respectability. Don't invest more than 3 cents in his 1990 cards. Our pick for his best 1990 card is Fleer.

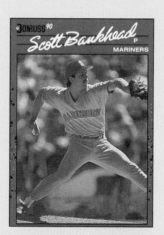

JESSE BARFIELD

	BA	G	AB	R	H	2B	3B	HR	RBI	SB
1989	.234	150	521	79	122	23	1	23	67	5
Life	.262	1161	3904	601	1025	181	28	197	583	60

Position: Outfield; designated hitter
Team: New York Yankees
Born: October 29, 1959   Joliet, IL
Height: 6'1" **Weight:** 200 lbs.
Bats: Right **Throws:** Right
Acquired: Traded from Blue Jays for
Al Leiter, 5/89

An early season slump and upcoming free agency caused Toronto to abandon Barfield early in 1989. Even though the Yankees knew that they might lose him at the end of the season, they still wanted his hitting talents. While he didn't match his normal numbers, he helped take up the offensive slack created by the season-long loss of Dave Winfield. Barfield's 23 homers tied for the team lead and marked the fourth time he topped the 20-homer mark. Before he left Toronto, he became the club's all-time homer leader. Barfield's best season came in 1986, when he hit a league-leading 40 homers and 108 RBI.

Barfield's future depends on where he ends up. If he continues with the Yankees, his 1990 cards could be sleeper investments at a dime apiece. Our pick for his best 1990 card is Score.

MARTY BARRETT

	BA	G	AB	R	H	2B	3B	HR	RBI	SB
1989	.256	86	336	31	86	18	0	1	27	4
Life	.281	867	3203	402	899	158	9	17	298	52

Position: Second base
Team: Boston Red Sox
Born: June 23, 1958   Arcadia, CA
Height: 5'10" **Weight:** 175 lbs.
Bats: Right **Throws:** Right
Acquired: First-round pick in secondary
phase of 6/79 free-agent draft

Barrett only displayed glimpses of his talents with the 1989 Red Sox. Injuries limited him to just 86 games, his lowest total since his 1983 rookie season. Barrett's .256 average hadn't dipped so low since that same year. His slump was a stark contrast from 1988, when he batted .283 with a career-high 65 RBI. Barrett was named the 1986 A.L.C.S. MVP after racking up a .367 mark. For an encore, he hit .433 in the World Series, belting out a record-tying 13 hits. One of the A.L.'s best fielders, he is a master of the hidden-ball trick. If he's healthy, Barrett will provide the 1990 Red Sox with assorted benefits.

Barrett is an underrated team player. But his statistics limit the investment value of his issues. Don't pay more than a nickel for Barrett's 1990 cards. Our pick for his best 1990 card is Score.

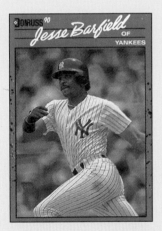

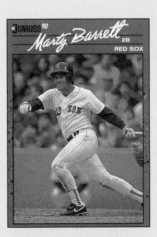

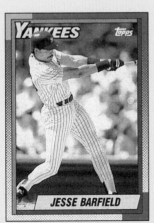

KEVIN BASS

	BA	G	AB	R	H	2B	3B	HR	RBI	SB
1989	.300	87	313	42	94	19	4	5	44	11
Life	.274	947	3135	401	862	161	29	78	396	111

Position: Outfield
Team: San Francisco Giants
Born: May 12, 1959 Redwood City, CA
Height: 6' **Weight:** 180 lbs.
Bats: Both **Throws:** Right
Acquired: Signed as a free agent, 11/89

The Giants signed Bass as an answer to their right field woes. Injuries hampered him in 1989 for the first time in five seasons. He has been one of Houston's most rugged performers, logging 157 games a year from 1986 through 1988. He toiled in the minor leagues for nearly six years before debuting in late 1982 with the Brewers. Traded to Houston that year, he became a full-time Astro in 1985 and finished second on the club in homers, RBI, and stolen bases. Bass earned his first spot on the N.L. All-Star team in 1986; he wound up the year with 20 homers, 79 RBI, and a .311 average. He hit .292 in the '86 N.L.C.S. In 1987, Bass tallied a career-best 85 RBI.

Take a chance on Bass's 1990 at a nickel apiece or less. If he recaptures that 1989 magic, Bass could be one of the league's finest hitters. Our pick for his best 1990 card is Score.

STEVE BEDROSIAN

	W	L	ERA	G	SV	IP	H	ER	BB	SO
1989	3	7	2.87	68	23	84	56	27	39	58
Life	56	61	3.24	484	161	909	769	327	395	736

Position: Pitcher
Team: San Francisco Giants
Born: December 6, 1957 Methuen, MA
Height: 6'3" **Weight:** 205 lbs.
Bats: Right **Throws:** Right
Acquired: Traded from Phillies for Dennis Cook, Terry Mulholland, and Charlie Hayes, 6/89

The pennant-hungry Giants were willing to part with three minor leaguers to obtain Bedrosian in mid-1989. The bullpen ace had seen only nine save opportunities with the struggling Phillies in 1989, but his career was revitalized when he relocated to the N.L. West contenders. In less than four seasons, Bedrosian became the Phillies all-time saves leader, surpassing Tug McGraw's 94. Bedrosian debuted with Atlanta in 1981 and was converted to a starter in 1985 before being traded to the Phils. When returned to the bullpen by his new team, Bedrosian promptly racked up 29 saves in 68 appearances. In 1987, he led the league with 40 saves, set a record of 13 straight saves, and won the Cy Young Award.

Now that Bedrosian is the pitching cornerstone of the Giants, his 1990 cards are bargain investments at a nickel each. Our pick for his best 1990 card is Fleer.

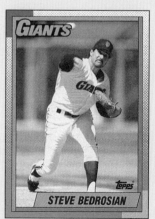

TIM BELCHER

	W	L	ERA	G	CG	IP	H	ER	BB	SO
1989	15	12	2.82	39	10	230	72	182	80	200
Life	31	20	2.82	71	14	443	139	355	138	375

Position: Pitcher
Team: Los Angeles Dodgers
Born: October 19, 1961 Sparta, OH
Height: 6'3" **Weight:** 210 lbs.
Bats: Right **Throws:** Right
Acquired: Traded from A's for
      Rick Honeycutt, 8/87

After striving in Orel Hershiser's shadow during 1988, Belcher established himself as another hurler for the Dodgers in 1989. He paced the Dodgers in complete games (ten), shutouts (eight), and strikeouts (200), while he tied Hershiser for the team lead in wins (15). Belcher spent four years in the Athletics' organization without getting any major league exposure. After going 4-2 in six games with the 1987 Dodgers, he sparkled in his 1988 rookie season. He earned a third-place finish in the N.L. Rookie of the Year balloting by going 12-6 with four saves. Belcher earned two victories in the 1988 N.L.C.S., followed with a win in the fourth game of the World Series.

Belcher may serve the Dodgers for another decade. His 1990 cards are great investments at a dime or less. Our pick for his best 1990 card is Score.

GEORGE BELL

	BA	G	AB	R	H	2B	3B	HR	RBI	SB
1989	.297	153	613	88	182	41	2	18	104	4
Life	.289	1035	3966	574	1145	212	32	181	654	56

Position: Outfield
Team: Toronto Blue Jays
Born: October 21, 1959 San Pedro de
      Macoris, Dominican Republic
Height: 6'1" **Weight:** 202 lbs.
Bats: Right **Throws:** Right
Acquired: Drafted from Phillies, 12/80

Even though Toronto was transplanted to a new stadium in 1989, Bell remained a fixture in the team's outfield. Fans have seen a lot of Bell through the years. From 1984 through 1988, he played in a yearly minimum of 156 games. The Blue Jays discovered him hidden in the Phillies' system and gave him his debut in 1981. He became a starter in 1984, hitting .292 with 26 homers and 87 RBI. His best season came in 1987, when he notched 47 homers, 134 RBI, and a .308 average to win the A.L. MVP. Bell's talent helped him become the first Blue Jay to be elected as an All-Star Game starter.

Propelling the Blue Jays to an A.L. East pennant gives Bell's cards even more popularity. Buying his 1990 issues for a dime or less will bring quick dividends if Toronto repeats. Our pick for his best 1990 card is Fleer.

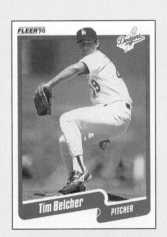

JAY BELL

	BA	G	AB	R	H	2B	3B	HR	RBI	SB
1989	.258	78	271	33	70	13	3	2	27	5
Life	.238	184	621	73	148	29	5	7	65	11

Position: Shortstop
Team: Pittsburgh Pirates
Born: December 11, 1965
      Eglin Air Force Base, FL
Height: 6'1" **Weight:** 180 lbs.
Bats: Right **Throws:** Right
Acquired: Traded from Indians for
      Felix Fermin, 2/89

Bell was one of the contenders for the shortstop job with the 1989 Pirates. He split his season between Pittsburgh and Triple-A Buffalo. While in Buffalo, Bell hit .285 with ten homers and 54 RBI. The Pirates then gave him ample opportunity to win the starting job. He had been unable to establish himself in three seasons with the Indians. Minnesota picked Bell as the eighth player taken in the first round of the 1984 draft. He became the 55th player in history to homer in his first major league at-bat when, ironically, Bell homered against the Twins on September 29, 1986.

After six seasons in pro baseball, Bell isn't a starter in the majors. Even though his 1990 cards should be priced at 3 cents, investing in his cards would be a gamble. Our pick for his best 1990 card is Donruss.

JOEY BELLE

	BA	G	AB	R	H	2B	3B	HR	RBI	SB
89 AA	.282	89	312	48	88	20	0	20	69	8
89 Major	.225	62	218	22	49	8	4	7	37	2

Position: Outfield
Team: Cleveland Indians
Born: August 25, 1966   Shreveport, LA
Height: 6'2" **Weight:** 200 lbs.
Bats: Right **Throws:** Right
Acquired: Second-round pick in 6/87
      free-agent draft

Belle was one of the surprises of the 1989 season for the Indians. When a sore back sidelined outfielder Cory Snyder, the Indians summoned Belle from Double-A, where he had 20 homers, 69 RBI, and a .282 average. On July 24, he blasted a grand slam against the Yankees to give his team a 7-3 victory. He is a legend at Louisiana State; after three years he holds all-time team records in home runs, RBI, runs, hits, slugging percentage, and total bases. After 49 college homers, Belle transported his power to Class-A Kinston in 1988, where he slugged eight homers and batted .301 in 41 games.

Expect Belle's 1990 rookie cards to end at a quarter or more if he stays a full year in Cleveland. Look for his issues at a dime and land a big windfall by season's end. Our pick for his best 1990 card is Score.

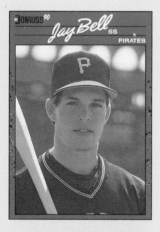

ANDY BENES

	W	L	ERA	G	CG	IP	H	ER	BB	SO
89 AA	8	4	2.16	16	5	108	79	26	39	115
89 Major	6	3	3.51	10	0	66	51	26	31	66

Position: Pitcher
Team: San Diego Padres
Born: August 20, 1967 Evansville, IN
Height: 6'6" **Weight:** 235 lbs.
Bats: Right **Throws:** Right
Acquired: First-round pick in 6/88
    free-agent draft

Once Benes got his pro career in gear, it took him less than a year to reach the majors. The Padres made Benes the first player chosen in the free-agent draft of June 1988. The rest of 1988, however, was devoted to pitching Team USA to an Olympic gold medal. He was a star in 1989 at Double-A Wichita, going 8-4 with 115 strikeouts in 108 innings. Texas League managers picked Benes as the circuit's best pitching prospect. He was nicked for six runs in his debut with the Padres, but he still tallied seven Ks in six innings. Benes was 16-3 with a 1.42 ERA at the University of Evansville in 1988.

If the Padres are contenders, Benes should be a key player. Find his 1990 cards at a quarter or less, and you'll have an investment bargain. Our pick for his best 1990 card is Donruss.

TODD BENZINGER

	BA	G	AB	R	H	2B	3B	HR	RBI	SB
1989	.245	161	628	79	154	28	3	17	76	3
Life	.254	354	1256	162	319	67	5	38	189	10

Position: First base
Team: Cincinnati Reds
Born: February 11, 1963 Dayton, KY
Height: 6'1" **Weight:** 185 lbs.
Bats: Both **Throws:** Right
Acquired: Traded from Red Sox with Jeff
    Sellers and Luis Vasquez for Rob
    Murphy and Nick Esasky, 12/88

Benzinger adjusted to a new league during his first season with the Cincinnati Reds. Although his batting average was forgettable, he was the Reds leader in doubles (28). His homers (17) and RBI (76), both career highs, trailed only team leader Eric Davis. The Reds were attracted to Benzinger after his 1988 campaign with the Boston Red Sox, his first full season in the majors. With Boston, he hit .254 with 13 home runs and 70 RBI. After starting out as the BoSox right fielder, the club moved him to first base in June. Benzinger played his first professional season in 1981, and needed more than six years in the minors before getting his break with Boston.

Benzinger's 1990 cards should be an affordable nickel or less. Based on his future home run potential, Benzinger's card values could grow quickly. Our pick for his best 1990 card is Donruss.

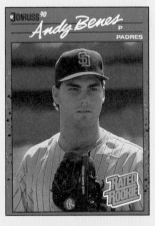
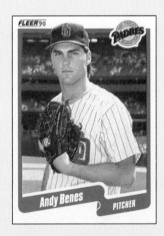

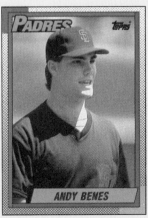

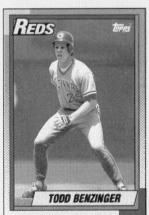

JUAN BERENGUER

	W	L	ERA	G	SV	IP	H	ER	BB	SO
1989	9	3	3.48	56	3	106	96	41	47	93
Life	55	49	3.93	343	14	963	829	421	490	800

Position: Pitcher
Team: Minnesota Twins
Born: November 30, 1954
       Aguadulce, Panama
Height: 5'11" **Weight:** 223 lbs.
Bats: Right **Throws:** Right
Acquired: Signed as a free agent, 1/87

Berenguer continued to excel in the Twins bullpen in 1989. His nine victories were third on the team, while his 93 strikeouts ranked second. In his three seasons with the Twins, the righty has topped 90 strikeouts each year. Berenguer made his major league debut on August 17, 1978, with the Mets. Besides the Mets, Berenguer has spent time with the Royals, Blue Jays, Tigers, and Giants. He won a career-high 11 games with the 1984 pennant-winning Tigers. In 1987, when he saved the second game of A.L.C.S. for Minnesota, Berenguer became the first Panamanian pitcher in history to appear in postseason play.

Berenguer has an unremarkable lifetime record. Due to his age, he's unlikely to achieve dazzling lifetime stats. His common-priced 1990 cards aren't appealing investments. Our pick for his best 1990 card is Topps.

DAVE BERGMAN

	BA	G	AB	R	H	2B	3B	HR	RBI	SB
1989	.268	137	385	38	103	13	1	7	37	1
Life	.260	1076	2099	251	545	77	14	44	224	14

Position: First base; outfield
Team: Detroit Tigers
Born: June 6, 1953 Evanston, IL
Height: 6'2" **Weight:** 190 lbs.
Bats: Left **Throws:** Left
Acquired: Traded from Phillies with
       Willie Hernandez for
       Glenn Wilson and
       John Wockenfuss, 3/84

Although Bergman's .268 average in 1989 wasn't his best, the mark was a team high for the Tigers. He played in a career-high 137 games and responded with a personal best of 103 hits, the most since he played at Triple-A Syracuse in 1977. Detroit acquired Bergman in 1984, and he hit .273 with seven homers and 44 RBI, and was a late-inning defensive replacement for the world champion Tigers. He began his career with the Yankees' organization in 1974. He won minor league batting titles in his first two years before getting a audition with the Yanks in 1975. Bergman then served stints with the Astros and Giants before excelling as a part-timer with Detroit.

Because he's played part-time during career, Bergman's cards are not high-demand items. Pass up his common-priced 1990 cards. Our pick for his best 1990 card is Fleer.

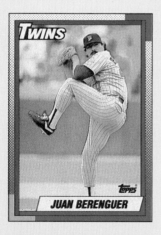

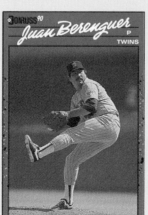

GERONIMO BERROA

	BA	G	AB	R	H	2B	3B	HR	RBI	SB
1989	.265	81	136	7	36	4	0	2	9	0
Life	.265	81	136	7	36	4	0	2	9	0

Position: Outfield
Team: Atlanta Braves
Born: March 18, 1965 Santo Domingo,
　　　Dominican Republic
Height: 6' **Weight:** 195 lbs.
Bats: Right **Throws:** Right
Acquired: Drafted from Blue Jays, 12/88

Berroa, after five years in the Toronto organization, got a chance at the major leagues when he was drafted out of the minors by Atlanta. He was a pinch hitter and substitute out-fielder for the 1989 Braves, marking his first full year in the major leagues. Berroa spent 1988 with Triple-A Syracuse, pacing the team with 64 RBI, and finishing second with eight homers, 122 hits, and 131 games played, while batting .260. He was a Double-A Southern League All-Star at Knoxville in 1987. His banner season included 36 homers, 108 RBI, and a .287 average. He was second in the league in RBI, hits (150), and slugging percentage (.568). Berroa has a lot of seasons to look forward to.

Don't consider investing any money in Berroa's 1990 cards, priced at a nickel apiece, until he cracks the Atlanta starting lineup. Our pick for his best 1990 card is Score.

DAMON BERRYHILL

	BA	G	AB	R	H	2B	3B	HR	RBI	SB
1989	.257	91	334	37	86	13	0	5	41	1
Life	.255	198	671	58	171	33	1	12	80	2

Position: Catcher
Team: Chicago Cubs
Born: December 3, 1963
　　　South Laguna, CA
Height: 6' **Weight:** 205 lbs.
Bats: Both **Throws:** Right
Acquired: First-round pick in 1/84
　　　free-agent draft

Just when it looked like Berryhill might get to play a full sea-son in the majors, he was sidelined for the last month of the 1989 season with a shoulder injury. Before the injury, he batted .257 with five homers and 41 RBI. Defensively, he threw out 24 of the first 51 potential basestealers. In 1988, Berryhill earned a spot on most N.L. all-rookie teams with a stellar first season. He appeared in 95 games, hitting .259 with seven homers and 38 RBI. In 1987, with Triple-A Iowa, he achieved career highs with 18 homers, 67 RBI, and a .287 average. Berryhill spent parts of five seasons in the minors before earning his starting job in Chicago.

Just because Berryhill hasn't displayed awesome power, investors haven't bothered with his cards. Be different. Spend a nickel or less on his 1990 issues. Our pick for his best 1990 card is Score.

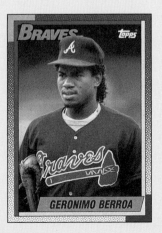

DANTE BICHETTE

	BA	G	AB	R	H	2B	3B	HR	RBI	SB
1989	.210	48	138	13	29	7	0	3	15	3
Life	.223	69	184	14	41	9	0	3	23	3

Position: Outfield
Team: California Angels
Born: November 18, 1963
West Palm Beach, FL
Height: 6'3" **Weight:** 212 lbs.
Bats: Right **Throws:** Right
Acquired: 17th-round pick in 6/84
free-agent draft

After starting the season at California in 1989, Bichette wound up with another stint at Triple-A Edmonton later in the season. His trip back to Edmonton was his third in three years. He had his most productive power season in 1988. Although his average dropped 33 points from 1987, Bichette had 14 homers and 81 RBI. He is a fine defensive outfielder, leading the 1988 Pacific Coast League with 22 assists in 129 games. In 1987 at Edmonton, Bichette batted a career-best .300 in 92 games. He was sidelined for six weeks with a broken finger that season. Bichette has time to gain a prominent role with Angels teams of the future.

Bichette has a decent chance to stick with the 1990 Angels. His 1990 cards should be a nickel or less, a price for safe, affordable investing. Our pick for his best 1990 card is Fleer.

MIKE BIELECKI

	W	L	ERA	G	CG	IP	H	ER	BB	SO
1989	18	7	3.14	33	4	212	187	74	81	147
Life	30	26	3.86	107	6	504	483	216	223	311

Position: Pitcher
Team: Chicago Cubs
Born: July 31, 1959 Baltimore, MD
Height: 6'3" **Weight:** 195 lbs.
Bats: Right **Throws:** Right
Acquired: Traded from Pirates for
Mike Curtis, 3/88

One major factor in the Cubs divisional pennant was Bielecki. He had the greatest season of his six-year major league career in 1989, setting career highs in virtually every pitching category. His 18 wins and 147 strikeouts were both second on the Cubs. Bielecki's success was unexpected considering his difficulties in 1988. He spent more than half the season in Triple-A, and wound up his brief stay in Chicago with a 2-2 mark in 19 appearances. Previously, his finest career mark was a 6-11 record with the 1986 Pirates. Bielecki stayed in the Pittsburgh system for six years before getting his first chance at the majors in 1984.

Bielecki was successful in 1989. However, he has a mediocre career record. Due to his limited chances at long-term success, avoid spending more than a nickel each on his 1990 cards. Our pick for his best 1990 card is Fleer.

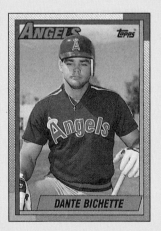

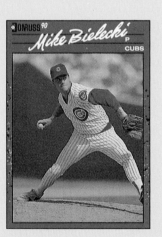

CRAIG BIGGIO

	BA	G	AB	R	H	2B	3B	HR	RBI	SB
1989	.257	134	443	64	114	21	2	13	60	21
Life	.247	184	566	78	140	27	3	16	65	27

Position: Catcher
Team: Houston Astros
Born: December 14, 1965 Smithtown, NY
Height: 5'11" **Weight:** 180 lbs.
Bats: Right **Throws:** Right
Acquired: First-round pick in 6/87
free-agent draft

Biggio nailed down a starting job with the Astros after beginning 1989 as a backup to Alan Ashby. Biggio won the job by late April. He was second on the team in homers and third in RBI. He displayed impressive speed for a catcher; his 21 stolen bases ranked among the best for backstops. He was even used briefly as a leadoff hitter. Defensively, he received praise from Astros coach Yogi Berra, himself a Hall of Fame catcher. It took just a season and a half for Biggio to advance through the Astros' system. When he was recalled from Triple-A Tucson in '88, he was hitting .320. Biggio is a long-term answer to Houston's catching needs.

Biggio's 1990 cards will be cheap. If you can get them for a nickel apiece, buy them in quantity. Our pick for his best 1990 card is Score.

BUD BLACK

	W	L	ERA	G	CG	IP	H	ER	BB	SO
1989	12	11	3.36	33	6	222	213	83	52	88
Life	70	71	3.72	267	19	1259	1216	521	367	640

Position: Pitcher
Team: Cleveland Indians
Born: June 30, 1957 San Mateo, CA
Height: 6'2" **Weight:** 185 lbs.
Bats: Left **Throws:** Left
Acquired: Traded from Royals for
Pat Tabler, 6/88

Black broke an extended slump and registered his first winning record in five years with the 1989 Indians, going 12-11. He hadn't notched a positive record since his 17-12 mark with the 1984 Royals. He finished third in wins with the 1989 Indians. Black had just four wins in 1988, a season marred by a strained pitching elbow and an extended stay on the disabled list. After pitching two games with the 1981 Mariners, Black pitched with the Royals for more than six seasons. He got the opening-day starting assignment from Kansas City three times, tying a team record. Black should be a busy member of the Indians rotation in 1990.

Despite his comeback, Black has a losing lifetime mark. It's hard to expect continued success, so you probably shouldn't invest in his common-priced 1990 cards. Our pick for his best 1990 card is Fleer.

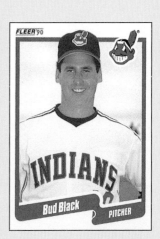

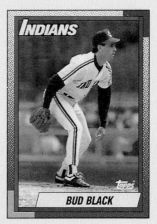

LANCE BLANKENSHIP

	BA	G	AB	R	H	2B	3B	HR	RBI	SB
1989	.232	58	125	22	29	5	1	1	4	5
Life	.227	68	128	23	29	5	1	1	4	5

Position: Infield; outfield
Team: Oakland Athletics
Born: December 6, 1963 Portland, OR
Height: 6' **Weight:** 185 lbs.
Bats: Right **Throws:** Right
Acquired: Tenth-round pick in 6/86
free-agent draft

One of the most versatile players on the A's, Blankenship won an opening-day roster spot with Oakland in 1989. He was returned briefly to Triple-A Tacoma in August before the September call-ups. In 1988, he batted .265 with nine homers, 52 RBI, 40 stolen bases, and 96 bases on balls for Tacoma. Blankenship was the Pacific Coast League's starting second baseman in the first Triple-A All-Star game. At Double-A Huntsville in 1987, he hit .254 average and had 34 stolen bases. Blankenship attended the University of California for four years, and was the first baseball player to be named All-Pac Ten for four consecutive seasons.

As with most rookie cards, Blankenship's first issues may be overpriced. His 1990 cards are risky buys until he has a solid shot at a starting job. Our pick for his best 1990 card is Score.

JEFF BLAUSER

	BA	G	AB	R	H	2B	3B	HR	RBI	SB
1989	.270	142	456	63	123	24	2	12	46	5
Life	.260	211	688	81	179	33	6	16	68	12

Position: Infield
Team: Atlanta Braves
Born: November 8, 1965 Los Gatos, CA
Height: 6' **Weight:** 170 lbs.
Bats: Right **Throws:** Right
Acquired: First-round pick in 6/84
free-agent draft

Blauser spread his talents around the Braves infield in 1989, dividing his time between second base, shortstop, and third base. The versatile infielder was one of Atlanta's most consistent hitters, posting the team's fourth highest batting average (.270). He battled back from a subpar 1988, in which he missed nearly half the season with a broken finger. Blauser made his major league debut July 5, 1987. After a brief demotion, he returned August 11 and started every game for the rest of the season. After the Cardinals made him their top pick in the January 1984 draft but failed to sign him, the Braves snared Blauser as their first pick in June that year.

Blauser should be a starter somewhere in the Atlanta infield in 1990. His 1990 issues, at 3 cents or less, are marginal but safe buys. Our pick for his best 1990 card is Fleer.

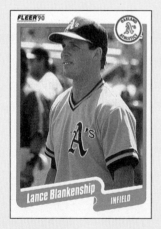

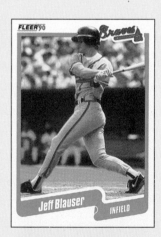

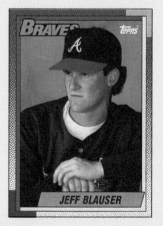

BERT BLYLEVEN

	W	L	ERA	G	CG	IP	H	ER	BB	SO
1989	17	5	2.73	33	8	241	225	76	44	131
Life	271	231	3.22	644	239	4703	4319	1868	1268	3562

Position: Pitcher
Team: California Angels
Born: April 6, 1951 Zeist, Netherlands
Height: 6'3" **Weight:** 205 lbs.
Bats: Right **Throws:** Right
Acquired: Traded from Twins for Mike
          Cook, Paul Sorreno, and Rob
          Wassenaar, 11/88

Blyleven marched closer to the Hall of Fame with another successful campaign in 1989. In his 20th major league season, he helped make the Angels into pennant contenders. His only no-hitter came as a Ranger in 1977, pitching against the Angels. One of the 1989 highlights for Blyleven was passing the 3,500 strikeout plateau, a feat only seven men in history have accomplished. He passed Hall of Famer Walter Johnson on the all-time strikeout list at mid-season. Among active pitchers, Blyleven trails only Nolan Ryan in career wins and strikeouts. Blyleven is one of only six foreign-born pitchers to win 200 or more career games.

    Blyleven is a certain Hall of Famer. People who don't snatch up his 1990 cards at a dime or less will miss out on healthy long-term gains. Our pick for his best 1990 card is Fleer.

MIKE BODDICKER

	W	L	ERA	G	CG	IP	H	ER	BB	SO
1989	15	11	4.00	34	3	211	217	94	71	145
Life	101	87	3.70	239	57	1573	1500	648	541	1037

Position: Pitcher
Team: Boston Red Sox
Born: August 23, 1957 Cedar Rapids, IA
Height: 5'11" **Weight:** 185 lbs.
Bats: Right **Throws:** Right
Acquired: Traded from Orioles for
          Brady Anderson and Curt
          Schiller, 7/88

After two seasons of frustration, Boddicker bounced back with the 1989 Red Sox. The veteran righty won 15 games, second highest on the team, and the second-best winning record of his long career. His last success came with the 1984 Orioles, when he led the A.L. with a 20-11 mark and 2.79 ERA. During his 1983 debut with Baltimore, he was 16-8. *The Sporting News* named Boddicker A.L. Rookie of the Year for his efforts. That year, he earned two complete-game wins in postseason play. He became the first rookie in the League Championship Series history to post a shutout, and Boddicker was named the Series MVP, the first pitcher to be so honored.

    Boddicker was 32 years old before he surpassed 100 wins. His chances for baseball immortality look slim, making his common-priced 1990 cards unattractive. Our pick for his best 1990 card is Topps.

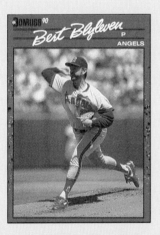

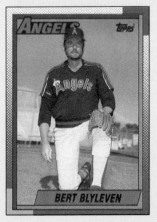
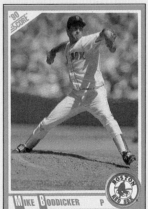

JOE BOEVER

	W	L	ERA	G	SV	IP	H	ER	BB	SO
1989	4	11	3.94	66	21	82	78	36	34	68
Life	5	14	3.81	120	22	158	155	67	62	121

Position: Pitcher
Team: Atlanta Braves
Born: October 4, 1960 St. Louis, MO
Height: 6'1" **Weight:** 200 lbs.
Bats: Right **Throws:** Right
Acquired: Traded from Cardinals for
Randy O'Neal, 7/87

All it took was one complete season in the majors for Boever to prove his ability. With the 1989 Braves, he led the club in appearances (66) and saves (21). Fans surprised at Boever's new status may forget that he has been in pro ball since 1982. He received two minor auditions with the Cardinals in 1985 and 1986 before being traded to Atlanta in 1987. The Braves demoted Boever to Triple-A Richmond to open 1988. However, he led the International League with 22 saves and was the circuit's reliever of the year before getting his recall.

Normally, relievers make poor card investments. However, Boever's sudden success could help move Atlanta back into contention. If you feel daring, buy a few Boever 1990 cards at 3 cents apiece. Our pick for his best 1990 card is Donruss.

WADE BOGGS

	BA	G	AB	R	H	2B	3B	HR	RBI	SB
1989	.330	156	621	113	205	51	7	3	54	2
Life	.352	1183	4534	823	1597	314	36	64	523	14

Position: Third base
Team: Boston Red Sox
Born: June 15, 1958 Omaha, NE
Height: 6'2" **Weight:** 190 lbs.
Bats: Left **Throws:** Right
Acquired: Seventh-round pick in 6/76
free-agent draft

Going into 1989, Boggs had earned five A.L. batting titles in the previous six years. He did not win the crown in 1989, but he still ended up with more than 200 hits. Each of his league-leading averages has been .357 or higher. Only Ty Cobb and Rogers Hornsby have higher lifetime batting averages. Boggs struck out a career-low 34 times in 1988 and continued to post amazing on-base percentages. In 1985, he set a new A.L. record by hitting safely in 135 games. His batting ability, combined with his defensive talents, makes Boggs one of the brightest stars in the sport.

Beat the pack in 1990. Just because Boggs missed out on a batting title, his cards may decrease in value. If his 1990 cards dip below 75 cents, stock up for some big financial gains. Our pick for his best 1990 card is Fleer.

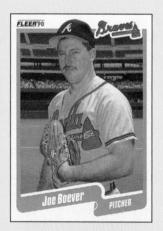
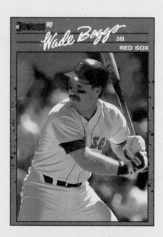

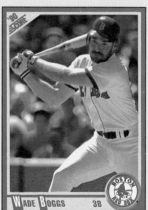
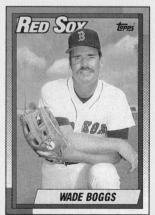

BARRY BONDS

	BA	G	AB	R	H	2B	3B	HR	RBI	SB
1989	.248	159	580	96	144	34	6	19	58	32
Life	.255	566	2082	364	532	124	24	84	223	117

Position: Outfield
Team: Pittsburgh Pirates
Born: July 24, 1964   Riverside, CA
Height: 6'1"   **Weight:** 185 lbs.
Bats: Left   **Throws:** Left
Acquired: First-round pick in 6/85
        free-agent draft

Speed and power continued to be Bonds's trademarks in 1989. Being the son of 14-year veteran outfielder Bobby Bonds put big expectations on Barry. He met the challenge and played 115 minor league games before winning a job with the Pirates in 1986. Bonds had a distinguished career at Arizona State, being named to *The Sporting News* All-America Team in 1985. He joined Dave Parker as the only Pirate ever in the "20/20" club with 25 home runs and 32 steals in 1987. Barry's lifetime homers combined with his father's 332 homers surpassed the previous all-time father-son mark of 407, co-held by Gus and Buddy Bell, and Yogi and Dale Berra.

Barry may rack up the same quality lifetime stats achieved by his father. Pick up his 1990 cards at a dime and look forward to some long-term profits. Our pick for his best 1990 card is Donruss.

BOBBY BONILLA

	BA	G	AB	R	H	2B	3B	HR	RBI	SB
1989	.281	163	616	96	173	37	10	24	86	8
Life	.278	601	2092	296	582	118	24	66	306	22

Position: Third base
Team: Pittsburgh Pirates
Born: February 23, 1963   New York, NY
Height: 6'3"   **Weight:** 230 lbs.
Bats: Both   **Throws:** Right
Acquired: Traded from White Sox for
        Jose DeLeon, 7/86

Bonilla has become a potent force for the Bucs. Bonilla began his pro career in the Pirates' organization in 1981 but labored in the minors for five years before being drafted by the White Sox. He played a half-season with Chicago before being reacquired in 1986. Bonilla played four different positions in Pittsburgh before winning the team's starting hot corner job in June 1987. He locked down the position by batting .300 with 15 homers and 77 RBI. Bonilla helped the Pirates chase the Mets for the division pennant in 1988, hitting .274 with 24 round-trippers and 100 RBI. As he continues his defensive improvements, Bonilla will be one of the league's stars.

Outside of Pittsburgh, Bonilla's 1990 cards should be a dime or less. If he returns to his All-Star form, expect that price to double quickly. Our pick for his best 1990 card is Fleer.

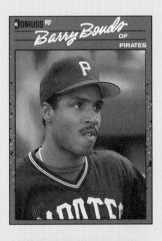

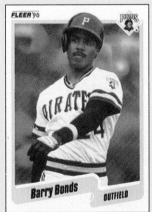

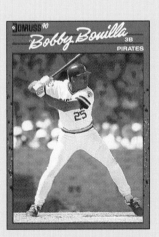

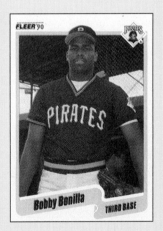

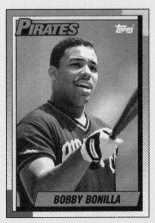

BOB BOONE

	BA	G	AB	R	H	2B	3B	HR	RBI	SB
1989	.274	131	405	33	111	13	2	1	43	3
Life	.254	2224	7128	668	1810	300	26	105	817	37

Position: Catcher
Team: Kansas City Royals
Born: November 19, 1947 San Diego, CA
Height: 6'2" **Weight:** 210 lbs.
Bats: Right **Throws:** Right
Acquired: Signed as a free agent, 11/88

Boone, the most active catcher in baseball history, continued his record-breaking reign behind the plate with the 1989 Royals. He showed few signs of age either with the glove or bat. His reputation as one of the finest receivers in the A.L. solidified in 1988 when he became the oldest nonpitcher ever to win a Gold Glove. Boone's 1989 batting average was his highest since his .286 season with the 1979 Phillies. He went to the Angels in 1982 and remained with California through 1988. This season will mark the fifth decade Boone's family has been represented in the majors. His father, Ray, was an A.L. infielder from 1948 to 1960.

Boone has a shot at the Hall of Fame. His 1990 cards should be a nickel or less, which offers inviting long-term profits to investors. Our pick for his best 1990 card is Fleer.

CHRIS BOSIO

	W	L	ERA	G	CG	IP	H	ER	BB	SO
1989	15	10	2.95	33	8	234	225	77	48	173
Life	33	37	3.93	127	19	620	643	271	149	436

Position: Pitcher
Team: Milwaukee Brewers
Born: April 3, 1963 Carmichael, CA
Height: 6'3" **Weight:** 225 lbs.
Bats: Right **Throws:** Right
Acquired: Second-round pick in 1/82
            free-agent draft

Staying in the starting rotation for the entire season gave Bosio a big boost in 1989. He was the Brewers leading winner in his fourth year with Milwaukee. In 1988, Bosio's stats suffered when he was split between starting and relieving, going 7-15 with six saves. He started for the Brewers through August, but was briefly demoted to Triple-A Denver. When he returned, he filled in for injured closer Dan Plesac. Bosio's first full season in Milwaukee came in 1987. He was 11-8 with two saves as a swing man. During his five minor league seasons, the Brewers groomed him both as a starter and reliever. Based on his 1989 success, Bosio will be a full-time starter.

Bosio had a good season, but his 1990 cards will be a nickel but seem like a risky investment. Our pick for his best 1990 card is Topps.

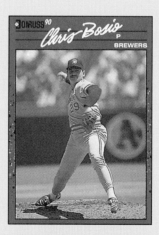

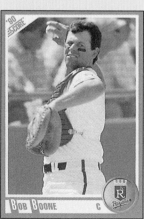

DARYL BOSTON

	BA	G	AB	R	H	2B	3B	HR	RBI	SB
1989	.252	101	218	34	55	3	4	5	23	7
Life	.239	495	1350	179	323	63	13	38	123	51

Position: Outfield
Team: Chicago White Sox
Born: January 4, 1963   Cincinnati, OH
Height: 6'3"   **Weight:** 203 lbs.
Bats: Left   **Throws:** Left
Acquired: First-round pick in 6/81
free-agent draft

In his ninth professional season, Boston was still fighting to win a starting assignment for the White Sox. He had a good season in 1989, hitting .252, but he played in just 101 games. He spent parts of the previous five seasons on the ChiSox roster, limited to part-time duty every year. In 1988, Boston hit .215 in 105 games, with nearly half of his hits going for extra bases, including 15 home runs. One of those clouts was a grand slam against Texas on June 26. His best pro season came in 1984. Boston was named the Triple-A American Association Rookie of the Year after batting .312 with 15 homers, 82 RBI, and a league-leading 19 triples.

Boston hasn't won a starting job with the Sox yet. His 1990 cards are commons, still too pricey for a part-time player. Our pick for his best 1990 card is Topps.

DENNIS BOYD

	W	L	ERA	G	CG	IP	H	ER	BB	SO
1989	3	2	4.42	10	0	59	57	29	19	26
Life	60	56	4.15	152	39	1016	1067	469	259	571

Position: Pitcher
Team: Boston Red Sox
Born: October 6, 1959   Meridian, MS
Height: 6'1"   **Weight:** 160 lbs.
Bats: Right   **Throws:** Right
Acquired: 16th-round pick in 6/80
free-agent draft

For the third straight season, Red Sox hurler "Oil Can" Boyd was haunted by an assortment of physical woes. He has averaged less than 15 appearances a year since 1987, when he was first sidelined with a sore right shoulder. Shoulder surgery after the All-Star break began the long streak of disability for him. Boyd had three straight double-digit winning seasons, going 12-12 in 1984, 15-13 in 1985, and a career-high 16-10 in 1986. He pitched three seasons in the minors before making his debut in the majors in 1982. After demotions the next two years, he joined Boston on May 30, 1984, and stayed the entire season. After three years of adversity, Boyd's once-promising career is struggling to survive.

Time is running out for the Boyd. Because of his health, don't invest is his common-priced 1990 cards. Our pick for his best 1990 card is Donruss.

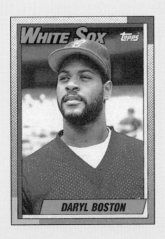

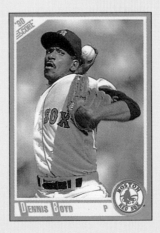

PHIL BRADLEY

	BA	G	AB	R	H	2B	3B	HR	RBI	SB
1989	.277	144	545	83	151	23	10	11	55	20
Life	.290	905	3273	506	950	165	41	74	345	138

Position: Outfield
Team: Baltimore Orioles
Born: March 11, 1959 Bloomington, IN
Height: 6' **Weight:** 185 lbs.
Bats: Right **Throws:** Right
Acquired: Traded from Phillies for
Gordon Dillard and Ken
Howell, 12/88

Bradley was a major factor in the 1989 rejuvenation of the Orioles. After spending just one year in the N.L. with Philadelphia, he seemed ready to return to the A.L. in 1989. He slumped to .264 in 1988, but stayed above the .300 mark starting in August. Bradley played with the Mariners from 1983 through 1987. His best season with the M's was his All-Star campaign of 1985, when he socked 26 homers, scored 100 runs, drove in 88 runners, and batted .300. In 1987, he swiped a career-high 40 bases. In college, Bradley was an All-Big Eight quarterback at Missouri from 1978 to '80, leading his club to three bowl appearances.

Bradley still has many good seasons ahead of him. His 1990 cards would be decent investments at a nickel or less. Our pick for his best 1990 card is Topps.

SCOTT BRADLEY

	BA	G	AB	R	H	2B	3B	HR	RBI	SB
1989	.274	103	270	21	74	16	0	3	37	1
Life	.271	413	1237	127	335	59	6	17	144	3

Position: Catcher
Team: Seattle Mariners
Born: March 22, 1960 Montclair, NJ
Height: 5'11" **Weight:** 185 lbs.
Bats: Left **Throws:** Right
Acquired: Traded from White Sox for
Ivan Calderon, 6/86

Bradley was one of baseball's busiest reserve catchers again in 1989. He played in a career-high 103 games in 1989 when starter Dave Valle was injured. Normally, the M's have used Bradley as a substitute at catcher, first base, third base, or the outfield. Additionally, he is one of the finest pinch-hitters in the A.L. In 1989, Bradley was third among Mariners regulars in hitting, with a .274 average. Active in pro baseball since 1981, he was the Triple-A International League MVP and batting champion with a .335 average at Columbus in 1984. With the Mariners, Bradley will be a valued part of the team's bench.

Unless Bradley becomes a full-timer, he'll never get the chance to rack up first-class stats. Until then, his common-priced 1990 cards shouldn't be investments. Our pick for his best 1990 card is Donruss.

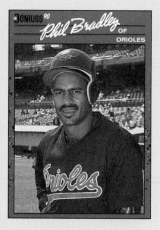

GLENN BRAGGS

	BA	G	AB	R	H	2B	3B	HR	RBI	SB
1989	.247	144	514	77	127	12	3	15	66	17
Life	.256	406	1506	193	385	62	12	42	203	36

Position: Outfield
Team: Milwaukee Brewers
Born: October 17, 1962
    San Bernardino, CA
Height: 6'3" **Weight:** 210 lbs.
Bats: Right **Throws:** Right
Acquired: Second-round pick in 6/83
    free-agent draft

A healthy Braggs was one of the offensive bright spots for the 1989 Brewers. After recovering from shoulder surgery in 1988, he achieved career highs in games played, runs scored, home runs, and stolen bases last year. Previously, Braggs was at his best in 1987, when he batted .269 with 13 homers and 77 RBI for Milwaukee. In four minor league seasons, he never batted below .296. Before the Brewers first called him up in 1986, he was batting .360 with 15 home runs and 75 RBI in 90 games at Triple-A Vancouver. *Baseball America* named him the Triple-A Player of the Year that season. Braggs earned three letters at the University of Hawaii.

    Braggs has been good but not great in three seasons with Milwaukee. His 1990 cards should be a nickel apiece, but they should be considered long-shot investments. Our pick for his best 1990 card is Topps.

JEFF BRANTLEY

	W	L	ERA	G	SV	IP	H	ER	BB	SO
1989	7	1	4.07	59	0	97	101	44	37	69
Life	7	1	4.07	59	0	97	101	44	37	69

Position: Pitcher
Team: San Francisco Giants
Born: September 5, 1963 Florence, AL
Height: 5'11" **Weight:** 180 lbs.
Bats: Right **Throws:** Right
Acquired: Sixth-round pick in 6/85
    free-agent draft

Brantley saw his fortunes reversed when he earned a spot on the 1989 Giants staff. In 1988, he wound up with an 0-1 record (in nine outings) after joining the Giants. When he earned a regular spot on San Francisco's roster in 1989, he won his first six decisions working in middle relief. A relief role was a new assignment for Brantley, who spent his first four seasons as a starter. At Triple-A Phoenix, he was second on the club in both wins and strikeouts, notching nine victories and 83 Ks. His 1988 performance was his first winning season since his 1985 debut with Fresno (8-2). Brantley played his college ball at Mississippi State, where he was an All-American.

    Long relievers don't become famous easily, nor do they enhance baseball card values. Therefore, skip over Brantley's 1990 commons. Our pick for his best 1990 card is Score.

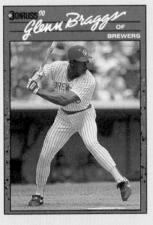
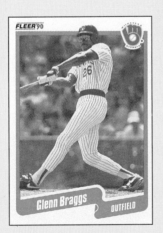

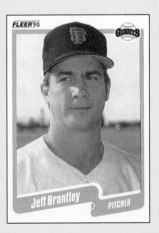

SID BREAM

	BA	G	AB	R	H	2B	3B	HR	RBI	SB
1989	.222	19	36	3	8	3	0	0	4	0
Life	.262	562	1744	210	457	112	8	45	240	32

Position: First base
Team: Pittsburgh Pirates
Born: August 13, 1960   Carlisle, PA
Height: 6'4" **Weight:** 220 lbs.
Bats: Left **Throws:** Left
Acquired: Traded from Dodgers with R.J.
Reynolds and Cecil Espy for Bill
Madlock, 6/85

A knee injury kept Bream out of all but 19 games for the 1989 Pirates. After three straight seasons of double-digit homers, Bucs fans hoped that he could finally live up to his potential. His best season in Pittsburgh was 1986, when he socked 16 homers and 77 RBI, batting .268 in 154 games. Bream's biggest professional season came in 1983, with Triple-A Albuquerque. He led the International League with 118 RBI, while he tied Kevin McReynolds for the league homer lead. Bream is widely respected for his defensive abilities. In 1988, he topped the N.L. with 140 assists, and his .995 fielding percentage was just one point behind the league leader.

Bream hasn't yet posted the consistent offensive marks to make him a serious card investment candidate. Bypass his 1990 commons. Our pick for his best 1990 card is Score.

GEORGE BRETT

	BA	G	AB	R	H	2B	3B	HR	RBI	SB
1989	.282	124	457	67	129	26	3	12	80	14
Life	.310	2137	8166	1300	2528	514	120	267	1311	58

Position: First base
Team: Kansas City Royals
Born: May 15, 1953   Glendale, WV
Height: 6' **Weight:** 200 lbs.
Bats: Left **Throws:** Right
Acquired: Second-round pick in 6/71
free-agent draft

Injuries limited Brett's accomplishments in 1989, but he continued to build up his impressive lifetime totals. After 13 years as a third baseman, he has played at first base since 1987, partially to preserve his fragile right shoulder. Prior to 1989, the lowest Brett ever batted was .282, during his rookie season of 1974. A 13-time All-Star, he's batted above .300 ten times, and he has slugged more than 20 home runs in eight different seasons. Brett has batted .340 with nine home runs in six League Championship Series. In two World Series, he's hit .373 with 19 hits. Brett was named the league MVP in 1980, the year he hit a stunning .390 to lead the league.

Brett has excellent chances for the Hall of Fame. Happily pay 35 cents or less for his 1990 cards, and be assured of some long-term profits. Our pick for his best 1990 card is Fleer.

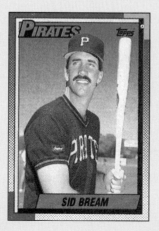

GREG BRILEY

	BA	G	AB	R	H	2B	3B	HR	RBI	SB
1989	.266	115	394	52	105	22	4	13	52	11
Life	.265	128	430	58	114	24	4	14	56	11

Position: Outfield
Team: Seattle Mariners
Born: May 24, 1965 Bethel, NC
Height: 5'9" **Weight:** 170 lbs.
Bats: Left **Throws:** Right
Acquired: First-round pick in secondary
phase of 6/86 free-agent draft

Known as "Pee Wee," Briley made an impression on Seattle in 1989. He was overlooked due to the acclaim received by rookie teammate Ken Griffey Jr. However, Briley won a starting outfield job primarily through his consistent hitting and his nonstop hustle. He topped double digits in the homer category in 1989 (surpassing his '88 minor league total of 11) and hit at the .270 mark. With Triple-A Calgary in 1988, he hit .313 in 112 games, ninth-best in the Pacific Coast League. He compiled hitting streaks of 18 and ten games and paced Calgary with 27 stolen bases that year. Briley should continue to be a key member of the Mariners.

Expect Briley's 1990 cards to quickly reach the quarter mark. Get in early and invest when his cards are 15 cents. Our pick for his best 1990 card is Topps.

GREG BROCK

	BA	G	AB	R	H	2B	3B	HR	RBI	SB
1989	.265	107	373	40	99	6	0	12	52	6
Life	.247	859	2775	369	686	114	6	102	406	36

Position: First base
Team: Milwaukee Brewers
Born: June 14, 1957 McMinnville, OR
Height: 6'3" **Weight:** 205 lbs.
Bats: Left **Throws:** Right
Acquired: Traded from Dodgers for
Tim Crews and Tim Leary, 12/86

While Brock's 1989 statistics with the Brewers don't seem impressive on the surface, his accomplishments are an improvement from his 1988 numbers. He played in just 107 games in 1989, his lowest total since his 1984 season with the Dodgers. However, he lifted his batting average more than 50 points from 1988, and he doubled his home run total. Brock hasn't neared his '87 stats, when he hit .299 with 13 homers and 85 RBI in his first year as a Brewer. During his five seasons with the Dodgers, he topped the 20-homer barrier twice, but he usually batted in the low .230s. He had a minor league career that included two league homer titles. In 1982, Brock hit 44 homers and 138 RBI in Triple-A.

Brock has played without much fanfare since joining the Brewers. Speculators won't find hope in his common-priced 1990 cards. Our pick for his best 1990 card is Donruss.

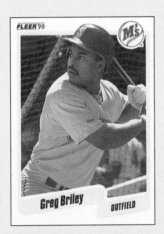
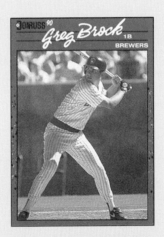

TOM BROOKENS

	BA	G	AB	R	H	2B	3B	HR	RBI	SB
1989	.226	66	168	14	38	6	0	4	14	1
Life	.245	1272	3711	459	909	168	38	70	411	86

Position: Infield
Team: New York Yankees
Born: August 10, 1953, Chambersburg, PA
Height: 5'10" **Weight:** 170 lbs.
Bats: Right **Throws:** Right
Acquired: Traded from Tigers for
Charlie Hudson, 5/89

The Tigers swapped Brookens, one of their senior members, to the Yankees in 1989 for pitching help. The trade ended a decade of major league service in Detroit for Brookens, who began his career in the Tigers' organization in 1975. He was the team's starting third baseman sporadically during his time in Detroit. His first season with the Tigers, in 1980, was his best. In 151 games, he batted .275 with ten homers and 66 RBI. Brookens pounded a career-high 13 homers in 1987. Although he has never stolen more than 14 bases in a single season, he swiped home against Yankee pitcher Ron Guidry in 1986. With superior defensive skills, Brookens fits in well around a team's infield.

Brookens' future with the Yankees will be as a utility player. His common-priced 1990 cards aren't worth the labor. Our pick for his best 1990 card is Score.

HUBIE BROOKS

	BA	G	AB	R	H	2B	3B	HR	RBI	SB
1989	.268	148	542	56	145	30	1	14	70	6
Life	.276	1198	4514	487	1244	224	29	103	609	55

Position: Outfield
Team: Montreal Expos
Born: September 24, 1956
Los Angeles, CA
Height: 6' **Weight:** 205 lbs.
Bats: Right **Throws:** Right
Acquired: Traded from Mets with Mike
Fitzgerald, Herm Winningham,
and Floyd Youmans for Gary
Carter, 12/84

Brooks continued his hitting exploits with the 1989 Expos, marking his sixth straight season of double-digit homers. He spent his second straight campaign in the Expos outfield after working for several years at shortstop, both with Montreal and the Mets. He played his first full season with the Mets in 1981, and hit .307 with four homers and 38 RBI. Brooks finished third in the N.L. Rookie of the Year balloting. He played third base through 1984 with the Mets, which was the longest of any third sacker in team history. Brooks set career highs with 100 RBI in 1985 and 20 homers in 1988.

The two-time All-Star hasn't gotten much recognition in Montreal. However, Brooks is capable of big numbers. At a nickel or less, his 1990 cards would be worthwhile investments. Our pick for his best 1990 card is Fleer.

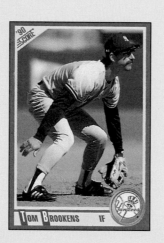

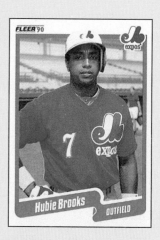

KEVIN BROWN

	W	L	ERA	G	CG	IP	H	ER	BB	SO
1989	12	9	3.35	28	7	191	167	71	70	104
Life	14	10	3.45	33	8	219	206	84	78	120

Position: Pitcher
Team: Texas Rangers
Born: March 14, 1965   McIntyre, GA
Height: 6'4"   **Weight:** 188 lbs.
Bats: Right   **Throws:** Right
Acquired: First-round pick in 6/86
free-agent draft

Brown tallied the best statistics of his career during his 1989 debut with the Rangers: Only Nolan Ryan won more games than did Brown. In fact, Brown reeled off seven complete games by mid-August, matching his career complete game total of the past three seasons. Previously, he had a personal best of 12 victories at Double-A Tulsa in 1988. He had brief late-season tryouts with the Rangers both in 1986 and 1988. He defeated the A's once each season. He set all-time records in both wins and strikeouts while pitching at Georgia Tech. Brown came to the college without a scholarship, joining the team as a freshman walk-on.

Brown could be a consistent winner in years to come. Paying 15 cents or less for his rookie 1990 cards would be a well-calculated risk. Our pick for his best 1990 card is Score.

JERRY BROWNE

	BA	G	AB	R	H	2B	3B	HR	RBI	SB
1989	.299	153	598	83	179	31	4	5	45	14
Life	.280	370	1290	178	361	58	12	7	103	48

Position: Second base
Team: Cleveland Indians
Born: February 13, 1966
Christiansted, Virgin Islands
Height: 5'10"   **Weight:** 170 lbs.
Bats: Both   **Throws:** Right
Acquired: Traded from Rangers with Pete
O'Brien and Oddibe McDowell for
Julio Franco, 12/88

One of the bright spots for the 1989 Indians was new second baseman Browne. He had the enormous chore of filling in for departed All-Star second sacker Julio Franco, a Tribe team favorite. However, Browne, a former Rangers hopeful, led the club in on-base percentage (.370), batting average (.299), hits (179), and stolen bases (14). His 1989 success, which included numerous career highs, was a marked contrast from his 1988 struggles. The Rangers, unhappy with Browne's initial .197 batting average, demoted him to Triple-A for a half-season. He regained the club's starting second base job after a September recall. Browne could be an Indians spark plug for years to come.

Browne is potential All-Star material. At 3 cents, his 1990 cards could be a sleeper investment for the upcoming season. Our pick for his best 1990 card is Fleer.

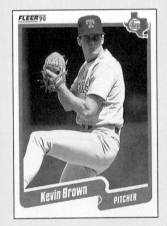

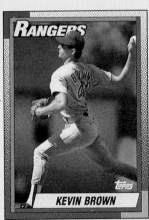

TOM BROWNING

	W	L	ERA	G	CG	IP	H	ER	BB	SO
1989	15	12	3.39	37	9	249	241	94	64	118
Life	37	19	3.73	185	26	1210	1141	501	337	675

Position: Pitcher
Team: Cincinnati Reds
Born: April 28, 1960 Casper, WY
Height: 6'1" **Weight:** 190 lbs.
Bats: Left **Throws:** Left
Acquired: Ninth-round pick in 6/82
      free-agent draft

It was hard for Browning in 1989 to match the excitement that he created in 1988, when on September 16, 1988, he tossed only the third perfect game in N.L. history, against the Dodgers. Browning earned his first no-hitter while pitching in 1984 in Triple-A. He ended 1988 with an 18-5 record, losing only two games after June 6. Browning was named N.L. Rookie Pitcher of the Year in 1985, when he debuted with a 20-9 season. This tireless performer has won in double figures in each major league season, averaging 15 wins a season. Browning is one of the top aces on the Reds staff.

If the Reds come back, Browning will surely fuel the team's rebound. His 10-cent 1990 cards could triple in value if the Reds win a pennant or if he wins 20 games. Our pick for his best 1990 card is Donruss.

MIKE BRUMLEY

	BA	G	AB	R	H	2B	3B	HR	RBI	SB
1989	.198	92	212	33	42	5	2	1	11	8
Life	.199	131	316	41	63	7	4	2	20	15

Position: Infield
Team: Detroit Tigers
Born: April 9, 1963 Oklahoma City, OK
Height: 5'10" **Weight:** 165 lbs.
Bats: Both **Throws:** Right
Acquired: Traded from Padres for
      Luis Salazar, 3/89

After playing with three organizations (Red Sox, Cubs, and Padres), Brumley finally found a home with the Tigers in 1989. He saw action in more than 80 games for Detroit, playing a variety of infield positions. Brumley played shortstop with the 1987 Cubs in 34 games. In 1988, he had the finest season of his seven-year pro career, hitting .315 with 41 stolen bases and 77 runs scored at Triple-A Las Vegas. He was named Triple-A's top shortstop by *Baseball America*. He polished his baseball skills at the University of Texas, playing in three straight College World Series. Brumley's father, Mike Sr., was a catcher for the Senators from 1964 to 1966.

Brumley hasn't proven his ability to hit major league pitching. Because of his offensive woes, there's no reason to invest any major money in his 1990 cards. Our pick for his best 1990 card is Topps.

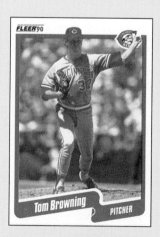

TOM BRUNANSKY

	BA	G	AB	R	H	2B	3B	HR	RBI	SB
1989	.239	158	556	67	133	29	3	20	85	5
Life	.247	1228	4425	593	1095	205	20	208	639	58

Position: Outfield
Team: St. Louis Cardinals
Born: August 20, 1960 Covina, CA
Height: 6'4" **Weight:** 215 lbs.
Bats: Right **Throws:** Right
Acquired: Traded from Twins for Tom Herr,
4/88

Brunansky continued as one of baseball's most dependable sluggers in 1989. The Cardinals outfielder belted 20 home runs, marking the eighth straight season he's topped the 20-homer milestone. St. Louis obtained "Bruno" in a 1988 trade because the team needed a power transfusion for their offense. He responded with 22 homers and 79 RBI in his first year with the Redbirds. Only eight previous Cardinals had hit 20 homers in a season while playing in Busch Stadium. He joined the Twins in 1982, after debuting with the Angels in 1981. With the Twins, he clobbered 166 dingers in seven full seasons, fourth highest in club history. Brunansky's highest round-tripper total was 32, which he achieved both in 1984 and 1987.

Brunansky's 1990 cards should sell for less than a nickel apiece. That's a price sure to climb when the Cardinals win their next pennant. Our pick for his best 1990 card is Donruss.

STEVE BUECHELE

	BA	G	AB	R	H	2B	3B	HR	RBI	SB
1989	.235	155	486	60	114	22	2	16	59	1
Life	.239	668	2032	249	486	88	11	69	242	13

Position: Third base
Team: Texas Rangers
Born: September 26, 1961 Lancaster, CA
Height: 6'2" **Weight:** 190 lbs.
Bats: Right **Throws:** Right
Acquired: Fifth-round pick in 6/82
free-agent draft

Despite suffering through the lowest batting average of his major league career, Buechele homered in double figures for his fourth straight season. He hit just .235, the lowest since he broke in with the Rangers in 1985. That year, the Rangers traded resident third sacker Buddy Bell and gave the job to Buechele. Before his 1985 call-up, he won the American Association MVP award by hitting .297 with nine homers and 64 RBI. While in the minors, he was groomed as a second baseman. Prior to starting his pro career in 1982, he played for the Stanford University baseball team. While in college, Buechele roomed with John Elway, current Denver Broncos quarterback.

Buechele will have to fight to keep his job in 1990. Buechele's erratic career statistics don't justify investment in his common-priced 1990 cards. Our pick for his best 1990 card is Donruss.

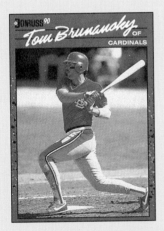

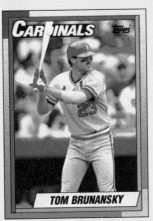

JAY BUHNER

	BA	G	AB	R	H	2B	3B	HR	RBI	SB
1989	.275	58	204	27	56	15	1	9	33	1
Life	.290	150	487	63	117	30	2	22	72	2

Position: Outfield
Team: Seattle Mariners
Born: August 13, 1964 Louisville, KY
Height: 6'3" **Weight:** 205 lbs.
Bats: Right **Throws:** Right
Acquired: Traded from Yankees with Rick
 Balabon and Troy Evers for Ken
 Phelps, 7/88

After a sensational debut with the Seattle Mariners in 1988, Buhner's first full season with the M's was anxiously await- ed. However, injuries and a minor league rehabilitation limit- ed his major league exposure. In just 58 games, Buhner raised his average more than 50 points and drove in a career-high 33 runs. After the Pirates drafted Buhner in the second round in January 1984, he was traded to the Yan- kees in December 1984. He spent nearly four seasons in the New York Yankees' minor league system but couldn't earn a starting job in the majors. At Triple-A Columbus in 1987, Buhner hit .279 with 31 homers and 85 RBI.

With speed, defense, and long-ball potential, Buhner has a promising future. Pick up his 1990 cards at a dime or less for a promising investment. Our pick for his best 1990 card is Fleer.

TIM BURKE

	W	L	ERA	G	SV	IP	H	ER	BB	SO
1989	9	3	2.55	68	28	84	68	24	22	54
Life	37	19	2.49	330	76	478	405	132	160	323

Position: Pitcher
Team: Montreal Expos
Born: February 19, 1959 Omaha, NE
Height: 6'3" **Weight:** 205 lbs.
Bats: Right **Throws:** Right
Acquired: Traded from Yankees for
 Pat Rooney, 12/83

Burke, a converted starter, was the major reason that the Expos were in the 1989 N.L. East pennant race. He joined the Montreal organization in 1983, and he became a reliev- er in Triple-A ball in 1984. In 1985, the Expos summoned Burke, and he led the N.L. with 78 appearances. He posted an incredible 1.19 ERA with a flawless 7-0 record in 1987, serving as the team closer. Burke earned 18 saves for a second time in 1988. It only took the first half of the season in 1989 to exceed his single-season mark for saves. Burke's season was highlighted by an appearance in the 1989 All- Star Game.

Burke could be a perennial All-Star. With his bright future, investing a dime apiece in his 1990 cards would be a rea- sonable venture. Our pick for his best 1990 card is Score.

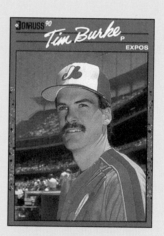

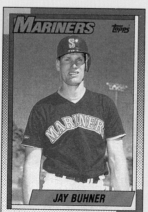

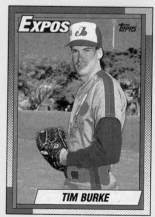

ELLIS BURKS

	BA	G	AB	R	H	2B	3B	HR	RBI	SB
1989	.303	97	399	73	121	19	6	12	61	21
Life	.289	374	1497	260	432	86	13	50	212	73

Position: Outfield
Team: Boston Red Sox
Born: September 11, 1964 Vicksburg, MS
Height: 6'2" **Weight:** 175 lbs.
Bats: Right **Throws:** Right
Acquired: First-round pick in 1/83
free-agent draft

Burks is one of the top hitters in the BoSox lineup. Playing with an All-Star team selected to play in Japan, he was the only player with two home runs. His accomplishments during his first three seasons in baseball have been even more impressive, considering the numerous injuries he's endured. When he's healthy, Burks displays impressive speed, as evidenced by his 27 steals in 1987 and 25 swipes in 1988. During 1987, he tied a major league mark for rookies with two grand slams. That year, Burks became only the third Boston player to post 20 homers and 20 stolen bases in the same year.

Cards for Burks may be as cheap as a quarter in 1990. Buy 'em up, then double your money fast if Boston joins the pennant race. Our pick for his best 1990 card is Donruss.

TODD BURNS

	W	L	ERA	G	SV	IP	H	ER	BB	SO
1989	6	5	2.24	50	8	96	66	24	28	49
Life	14	7	2.73	67	9	198	159	60	62	106

Position: Pitcher
Team: Oakland Athletics
Born: July 6, 1963 Maywood, CA
Height: 6'2" **Weight:** 185 lbs.
Bats: Right **Throws:** Right
Acquired: Seventh-round pick in 6/84
free-agent draft

In just his second major league season, Burns made the conversion from the starting rotation to the bullpen and became a vital member of the 1989 A's pitching staff. He racked up six wins and eight saves, second in the Oakland relief corps. Previously, Burns started 14 games for the Athletics in 1988 and went 8-2. He notched two seven-hitters in 1988, and struck out a season-high seven batters versus California on July 27. He perfected his craft through five minor league seasons. Burns pitched as a reliever in three of those campaigns, then prepared for the job of set-up man during his time at Triple-A Tacoma.

Until he becomes a righty closer for the A's or moves back to the starting rotation, Burns's common-priced 1990 cards won't be good buys. Our pick for his best 1990 card is Score.

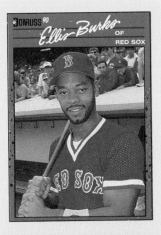

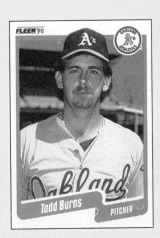

RANDY BUSH

	BA	G	AB	R	H	2B	3B	HR	RBI	SB
1989	.263	141	391	60	103	17	4	14	54	5
Life	.252	931	2472	335	623	126	24	82	343	32

Position: Outfield
Team: Minnesota Twins
Born: October 5, 1958 Dover, DE
Height: 6'1" **Weight:** 185 lbs.
Bats: Left **Throws:** Left
Acquired: Second-round pick in 6/79
          free-agent draft

Bush was at his best with the 1989 Minnesota Twins, reaching career highs in many offensive categories. The eight-year veteran set personal bests in games played (141), runs (60), and triples (four). His hits (103) and homers (14) matched his previous career-highs, both achieved in 1988. Bush cracked double figures for home runs for the sixth time in seven full seasons with Minnesota. He first broke into the starting lineup in 1983, when he batted .249 with 11 homers and 56 RBI in 124 games. Bush has served the Twins well as a pinch-hitter through the years. He tied for the American League pinch-hitting lead in 1984, going eight for-20. In 1986, Bush set a club record with a .433 pinch-hitting mark.

Playing in Kirby Puckett's shadow keeps Bush's card prices low. Don't expect to see any value increases for his 1990 commons. Our pick for his best 1990 card is Donruss.

BRETT BUTLER

	BA	G	AB	R	H	2B	3B	HR	RBI	SB
1989	.283	154	594	100	168	22	4	4	36	31
Life	.281	1200	4379	742	1232	169	74	36	318	307

Position: Outfield
Team: San Francisco Giants
Born: June 15, 1957 Los Angeles, CA
Height: 5'10" **Weight:** 160 lbs.
Bats: Left **Throws:** Left
Acquired: Signed as a free agent, 12/87

A talented leadoff hitter and fine defensive player, Butler continued to be a potent ingredient for the Giants in 1989. Butler was a free-agent acquisition following the 1987 season. He is one of baseball's most gifted bunters. In 1988, he bunted safely 20 out of 37 times to lead the league. His personal best of 109 runs scored was another league high. When he tripled 14 times in 1986 for Cleveland, he became the first player since Hall of Famer Sam Crawford to lead both leagues in triples. In Butler's first full season, 1983, he set a Braves' single-season record with 39 stolen bases. A four-sport star in high school, Butler attended Southeastern Oklahoma State.

Butler's 1990 cards should be an affordable dime or less. His lack of homers and a .300 average limit his stardom and card investment potential. Our pick for his best 1990 card is Fleer.

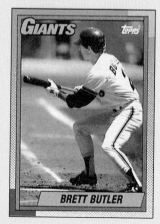

GREG CADARET

	W	L	ERA	G	CG	IP	H	ER	BB	SO
1989	5	5	4.05	46	3	120	130	54	57	80
Life	16	9	3.78	133	3	231	227	97	117	174

Position: Pitcher
Team: New York Yankees
Born: February 27, 1962 Detroit, MI
Height: 6'3" **Weight:** 205 lbs.
Bats: Left **Throws:** Left
Acquired: Traded from Athletics with Eric
　　　　　　Plunk and Luis Polonia for
　　　　　　Rickey Henderson, 6/89

The Yankees were delighted to obtain Cadaret from the Athletics in mid-1989. He had worked as a reliever in his first two seasons with the A's, but he divided his 1989 outings between the bullpen and starting rotation. As a result, he earned three complete games along with five victories. Cadaret had nearly five seasons of minor league experience in the A's system before getting his big league debut on July 5, 1987, against Boston. While in the minors, he won 44 games. Prior to 1987, he worked exclusively as a starter. In 1988, Cadaret was used by Oakland as a left-handed set-up man for closer Dennis Eckersley.

Cadaret's career won't spur card investments if he stays in middle relief. Until he gains a more prominent role on the Yankees staff, bypass his 1990 commons. Our pick for his best 1990 card is Fleer.

IVAN CALDERON

	BA	G	AB	R	H	2B	3B	HR	RBI	SB
1989	.286	157	622	83	178	34	9	14	87	7
Life	.273	502	1826	271	499	110	16	67	249	29

Position: Outfield
Team: Chicago White Sox
Born: March 19, 1962
　　　　　Fajardo, Puerto Rico
Height: 6'1" **Weight:** 205 lbs.
Bats: Right **Throws:** Right
Acquired: Traded from Mariners for
　　　　　　Scott Bradley, 6/86

Calderon was the cornerstone of the White Sox offense in 1989, leading the team in eight different categories. His total hits (178) and triples (nine) were both personal highs during his five-year major league career. His 1989 achievements capped a turnaround from a slump during the previous season. In 1988, Calderon batted just .212 in 73 games, with 14 homers and 35 RBI. Pulled rib cage muscles and an injured shoulder limited his action. He collected a career-high 28 round-trippers in 1987, with 83 RBI. Calderon played in the Seattle organization for more than four years before his debut on August 10, 1984.

When he's healthy, Calderon can hit. However, he's only played in more than 100 games twice in his career. Don't invest in his 5-cent 1990 cards until he can stay in the line-up for two straight years. Our pick for his best 1990 card is Score.

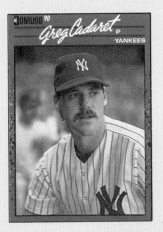

KEN CAMINITI

	BA	G	AB	R	H	2B	3B	HR	RBI	SB
1989	.255	161	585	71	149	31	3	10	72	4
Life	.246	254	871	86	214	40	4	14	102	4

Position: Third base
Team: Houston Astros
Born: April 21, 1963   Hanford, CA
Height: 6'   **Weight:** 200 lbs.
Bats: Both   **Throws:** Right
Acquired: Third-round pick in 6/84
free-agent draft

Caminiti earned the Astros third baseman's job in 1989 by leading Houston in games played (161), at-bats (585), and doubles (31). He became a full-timer with Houston after failing to win the third base job in 1987 and 1988. His major league debut was a memorable one. On July 15, 1987, he tripled and homered off Philadelphia's Kevin Gross, the only hits allowed by Gross in the game. Caminiti was named N.L. Player of the Week for his early efforts, which included hitting in ten of his first 12 games. Caminiti played at San Jose State, where he was named a second-team All-American by *The Sporting News.*

Here's a good spot for an affordable investment. Caminiti's 1990 cards should sell for a nickel or less. You'll be surprised at the future profits. Our pick for his best 1990 card is Score.

JOHN CANDELARIA

	W	L	ERA	G	CG	IP	H	ER	BB	SO
89 NL	0	2	3.31	12	0	16	17	8	4	14
Life	164	104	3.23	410	165	2318	2187	930	527	1481

Position: Pitcher
Team: Montreal Expos
Born: November 6, 1953   Brooklyn, NY
Height: 6'6"   **Weight:** 225 lbs.
Bats: Right   **Throws:** Left
Acquired: Traded from Yankees for
Mike Blowers, 8/89

When the Expos wanted an arm to help them in their 1989 pennant race, they requested Candelaria. The lefthander worked in 12 relief appearances with Montreal, going 0-2 with a 3.31 ERA. The bullpen is a strange place for him. Beginning with his 1975 debut with the Pirates, he was a starter for all but one season prior to 1989. His only real taste of relief came in 1985, when Candelaria made 37 relief appearances (with nine saves) before being traded from Pittsburgh. In ten seasons with the Pirates, he had 124 wins (ninth-best in team history). His 1,142 strikeouts rank fourth on the Pirates' top-ten list. Candelaria owns the last no-hitter ever pitched for the team (in 1976).

If Candelaria doesn't reach 200 lifetime wins, his cards have no long-term profit prospects. Investing in his 1990 commons isn't suggested. Our pick for his best 1990 card is Topps.

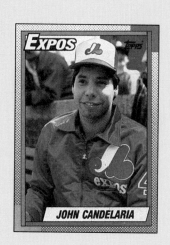

54

TOM CANDIOTTI

	W	L	ERA	G	CG	IP	H	ER	BB	SO
1989	13	10	3.10	31	4	206	188	71	55	124
Life	56	54	3.70	148	41	964	940	396	333	583

Position: Pitcher
Team: Cleveland Indians
Born: August 31, 1957   Walnut Creek, CA
Height: 6'2" **Weight:** 205 lbs.
Bats: Right **Throws:** Right
Acquired: Signed as a free agent, 12/85

One of baseball's few remaining knuckleball artists, Candiotti led the 1989 Indians in wins. His success marked his third double-figure victory season in the last four years. He appeared from virtually nowhere as a minor league free agent to win a spot on the Cleveland roster in 1986. He had been released by Milwaukee after spending five years in the minors. The Brewers regretted their impatience when he went 16-12 with the Tribe. Veteran Phil Niekro taught Candiotti the knuckler, a pitch which revived a floundering career. With his trick pitch and effortless delivery, Candiotti could be baffling hitters for at least another decade.

Candiotti's 1990 commons are long-shot investments. He may never achieve greatness with the Indians but could thrive with a contender. Our pick for his best 1990 card is Score.

JOHN CANGELOSI

	BA	G	AB	R	H	2B	3B	HR	RBI	SB
1989	.219	112	160	18	35	4	2	0	9	11
Life	.242	433	900	147	218	32	9	6	67	91

Position: Outfield
Team: Pittsburgh Pirates
Born: March 10, 1963   Brooklyn, NY
Height: 5'8" **Weight:** 150 lbs.
Bats: Both **Throws:** Left
Acquired: Traded from White Sox for
Jim Winn, 3/87

Cangelosi was one of the most active members of the Pittsburgh bench in 1989, appearing in more than 100 games for the third time in his career. The Bucs used him as a pinch-runner and defensive substitute to make the most of his speed. Speed is Cangelosi's biggest asset, as evidenced by his career-high 50 stolen bases with the 1986 White Sox. During his second pro season, with Class-A Appleton in 1983, he stole 87 bases to lead the Midwest League. A willingness to serve has kept Cangelosi on the Pirate roster. In 1988, he even worked as a relief pitcher for the first time in his career. Cangelosi was successful, tossing two scoreless innings against the Dodgers.

Until he becomes a full-timer, Cangelosi won't be a worthy card investment. Avoid his 1990 commons. Our pick for his best 1990 card is Topps.

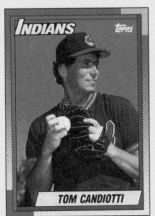

JOSE CANSECO

	BA	G	AB	R	H	2B	3B	HR	RBI	SB
1989	.269	65	227	40	61	9	1	17	57	6
Life	.270	568	2163	342	583	110	5	128	424	86

Position: Outfield
Team: Oakland Athletics
Born: July 2, 1964   Havana, Cuba
Height: 6'3"   **Weight:** 230 lbs.
Bats: Right   **Throws:** Right
Acquired: 15th-round pick in 6/82
   free-agent draft

A fractured wrist sharply curtailed Canseco's accomplishments in 1989. Despite his inactivity, fans made him a top vote-getter in All-Star balloting. Canseco had a spectacular 1988 campaign when he won the A.L. MVP. He became the first player in history to join the "40/40" club by slamming 42 homers and swiping 40 bases. Canseco topped the league in RBI, extra-base hits, and slugging percentage as well. He usually comes through in the clutch; he had a .313 average in the '88 A.L.C.S. and he hit .357 in the '89 World Series. Jose's twin brother, Ozzie, is in the A's minor league system.

Despite his injury, Jose remained awesome at the plate. If you can get his 1990 cards for under a dollar, do it fast. His card values seem to be limitless. Our pick for his best 1990 card is Topps.

DON CARMAN

	W	L	ERA	G	SV	IP	H	ER	BB	SO
1989	5	15	5.24	49	0	149	152	87	86	81
Life	47	50	4.05	253	9	796	736	358	321	523

Position: Pitcher
Team: Philadelphia Phillies
Born: August 14, 1959   Oklahoma City, OK
Height: 6'3"   **Weight:** 195 lbs.
Bats: Left   **Throws:** Left
Acquired: Signed as a free agent, 8/78

In 1989, Carman tied for the N.L. lead in losses. He and St. Louis rookie Ken Hill each had 15 losses; Carman's defeats often came as the result of brief relief appearances. He's toiled in the role of swing man during his career with the Phillies, working both as a starter and reliever. However, he posted double-digit win totals in 1986 to 1988, including a career-high 13 victories in 1987. As a reliever, his finest season came in 1985, when he went 9-4 with seven saves and a 2.08 ERA in 71 appearances. Carman spent nearly six full seasons in the minors before sticking with the Phillies in 1984.

Wait to see how well Carman performs before investing in his 1990 commons. After such a poor 1989, his major league future hangs in the balance. Our pick for his best 1990 card is Donruss.

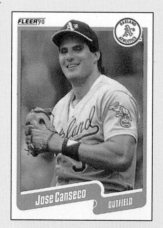

CRIS CARPENTER

	W	L	ERA	G	CG	IP	H	ER	BB	SO
1989	4	4	3.18	36	0	68	70	24	26	35
Life	6	7	3.83	44	1	115	126	49	35	59

Position: Pitcher
Team: St. Louis Cardinals
Born: April 5, 1965   St. Augustine, FL
Height: 6'1" **Weight:** 185 lbs.
Bats: Right **Throws:** Right
Acquired: First-round pick in 6/87
        free-agent draft

Carpenter jumped from the University of Georgia to St. Louis in less than one year. In 1987 he posted nine wins and 11 saves as a reliever in college. Carpenter won the MVP award in the 1987 Pan American Games with six wins, five saves, and a 1.37 ERA. After playing winter instructional ball in 1987, he started the 1988 season at Triple-A Louisville, going 6-2 with a 2.87 ERA. He earned a call-up to St. Louis, but after winning two games he went on the disabled list with a rotator cuff strain. Carpenter was a noted punter for the Georgia football team.

Frustrated at his lack of success in the majors, Carpenter has contemplated becoming an NFL punter. If he does this, he'll raise interest in his cards. Buy his 1990 cards at a nickel apiece. Our pick for his best 1990 card is Topps.

MARK CARREON

	BA	G	AB	R	H	2B	3B	HR	RBI	SB
1989	.308	68	133	20	41	6	0	6	16	2
Life	.318	84	154	25	49	8	0	7	18	2

Position: Outfield
Team: New York Mets
Born: July 19, 1963   Chicago, IL
Height: 6' **Weight:** 194 lbs.
Bats: Right **Throws:** Left
Acquired: Seventh-round pick in 6/81
        free-agent draft

Carreon's greatest talent may be patience. After seven minor league seasons in the Mets' farm system, he earned a spot on the 1989 big league roster as an outfielder and pinch hitter. In his first 45 games with New York in 1989, he batted .293 with four home runs and nine RBI. In 1988 with Triple-A Tidewater, Carreon slammed a career high of 14 home runs. He was a starter in the first annual Triple-A All-Star game. With Tidewater in 1987, Carreon had 19 game-winning RBI and 41 doubles. He batted .312 with ten homers and 89 RBI. Carreon's father, Camilo, was a catcher from 1959 to 1966 with the White Sox, Indians, and Orioles.

Mark isn't guaranteed of starting time with the 1990 Mets. Don't invest in his common-priced 1990 cards until he gets a full-time job. Our pick for his best 1990 card is Donruss.

  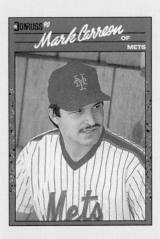 

  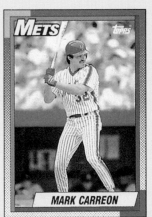

GARY CARTER

	BA	G	AB	R	H	2B	3B	HR	RBI	SB
1989	.183	50	153	14	28	8	0	2	15	0
Life	.265	2008	7194	955	1907	329	30	305	1143	36

Position: Catcher
Team: New York Mets
Born: April 8, 1954 Culver City, CA
Height: 6'2" **Weight:** 214 lbs.
Bats: Right **Throws:** Right
Acquired: Traded from Expos for Hubie
Brooks, Mike Fitzgerald, Herm
Winningham,and Floyd Youmans,
12/84

After an injury-plagued 1989 season, Carter's career was thrown in limbo when the Mets announced they wouldn't offer him a contract for 1990. As the team said goodbye to Carter, his brief career in the Big Apple was snuffed out. He starred with the Expos from 1974 to 1984, landing seven of his first 11 All-Star nominations. He gained national acclaim in the 1981 All-Star Game, when he became just the fifth player in history to crack two All-Star homers in one game. In 1986, Carter hit 24 homers and 105 RBI to lead the Mets to a World Series.

Carter has a remote shot at the Hall of Fame and may be making his last appearance in card sets if his career is over. However, no short-term profits will be available on his 5-cent 1990 cards. Our pick for his best 1990 card is Score.

JOE CARTER

	BA	G	AB	R	H	2B	3B	HR	RBI	SB
1989	.243	162	651	84	158	32	4	35	105	13
Life	.268	862	3307	462	885	165	23	151	531	127

Position: Outfield
Team: Cleveland Indians
Born: March 7, 1960 Oklahoma City, OK
Height: 6'3" **Weight:** 215 lbs.
Bats: Right **Throws:** Right
Acquired: Traded from Cubs with Darryl
Banks, Don Schulze, and Mel Hall
for Rick Sutcliffe, Ron Hassey,
and George Frazier, 6/84

The offensive centerpiece of the Indians, Carter topped the 20-homer plateau for the fourth time in five years. He remained a consistent threat to A.L. pitchers in 1989, ranking among leaders in home runs and RBI. He ranks eighth on the all-time Indians' home run list. A four-sport star in high school, Carter was a star baseball player at Wichita State. In 1981, he was named College Player of the Year by *The Sporting News*, then he became the second player in the nation selected in 1981. Carter spent nearly three seasons in the Cubs' minor league system before being traded to the Indians.

Carter is an accomplished long-ball threat. Buy his 1990 cards at a dime or less. The value of those cards could skyrocket if he joins a contender. Our pick for his best 1990 card is Donruss.

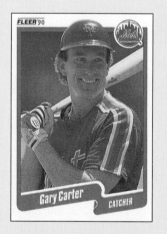

CARMEN CASTILLO

	BA	G	AB	R	H	2B	3B	HR	RBI	SB
1989	.257	94	218	23	56	13	3	8	33	1
Life	.230	290	683	83	157	24	8	11	68	19

Position: Outfield
Team: Minnesota Twins
Born: June 8, 1958
San Francisco de Macoris,
Dominican Republic
Height: 6'1" **Weight:** 190 lbs.
Bats: Right **Throws:** Right
Acquired: Traded from Indians for
Keith Atherton, 3/89

Castillo set a career high for games played with the 1989 Twins. Although he continued as a part-time player, he appeared in 94 games with his new team. He showed his power potential, however, by attaining a .454 slugging percentage and popping eight home runs. He has been battling since his 1982 major league debut to win a full-time job somewhere. After beginning his career in the Philadelphia organization in 1978 as an undrafted free agent, he first reached the majors with the 1982 Indians. In 1984, 1985, and 1987, he earned double-digit totals in home runs. The Indians traded him for pitching, and the Twins were anxious to gain Castillo's batting ability.

Castillo can't crack a starting lineup, which makes his cards unpopular. His 1990 commons are undesirable investments. Our pick for his best 1990 card is Score.

RICK CERONE

	BA	G	AB	R	H	2B	3B	HR	RBI	SB
1989	.243	102	296	28	72	16	1	4	48	0
Life	.241	1157	3640	343	877	167	15	54	402	4

Position: Catcher
Team: Boston Red Sox
Born: May 19, 1954   Newark, NJ
Height: 5'11" **Weight:** 185 lbs.
Bats: Right **Throws:** Right
Acquired: Signed as a free agent, 4/88

Cerone completed his 15th season in the major leagues with a respectable effort for the 1989 Red Sox. The injury-prone receiver played in more than 100 games for just the third time this decade, and had the most hits (72) and RBI (48) since his 1980 campaign with the Yankees. He hit a homer for the Yanks in the 1981 World Series. Boston discovered his availability just two weeks into the 1988 season and put him to work. Cerone began his pro career in 1975, and was promoted to the Indians during that first season. He has played with the Blue Jays, Yankees, Braves, Brewers, and Red Sox.

Cerone's 1990 cards will be commons. Because he is in the twilight of his career and will be struggling to keep a starting job, his cards will not offer any investment potential. Our pick for his best 1990 card is Fleer.

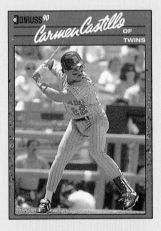

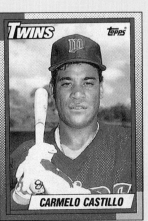

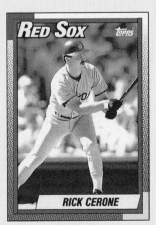

JOHN CERUTTI

	W	L	ERA	G	CG	IP	H	ER	BB	SO
1989	11	11	3.07	33	3	205	214	70	53	69
Life	37	28	3.67	161	7	632	638	258	205	320

Position: Pitcher
Team: Toronto Blue Jays
Born: April 28, 1960 Albany, NY
Height: 6'2" **Weight:** 200 lbs.
Bats: Left **Throws:** Left
Acquired: First-round pick in 6/81
  free-agent draft

Cerutti spent a full season in the 1989 Blue Jays starting rotation and tied his career-high victory total. He won 11 games, which matched his record from 1987. Although he has been a Blue Jays regular since 1986, he marked his first season as solely in the starting rotation in 1989. His two relief appearances were his fewest since he earned a four-game debut with the 1985 Blue Jays. Out of 133 minor league appearances during five seasons, Cerutti relieved in just nine games. Unlike many other pitchers, he has shown equal success both as a starter and reliever. However, Cerutti's potential could be unlimited if Toronto keeps his role well defined.

Cerutti's 1990 cards sell as commons. The cards are good investments, providing that the talented lefthander maintains his starter status. Our pick for his best 1990 card is Score.

NORM CHARLTON

	W	L	ERA	G	SV	IP	H	ER	BB	SO
1989	8	3	2.93	69	0	95	67	31	40	96
Life	12	8	3.35	79	0	156	127	58	60	137

Position: Pitcher
Team: Cincinnati Reds
Born: January 6, 1963 Ft. Polk, LA
Height: 6'3" **Weight:** 195 lbs.
Bats: Both **Throws:** Left
Acquired: Traded from Expos with Tim
  Barker for Wayne Krenchicki,
  3/86

Charlton made a successful move to the bullpen with the Reds in 1989, his second year in the majors. The transition was surprising, because he had made just one relief appearance in his first 109 pro games. Charlton wrapped up his rookie season in fine fashion. After joining the Reds in mid-August, he allowed three runs or less in eight of his last nine starts. As a reliever in 1989, he consistently overwhelmed batters, averaging more than one strikeout per inning. He was an All-American at Rice University. Charlton was a first-round selection in the June 1984 draft by the Expos.

It's possible to find Charlton's 1990 cards for a nickel apiece. He is too talented to be in the bullpen forever. Invest in his cards before he becomes a starter. Our pick for his best 1990 card is Topps.

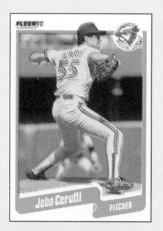
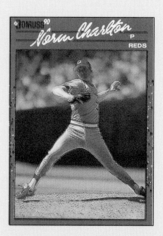

JIM CLANCY

	W	L	ERA	G	CG	IP	H	ER	BB	SO
1989	7	14	5.08	33	1	147	155	83	66	91
Life	135	154	4.16	385	74	2353	2340	1088	880	1328

Position: Pitcher
Team: Houston Astros
Born: December 18, 1955 Chicago, IL
Height: 6'4" **Weight:** 220 lbs.
Bats: Right **Throws:** Right
Acquired: Signed as a free agent, 12/88

Clancy made news before the 1989 season started. When he signed a free-agent contract with the Astros on December 16, 1988, he ended his reign as the last original Blue Jay. He began his pro career in 1974 with the Texas organization. Toronto made Clancy its third selection in the 1977 expansion draft. He had eight seasons of double-digit wins in 12 years with the Blue Jays. Clancy's career-best record came in 1982, when he was 16-14. He won a spot on the A.L. All-Star team, and he led the league with 40 starts. Clancy suffered through a horrendous 1989 campaign, but he's still respected for his pitching stamina.

Clancy has a lifetime losing record, an automatic warning that his common-priced 1990 cards won't bring long-term profits. Our pick for his best 1990 card is Fleer.

DAVE CLARK

	BA	G	AB	R	H	2B	3B	HR	RBI	SB
1989	.237	102	253	21	60	12	0	8	29	0
Life	.244	212	554	53	135	22	1	17	68	2

Position: Outfield
Team: Chicago Cubs
Born: September 3, 1962 Tupelo, MS
Height: 6'2" **Weight:** 200 lbs.
Bats: Left **Throws:** Right
Acquired: Traded from Indians for
       Mitch Webster, 11/89

The Cubs acquired Clark for some lefthanded power and as a backup to Andre Dawson. In 1989, Clark's fourth season with the Indians, he reached major league career highs in nearly every offensive category, including 102 games played, eight homers, and 29 RBI. He hit .263 in 63 games for the 1988 Indians. He was named All-American by *The Sporting News* from Jackson State in 1983, prior to becoming Cleveland's first-round selection in the June draft, the 11th player taken overall. His finest season was in 1987 at Triple-A Buffalo, when he batted .340 with 30 homers and 80 RBI, and led the American Association with 22 outfield assists. Clark's brother, Louis, plays wide receiver for the Seattle Seahawks.

Clark's 1990 cards are commons. Those investors hopeful that he can gain a starting job should invest in his cards. Our pick for his best 1990 card is Topps.

JACK CLARK

	BA	G	AB	R	H	2B	3B	HR	RBI	SB
1989	.242	142	455	76	110	19	1	26	94	6
Life	.271	1658	5775	952	1563	291	37	282	998	72

Position: First base
Team: San Diego Padres
Born: November 10, 1955
New Brighton, PA
Height: 6'3" **Weight:** 205 lbs.
Bats: Right **Throws:** Right
Acquired: Traded from Yankees with Pat
Clements for Lance McCullers,
Jimmy Jones, and Stan
Jefferson, 10/88

Clark returned to both the National League and California in 1989 when he was traded to the Padres. He was obtained to help jump start the team's sluggish offense, and he delivered with team-leading marks of 26 homers and 94 RBI. Clark surpassed the 90-RBI horizon for the fourth time in his 14-year career. When the Padres obtained him from the Yankees, they hoped that he could rekindle the fire he displayed with the 1987 Cardinals. He reached career highs in both homers (35) and RBI (106). He grew up in California, and starred with the Giants from 1976 to 1984. Upon San Francisco's 25th anniversary in 1982, Clark was elected to the "Dream Team" of the top players in team history.

Clark's 1990 cards will sell for 15 cents apiece. That's a bargain price for a future Hall of Famer. Our pick for his best 1990 card is Donruss.

JERALD CLARK

	BA	G	AB	R	H	2B	3B	HR	RBI	SB
1989	.195	17	41	5	8	2	0	1	7	0
Life	.196	23	56	5	11	3	0	1	10	0

Position: Outfield
Team: San Diego Padres
Born: August 10, 1963 Crockett, TX
Height: 6'4" **Weight:** 189 lbs.
Bats: Right **Throws:** Right
Acquired: 12th-round pick in 6/85
free-agent draft

Although he got just a brief shot with the Padres, Clark proved his readiness with another banner season in the minors. He hit .313 with 22 homers and 83 RBI at Triple-A Las Vegas in 1989. Since he began his pro career in 1985, he's never batted below .301. In 1987, with Double-A Wichita, he batted .313 with a career high of 95 RBI. Clark was ignored in the June 1985 draft until the Padres made him a 12th-round pick. After five years in the minors, look for Clark to win at least a reserve role with the 1990 Padres.

While Clark hasn't distinguished himself as a major leaguer yet, he has proven it all in the minors. Make a modest investment in his 15-cent 1990 cards. Then hope the Padres give Clark a chance in the bigs. Our pick for his best 1990 card is Donruss.

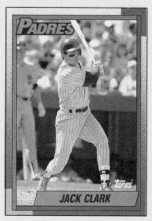

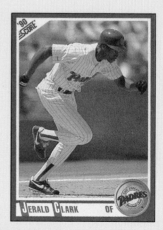

WILL CLARK

	BA	G	AB	R	H	2B	3B	HR	RBI	SB
1989	.333	159	588	104	196	38	9	23	111	8
Life	.304	582	2100	361	638	125	22	98	352	26

Position: First base
Team: San Francisco Giants
Born: March 13, 1964   New Orleans, LA
Height: 6'1" **Weight:** 190 lbs.
Bats: Left **Throws:** Left
Acquired: First-round pick in 6/85
free-agent draft

Will "The Thrill" Clark was the overwhelming choice as the N.L.'s starting first baseman in the 1989 All-Star Game, an honor he earned for the second straight year. Clark first gained fame as a member of the 1984 U.S. Olympic team. Since missing 47 games in '86, Clark has remained virtually injury-free, building a respectable consecutive-game streak. In 1988, he became the first player in Giants' history to play in all 162 games. Despite playing in the shadow of Kevin Mitchell's hitting explosion in '89, Clark was in the league's top five in runs, RBI, hits, on-base percentage, and slugging percentage.

After 1989, America knows that Clark is capable of anything. The 75-cent cost of his 1990 cards may seem steep, but that price could double if Clark duplicates his success in 1990. Our pick for his best 1990 card is Score.

ROGER CLEMENS

	W	L	ERA	G	CG	IP	H	ER	BB	SO
1989	17	11	3.13	35	8	253	215	101	93	230
Life	95	45	3.06	175	58	1284	1088	476	371	1215

Position: Pitcher
Team: Boston Red Sox
Born: August 4, 1962   Dayton, OH
Height: 6'4" **Weight:** 220 lbs.
Bats: Right **Throws:** Right
Acquired: First-round pick in 6/83
free-agent draft

Like clockwork, Clemens in 1989 continued to be a main contender for the A.L. strikeout crown. He spent his fourth year as the Red Sox pitching ace in 1989. He enjoyed the finest years of his young career in 1986 and 1987, when he won back-to-back Cy Youngs. A late-season slump in 1988, following a 15-5 beginning through July, cost Clemens his third straight 20-win season. In 1986, after hurling the Red Sox to the World Series, his honors included the league MVP Award, the All-Star MVP, and the Cy Young. In 1983, Clemens was the winning pitcher in the last game of the NCAA World Series for the Texas Longhorns.

Invest in Clemens's 1990 cards, which may be less than 50 cents. Those cards will hit the 75-cent mark as soon as he shoots for 20 wins. Our pick for his best 1990 card is Donruss.

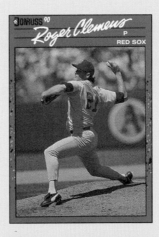

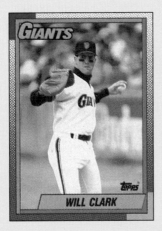

PAT CLEMENTS

	W	L	ERA	G	SV	IP	H	ER	BB	SO
1989	4	1	3.92	23	0	39	39	17	15	18
Life	12	10	3.90	217	12	284	281	123	121	124

Position: Pitcher
Team: San Diego Padres
Born: February 2, 1962   McCloud, CA
Height: 6'   **Weight:** 180 lbs.
Bats: Right   **Throws:** Left
Acquired: Traded from Yankees with Jack
Clark for Lance McCullers, Jimmy
Jones, and Stan Jefferson, 10/88

Clements played part of 1989 with the Padres, his fourth
major league team in his seven-year career. After 18 games
with the Triple-A Las Vegas, the Padres called him up. In
long relief, he finished eight of 23 appearances in 1989.
Clements was a much-heralded rookie coming out of UCLA.
In 1983, the Angels drafted Clements in the fourth round. By
1985, he was in the majors. His rookie season was memorable, a 5-0 record with one save and a 3.34 ERA in 41
appearances. He earned a career-high seven saves with
the Yankees in 1987. At San Diego, however, it seems like
Clements will have to battle just to keep a job in the majors.

Clements has forgettable lifetime stats, and could be
spending 1990 back in the minors. Investing in his 1990
cards is too risky. Our pick for his best 1990 card is Topps.

DAVE COCHRANE

	BA	G	AB	R	H	2B	3B	HR	RBI	SB
1989	.235	54	102	13	24	4	1	3	7	0
Life	.220	73	164	17	36	6	1	4	9	0

Position: Infield; outfield
Team: Seattle Mariners
Born: January 31, 1963   Riverside, CA
Height: 6'2"   **Weight:** 180 lbs.
Bats: Both   **Throws:** Right
Acquired: Traded from Royals for
Ken Spratke, 2/88

Cochrane's 54-game exposure with the 1989 Mariners was
his chance of a lifetime, and he made a strong bid to
become the M's top utility player. He started his long march
to the majors in 1982 with the Mets' organization. In mid-
1985, he was traded to the White Sox for Tom Paciorek but
was sidelined that year with a broken ankle. The next year,
Cochrane appeared in 19 games for the White Sox, batting
.194. Finally, in 1989, he got another opportunity. In the
minors, Cochrane has hit 15 or more homers in six different
seasons. However, his time is running out to equal those
stats in the majors.

Don't invest in Cochrane's 1990 commons until he wins a
starting job in the majors. At this point, his future doesn't
look promising. Our pick for his best 1990 card is Topps.

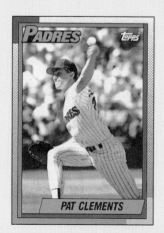

VINCE COLEMAN

	BA	G	AB	R	H	2B	3B	HR	RBI	SB
1989	.254	145	563	94	143	21	9	2	28	65
Life	.247	754	3038	493	792	88	47	9	178	472

Position: Outfield
Team: St. Louis Cardinals
Born: September 22, 1961
    Jacksonville, FL
Height: 6' **Weight:** 170 lbs.
Bats: Both **Throws:** Right
Acquired: Tenth-round pick in 6/82
    free-agent draft

Coleman carved out a place in sports history in 1989. The N.L.'s stolen base champion for the fifth straight year reeled off a record 50 consecutive stolen bases from 1988 to '89. He was thrown out by Chicago's Damon Berryhill in September 1988, then remained untouched until Montreal's Nelson Santovenia gunned him down on July 28, 1989. In 1985, Coleman was the unanimous selection as the N.L. Rookie of the Year with a league-leading 110 steals. Coleman is the only player to swipe 100-plus bases in each of his first three major league seasons. In 1983, his second minor league season, Coleman set a pro baseball record with 145 steals in 113 games.

Stolen bases alone won't make Coleman a superstar. Until he hits for a better average and fields decently, his 1990 cards will be overpriced at 15 cents each. Our pick for his best 1990 card is Score.

DARNELL COLES

	BA	G	AB	R	H	2B	3B	HR	RBI	SB
1989	.252	146	535	54	135	21	3	10	59	5
Life	.247	606	2024	239	500	101	9	57	271	18

Position: Third base; outfield
Team: Seattle Mariners
Born: June 2, 1962 San Bernadino, CA
Height: 6'1" **Weight:** 185 lbs.
Bats: Right **Throws:** Right
Acquired: Traded from Pirates for
    Glenn Wilson, 7/88

Coles won the starting third base job during the 1989 season for the Mariners. He wound up at the hot corner during the last month of the season when the team was unhappy with Jim Presley and Edgar Martinez. The extra duty satisfied Coles, who demanded a trade earlier in the year. He saw his greatest success with the 1986 Tigers, hitting .273 with 20 homers and 86 RBI. However, the Bengals traded him after the 1987 campaign, and Pittsburgh shuttled him back to Seattle in July 1988. If Coles stays happy, he could be an important starter for the 1990 M's.

Coles is a potential All-Star. However, his attitude has hampered his production in the past. Risk-loving investors could grab a handful of his 1990 commons and hope that Coles retains a starting job for the M's. Our pick for his best 1990 card is Fleer.

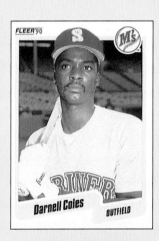

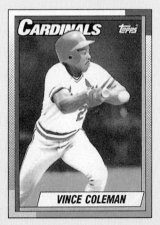

PAT COMBS

	W	L	ERA	G	CG	IP	H	ER	BB	SO
1989	4	0	2.09	6	1	38	36	9	6	30
Life	4	0	2.09	6	1	38	36	9	6	30

Position: Pitcher
Team: Philadelphia Phillies
Born: October 29, 1966 Newport, RI
Height: 6'4" **Weight:** 205 lbs.
Bats: Left **Throws:** Left
Acquired: First-round pick in 6/88
free-agent draft

Combs began his pro career in 1989 at Double-A Reading, and by season's end he was pitching for the Phillies. At Reading, he was 8-7. Following a promotion to Triple-A Scranton-Wilkes Barre, Combs was unstoppable. He notched a 3-0 record with two complete games and a 0.37 ERA. After winning seven straight he was promoted to Philadelphia. Combs was 4-0 there, and his strikeout-to-walk ratio was five-to-one. He played college ball for Stanford, and he was 5-1 for the '88 USA Olympic team. The team's coach ranked him equal to Jim Abbott but said that Combs threw a better breaking ball.

Combs has a good shot to make the 1990 Phillies. His rookie 1990 cards will start at as much as 50 cents. If he opens the season in Philadelphia, that price could quickly double. Our pick for his best 1990 card is Score.

DAVID CONE

	W	L	ERA	G	CG	IP	H	ER	BB	SO
1989	14	8	3.52	34	7	219	183	86	74	190
Life	39	17	3.12	101	16	572	477	198	211	492

Position: Pitcher
Team: New York Mets
Born: January 2, 1963 Kansas City, MO
Height: 6'1" **Weight:** 185 lbs.
Bats: Left **Throws:** Right
Acquired: Traded from Royals with
Chris Jelic for Ed Hearn,
Rick Anderson, and
Mauro Gozzo, 3/87

Although Cone didn't repeat his 1988 success, he was a leading winner on the Mets staff again in 1989. He tied for the team lead with 14 victories. Cone's 190 strikeouts put him among N.L. leaders for a second straight season. He was coming off an incredible 20-3 effort in 1988. His .870 winning percentage was the sixth-best in history for any pitcher with 20 or more wins. For three straight seasons, Cone has tallied double-digit hit totals. In 1989, he was the senior circuit's top-hitting pitcher. Cone was a high school star in football and basketball; his Kansas City school did not field a baseball team.

A never-ending demand for any Mets cards should inflate Cone's 1990 card prices to 35 cents. It will be best to sell as soon as he reaches 20 wins again. Our pick for his best 1990 card is Fleer.

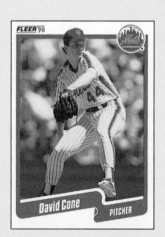

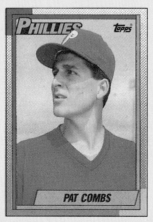

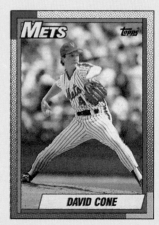

DENNIS COOK

	W	L	ERA	G	CG	IP	H	ER	BB	SO
1989	7	8	3.72	23	2	121	110	50	38	67
Life	9	9	3.59	27	3	143	119	57	49	80

Position: Pitcher
Team: Philadelphia Phillies
Born: October 4, 1962 La Marque, TX
Height: 6'3" **Weight:** 185 lbs.
Bats: Left **Throws:** Left
Acquired: Traded from Giants with Charlie
　　　　　Hayes and Terry Mulholland for
　　　　　Steve Bedrosian, 7/89

The Phillies call Cook the key to the trade that sent former Cy Young winner Steve Bedrosian to the Giants. In his first three starts with the 1989 Phillies, Cook was 2-1 with a 1.96 ERA. After leading Triple-A Phoenix in wins, complete games, innings, and strikeouts in 1988, he got four starts with the Giants. His 2-1 record included a September 25 two-hit win that stopped the Dodgers from clinching the pennant at Candlestick. In 1987, he was the Texas League Pitcher of the Year after going 9-2 with a 2.13 ERA in 16 starts. In 1986, Cook topped the California League with 173 strikeouts in 170 innings.

Cook's 1990 cards seem like good buys at 15 cents or less. If the Phillies give him even a small lead to work with, he should go far. Our pick for his best 1990 card is Score.

SCOTT COOLBAUGH

	BA	G	AB	R	H	2B	3B	HR	RBI	SB
89 AA	.260	144	527	66	137	28	0	18	74	1
89 Major	.275	25	51	7	14	1	0	2	7	0

Position: Third base
Team: Texas Rangers
Born: June 1, 1966 Binghamton, NY
Height: 5'11" **Weight:** 185 lbs.
Bats: Right **Throws:** Right
Acquired: Third-round pick in 6/87
　　　　　free-agent draft

With just two full minor league seasons under his belt, Coolbaugh got his first shot at the majors with the 1989 Rangers. He got a late-season call-up to the Rangers after popping a career-high 18 homers with Triple-A Oklahoma City. Coolbaugh became one of the offensive terrors of the American Association in 1989, challenging for league leads in homers and RBI. With Texas, he started six of his first 11 games after joining the team. He played collegiate ball at the University of Texas in Austin. Coolbaugh was the team's MVP and was named to the College World Series All-Tournament team.

Coolbaugh may have the inside tracking for the Rangers third base job in 1990. His rookie 1990 cards could be a steal at 15 cents or less. Our pick for his best 1990 card is Score.

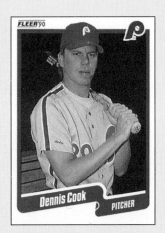

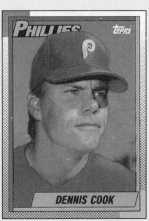

SCOTT COOPER

	BA	G	AB	R	H	2B	3B	HR	RBI	SB
1989	.247	117	421	50	104	24	2	7	39	1
Life	.298	130	497	90	148	45	7	9	73	0

Position: Third base
Team: Boston Red Sox
Born: October 13, 1967   St. Louis, MO
Height: 6'3"   **Weight:** 200 lbs.
Bats: Left   **Throws:** Right
Acquired: Third-round pick in 6/86
free-agent draft

Cooper has the unenviable task of being a third baseman in the Boston system, knowing that Wade Boggs is the Red Sox hot corner man. However, Cooper has battled on for four seasons, making progress at each level. In 1989 at Double-A New Britain, he ranked among team leaders in homers and RBI. His 1988 season at Class-A Lynchburg made him a Carolina League All-Star. He batted .298 with nine homers and 73 RBI. His 45 doubles were a league best. He drilled 15 homers at Class-A Greensboro in 1987. Despite his limited opportunities with the Red Sox, Cooper has the talent to be a major leaguer.

The best advice concerning Cooper's 15-cent 1990 cards is to wait on investing until the Red Sox give him a substantial trial in the coming season. Our pick for his best 1990 card is Score.

JOHN COSTELLO

	W	L	ERA	G	SV	IP	H	ER	BB	SO
1989	5	4	3.32	48	3	62	48	23	20	40
Life	10	6	2.68	84	4	111	92	33	45	78

Position: Pitcher
Team: St. Louis Cardinals
Born: December 24, 1960   New York, NY
Height: 6'1"   **Weight:** 180 lbs.
Bats: Right   **Throws:** Right
Acquired: 25th-round pick in 6/83
free-agent draft

Costello spent his first full season with the Cardinals in 1989, and provided stability to the team's bullpen. He appeared in a career-high 48 games and earned three saves and five wins while helping keep the Cardinals in pennant contention down to the last week of the season. He worked in the Cardinals' minor league system for more than five seasons for a chance at the majors. He proved his readiness in 1988, when he was 1-1 with 11 saves in his first 20 appearances for Triple-A Louisville. During his 1988 rookie season in St. Louis, Costello ranked second in the league among rookie relievers, holding opponents scoreless in 29 of 36 games pitched. For 1990, Costello will be a middle reliever for the Cards.

Unless Costello becomes a closer, his 1990 commons won't have much long-term investment appeal. Our pick for his best 1990 card is Topps.

HENRY COTTO

	BA	G	AB	R	H	2B	3B	HR	RBI	SB
1989	.264	100	295	44	78	11	2	9	33	10
Life	.258	475	1112	154	287	48	3	24	106	54

Position: Outfield
Team: Seattle Mariners
Born: January 5, 1961   Bronx, NY
Height: 6'2"   **Weight:** 178 lbs.
Bats: Right   **Throws:** Right
Acquired: Traded from Yankees with
Steve Trout for Lee Guetterman,
Clay Parker, and Shane Taylor,
12/87

Although he lost the starting Mariners center fielder's job to rookie Ken Griffey Jr., Cotto still served the team as a top reserve in 1989. He surpassed the 100-game barrier for the third time in six major league seasons and set a career-high for homers. When Griffey was injured, Cotto filled in ably. In 1988, he hit .259 with eight homers, 33 RBI, 50 runs, and 18 doubles. He stole a career-high 27 bases, including his first 17 attempts. His speed has helped him become a solid defensive outfielder. In 1984, Cotto's .984 fielding percentage topped Cubs outfielders during that pennant-winning year.

Cotto will likely be the M's fourth outfielder as long as he's in Seattle. Such part-time status makes his 1990 commons uninviting card investments. Our pick for his best 1990 card is Fleer.

DANNY COX

	W	L	ERA	G	CG	IP	H	ER	BB	SO
1989				Did not play						
Life	56	56	3.40	152	21	985	991	372	297	493

Position: Pitcher
Team: St. Louis Cardinals
Born: September 21, 1959
Northampton, England
Height: 6'4"   **Weight:** 225 lbs.
Bats: Right   **Throws:** Right
Acquired: 12th-round pick in 6/81
free-agent draft

Cox suffered a torn ligament in his pitching elbow and missed the 1989 season. The Cardinals were looking forward to seeing him rebound from a poor 1988 season, when he was plagued by elbow troubles. He wound up with a 3-8 mark after starting just 13 games. He had double-digit win totals from 1985 to 1987. His career-best record came in 1985, when he was 18-9 with ten complete games. Cox added a victory in the N.L.C.S. that turned the playoffs around after two straight Cardinal losses. In 1987, he won the seventh and decisive game of the N.L.C.S. If healthy, Cox will be the senior member of the Cardinals pitching staff.

The verdict is still out on Cox's health. See if he makes a comeback before investing anything in his 1990 commons. Our pick for his best 1990 card is Topps.

TIM CREWS

	W	L	ERA	G	SV	IP	H	ER	BB	SO
1989	0	1	3.21	44	1	61	69	22	23	56
Life	5	2	3.07	106	4	161	176	55	47	121

Position: Pitcher
Team: Los Angeles Dodgers
Born: April 3, 1961 Tampa, FL
Height: 6' **Weight:** 190 lbs.
Bats: Right **Throws:** Right
Acquired: Traded from Brewers with Tim
Leary for Greg Brock, 12/86

Crews spent his first full season with the Dodgers in 1989, making the most of his middle-relief assignment. He appeared in a career-high 44 games, finishing 16. He averaged nearly one strikeout per inning last season coming in from the Dodgers bullpen. Crews began his pro career in 1981 as a starter. Working in the Milwaukee organization through 1986, he made just 11 relief appearances in 116 games. When the Dodgers acquired him they began grooming him as a reliever for the start of the 1987 season. After seven victories and 12 saves in his first 42 games at Triple-A Albuquerque in 1987, the Dodgers gave Crews his major league debut in July.

Middle relief is a tough role to become a hero in, as Crews has found out. His little-known career inhibits investment in his 1990 commons. Our pick for his best 1990 card is Donruss.

CHUCK CRIM

	W	L	ERA	G	SV	IP	H	ER	BB	SO
1989	9	7	2.83	76	7	117	114	37	36	59
Life	22	21	3.17	199	28	352	342	124	103	173

Position: Pitcher
Team: Milwaukee Brewers
Born: July 23, 1961 Van Nuys, CA
Height: 6' **Weight:** 190 lbs.
Bats: Right **Throws:** Right
Acquired: 17th-round pick in 6/82
free-agent draft

Crim led the A.L. in appearances for the second straight year while pitching for the 1989 Brewers. He worked in a league-leading 76 contests (compared to an A.L. best of 70 for 1988). He has made middle relief an art form, paving the way for Brewers bullpen stopper Dan Plesac. Crim reached additional career bests in wins, ERA, and strikeouts. He won his first Brewers roster spot in 1987 and notched 12 saves that year, even though he was pressed into starting duty five times. He was a college baseball star at Hawaii, earning All-American honors in 1980 and leading his club to the College World Series.

Although Crim does his job in the thankless position of middle reliever, a scattering of his 1990 commons might not be a bad investment. Our pick for his best 1990 card is Fleer.

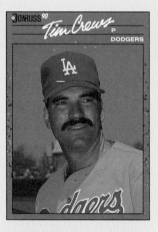

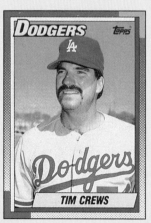

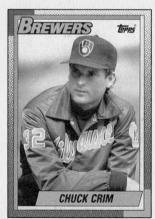

MILT CUYLER

	BA	G	AB	R	H	2B	3B	HR	RBI	SB
89 AA	.262	100	366	69	96	8	7	7	34	32
Life	.296	132	483	100	143	11	3	2	32	50

Position: Outfield
Team: Detroit Tigers
Born: October 7, 1968 Macon, GA
Height: 5'10" **Weight:** 175 lbs.
Bats: Both **Throws:** Right
Acquired: Second-round pick in 6/86
free-agent draft

Cuyler is slated as the center fielder of the future for the Tigers. In his fourth minor league season in 1989, he paced Double-A London in runs scored, and he was chosen as the best defensive outfielder in the Eastern League by circuit managers. His speed allows him to reach hits other outfielders couldn't touch. Cuyler displayed his potential in 1988 at Class-A Lakeland. He topped the Florida State League with 100 runs scored and was second with 143 hits, batting .296. He stole 50 bases in 75 attempts and was named a league All-Star in center field. Cuyler should contend for Detroit's center field job in the near future.

It's likely that nearly all of Detroit's roster spots will be open for 1990. Cuyler's 1990 rookie cards could be tempting investments at a dime or less. Our pick for his best 1990 card is Score.

KAL DANIELS

	BA	G	AB	R	H	2B	3B	HR	RBI	SB
1989	.246	55	171	33	42	13	0	4	17	9
Life	.302	377	1215	235	367	76	6	54	168	77

Position: Outfield
Team: Los Angeles Dodgers
Born: August 20, 1963 Vienna, GA
Height: 5'11" **Weight:** 195 lbs.
Bats: Left **Throws:** Right
Acquired: Traded from Reds with Lenny
Harris for Mariano Duncan and
Tim Leary, 7/89

Daniels endured knee problems with the 1989 Dodgers, limiting him to his fewest games in four years. He was active in just 55 games, his lowest total since he broke in with the 1986 Reds. Even when Daniels was in the lineup, he maintained just some of his once-admirable speed because of six knee operations. He carved his niche with the Reds by hitting .320 in 1986, adding six home runs, 23 RBI, and 15 stolen bases. In 1987, he batted a career-high .334, including 26 homers, 64 RBI, and 26 stolen bases. While his stats dipped to .291 with 18 dingers and 64 RBI in 1988, Daniels stayed healthy enough to play in a personal-best 140 games.

Before investing, speculators should decide whether Daniels can play several more years. For now, don't pay the going rate of a dime apiece for his 1990 cards. Our pick for his best 1990 card is Donruss.

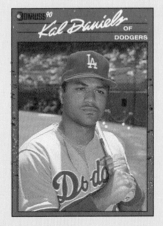

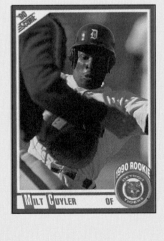

RON DARLING

	W	L	ERA	G	CG	IP	H	ER	BB	SO
1989	14	14	3.52	33	4	217	214	85	70	153
Life	87	55	3.38	207	24	1391	1242	523	542	991

Position: Pitcher
Team: New York Mets
Born: August 19, 1960   Honolulu, HI
Height: 6'3"   **Weight:** 195 lbs.
Bats: Right   **Throws:** Right
Acquired: Traded from Rangers with
Walt Terrell for Lee Mazzilli,
4/82

Darling breezed through his sixth-straight season of double-digit wins with the 1989 Mets. He tied David Cone for the team lead in wins (14). Darling's losses (14) were a career high, however. Previously, he had never lost more than nine games in a season. He has been the foundation of the Met pitching staff since 1984, his first full season in New York. Fans count on at least ten wins and 200 innings pitched from Darling each year. He was buried treasure that the Mets uncovered during a 1982 trade. After spending 1982 and most of 1983 at Triple-A Tidewater, Darling got his major league debut on September 6, 1983.

As with teammates Cone and Dwight Gooden, Darling gets much acclaim for his efforts. His 1990 cards will be a nickel, a wise investment for a potential 20-game winner. Our pick for his best 1990 card is Score.

DANNY DARWIN

	W	L	ERA	G	SV	IP	H	ER	BB	SO
1989	11	4	2.36	68	7	122	92	32	33	104
Life	100	105	3.51	440	27	1750	1640	682	550	1156

Position: Pitcher
Team: Houston Astros
Born: October 25, 1955   Bonham, TX
Height: 6'3"   **Weight:** 190 lbs.
Bats: Right   **Throws:** Right
Acquired: Traded from Brewers for Don
August and Mark Knudson, 8/86

In 1989, Darwin posted his best record while anchoring the Houston bullpen. His mark of 11-4 with seven saves was his best since 1980 with the Rangers, when he was 13-4 with eight saves. He achieved a personal high in appearances (68), marking the first season in a 14-year career that was devoted solely to relief pitching. The Astros acquired Darwin in 1986 as pennant insurance, and he's been a vital part of the pitching staff ever since. He debuted with the Rangers in 1978, and stayed with the team for seven seasons. He was a Brewer in 1985 and 1986 before joining Houston. Darwin's stats have suffered from dividing his career between starting and relieving.

Darwin's age and Houston's urge to switch him from the bullpen to the starting rotation will cloud his 1990 commons investment future. Our pick for his best 1990 card is Donruss.

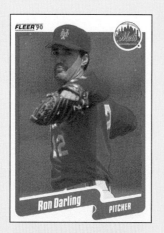

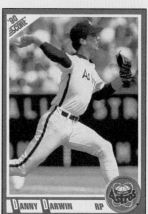
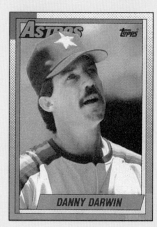

JACK DAUGHERTY

	BA	G	AB	R	H	2B	3B	HR	RBI	SB
1989	.302	52	106	15	32	4	2	1	10	2
Life	.285	63	116	16	33	5	2	1	11	2

Position: First base
Team: Texas Rangers
Born: July 3, 1960   Hialeah, FL
Height: 6'   **Weight:** 185 lbs.
Bats: Both   **Throws:** Left
Acquired: Traded from Expos for
　　　　Tom O'Malley, 9/88

At age 29, Daugherty wasn't the typical portrait of a rookie in 1989. However, the hard-hitting first baseman was a consistent part-timer for the Rangers, hitting above .300 during the season. His only prior major league experience came with the Expos during an 11-game trial in 1987. His professional career began in the Oakland farm system in 1983 before joining the Expos' organization the following season. In 1984, Daugherty was named Class-A Pioneer League Player of the Year. He hit .402 with 15 homers and 82 RBI, leading the loop in five offensive categories. He batted above .300 during the next three seasons, the latest being 1987 at Triple-A Indianapolis. Daugherty should provide the Rangers with depth in 1990.

Daugherty's rookie batting average looks promising. If you can invest in his rookie 1990 cards for 15 cents or less, consider yourself lucky. Our pick for his best 1990 card is Score.

DARREN DAULTON

	BA	G	AB	R	H	2B	3B	HR	RBI	SB
1989	.201	131	368	29	74	12	2	8	44	2
Life	.206	329	885	85	182	31	3	24	101	9

Position: Catcher
Team: Philadelphia Phillies
Born: January 3, 1962   Arkansas City, KS
Height: 6'2"   **Weight:** 190 lbs.
Bats: Left   **Throws:** Right
Acquired: 25th-round pick in 6/80
　　　　free-agent draft

Although Daulton had an anemic batting average in 1989, he racked up some accomplishments for the Phillies. In his first full season, he achieved career highs in games played and numerous offensive categories. His eight home runs tied his 1986 efforts, when he clubbed eight homers in just 49 games. Constant shoulder ailments have haunted him. A career-threatening injury occurred on June 21, 1986, when Mike Heath banged into his knee during a play at the plate. Daulton was sidelined for the rest of the season and underwent surgery. But after ten months of recuperation, Daulton returned on May 24, 1987, hitting a three-run homer in his first game.

The Phillies will be housecleaning in 1990. Daulton's sickly batting average makes him expendable. At this point, his 1990 commons look like poor investments. Our pick for his best 1990 card is Score.

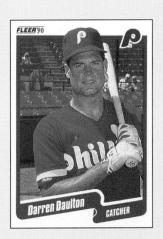

73

ALVIN DAVIS

	BA	G	AB	R	H	2B	3B	HR	RBI	SB
1989	.305	142	498	84	152	30	1	21	95	0
Life	.290	881	3180	461	921	176	9	131	530	7

Position: First base
Team: Seattle Mariners
Born: September 9, 1960 Riverside, CA
Height: 6'1" **Weight:** 190 lbs.
Bats: Left **Throws:** Right
Acquired: Sixth-round draft pick in 6/82
　　　　　free-agent draft

Davis is the owner of many Seattle offensive records. A Mariner since 1984, he has established team records in games, runs, hits, doubles, home runs, RBI, total bases, and walks. A star at Arizona State, he was named All-Pac Ten three times. He was the first Mariner in history to win a major award when he was named the 1984 A.L. Rookie of the Year. His rookie season consisted of 27 home runs, 116 RBI, and a .284 batting average. After hitting 18 home runs both in 1985 and 1986, "A.D." rebounded to 29 homers, 100 RBI, and a .295 average in 1987. On May 9, 1986, against Toronto, Davis drove in eight runs.

　Davis's 1990 cards won't cost more than a dime each. Invest at that bargain price. If he tops the league in any hitting categories, those prices will soar. Our pick for his best 1990 card is Donruss.

CHILI DAVIS

	BA	G	AB	R	H	2B	3B	HR	RBI	SB
1989	.271	154	560	81	152	24	1	22	90	3
Life	.268	1186	4308	594	1153	197	24	144	601	107

Position: Outfield
Team: California Angels
Born: January 17, 1960 Kingston, Jamaica
Height: 6'3" **Weight:** 210 lbs.
Bats: Both **Throws:** Right
Acquired: Signed as a free agent, 12/87

Davis fueled the Angels for a second straight year, leading the 1989 club in home runs and RBI. Since joining the Angels as a free agent prior to the 1988 season, he has reached 20 homers and 90 RBI in both years. In 1989, he made six errors in the outfield, a marked improvement over his 19 errors in 1988. It's obvious that Davis seems most comfortable at the plate. Ever since he broke in with the San Francisco organization in 1978, he's been a hard hitter. In every one of his 12 pro seasons, Davis has homered in double digits.

　Buy Davis's 1990 cards at a dime or less. His stats have never been better since joining the Angels. If he leads the Halos to a pennant soon, his card prices will explode. Our pick for his best 1990 card is Score.

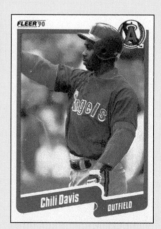

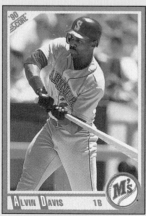

ERIC DAVIS

	BA	G	AB	R	H	2B	3B	HR	RBI	SB
1989	.281	131	462	74	130	14	2	34	101	21
Life	.275	640	2119	431	582	83	16	142	413	212

Position: Outfield
Team: Cincinnati Reds
Born: May 29, 1962   Los Angeles, CA
Height: 6'3"   **Weight:** 185 lbs.
Bats: Right   **Throws:** Right
Acquired: Eighth-round pick in 6/80
      free-agent draft

Davis highlighted his 1989 season with his second career All-Star appearance. He broke into Cincinnati's starting line-up in mid-1984 after spending more than four years in the minors. The Reds originally tried to make Davis a shortstop but abandoned the idea after one year. After a return to the minors in 1985, he enjoyed his first full major league season in 1986. He wound up the year with 27 home runs and 80 steals. Davis belted a career-high 37 homers and drove in 100 runs in 1987. In 1988, he set a club record with an N.L.-best 21 game-winning RBI. With sterling defensive skills, Davis could maintain his stardom for another decade.

Plan on paying at least 50 cents for Davis's 1990 cards. His cards are consistent price gainers, and could skyrocket in value if he lands an MVP award. Our pick for his best 1990 card is Score.

GLENN DAVIS

	BA	G	AB	R	H	2B	3B	HR	RBI	SB
1989	.269	158	581	87	156	26	1	34	89	4
Life	.264	737	2705	383	713	135	6	144	454	15

Position: First base
Team: Houston Astros
Born: March 28, 1961   Jacksonville, FL
Height: 6'3"   **Weight:** 210 lbs.
Bats: Right   **Throws:** Right
Acquired: First-round pick in secondary
      phase of 1/81 free-agent draft

After just five major league seasons, Davis has established himself as one of the National League's biggest power threats. He drove in 93 or more runs each year from 1986 through 1988, peaking at 101 RBI in 1986. Davis in 1989 became the first Houston player to have three seasons of 30 or more round-trippers. Prior to 1989, Davis already had 53 home runs in the cavernous Astrodome, the fourth-highest total in that stadium's history. In the minors, Davis tied for league leads in home runs in 1982 and 1983. He broke into the Astros starting lineup in 1985. Davis remains as the Astros resident manufacturer of home runs.

Quickly pay up to 15 cents each for Davis's 1990 cards. The heir apparent to the N.L. homer crown has unlimited possibilities as a card investment. Our pick for his best 1990 card is Fleer.

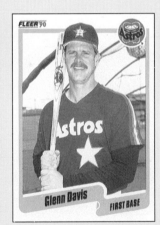
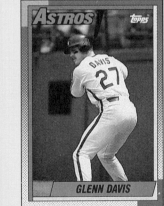

MARK DAVIS

	W	L	ERA	G	SV	IP	H	ER	BB	SO
1989	4	3	1.85	70	44	93	66	19	31	92
Life	40	65	3.76	416	85	858	758	359	340	754

Position: Pitcher
Team: San Diego Padres
Born: October 19, 1960 Livermore, CA
Height: 6'4" **Weight:** 200 lbs.
Bats: Left **Throws:** Left
Acquired: Traded from Giants with Chris
 Brown, Mark Grant, and Keith
 Comstock for Dave Dravecky,
 Craig Lefferts, and Kevin
 Mitchell, 7/87

The 1989 Cy Young Award winner, Davis continued to be one of the N.L.'s most effective relievers. He compiled a career high for saves with 44. He got his first chance to serve as the San Diego stopper in 1988, and he responded with 28 saves and a sparkling 2.01 ERA in 62 games pitched. His efforts earned him a postseason spot on the All-Star team selected to tour Japan. In 1989, Davis pitched one scoreless inning, striking out two, in his first-ever All-Star Game. He had spent five years with the Giants, working both as a starter and reliever. Davis averages at least one strikeout per inning pitched.

Davis will have 1990 cards selling for up to a quarter. Until he shows his 1989 exploits weren't a fluke, his cards won't be prudent buys. Our pick for his best 1990 card is Donruss.

MIKE DAVIS

	BA	G	AB	R	H	2B	3B	HR	RBI	SB
1989	.249	67	173	21	43	7	1	5	19	6
Life	.259	963	2999	419	778	161	16	91	371	134

Position: Outfield
Team: Los Angeles Dodgers
Born: June 11, 1959 San Diego, CA
Height: 6'3" **Weight:** 185 lbs.
Bats: Left **Throws:** Left
Acquired: Signed as a free agent, 12/87

Davis saw limited action with the 1989 Dodgers, playing in fewer than 100 games for the first time since 1982, when he was first breaking in with the Athletics. He had his glory years with the A's through 1987, when he became a free agent and signed with Los Angeles. His greatest year in Oakland came in 1985, when he batted .287 with 24 homers and 82 RBI in 154 games. He followed with 19 round-trippers in 1986 and 22 more in 1987. His first season with the Dodgers in 1988 was anything but memorable, as he batted a career-low .196 with two homers and 17 RBI in 108 games. But in the '88 World Series, Davis clouted a two-run shot in the fifth game against his old team.

Davis once was one of Oakland's finest power men. Now, he can't rack up piles of homers without getting to play. Avoid buying his 1990 commons until he earns a starting position. Our pick for his best 1990 card is Topps.

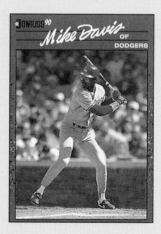

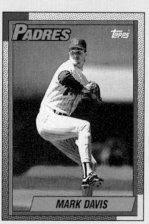

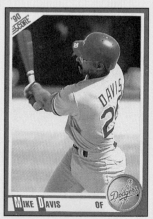

STORM DAVIS

	W	L	ERA	G	CG	IP	H	ER	BB	SO
1989	19	7	4.36	31	1	169	187	82	68	91
Life	92	62	3.86	244	28	1318	1315	566	488	769

Position: Pitcher
Team: Oakland Athletics
Born: December 16, 1961 Dallas, TX
Height: 6'4" **Weight:** 200 lbs.
Bats: Right **Throws:** Right
Acquired: Traded from Padres for
　　　　　　 Dave Leiper, 8/87

Despite tallying one of the highest ERAs of his career, Davis earned a career high for wins with the 1989 Athletics. Davis missed 20-win seasons by a single victory. During the 1989 World Series, Oakland manager Tony LaRussa shuffled the pitching rotation after the San Francisco earthquake interrupted the third game, yanking Davis out of the starting rotation. Davis then said that he'd declare free agency after the Series was finished. Many teams might want him if he's available. Since his 1982 debut with Baltimore, Davis has reached double figures in wins three times.

If the A's don't retain Davis, he could gain lots of attention with his possible free agency. His 1990 cards, at a dime or less, are reasonable investments. Our pick for his best 1990 card is Donruss.

ANDRE DAWSON

	BA	G	AB	R	H	2B	3B	HR	RBI	SB
1989	.252	118	416	62	105	18	6	21	77	8
Life	.281	1871	7256	1058	2037	368	83	319	1131	288

Position: Outfield
Team: Chicago Cubs
Born: July 10, 1954 Miami, FL
Height: 6'3" **Weight:** 195 lbs.
Bats: Right **Throws:** Right
Acquired: Signed as a free agent, 3/87

Although Dawson didn't match his incredible 1987 output, he continued to be a vital force for the Cubs in 1989. He provided his team with clutch hitting and polished defense. In 1989, Dawson broke both the 2,000-hit and 300-home run barriers, adding to his career statistics. In 1987, he led the league with 49 homers and 137 RBI, winning the N.L. MVP Award. He began his career with the Expos by winning the Rookie of the Year Award in 1977. He holds the Montreal all-time home run record. When he hangs up his spikes, Dawson will be a strong candidate for the Hall of Fame.

Dawson hasn't neared the stats he posted in his MVP season of 1987. The hobby probably won't offer a solid resale market for his 15-cent 1990 cards for years. Our pick for his best 1990 card is Donruss.

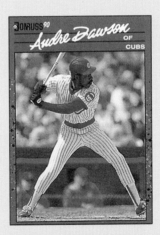

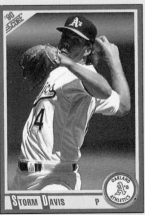

KEN DAYLEY

	W	L	ERA	G	SV	IP	H	ER	BB	SO
1989	4	3	2.87	71	12	75	63	24	30	40
Life	29	41	3.64	317	37	495	493	200	186	350

Position: Pitcher
Team: St. Louis Cardinals
Born: February 25, 1959, Jerome, ID
Height: 6' **Weight:** 180 lbs.
Bats: Left **Throws:** Left
Acquired: Traded from Braves with Mike
      Jorgensen for Ken Oberkfell,
      6/84

Dayley established new career highs for appearances (71) and saves (12) for the 1989 St. Louis Cardinals. When team stopper Todd Worrell was ailing, Dayley shouldered the extra load and kept the Cardinals in the pennant race down to the last week of the season. Simply remaining in the majors today is one of his greatest achievements. He was sidelined for nearly half of 1987 with elbow stiffness. Dayley's career could have ended with off-season surgery, but he was back on the mound in late May of 1988. He has excelled in postseason play. Dayley owns ten scoreless innings of League Championship Series work, along with four L.C.S. career saves.

    Once Worrell returns, Dayley will resume his short man work in relief, setting up save situations. His 1990 commons won't offer much investment potential. Our pick for his best 1990 card is Topps.

ROB DEER

	BA	G	AB	R	H	2B	3B	HR	RBI	SB
1989	.210	130	466	72	98	18	2	26	65	4
Life	.229	624	2084	316	477	79	8	121	339	41

Position: Outfield
Team: Milwaukee Brewers
Born: September 29, 1960 Mesa, AZ
Height: 6'3" **Weight:** 210 lbs.
Bats: Right **Throws:** Right
Acquired: Traded from Giants for Dean
      Freeland and Eric Pilkington,
      12/85

In 1989, Deer paced the Brewers in round-trippers for the fourth straight season. In 1988, he posted a career-high .252 average despite tying for the A.L. lead in strikeouts with 153. After the All-Star break, he hit a respectable .296. Deer was an unknown commodity in the Giants' farm system for almost seven seasons before joining Milwaukee. He won three minor league home run titles before getting a 13-game trial with San Francisco in 1984. Playing part-time with the Giants in 1985 gave him little opportunity, and he wound up with eight homers and a .185 average. After the Brewers obtained Deer, he clobbered 33 home runs during his 1985 debut.

    Vote this guy "most likely to strike out." Deer isn't a good 1990 card investment choice at current prices of a nickel or less. Our pick for his best 1990 card is Donruss.

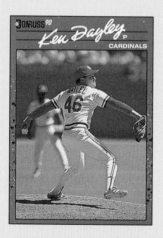

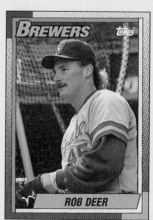

JOSE DeJESUS

	W	L	ERA	G	CG	IP	H	ER	BB	SO
1989	0	0	4.50	3	0	8	7	4	8	2
Life	0	1	10.80	5	0	10	13	12	13	4

Position: Pitcher
Team: Kansas City Royals
Born: January 6, 1965 Brooklyn, NY
Height: 6'5" **Weight:** 175 lbs.
Bats: Right **Throws:** Right
Acquired: Signed as a free agent, 5/83

In 1989, Triple-A American Association managers ranked DeJesus as the league's best fastball pitcher and best prospect. He was among the top strikeout pitchers in all of Triple-A in 1989. He surpassed his career high of 149 strikeouts in August at Omaha, a mark that he achieved in 1988 with Double-A Memphis. DeJesus finished second in the Southern League in Ks that year, despite being called up to Triple-A Omaha in late July. He joined the Royals in late 1988 and went 0-1 in two appearances. After seven seasons in professional baseball, DeJesus should face major league hitters in 1990.

Although DeJesus has only pitched five games for the Royals, his future isn't that promising. Be conservative, and don't spend much on his rookie 1990 cards. Our pick for his best 1990 card is Topps.

JOSE DeLEON

	W	L	ERA	G	CG	IP	H	ER	BB	SO
1989	16	12	3.05	36	5	244	173	83	80	201
Life	61	77	3.70	201	20	1233	974	507	550	1061

Position: Pitcher
Team: St. Louis Cardinals
Born: December 20, 1960
  Rancho Viejo, Dominican Republic
Height: 6'3" **Weight:** 215 lbs.
Bats: Right **Throws:** Right
Acquired: Traded from White Sox for Lance
  Johnson and Ricky Horton, 2/88

DeLeon enjoyed the best season of his 11-year pro career in 1989. He reached a career high for wins with a 16-12 record, second-best on the club. Although his 201 strikeouts were seven fewer than his 1988 total, DeLeon had enough to lead the N.L. in Ks. In 1988, he went 13-10 in his first year with the Cardinals. His athletic ability was highlighted in 1988, when he was used as an outfielder in an extra-innings game. He demonstrated that he can win with a winner. He was 2-19 with the 1985 Pirates, worst in the N.L. Pittsburgh, however, gave DeLeon just two runs or less in 14 of his 19 starts.

DeLeon's strikeout title is a start toward recognition. However, he still has a lackluster lifetime record, tossing doubt on the investment potential of his nickel-priced 1990 cards. Our pick for his best 1990 card is Donruss.

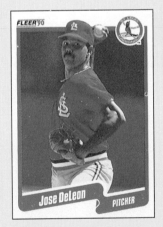

LUIS de los SANTOS

	BA	G	AB	R	H	2B	3B	HR	RBI	SB
1989	.253	28	87	6	22	3	1	0	6	0
Life	.220	39	109	7	24	4	2	0	7	0

Position: First base
Team: Kansas City Royals
Born: December 29, 1966
     San Cristobal, Dominican Republic
Height: 6'5" **Weight:** 195 lbs.
Bats: Right **Throws:** Right
Acquired: Second-round pick in 6/84
     free-agent draft

After spending most of the 1989 season with the Royals, de los Santos went back to Triple-A Omaha and batted near .300. He first made the 1989 Royals when George Brett was injured. At the time, de los Santos was batting .361 at Omaha. He batted .375 in spring training in 1989. One of his career highlights was on May 2, 1989, at Yankee Stadium. With 40 of his friends and relatives in attendance, the Queens resident stroked a two-run single to give the Royals a 5-3 victory. In 1988, he was the American Association MVP and first baseman in the Triple-A All-Star Game. De los Santos led the league with 164 hits and tied for the lead with 87 RBI.

De los Santos's 1990 cards will cost a nickel. He hasn't shown the consistency to make his cards investment-worthy yet. Our pick for his best 1990 card is Topps.

JIM DESHAIES

	W	L	ERA	G	CG	IP	H	ER	BB	SO
1989	15	10	2.91	34	6	225	180	73	79	153
Life	49	36	3.43	121	11	738	632	281	274	519

Position: Pitcher
Team: Houston Astros
Born: June 23, 1960 Massena, NY
Height: 6'4" **Weight:** 225 lbs.
Bats: Left **Throws:** Left
Acquired: Traded from Yankees with
     Neder de Jesus Horta and
     Dody Rather for Joe Niekro,
     9/85

Deshaies earned a career high in victories while pitching for the 1989 Astros. His 15 wins also marked the fourth straight year the lefty won at least 11 games. He began his pro career in the Yankees' organization in 1982. However, New York gave him just a two-game audition in the majors during five minor league seasons. Houston promoted him immediately. He was 12-5 in 1986, notching the best record of any N.L. rookie pitcher. Deshaies finished seventh in the league's Rookie of the Year balloting. He earned a lasting place in baseball history on September 23, 1986, against the Dodgers. To start the game, Deshaies struck out eight consecutive Dodgers—seven went down swinging.

Deshaies could be Houston's next 20-game winner. Investors would be wise to soak up his 1990 cards, priced at a nickel or less. Our pick for his best 1990 card is Score.

DELINO DeSHIELDS

	BA	G	AB	R	H	2B	3B	HR	RBI	SB
89 AAA	.260	53	233	36	50	10	7	1	23	9
88 A	.252	127	460	97	116	26	6	12	46	61

Position: Shortstop
Team: Montreal Expos
Born: January 15, 1969 Seaford, DE
Height: 6'1" **Weight:** 170 lbs.
Bats: Left **Throws:** Right
Acquired: First-round pick in 6/87
 free-agent draft

In his third pro season, DeShields continued his steady progress through the Montreal farm system, solidifying his reputation as the Expo shortstop of the future. At Double-A Jacksonville in 1989, he hit .270 with three homers, 35 RBI, and a team-leading 37 stolen bases. Deshields was ranked the fifth-best major league prospect by *Baseball America*. He landed a midseason promotion to Triple-A Indianapolis. He displayed awesome speed in 1988 at Class-A Rockford. His .252 average was complemented by 12 homers, 46 RBI, and 61 stolen bases. While he struck out 110 times, he also drew 95 bases on balls. DeShields turned down a basketball scholarship to Villanova to start his baseball career.

Deshields may not make the majors until 1991, but he definitely will make it. Invest in his rookie 1990 cards at 15 cents each. Our pick for his best 1990 card Score.

MIKE DEVEREAUX

	BA	G	AB	R	H	2B	3B	HR	RBI	SB
1989	.266	122	391	55	104	14	3	8	46	22
Life	.248	171	488	66	121	18	3	8	52	25

Position: Outfield
Team: Baltimore Orioles
Born: April 10, 1963 Casper, WY
Height: 6' **Weight:** 195 lbs.
Bats: Right **Throws:** Right
Acquired: Traded from Dodgers for
 Mike Morgan, 3/89

Devereaux's acquisition by the 1989 Orioles helped get the O's back on the winning track. As a part-timer with Baltimore, he batted in the .270s for most of 1989. Devereaux and his double-digit swipe total helped make basestealing a major part of the O's game. Speed has always been one of his major assets. Devereaux stole 33 bases in 1988 at Triple-A Albuquerque. His .340 batting average, 13 homers, and 76 RBI won him a spot on the Pacific Coast League All-Star team. In 1987 at Double-A San Antonio, he hit .301 with 26 homers, 91 RBI, and 33 steals in 135 games. Devereaux hit .302 at San Antonio in 1986, with 31 stolen bases and 53 RBI.

All Devereaux needed was some playing time in order to prove his ability. His 1990 cards are decent buys at a nickel or less. Our pick for his best 1990 card is Donruss.

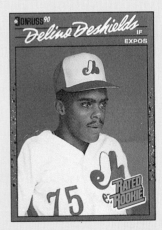

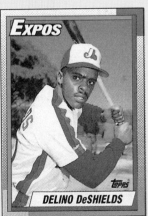

ROB DIBBLE

	W	L	ERA	G	SV	IP	H	ER	BB	SO
1989	10	5	2.09	74	2	99	62	23	39	141
Life	11	6	1.99	111	2	158	105	35	60	200

Position: Pitcher
Team: Cincinnati Reds
Born: January 24, 1964 Bridgeport, CT
Height: 6'4" **Weight:** 235 lbs.
Bats: Left **Throws:** Right
Acquired: First-round pick in 6/83
free-agent draft

The only man to have a better strikeouts-to-innings pitched ratio than Nolan Ryan in 1989 was Dibble. The reliever amassed an incredible total of 141 strikeouts in only 99 innings. He also got some unwanted publicity during his first full season in the majors. A fiery temper and some confrontations with umpires found Dibble suspended briefly during the year. Despite the time off, he still led the Reds in appearances, ERA, and strikeouts (surpassing each of the Cincinnati starters). He earned his promotion to the majors with two wins and 13 saves in 31 outings at Triple-A Nashville in 1988. In his first 37 games with the Reds, Dibble went 1-1 with a 1.82 ERA.

Dibble's personality and high strikeout totals make him visible with card collectors. His 1990 cards would be a good investment at a nickel. Our pick for his best 1990 card is Fleer.

FRANK DiPINO

	W	L	ERA	G	SV	IP	H	ER	BB	SO
1989	9	0	2.45	67	0	88	73	24	20	44
Life	29	35	3.70	432	53	591	551	243	229	453

Position: Pitcher
Team: St. Louis Cardinals
Born: October 22, 1956 Syracuse, NY
Height: 6' **Weight:** 180 lbs.
Bats: Left **Throws:** Left
Acquired: Signed as a free agent, 12/88

DiPino earned the finest record of his career with the 1989 Cardinals. He took a two-game winning streak into 1989 and then reeled off nine more consecutive victories. He exceeded 60 appearances for the third straight season, the last two of which were spent with the Cubs. DiPino floundered for six seasons in the Milwaukee organization, getting only two games in the majors. In September 1982, he was traded with Kevin Bass for Don Sutton. In 1983, DiPino's first full season in the N.L., he achieved a career-high 20 saves. DiPino claimed 23 more saves in the next three seasons before joining the Cubs in mid-1986.

Middle relievers have little control over their statistics because they pitch in varied game situations. DiPino's unlikely to rack up enough numbers to make his 1990 commons worthwhile investments. Our pick for his best 1990 card is Score.

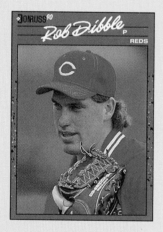

BENNY DISTEFANO

	BA	G	AB	R	H	2B	3B	HR	RBI	SB
1989	.247	96	154	12	38	8	0	2	15	1
Life	.227	188	300	31	68	13	3	7	35	1

Position: Infield; outfield
Team: Pittsburgh Pirates
Born: January 23, 1962   Brooklyn, NY
Height: 6'1"   **Weight:** 200 lbs.
Bats: Left   **Throws:** Left
Acquired: Second-round pick in 1/82
free-agent draft

Distefano spent his first full season with Pittsburgh in 1989 and provided the Bucs' bench with a versatile lefty. He began his pro career in 1982, and in 1983 he bashed a career-high 25 home runs. By 1984, he earned his first brief jump to the majors, arriving to stay in 1988 with a .345 batting average over 16 games with the Bucs. He batted .455 in his last three games of the 1988 season. Distefano was drafted by Los Angeles in the 16th round in January 1981, and Toronto chose him in the second round in June 1981 before he went to college. One of Distefano's high school teammates was star reliever John Franco.

Distefano began working out as a lefthanded catcher in late 1988, a reserve role in which he could make history. His 1990 commons are long-shot investments. Our pick for his best 1990 card is Fleer.

JOHN DOPSON

	W	L	ERA	G	CG	IP	H	ER	BB	SO
1989	12	8	3.99	29	2	196	166	75	69	95
Life	15	21	3.53	59	3	377	341	148	131	200

Position: Pitcher
Team: Boston Red Sox
Born: July 14, 1963   Baltimore, MD
Height: 6'4"   **Weight:** 205 lbs.
Bats: Left   **Throws:** Right
Acquired: Traded from Expos with Luis
Rivera for Spike Owen and Don
Gakeler, 12/88

Dopson was one of Boston's biggest gambles in 1989, but the hurler paid off in a big way. He was third in wins for the BoSox, marking his first full season in the majors. Anyone who viewed him struggle with the '88 Expos would be the most surprised by his 1989 success. In 1988, Dopson went 3-13, although he posted an adequate 3.04 ERA. The Expos averaged just 3.3 runs for him during his 26 starts. He worked for six seasons in the Montreal farm system to earn a job in the majors. The Expos gave him a brief chance in 1985, when he pitched in four games. Dopson had a horrendous 11.08 ERA and an 0-2 record.

Dopson's success could determine Boston's pennant hopes. His 1990 commons would be a low-risk gamble. Our pick for his best 1990 card is Donruss.

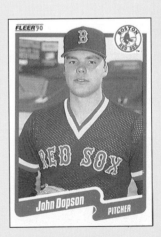

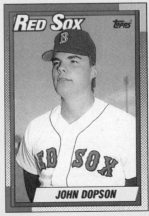

BILL DORAN

	BA	G	AB	R	H	2B	3B	HR	RBI	SB
1989	.219	142	507	65	111	25	2	8	58	22
Life	.265	1056	3920	562	1040	159	33	63	372	173

Position: Second base
Team: Houston Astros
Born: May 28, 1958 Cincinnati, OH
Height: 6' **Weight:** 175 lbs.
Bats: Both **Throws:** Right
Acquired: Sixth-round pick in 6/79
  free-agent draft

Doran's restored health was a reason why the Astros managed to stay in the 1989 N.L. West race. He returned to the Houston lineup in 1989 after missing 30 games in 1988 due to a strained hamstring and an injured left shoulder. His health seemed questionable after undergoing postseason surgery to repair the rotator cuff in his left shoulder. In 1989, he became the eighth Astro to reach 1,000 hits. He stole a career-high 42 bases in 1986. In 1987, Doran was named the team's MVP after popping a career-high 16 homers and playing in all 162 games.

Aside from Ryne Sandberg, Doran may be one of the best all-around second sackers in the N.L. His 1990 cards, at a nickel or less, seem like a solid investment. Our pick for his best 1990 card is Fleer.

BRIAN DOWNING

	BA	G	AB	R	H	2B	3B	HR	RBI	SB
1989	.283	142	544	59	154	25	2	14	59	0
Life	.266	2018	6796	1012	1807	307	24	234	934	48

Position: Designated hitter
Team: California Angels
Born: October 9, 1950 Los Angeles, CA
Height: 5'10" **Weight:** 200 lbs.
Bats: Right **Throws:** Right
Acquired: Traded from White Sox with
  David Frost and Chris Knapp for
  Bobby Bonds, Rich Dotson, and
  Thad Bosley, 12/77

In his 16th full major league season, Downing was one of the league's best designated hitters in 1989. He hit .283 with 14 homers in 1989. The holder of many of the Angels' all-time offensive marks, he also holds team records for highest single-season fielding percentage both as a catcher and outfielder. Downing became a full-time designated hitter in 1987. Offensively, his best years have been in 1987 (29 home runs), 1986 (95 RBI), and 1979 (.326 average). He had 19 or more home runs yearly from 1982 through 1988. He drove in seven runs against Boston in the 1986 A.L.C.S. Downing played his first five seasons with the White Sox before coming home to California in 1978.

Downing is in the twilight of a respectable career. However, his common-priced 1990 cards won't produce short-term gains due to his declining stats. Our pick for his best 1990 card is Topps.

KELLY DOWNS

	W	L	ERA	G	CG	IP	H	ER	BB	SO
1989	4	8	4.79	18	0	82	82	44	26	49
Life	33	30	3.57	100	11	524	485	208	170	368

Position: Pitcher
Team: San Francisco Giants
Born: October 25, 1960 Ogden, UT
Height: 6'4" **Weight:** 200 lbs.
Bats: Right **Throws:** Right
Acquired: Traded from Phillies with
George Riley for Al Oliver and
Renie Martin, 9/84

In 1989, Downs was stymied by a shoulder injury that occurred in late 1988. He pitched in just 18 games, his lowest total in the last three seasons. He was first called up to the Giants in mid-1986, on the same day his wife gave birth to their first child. Although he was 4-4 in 28 games that year, he posted a 4-0 mark in his last eight starts. He won 12 games in 1987 as a starter and reliever, and he won 13 in 1988 as a full-time starter. Until he proves that he's fully healthy, Downs should see duty both as a starter and reliever for the 1990 Giants.

If Downs spends some time in the bullpen, his stats will suffer. Don't bother investing in his 1990 commons unless he finds a spot in the Giants rotation. Our pick for his best 1990 card is Fleer.

DOUG DRABEK

	W	L	ERA	G	CG	IP	H	ER	BB	SO
1989	14	12	2.80	35	8	244	215	76	69	123
Life	47	39	3.35	124	12	771	700	287	215	446

Position: Pitcher
Team: Pittsburgh Pirates
Born: July 25, 1962 Victoria, TX
Height: 6'1" **Weight:** 185 lbs.
Bats: Right **Throws:** Right
Acquired: Traded from Yankees with Logan
Easley and Brian Fisher for Rick
Rhoden, Cecilio Guante, and Pat
Clements, 11/86

Pittsburgh's leading starter in 1989, Drabek continued to live up to the faith that the Bucs put in him. Tallying career bests in ERA (2.80) and complete games (eight), he had a team-leading 14 triumphs in 1989. He earned a career-high 15 wins during the 1988 campaign. In that year, Drabek tied for the N.L. lead in double plays, cementing a reputation as a fine fielder. During his first full major league season, with the 1987 Pirates, he led the club with 120 strikeouts, a total that he has consistently surpassed since. One of the first honors Drabek won was the N.L. Pitcher of the Month Award in August 1987.

Drabek improves yearly, which investors should notice. His 1990 cards will be a nickel apiece, a price that will triple if he helps the Bucs to a pennant. Our pick for his best 1990 card is Fleer.

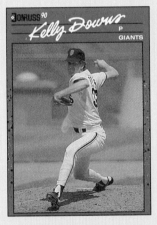

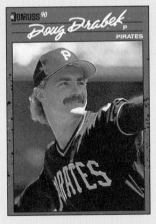
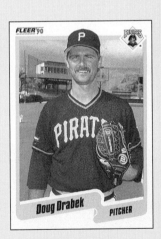

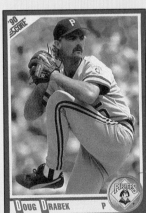

DAVE DRAVECKY

	W	L	ERA	G	CG	IP	H	ER	BB	SO
1989	2	0	3.46	2	0	13	8	5	4	5
Life	64	57	3.13	226	28	1062	968	370	315	558

Position: Pitcher
Team: San Francisco Giants
Born: February 14, 1956 Youngstown, OH
Height: 6'1" **Weight:** 200 lbs.
Bats: Right **Throws:** Left
Acquired: Traded from Padres with Craig
Lefferts and Kevin Mitchell for
Chris Brown, Keith Comstock,
Mark Davis, and Mark Grant,
7/87

Dravecky provided fans with ecstasy and agony in 1989. After missing all but seven games in 1988, he underwent successful surgery to remove a cancerous tumor from his pitching arm. Not only did he beat the cancer, he was back on the mound in 1989. His first victory made national news as one of America's most inspiring stories of the year. Sadly, in his second appearance, his left arm broke while delivering a pitch. Dravecky reinjured the arm while rushing onto the field to celebrate the team's pennant clinching, and he had to announce his retirement.

Dravecky's 1990 cards will sell for a nickel. Considering that his playing days are done, his cards aren't good short-term investments. However, in the coming years, he may gain even bigger fame for his courageous comeback. His cards could provide long-term profit. Our pick for his best 1990 card is Score.

BRIAN DuBOIS

	W	L	ERA	G	SV	IP	H	ER	BB	SO
89 Major	0	4	1.75	6	1	36	29	7	17	13
89 AAA	4	2	2.00	7	0	54	41	12	18	29

Position: Pitcher
Team: Detroit Tigers
Born: April 18, 1967 Joliet, IL
Height: 6' **Weight:** 170 lbs.
Bats: Left **Throws:** Left
Acquired: Traded from Orioles for
Keith Moreland, 7/89

After escaping a five-year entombment in the Baltimore minor league system, DuBois emerged as one of Detroit's most exciting rookie hurlers of 1989. He was 0-4 in six games, but he received little offensive support. His ERA was at 1.75 after five starts. In his only relief appearance, he earned his first major league save. He joined the Tigers on August 16, 1988, after making just three starts at Triple-A Toledo. DuBois had his biggest winning season in the minors at Double-A Hagerstown in 1987. He was 12-4 with seven complete games. He picked off 33 baserunners without committing a single balk. The Orioles picked DuBois in the fourth round of the 1985 draft.

DuBois's rookie 1990 cards will be at the 15-cent level. Since the pitching-hungry Tigers will give him a chance, his cards are promising investments. Our pick for his best 1990 card is Topps.

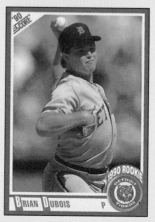

ROB DUCEY

	BA	G	AB	R	H	2B	3B	HR	RBI	SB
1989	.211	41	76	5	16	4	0	0	7	2
Life	.236	102	178	32	42	9	1	1	19	5

Position: Outfield
Team: Toronto Blue Jays
Born: May 24, 1965 Toronto, Ontario
Height: 6'2" **Weight:** 175 lbs.
Bats: Left **Throws:** Right
Acquired: Signed as a free agent, 5/84

Ducey played his third straight season with the Toronto Blue Jays, yet he again failed to remain in the majors for an entire season. His 41 games were a career high, yet his batting average fell more than 100 points from his 1988 efforts. After hitting his first major league home run against Baltimore on September 14, 1987, he's been waiting more than two years for his second round-tripper. He was a contender for Toronto's starting center field job in spring training of 1988 before being demoted before the start of the season. His total minor league experience amounts to more than five seasons. Ducey is the only Canada-born player active on the Blue Jays' roster, and just the third Canadian to play with Toronto.

Ducey hasn't shown much promise in more than 100 major league games. Investors should remain skeptical on his 1990 commons. Our pick for his best 1990 card is Topps.

SHAWON DUNSTON

	BA	G	AB	R	H	2B	3B	HR	RBI	SB
1989	.278	138	471	52	131	20	6	9	60	19
Life	.256	612	2223	267	569	109	22	44	224	85

Position: Shortstop
Team: Chicago Cubs
Born: March 21, 1963 Brooklyn, NY
Height: 6'1" **Weight:** 175 lbs.
Bats: Right **Throws:** Right
Acquired: First-round pick in 6/82
free-agent draft

Dunston had the best average of his career in 1989 for the Cubs. His .278 mark was his highest since he hit .329 at Double-A Midland in 1984. Everyone expected Dunston to become an immediate superstar after he was the first player chosen in the 1982 free-agent draft. The Cubs rushed him to the majors in 1985, making him the opening-day shortstop. After nine errors and a .194 average, he was sent back to Triple-A Iowa. When he returned to Chicago in August, he hit .320 in his final 40 games. Dunston improves his defense every year, and his efforts to become the league's best shortstop are paying off.

Dunston's popularity will grow due to his and Chicago's great season. His 1990 cards may be a nickel or less, a good price for investment. Our pick for his best 1990 card is Score.

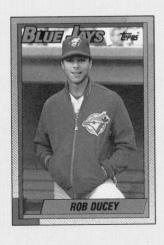

MIKE DYER

	W	L	ERA	G	CG	IP	H	ER	BB	SO
89 Major	4	7	4.87	16	1	71	74	38	37	37
89 AAA	3	6	4.43	15	2	89	80	44	51	63

Position: Pitcher
Team: Minnesota Twins
Born: September 8, 1966   Upland, CA
Height: 6'3"   **Weight:** 195 lbs.
Bats: Right   **Throws:** Right
Acquired: Third-round pick in 6/86
      free-agent draft

Dyer was one of a parade of rookie pitchers auditioning for the Twins in 1989. Although he had an unspectacular Triple-A record (3-6 with Portland in 1989), he got a midseason call-up from Minnesota. His four victories in 16 games topped all Twins rookies, although his ERA was passable at best. The Twins are high on Dyer. In 1987 with Class-A Kenosha, he led the entire Twins' minor league system with a 16-5 record and was honored as the Minnesota Minor League Player of the Year. He struck out a career-high 163 in 167 innings. Dyer moved up to Double-A Orlando in 1988, where he was 11-13.

Everyone has a chance of making the Twins pitching staff in 1990, including Dyer. Based on his modest success, don't pay more than a dime each for his rookie 1990 cards. Our pick for his best 1990 card is Fleer.

LENNY DYKSTRA

	BA	G	AB	R	H	2B	3B	HR	RBI	SB
1989	.237	146	511	66	121	32	4	7	32	30
Life	.268	634	2038	326	547	124	20	31	172	133

Position: Outfield
Team: Philadelphia Phillies
Born: February 10, 1963   Santa Ana, CA
Height: 5'10"   **Weight:** 160 lbs.
Bats: Left   **Throws:** Left
Acquired: Traded from Mets with Roger
      McDowell for Juan Samuel, 7/89

Dykstra escaped the Mets platoon system and won a starting outfield spot after a mid-1989 trade to the Phillies. He hit a career-low .237 with other lows in homers and RBI. The Phillies hope that his gung-ho style will be an additional benefit to the team. His aggressiveness contributed to 30 or more stolen bases in three of the last four seasons. He's known for his defensive talent, with just four errors in 1989. Dykstra began his pro career in 1981 and spent about four seasons in the minors before making the Mets. In 1983 with Class-A Lynchburg, Dykstra set a record with 105 stolen bases.

Phillie fans, hungry for a hero now that Mike Schmidt retired, will idolize Dykstra if he rebounds. Picking up his 1990 cards for a nickel could be a smart move. Our pick for his best 1990 card is Donruss.

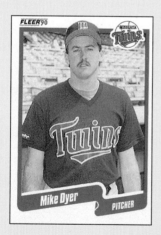

GARY EAVE

	W	L	ERA	G	CG	IP	H	ER	BB	SO
89 Major	2	0	1.31	3	0	20	15	3	12	9
89 AAA	13	3	2.80	23	1	141	111	44	57	93

Position: Pitcher
Team: Atlanta Braves
Born: July 22, 1963 Monroe, LA
Height: 6'4" **Weight:** 190 lbs.
Bats: Right **Throws:** Right
Acquired: 12th-round pick in 6/85
free-agent draft

In 1989, his second year at Triple-A Richmond, reliever Eave established himself as one of Atlanta's top arms. The Braves have tried him both as a starter and reliever. When he posted an 8-3 record with Richmond in early August, he established a new personal high for wins. Additionally, he surpassed his previous high for innings worked. He was the last pitcher cut from the major league roster at the beginning of 1988. Eave returned to Atlanta in April to make five relief appearances. In 1987, he had a cumulative total of 139 Ks in 141 innings pitched. Eave's pitching might help the Braves escape from the cellar in 1990.

Eave has a promising future, but relievers for inferior teams can be overlooked. Wait to see if he cracks the starting rotation before investing in his 15-cent 1990 cards. Our pick for his best 1990 card is Donruss.

DENNIS ECKERSLEY

	W	L	ERA	G	SV	IP	H	ER	BB	SO
1989	4	0	1.56	51	33	57	32	10	3	55
Life	165	138	3.57	541	97	2741	2584	1086	655	1865

Position: Pitcher
Team: Oakland Athletics
Born: October 3, 1954 Oakland, CA
Height: 6'2" **Weight:** 195 lbs.
Bats: Right **Throws:** Right
Acquired: Traded from Cubs with Dan Rohn
for Brian Guinn, Mark Leonette,
and Dave Wilder, 4/87

Eckersley anchored the A's bullpen for a second straight season in 1989. He racked up 33 saves, tying for third-highest in the American League. It was tough to match his 1988 success, when he earned 45 saves (just one short of the major league record). "Eck" has pitched for his hometown Athletics since a trade from the Cubs. He had been a starter for the previous 12 seasons. He revitalized his career by switching to relief after 301 starts dating back to his 1975 rookie season with the Indians. As a starter, Eckersley enjoyed nine seasons of double-digit wins, including a 20-8 campaign with the 1978 Red Sox.

Despite Eckersley's reputation as one of the best stoppers in baseball, many dealers still sell his 1990 card for a nickel. His cards will not bring much in short-term profits. Our pick for his best 1990 card is Score.

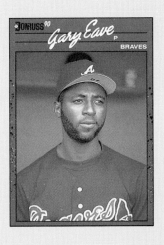

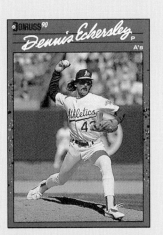

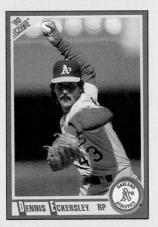

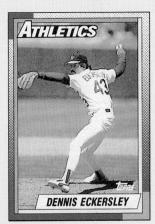

JIM EISENREICH

	BA	G	AB	R	H	2B	3B	HR	RBI	SB
1989	.293	134	475	64	139	33	7	9	59	27
Life	.268	308	904	97	202	39	3	19	93	6

Position: Outfield; designated hitter
Team: Kansas City Royals
Born: April 18, 1959   St. Cloud, MN
Height: 5'11"   **Weight:** 195 lbs.
Bats: Left   **Throws:** Left
Acquired: Signed as a free agent, 10/86

Eisenreich paced the 1989 Royals with a .293 batting average as he established new highs in nearly every offensive category during his eight-year career. He led the 1989 club with 27 stolen bases, and his 139 hits were second. After a stunning rookie debut with the 1982 Twins (including a .303 batting average in 34 games), Eisenreich was placed on the voluntarily retired list in 1984 after playing just 14 games in two years because of Tourette's syndrome. The nervous system disorder was successfully treated, and after two years of playing amateur baseball, he was given a minor league contract by Kansas City. Eisenreich made it back to the majors on June 17, 1987.

Eisenreich will be a regular in 1990. His 1990 cards will be 3 cents or less, a decent investment price for a courageous player with untapped potential. Our pick for his best 1990 card is Donruss.

KEVIN ELSTER

	BA	G	AB	R	H	2B	3B	HR	RBI	SB
1989	.231	151	458	52	106	25	2	10	55	4
Life	.223	308	904	97	202	39	3	19	93	6

Position: Shortstop
Team: New York Mets
Born: August 3, 1964   San Pedro, CA
Height: 6'2"   **Weight:** 195 lbs.
Bats: Right   **Throws:** Right
Acquired: Second-round pick in 1/84
   free-agent draft

In his sophomore season with the 1989 New York Mets, Elster set new highs in every offensive category. The shortstop still had a modest batting average, but he was one of six Mets to achieve double-digit totals in home runs. His homer totals have grown consistently since 1984, his first professional season, to a career-high ten in 1989. He continued to shine defensively, one year after he had established an N.L. record with 60 consecutive errorless games. He joined the Mets on August 30, 1986. He was first promoted to the Mets on the basis of a banner 1986 at Triple-A Tidewater. He set a team record with 170 hits that year, a .310 average, eight homers, and 74 RBI.

Elster won't reach stardom until he ups his batting average. For now, his 1990 commons are borderline investments. Our pick for his best 1990 card is Fleer.

NICK ESASKY

	BA	G	AB	R	H	2B	3B	HR	RBI	SB
1989	.277	154	564	79	156	26	5	30	108	1
Life	.251	801	2668	334	671	120	21	122	427	18

Position: First base
Team: Boston Red Sox
Born: February 14, 1960   Hialeah, FL
Height: 6'3"   **Weight:** 215 lbs.
Bats: Right   **Throws:** Right
Acquired: Signed as a free agent, 11/89

Esasky joined the Braves to provide some punch. In 1989, he became best friends with the "green monster" when he joined the Red Sox. The righthanded slugger cashed in on Fenway Park's left field wall to lead the BoSox with 30 homers and 108 RBI, both career highs. He finished third in the A.L. home run derby and second in RBI. Esasky played for Cincinnati from 1983 through 1988. The Reds had hoped to make him a third baseman, but due to defensive lapses at the hot corner he was shuttled between first base and left field starting in 1984. Prior to his 1989 campaign, Esasky's personal bests were 22 homers (in 1987) and 66 RBI (in 1985).

Esasky's banner season will gain new popularity for his 1990 cards. Homer hitters are good card investments, so spend up to a dime apiece. Our pick for his best 1990 card is Donruss.

ALVARO ESPINOZA

	BA	G	AB	R	H	2B	3B	HR	RBI	SB
1989	.282	146	503	51	142	23	1	0	41	3
Life	.274	218	605	60	166	26	1	0	51	3

Position: Shortstop
Team: New York Yankees
Born: February 19, 1962
          Valencia, Venezuela
Height: 6'   **Weight:** 170 lbs.
Bats: Right   **Throws:** Right
Acquired: Signed as a free agent, 11/87

After two failed experiences with other organizations, Espinoza became the Yankees starting shortstop in 1989. He had just 73 games of major league experience before winning a full-time job with the Yanks. He had the fifth-highest batting average among 1989 regulars, but trailed only Steve Sax and Don Mattingly in total hits. Espinoza committed 22 errors, the second-worst total in the league. His long career began in 1979. After two seasons, The Astros released him, and he sat out the 1981 campaign. Signed as a free agent by the Twins' farm system, he first appeared in the majors in 1985. After playing in Triple-A in 1987, Espinoza became a six-year minor league free agent and signed with the Yankees.

Espinoza needs to prove he's for real before card investors pursue his common-priced 1990 cards. Our pick for his best 1990 card is Fleer.

CECIL ESPY

	BA	G	AB	R	H	2B	3B	HR	RBI	SB
1989	.257	142	475	65	122	12	7	3	31	45
Life	.251	299	841	166	211	30	13	5	71	80

Position: Outfield
Team: Texas Rangers
Born: January 20, 1963 San Diego, CA
Height: 6'3" **Weight:** 195 lbs.
Bats: Both **Throws:** Right
Acquired: Traded from Pirates for
Mike Dotzler, 4/87

Espy kept running for the 1989 Rangers, finishing second in the A.L. in stolen bases. Only Oakland's Rickey Henderson (with 77 steals) surpassed Espy's career-high 45 steals. Even though he's been active in pro baseball since 1980, he registered just his second full season in the majors in 1989. Espy first displayed his speed in 1983, playing for Vero Beach and leading the Florida State League with 74 steals, 523 at-bats, 100 runs scored, and 166 hits. He spent his first three years in the White Sox' organization, then worked in the Dodgers' system for four seasons. Espy played one year at Triple-A for Pittsburgh in 1986 before going to Texas.

Espy is a fixture in the Rangers outfield. However, he'll have to hit for more power or a higher average before his 1990 cards raise from their commons prices. Our pick for his best 1990 card is Donruss.

DWIGHT EVANS

	BA	G	AB	R	H	2B	3B	HR	RBI	SB
1989	.285	146	520	82	148	27	3	20	100	3
Life	.273	2382	8281	1369	2262	456	69	366	1283	73

Position: Outfield
Team: Boston Red Sox
Born: November 3, 1951
　　　Santa Monica, CA
Height: 6'3" **Weight:** 208 lbs.
Bats: Right **Throws:** Right
Acquired: Fifth-round pick in 6/69
　　　free-agent draft

One of the A.L.'s unsung heroes, Evans made his 16th major league season a memorable one in 1988. He drove in 111 runs and hit 21 homers (reaching 20 homers for the tenth time). He attained his coveted 2,000th career hit against Oakland May 27, 1988. That same day, he set single-game career highs with seven RBI and 12 total bases. Despite his hitting exploits, the eight-time Golden Glove winner is known mostly for his defensive skills. Only Ted Williams and Carl Yastrzemski have logged more games as Boston outfielders. A veteran of two World Series, Evans has a lifetime average of .300 with three home runs and 14 RBI.

Evans has a shot at the Hall of Fame, so his 1990 cards could be safe long-term investment vehicles at a dime or less. Our pick for his best 1990 card is Score.

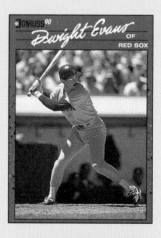

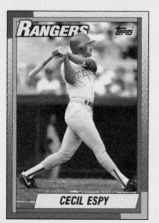
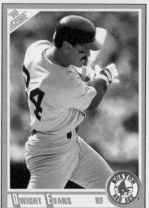

STEVE FARR

	W	L	ERA	G	SV	IP	H	ER	BB	SO
1989	2	5	4.12	51	18	63	75	29	22	56
Life	24	28	3.68	263	49	499	476	204	201	418

Position: Pitcher
Team: Kansas City Royals
Born: December 12, 1956 Cheverly, MD
Height: 5'11" **Weight:** 200 lbs.
Bats: Right **Throws:** Right
Acquired: Signed as a free agent, 5/85

Farr became the fourth-highest save leader in Kansas City history with another strong season in 1989. He tied Jeff Montgomery for the team lead with 18 saves. Although Farr has been with the Royals since 1985, he has been used as a closer for only the last two seasons. He has been in pro baseball since 1977. After rambling in the Pirates' system, he was traded to the Indians following the 1983 campaign. He made his major league debut in 1984 but then signed as a free agent with the Royals. Farr won the third game of the 1985 A.L.C.S., helping the Royals erase a two-game deficit.

Farr got a late start on compiling his string of accomplishments. He'll need to grab more headlines before his common-priced 1990 cards gain in value. Our pick for his best 1990 card is Donruss.

JOHN FARRELL

	W	L	ERA	G	CG	IP	H	ER	BB	SO
1989	9	14	3.63	31	7	208	196	84	71	132
Life	28	25	3.86	72	12	487	480	209	160	252

Position: Pitcher
Team: Cleveland Indians
Born: August 4, 1962 Neptune, NJ
Height: 6'4" **Weight:** 210 lbs.
Bats: Right **Throws:** Right
Acquired: Second-round pick in 6/84 free-agent draft

Farrell reversed his fortunes in 1989, seeing his 14 wins in 1988 turn into the same number of losses. After going 14-10 with the 1988 Indians, he seemed ready to achieve new prominence in the A.L. However, 1989 wasn't as kind to him, and his record fell to 9-14. One slight consolation was that his 132 strikeout mark was tops for the team. Also, he led the team with seven complete games. Farrell's first pro season came in 1984, following a notable collegiate career at Oklahoma State University as a four-year letterman. He first joined the Indians on August 18, 1987, and earned a relief win against the Brewers. Farrell went 5-1 that first season, pitching into at least the seventh inning for all nine starts.

Don't invest in Farrell's 1990 commons. He faces an uphill battle trying to win with the Indians. Our pick for his best 1990 card is Donruss.

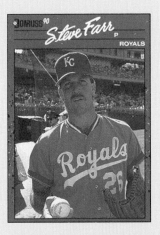

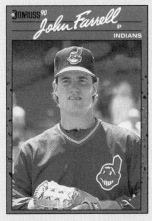

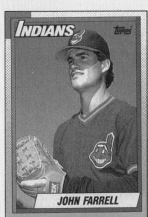

MIKE FELDER

	BA	G	AB	R	H	2B	3B	HR	RBI	SB
1989	.241	117	315	50	76	11	3	3	23	26
Life	.240	334	896	144	215	20	14	6	72	88

Position: Outfield
Team: Milwaukee Brewers
Born: November 18, 1962 Richmond, CA
Height: 5'8" **Weight:** 160 lbs.
Bats: Both **Throws:** Right
Acquired: Third-round pick in 1/81
    free-agent draft

Staying healthy was Felder's biggest feat for the 1989 Brewers. "Tiny" played in a career-high 117 games in 1989. He bounced back from hamstring problems that plagued him throughout the 1988 season and limited his action to just 50 games. The injury also curtailed his speed, the asset that brought him to the major leagues first in 1985. He swiped 34 bases in 1987, the sixth-highest single-season total in club history; only Tommy Harper and Paul Molitor have exceeded Felder's mark. He spent five years in the minors, stealing 323 bases before his promotion. His four league stolen base crowns, accumulated from 1982 to 1985, include a personal best of 92 steals in the California League in 1982.

With a passable batting average and little power, Felder stands little chance of being a major league starter. Don't invest in his 1990 commons. Our pick for his best 1990 card is Fleer.

JUNIOR FELIX

	BA	G	AB	R	H	2B	3B	HR	RBI	SB
89 AAA	.276	21	87	17	24	4	2	1	10	13
89 Major	.258	110	415	62	107	14	8	9	46	18

Position: Outfield
Team: Toronto Blue Jays
Born: October 3, 1967
    Laguna Sabada, Dominican Republic
Height: 5'11" **Weight:** 165 lbs.
Bats: Both **Throws:** Right
Acquired: Signed as a free agent, 9/85

Yes, his first name really is Junior. And yes, the young outfielder really has talent. Felix helped keep Toronto at the top of the A.L. East. After his first 80 games, he hit .274 with eight home runs, 43 RBI, and 14 stolen bases. He ended the season with 18 stolen bases, third on the team. His sudden success prompted the Blue Jays to trade Jesse Barfield. At Double-A Knoxville in 1988, Felix hit .253 with 52 runs, 16 doubles, three home runs, 25 RBI, and 40 stolen bases. Felix's best season came in 1987 at Class-A Myrtle Beach, batting .290 with 12 homers, 51 RBI, and 64 stolen bases.

Felix's rookie 1990 cards could be overpriced, because some collectors go overboard on prospects. He has talent, but don't pay more than a dime apiece for his cards. Our pick for his best 1990 card is Donruss.

FELIX FERMIN

	BA	G	AB	R	H	2B	3B	HR	RBI	SB
1989	.238	156	484	50	115	9	1	0	21	6
Life	.241	222	639	65	154	9	3	0	27	9

Position: Shortstop
Team: Cleveland Indians
Born: October 9, 1963
      Mao, Dominican Republic
Height: 5'11" **Weight:** 170 lbs.
Bats: Right **Throws:** Right
Acquired: Traded from Pirates for Jay Bell,
      2/89

A change of scenery worked wonders for Fermin, as he played his first full season with the Indians. He had been in the Pirates' organization since 1983, but he had abbreviated stays with Pittsburgh only in 1987 and 1988. When the Indians and Pirates swapped shortstops, it gave him a new chance at a major league career. He was one of Cleveland's most durable players, playing in 156 games. Fermin led all junior circuit shortstops with 26 errors in 1989. He had been widely respected for his fielding quickness. Teammates nicknamed him "Gato," the Spanish word for cat. In seven pro seasons, Fermin has never hit a home run.

If Fermin wants to last in the majors, he better increase his batting average. For now, investors should remain cautious and avoid his 1990 commons. Our pick for his best 1990 card is Donruss.

SID FERNANDEZ

	W	L	ERA	G	CG	IP	H	ER	BB	SO
1989	14	5	2.83	35	6	219	157	69	75	198
Life	69	45	3.23	169	15	1032	764	370	424	972

Position: Pitcher
Team: New York Mets
Born: October 12, 1962 Honolulu, HI
Height: 6'1" **Weight:** 230 lbs.
Bats: Left **Throws:** Left
Acquired: Traded from Dodgers with
      Ross Jones for Carlos Diaz and
      Bob Bailor, 12/83

Fernandez had a sterling season for the New York Mets in 1989, leading the squad in ERA and strikeouts. He tied Ron Darling and David Cone for the lead in wins with 14. Fernandez spent 1981 to 1983 in the Los Angeles farm system, but pitched only two games with the Dodgers in 1983. Meanwhile, the Mets saw Fernandez win in double digits for four straight years. His brightest season came in 1986, when he was 16-6 in helping the Mets win a World Series. Fernandez made consecutive All-Star game appearances in 1986 and 1987, throwing scoreless innings of relief on both occasions.

Fernandez's 1990 cards will be a nickel or less. While he may never be a Hall of Famer, he is capable of a few blockbuster seasons. Invest heartily. Our pick for his best 1990 card is Fleer.

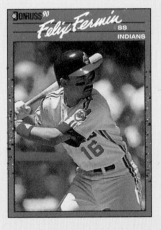

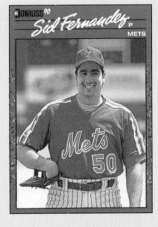

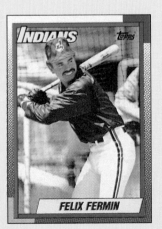

TONY FERNANDEZ

	BA	G	AB	R	H	2B	3B	HR	RBI	SB
1989	.257	140	573	64	147	25	9	11	64	22
Life	.291	867	3317	426	967	165	44	36	338	112

Position: Shortstop
Team: Toronto Blue Jays
Born: August 6, 1962
San Pedro de Macoris,
Dominican Republic
Height: 6'2" **Weight:** 175 lbs.
Bats: Both **Throws:** Right
Acquired: Signed as a free agent, 4/79

Fernandez enjoyed his third consecutive All-Star season with Toronto in 1989. Although his average was the lowest of his six-year major league career, he belted a career-high 11 home runs. His high had been ten with the 1986 Toronto and 1981 Syracuse clubs. He made up for his shortcomings with another superb season in the field. In 140 games, he made just six errors. In 1988, Fernandez compiled a 65-game errorless streak. His personal best average in the majors is a .322 mark, attained with the 1987 club. Although he first made Toronto in 1983, Fernandez wasn't the team's starting shortstop until 1985, due to the presence of Alfredo Griffin.

Fernandez is one of the best shortstops in the business, but his 1990 cards are available for commons prices. Stock up, and then sell when his card prices triple. Our pick for his best 1990 card is Fleer.

TOM FILER

	W	L	ERA	G	CG	IP	H	ER	BB	SO
1989	7	3	3.61	13	0	72	74	29	23	20
Life	20	13	4.28	51	21	263	270	125	92	98

Position: Pitcher
Team: Milwaukee Brewers
Born: December 1, 1956 Philadelphia, PA
Height: 6'1" **Weight:** 198 lbs.
Bats: Right **Throws:** Right
Acquired: Purchased from Blue Jays,
10/87

Filer made 13 starts with the 1989 Brewers, enough to equal his career high in victories. He split the season between Triple-A Denver and Milwaukee and went 7-3, matching his seven wins that came in an undefeated season with the Blue Jays in 1985. Those seven wins helped him compile a 12-game winning streak that stretched over seven years. His first victory came in 1982, as a member of the Cubs. After spending the next two seasons in Double-A, Filer was purchased by the Blue Jays in 1985. A torn ligament in his right elbow kept him inactive through 1986. He toiled back in the minors in 1987, and joined the Brewers in 1988. Filer went 4-0 (with a 1.80 ERA) before finally getting beaten.

Filer is 33 and has just 20 career victories. His common-priced 1990 cards would be poor investments. Our pick for his best 1990 card is Donruss.

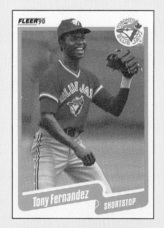
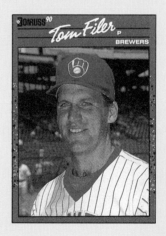

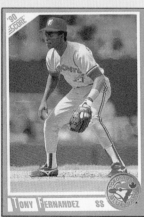

CHUCK FINLEY

	W	L	ERA	G	CG	IP	H	ER	BB	SO
1989	16	9	2.57	29	9	199	171	57	82	156
Life	30	32	3.58	120	11	530	504	211	230	367

Position: Pitcher
Team: California Angels
Born: November 16, 1962 Monroe, LA
Height: 6'6" **Weight:** 215 lbs.
Bats: Left **Throws:** Left
Acquired: First-round pick in secondary
  phase of 1/85 free-agent draft

A former relief specialist, Finley found his niche in the Angels starting rotation in 1989. The Angels became pennant contenders in the A.L. West, thanks in part to Finley's best season. For the first half of 1989 he was California's leading winner, and he topped the squad in complete games. He first made the Angels roster in 1986 as a reliever. Before his advancement to the majors, he had appeared in just 28 games in the minor leagues. He totaled 57 games in relief before getting into the team's rotation. In 1988, Finley's year was dominated by two notable outings, a ten-strikeout performance against Milwaukee and a five-hitter against Toronto.

Finley's 1990 cards will be a nickel or less. See if he can duplicate his 1989 exploits before investing anything in his cards. Our pick for his best 1990 card is Donruss.

STEVE FINLEY

	BA	G	AB	R	H	2B	3B	HR	RBI	SB
1989	.249	81	217	35	54	5	2	2	25	17
Life	.249	81	217	35	54	5	2	2	25	17

Position: Outfield
Team: Baltimore Orioles
Born: May 12, 1965 Union City, TN
Height: 6'2" **Weight:** 175 lbs.
Bats: Left **Throws:** Left
Acquired: 14th-round pick in 6/87
  free-agent draft

Finley was another face in the Baltimore youth movement of 1989. A part-timer for the O's, he batted .249 with two homers and 25 RBI. He began the 1988 season (his first full year in pro baseball) at Class-A Hagerstown but was elevated to Triple-A Rochester just 18 games later. With Rochester, Finley won the International League batting title with a .314 mark. He was the first Oriole minor leaguer in 12 years to accomplish the feat. The starting center fielder for the league All-Star game, he was named the league's Rookie of the Year. His 143 hits were another league best. Finley played college baseball for Southern Illinois-Carbondale.

Let Finley gain some more major league experience before investing in his 1990 cards. For now, the jury's still out on his potential. Our pick for his best 1990 card is Score.

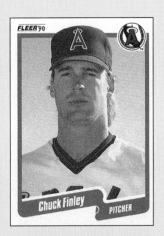

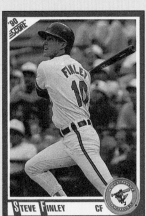

CARLTON FISK

	BA	G	AB	R	H	2B	3B	HR	RBI	SB
1989	.293	103	375	47	110	25	2	13	68	1
Life	.271	2141	7603	1155	2063	371	46	336	1161	117

Position: Catcher
Team: Chicago White Sox
Born: December 26, 1947   Bellow Falls, VT
Height: 6'2"   **Weight:** 225 lbs.
Bats: Right   **Throws:** Right
Acquired: Signed as a free agent, 3/81

Injuries early in 1989 hampered Fisk, but he continued to carve a deeper niche in baseball record books. "Pudge," in his ninth season with the White Sox, obtained his 2,000th career hit. During his nine years with Boston, he was named to seven All-Star teams. He notched a career-best 37 home runs and 107 RBI in 1985. Fans still remember Fisk's 12th-inning, game-winning home run in Game Six of the 1975 World Series against Cincinnati. Ranking second in lifetime home runs for catchers and first in the A.L. in games caught, Fisk moves closer to the Hall of Fame with every game.

Try to pay 15 cents or less for 1990 cards. This may be the last card of the future Hall of Famer, offering sparkling long-term dividends. Our pick for his best 1990 card is Score.

MIKE FITZGERALD

	BA	G	AB	R	H	2B	3B	HR	RBI	SB
1989	.238	100	290	33	69	18	2	7	42	3
Life	.241	571	1616	148	389	70	6	29	207	17

Position: Catcher
Team: Montreal Expos
Born: July 13, 1960   Long Beach, CA
Height: 5'11"   **Weight:** 190 lbs.
Bats: Right   **Throws:** Right
Acquired: Traded from Mets with Hubie Brooks, Floyd Youmans, and Herm Winningham for Gary Carter, 12/84

Fitzgerald broke the 100-game mark for just the fourth time in his career with the 1989 Expos. Since he joined the Expos, he has been hampered by injuries. However, Fitzgerald made the most of his limited playing time in 1989 and set career highs in both home runs and RBI. He never had an easy beginning with the Expos. He was one of four Mets included in the 1984 deal for Gary Carter. In 1986, Fitzgerald hit a career-high .282 with six homers and 37 RBI. The next year, he took revenge against the Mets. On July 17, 1987, Fitzgerald picked an opportune time to slug his first career grand-slam homer.

In 1990, Fitzgerald will be busy fighting to keep his starting job. Because the Expos aren't as committed to him as their top receiver, don't invest in his 1990 commons. Our pick for his best 1990 card is Fleer.

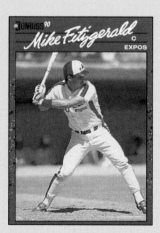

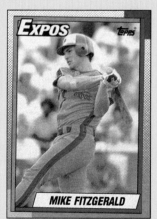

MIKE FLANAGAN

	W	L	ERA	G	CG	IP	H	ER	BB	SO
1989	8	10	3.93	30	1	171	186	75	47	47
Life	163	134	3.89	415	101	2616	2644	1130	834	1414

Position: Pitcher
Team: Toronto Blue Jays
Born: December 16, 1951 Manchester, NH
Height: 6' **Weight:** 195 lbs.
Bats: Left **Throws:** Left
Acquired: Traded from Orioles for Oswald
          Pereza and Jose Mesa, 8/87

Flanagan logged his 15th season in the majors while pitching for the 1989 Blue Jays. He assisted in Toronto's divisional title. He pitched for pennant winners in Baltimore both in 1979 and 1983, and pitched in two World Series. Flanagan's finest season occurred in 1979. He was 23-9 with 16 complete games and five shutouts. He earned one A.L.C.S. victory and a win in the World Series. Flanagan won the A.L. Cy Young Award and finished sixth in MVP balloting. During his reign with the Orioles, he won in double figures seven times, including four straight years of 15 or more wins from 1977 to 1980. Flanagan's best record with Toronto came in 1988, a 13-13 effort.

Flanagan isn't Hall of Fame material. He's nearing the end of a respectable career, but his 1990 commons are unlikely short-term investments. Our pick for his best 1990 card is Donruss.

SCOTT FLETCHER

	BA	G	AB	R	H	2B	3B	HR	RBI	SB
1989	.253	142	546	77	138	25	2	1	43	2
Life	.268	997	3268	436	875	147	24	17	302	56

Position: Second base
Team: Chicago White Sox
Born: July 30, 1958 Fort Walton Beach, FL
Height: 5'11" **Weight:** 172 lbs.
Bats: Right **Throws:** Right
Acquired: Traded from Rangers with Wilson
          Alvarez and Sam Sosa for Harold
          Baines and Fred Manrique, 6/89

Fletcher got a new position when he was reacquired by the White Sox in 1989. The former Rangers shortstop was part of the deal that sent slugger Harold Baines to Texas. The ChiSox have Ozzie Guillen installed at short, so Fletcher was shifted to second base. His last work at second was in 1986. He had been a utility player for Chicago in 1985, but had started at shortstop for the Sox in 1983 and 1984. With Texas, he had led the team in batting for three straight seasons, including a career-high mark of .300 in 1986. Fletcher began his pro career with the Cubs and was their opening-day shortstop in 1982.

Fletcher is a scrappy hitter and superb fielder. However, he seems unlikely to build outstanding offensive numbers. His common-priced 1990s are unpredictable investments. Our pick for his best 1990 card is Score.

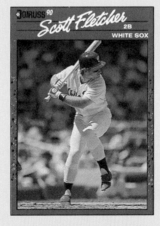

TOM FOLEY

	BA	G	AB	R	H	2B	3B	HR	RBI	SB
1989	.229	122	375	34	86	19	2	7	39	2
Life	.254	721	1920	185	488	98	16	26	192	26

Position: Infield
Team: Montreal Expos
Born: September 9, 1959 Columbus, GA
Height: 6'1" **Weight:** 180 lbs.
Bats: Left **Throws:** Right
Acquired: Traded from Phillies with Larry
    Sorensen for Dan Schatzeder and
    Skeeter Barnes, 7/86

Foley served as the Montreal utility infielder in 1989. He seemed groomed for the starting shortstop job in Philadelphia in 1986, but a broken wrist in spring training kept him out of action for five weeks. Blessed with hitting as well as fielding ability, he notched a career-high seven homers in 1989. His personal-best batting average came in 1987 with Montreal, a .293 effort. Foley has been active in pro baseball since 1977, when Cincinnati drafted him in the seventh round. He has remained righthanded in the seven years he has spent in the majors, although he is a rare ambidextrous athlete. In high school in Miami, Foley played as a lefthanded quarterback.

Foley will likely remain a reserve infielder with the 1990 Expos. There is little investment future in his 1990 commons. Our pick for his best 1990 card is Donruss.

CURT FORD

	BA	G	AB	R	H	2B	3B	HR	RBI	SB
1989	.218	108	142	13	31	5	1	1	13	5
Life	.249	384	724	88	180	37	8	7	89	36

Position: Outfield
Team: Philadelphia Phillies
Born: October 11, 1960 Jackson, MS
Height: 5'10" **Weight:** 150 lbs.
Bats: Left **Throws:** Right
Acquired: Traded from Cardinals with
    Steve Lake for Milt Thompson,
    12/88

The Phillies had high hopes for Ford when they obtained him from the Cardinals, but he was employed primarily in a utility role. Unfortunately, he had the second-lowest batting average of his career. He improved his poor 1988 showing, a .195 average in 92 games. With Philly, he batted .218. Ford's finest season occurred in 1987, when he played in 89 games (including 56 games as a starter). He batted .285 with five triples, three homers, and 26 RBI. He hit .333 in the National League Championship Series against San Francisco, and .308 against Minnesota in the World Series. Before Ford began his pro career in 1981, he played college baseball at Jackson State.

Unless Ford wins a starting position with the Phillies, there will be little interest in his 1990 commons. See how he does in spring training before deciding on investing. Our pick for his best 1990 card is Topps.

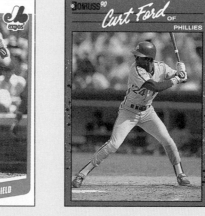

100

BOB FORSCH

	W	L	ERA	G	CG	IP	H	ER	BB	SO
1989	4	5	5.32	37	0	108	133	64	46	40
Life	168	136	3.77	498	67	2794	2777	1169	832	1133

Position: Pitcher
Team: Houston Astros
Born: January 13, 1950 Sacramento, CA
Height: 6'3" **Weight:** 215 lbs.
Bats: Right **Throws:** Right
Acquired: Traded from Cardinals for
    Denny Walling, 9/88

Forsch wound down a long, impressive career with minor action for the 1989 Astros. He is the third-highest winner and strikeout leader in Cardinal history (with 163 victories and 1,079 Ks). His '89 win total was his lowest since 1984, when he missed more than half the season due to back surgery. Forsch owns two no-hitters, one in 1978 and one in 1983. His brother Ken pitched for the Astros before Bob joined the team. They are the only siblings in major league history to each toss no-hitters. Bob has gained minor fame in his career as a fine-hitting pitcher. Forsch has won two Silver Slugger Awards for his batting talent.

    Forsch will play a minor role in the Astros' plans. Don't expect his 1990 cards to be worth more than a nickel. Our pick for his best 1990 card is Score.

JOHN FRANCO

	W	L	ERA	G	SV	IP	H	ER	BB	SO
1989	4	8	3.12	60	32	81	77	28	36	60
Life	42	30	2.49	393	148	528	460	146	210	367

Position: Pitcher
Team: Cincinnati Reds
Born: September 17, 1960 Brooklyn, NY
Height: 5'10" **Weight:** 185 lbs.
Bats: Left **Throws:** Left
Acquired: Traded from Dodgers with
    Brett Wise for Rafael Landestoy,
    5/83

Cincinnati had only 24 saves through late July 1989—and Franco earned 23 of them. He has topped 20 saves a season in his last four campaigns with the Reds. His career high came in 1988, when he registered a league-leading 39 saves (in 42 opportunities). He now holds both single-season and career save marks for the Reds. His 13 saves in July 1988 set a major league record for most saves in one month. Franco's acquisition remains as one of Cincinnati's smartest trades of the decade. He began his career in 1981 in the Dodgers' system but spent more than two seasons without getting a shot at the majors. Franco earned his first pro save in late 1983.

    Like many successful relief artists, Franco is perpetually ignored by card buffs. His 1990 cards will be commons, a bad omen for investors. Our pick for his best 1990 card is Donruss.

JULIO FRANCO

	BA	G	AB	R	H	2B	3B	HR	RBI	SB
1989	.316	150	548	80	173	31	5	13	92	21
Life	.298	1064	4138	584	1232	188	36	58	524	152

Position: Second base
Team: Texas Rangers
Born: August 23, 1961
San Pedro de Macoris,
Dominican Republic
Height: 6' **Weight:** 165 lbs.
Bats: Right **Throws:** Right
Acquired: Traded from Indians for Pete
O'Brien, Jerry Browne, and
Oddibe McDowell, 12/88

Franco was a key acquisition for the Rangers in 1989, helping the Texas team refuel its once-sputtering offense. He was one of the A.L.'s top hitters all season long, as his average stayed above .300 for the fourth straight season. Franco and Ruben Sierra dueled all season long for the club leads in RBI and batting average. Franco matched his 1988 totals of ten home runs and 54 RBI just after the All-Star break. He was rewarded by being voted the A.L.'s starting second baseman in the All-Star Game. Going into 1989, Franco ranked fifth among baseball's hit leaders from 1984 through 1988 with 898 safeties.

Paying a dime or less for Franco's 1990 cards is a shrewd investment. For a short-term profit, sell as soon as Franco gets another All-Star invitation. Our pick for his best 1990 card is Topps.

TERRY FRANCONA

	BA	G	AB	R	H	2B	3B	HR	RBI	SB
1989	.232	90	233	26	54	10	1	3	23	2
Life	.274	705	1727	162	474	74	6	16	143	12

Position: First base; outfield
Team: Milwaukee Brewers
Born: April 22, 1959 Aberdeen, SD
Height: 6' **Weight:** 175 lbs.
Bats: Left **Throws:** Left
Acquired: Signed as a free agent, 4/89

Francona earned some fame during his first month with the 1989 Brewers. He broke up a no-hit bid by Nolan Ryan. Ryan struck out 13 of the first 19 hitters, but Francona's eighth-inning single stopped Ryan from a sixth no-hitter. In 1989, Francona filled in at first base for the Brewers when Greg Brock was injured. Francona has played more than 100 games just three times in his eight-year career. His pro career began in 1980. The Expos promoted him in 1981, and he stayed in Montreal through 1985. He then made stops with the Cubs, the Reds, and Indians. Francona's busiest season came in 1983, when he played in 120 games, hitting .257 with three homers and 22 RBI.

Francona will be a part-timer for the rest of his career. His 1990 commons aren't good investment choices. Our pick for his best 1990 card is Score.

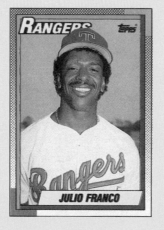

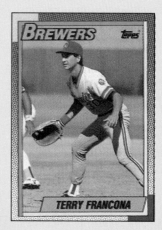

WILLIE FRASER

	W	L	ERA	G	SV	IP	H	ER	BB	SO
1989	4	7	3.24	44	2	91	80	33	23	40
Life	26	30	4.45	115	3	467	449	231	167	240

Position: Pitcher
Team: California Angels
Born: May 26, 1964   New York, NY
Height: 6'1"   **Weight:** 208 lbs.
Bats: Right   **Throws:** Right
Acquired: First-round pick in 6/85
       free-agent draft

After two seasons of moderate success as a starter, the Angels switched Fraser to the bullpen in 1989. He was 4-7 with two saves, finishing 21 of the 44 games he relieved in. His first full season with California came in 1987. He was 10-10 in 36 games, 23 as a starter. In 1988, he notched a 12-13 record in 32 starts and two relief appearances. On August 10, 1988, he hurled a one-hitter against Seattle. In 1986, Fraser went 9-2 at Class-A Palm Springs. After just six starts at Triple-A that year, he was called up to Anaheim. California discovered Fraser at Concordia College, where twice he was an All-State player.

As a middle reliever, Fraser probably won't accumulate the lifetime stats to make his 1990 commons worth investing in. Wait to see if he is put back in the starting rotation. Our pick for his best 1990 card is Score.

TODD FROHWIRTH

	W	L	ERA	G	SV	IP	H	ER	BB	SO
1989	1	0	3.59	45	0	62	56	25	18	39
Life	3	2	3.81	67	0	85	84	36	31	59

Position: Pitcher
Team: Philadelphia Phillies
Born: September 28, 1962   Milwaukee, WI
Height: 6'4"   **Weight:** 195 lbs.
Bats: Right   **Throws:** Right
Acquired: 13th-round pick in 6/84
       free-agent draft

Frohwirth joined the Phillies for a third season in 1989. He split his season between Triple-A and the majors for the third consecutive year. Philadelphia gave him ample opportunities in 1989, using him in 45 games. He was promoted from Scranton-Wilkes Barre in 1989 after 21 games, going 3-2 with seven saves, with 29 strikeouts in 32 innings. He was named the Phillies Minor League Pitcher of the Year in 1987, when he was 2-4 with a 1.86 ERA and a league-leading 19 saves at Double-A Reading. Frohwirth, who started his pro career in 1984, patterned his delivery after another great Phillies reliever, sidewinder Kent Tekulve.

Relief pitchers' cards normally have little investment appeal. Because Frohwirth won't be used as a stopper, his rookie 1990 cards will be overpriced at any amount over a dime apiece. Our pick for his best 1990 card is Donruss.

GARY GAETTI

	BA	G	AB	R	H	2B	3B	HR	RBI	SB
1989	.251	130	498	63	125	11	4	19	75	6
Life	.259	1207	4412	585	1144	225	20	185	673	68

Position: Third base
Team: Minnesota Twins
Born: August 19, 1958 Centralia, IL
Height: 6' **Weight:** 200 lbs.
Bats: Right **Throws:** Right
Acquired: First-round pick in 6/79
free-agent draft

Gaetti was a powerhouse for the 1989 Twins, among team leaders in both home runs and RBI. He remains at the top of his game, coming off an impressive 1988 campaign of 28 homers, 88 RBI, and a personal-best .301 batting average. He pounded a career-high 34 homers in 1986, with 108 RBI and 91 runs scored. He supplied 109 RBI for the 1987 World Championship team, slugging 31 homers and scoring 95 runs. Gaetti batted .300 in the A.L.C.S., winning the MVP. He has slugged 30-plus homers and driven in 100-plus runs in two seasons. A Gold Glove winner, Gaetti is one of the best all-around third basemen in the A.L.

Investors overlooked Gaetti during the 1989 season. This could drive his 1990 card prices below a dime, which could double in weeks if he rediscovers his home run stroke. Our pick for his best 1990 card is Donruss.

GREG GAGNE

	BA	G	AB	R	H	2B	3B	HR	RBI	SB
1989	.272	149	460	69	125	29	7	9	48	11
Life	.250	717	2151	309	537	115	29	47	216	54

Position: Shortstop
Team: Minnesota Twins
Born: November 12, 1961 Fall River, MA
Height: 5'11" **Weight:** 175 lbs.
Bats: Right **Throws:** Right
Acquired: Traded from Yankees with Ron
Davis and Paul Boros for Roy
Smalley, 4/82

Gagne celebrated his fifth year as the Twins starting short-stop in 1989. After being tutored by former designated hitter Don Baylor, Gagne batted a career-high .272. He hit nine homers, and just missed reaching double digits in round-trippers for a fourth consecutive season. In 1988, he slammed a personal high of 14 homers. One of Gagne's career highlights was slugging two home runs in the 1987 A.L.C.S. to help the Twins to the World Series against the Cardinals. His sixth-inning RBI single drove in the winning run of the decisive seventh game. Gagne started his pro career in the Yankees' organization in 1979 and debuted with the Twins in 1983.

Gagne is an adequate shortstop and decent hitter. Yet, he's far from stardom. Don't bother investing in his 1990 commons. Our pick for his best 1990 card is Score.

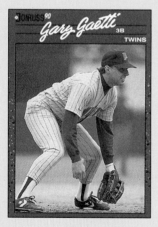

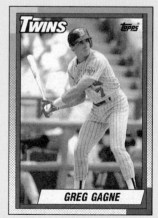

ANDRES GALARRAGA

	BA	G	AB	R	H	2B	3B	HR	RBI	SB
1989	.257	152	572	76	147	30	1	23	83	12
Life	.282	585	2128	295	600	126	12	77	313	39

Position: First base
Team: Montreal Expos
Born: June 18, 1961 Caracas, Venezuela
Height: 6'3" **Weight:** 235 lbs.
Bats: Right **Throws:** Right
Acquired: Signed as a free agent, 1/79

When power was needed by Montreal in 1989, the team called upon Galarraga. He led the Expos in home runs for a second straight year, and continued his excellent defensive work around first base. In fact, Galarraga is nicknamed "Cat" for his quickness with the glove. He was the talk of the '88 N.L., pacing the circuit in hits (184), doubles (42), and total bases (329). He was fourth in the league with a .302 average, along with 29 homers and 92 RBI. Galarraga set a major league record by leading the league in both hits and strikeouts (153). He was seventh in MVP balloting. In 1987, his first full season, Galarraga batted .305 with 90 RBI.

Grab Galarraga's 1990 cards at a dime. He has the potential to challenge for a batting title, making his cards worth the risk. Our pick for his best 1990 card is Score.

DAVE GALLAGHER

	BA	G	AB	R	H	2B	3B	HR	RBI	SB
1989	.266	161	601	74	160	22	2	1	46	5
Life	.273	277	984	135	269	38	6	6	78	12

Position: Outfield
Team: Chicago White Sox
Born: September 20, 1960 Trenton, NJ
Height: 6' **Weight:** 180 lbs.
Bats: Right **Throws:** Right
Acquired: Signed as a free agent, 1/88

Gallagher, one of the most consistent members of the White Sox in 1989, is one of baseball's little-told success stories. He set career highs in hits, runs, and RBI in 1989, surpassing his 1988 totals by the All-Star break. Gallagher spent his first full season in the majors in 1988. The White Sox rescued him from baseball oblivion after eight seasons in the minor leagues, signing him as a free agent. His rookie season included five homers, 59 runs scored, and a .303 batting average. Gallagher was the only White Sox regular with a .300-plus average. Prior to '88, Gallagher spent more than seven years in the Indians' farm system before getting a 15-game trial in 1987.

Gallagher is a dependable player. However, he'll need a .300 average before his common-priced 1990 cards will be worthwhile investments. Our pick for his best 1990 card is Fleer.

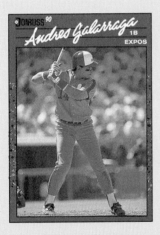

MIKE GALLEGO

	BA	G	AB	R	H	2B	3B	HR	RBI	SB
1989	.252	133	357	45	90	14	2	3	30	7
Life	.235	430	872	116	205	35	3	8	77	10

Position: Infield
Team: Oakland Athletics
Born: October 31, 1960   Whittier, CA
Height: 5'8" **Weight:** 160 lbs.
Bats: Right **Throws:** Right
Acquired: Second-round pick in 6/81
   free-agent draft

When the Oakland Athletics needed help at shortstop in 1989, they called on Gallego. He filled in at short when starter Walt Weiss injured a knee. Gallego proceeded to play in a career high of 133 games. Never before in his nine-year career had the defensive whiz appeared in so many games. He set numerous career highs in 1989, as he continued to fill in around the infield. His average climbed more than 40 points from his 1988 total. Gallego first joined the Athletics in 1985, and played in 76 games his rookie season. His defensive adaptability and his enthusiasm makes Gallego a valuable asset to the A's.

   Gallego is a prototype utility infielder. He's not slated as a starter for the 1990 club. Cards of part-timers aren't good investments, and Gallego's 1990 commons are no exceptions. Our pick for his best 1990 card is Score.

RON GANT

	BA	G	AB	R	H	2B	3B	HR	RBI	SB
1989	.177	75	260	26	46	8	3	9	25	9
Life	.236	242	906	120	214	40	11	30	94	32

Position: Outfield; infield
Team: Atlanta Braves
Born: March 2, 1965   Victoria, TX
Height: 6' **Weight:** 172 lbs.
Bats: Right **Throws:** Right
Acquired: Fourth-round pick in 6/83
   free-agent draft

Gant fell from grace with the Braves in 1989, losing his starting second baseman's job and getting demoted to the minor leagues. He was knocked out of the lineup by Jeff Treadway. The Braves' brass then decided that Gant should learn to play the outfield. He was shuttled to the minors to polish his swing and learn a new position. He battled his way back to Triple-A Richmond, where he batted .262 with 11 homers and 27 RBI. The new outfielder got recalled by Atlanta, and played in a total of 75 games in 1989. In 1988, Gant led all major league rookies with 19 homers and 60 RBI, finishing fourth in N.L. Rookie of the Year balloting.

   The Braves lost faith in Gant in 1989. See if they find a job for him before investing anything in his 1990 commons. Our pick for his best 1990 card is Topps.

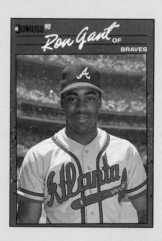

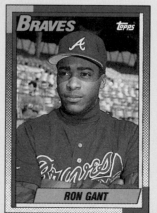

JIM GANTNER

	BA	G	AB	R	H	2B	3B	HR	RBI	SB
1989	.274	116	409	51	112	18	3	0	34	20
Life	.275	1472	5084	605	1399	215	28	44	478	109

Position: Second base
Team: Milwaukee Brewers
Born: January 5, 1954   Eden, WI
Height: 5'11"   **Weight:** 175 lbs.
Bats: Left   **Throws:** Right
Acquired: 12th-round pick in 6/74
free-agent draft

Gantner's 1989 season was snuffed out prematurely when he was taken out by a rolling block by Yankee Marcus Lawton on a double play. Lawton's illegal slide damaged Gantner's knee and shelved him for the season. Some doubts arose about his health as fans wondered if he could rebound from surgery. "Gumby" is an institution on the Brewers, a contributing member of the team since 1976. Despite playing for a losing team in the 1982 World Series, he hit .333 in seven games against the St. Louis Cardinals. The following season, he established career highs with 11 homers and 74 RBI. The Wisconsin native ranks among the top ten in 13 offensive career categories for the Brewers.

Avoid investing in Gantner's 1990 commons. Even if he can play with a mended knee in 1990, his ability could be hampered forever. Our pick for his best 1990 card is Topps.

MARK GARDNER

	W	L	ERA	G	CG	IP	H	ER	BB	SO
89 AAA	12	4	2.37	24	4	163	122	43	59	175
89 Major	0	3	5.13	7	0	26	26	15	11	21

Position: Pitcher
Team: Montreal Expos
Born: March 1, 1962   Los Angeles, CA
Height: 6'1"   **Weight:** 190 lbs.
Bats: Right   **Throws:** Right
Acquired: Eighth-round pick in 6/85
free-agent draft

The Expos indicated their faith in Gardner when they placed him on the 40-man major league roster after the 1988 season. In 1989, as Triple-A Indianapolis ran away with its American Association division during the first two months of the season, he started the season with five straight wins and recorded an August one-hitter versus Buffalo. In 1988 at Indianapolis, he was 4-2 with three complete games and a 2.77 ERA. With Double-A Jacksonville in '88, he was 6-3 with a 1.60 ERA. One of his wins was a two-hit, 15-strikeout complete game. The owner of an impressive fastball, Gardner got a brief stay at Montreal in 1989 and should be able to land a job there soon.

Gardner's 1989 performance won't enhance much interest in his 1990 cards. Don't pay more than a dime apiece for his issues. Our pick for his best 1990 card is Score.

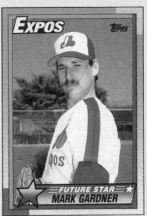

SCOTT GARRELTS

	W	L	ERA	G	CG	IP	H	ER	BB	SO
1989	14	5	2.28	30	2	193	149	49	46	119
Life	56	41	3.01	313	5	757	600	253	334	615

Position: Pitcher
Team: San Francisco Giants
Born: October 30, 1961 Urbana, IL
Height: 6'4" **Weight:** 205 lbs.
Bats: Right **Throws:** Right
Acquired: First-round pick in 6/79
free-agent draft

Despite unsuccessfully trying to switch from relieving to starting in 1986, Garrelts was a star in the rotation for the 1989 Giants and helped them win a pennant. He led the '89 team in wins, ERA, and strikeouts. He started and lost the first and third games of the 1989 World Series, getting an extra appearance because of the Bay area earthquake. Relief had been Garrelts's specialty in the past. Called up to stay at age 22, he served as a bullpen man for the Giants from 1985 to 1988; he led the N.L. with 11 relief wins in '87. Twice, he's collected a personal high of 13 saves, and Garrelts ranks fifth on the team's all-time save list with 48.

Garrelts needs to establish himself as a starter for a second season before the hobby will seriously pursue his 1990 commons. Our pick for his best 1990 card is Score.

BOB GEREN

	BA	G	AB	R	H	2B	3B	HR	RBI	SB
1989	.288	65	205	26	59	5	1	9	27	0
Life	.279	75	215	26	60	5	1	9	27	0

Position: Catcher
Team: New York Yankees
Born: September 22, 1961 San Diego, CA
Height: 6'3" **Weight:** 205 lbs.
Bats: Right **Throws:** Right
Acquired: Signed as a free agent, 11/85

In what looked like his last chance with the Yankees, Geren made the most of his 1989 call-up. In his first 35 games, he hit .355 with five homers and 16 RBI. Also, the player known for his defense had just one error. The Yankees acquired Geren as a minor league free agent in 1985, after he had spent six of his first seven seasons in the St. Louis organization. His best season in the minors came in 1983 with Class-A Springfield when he hit .265 with 24 homers and 73 RBI. In 1987, he led Double-A Eastern League catchers with a .994 fielding percentage. If Geren continues to hit major league pitching, he could become the Yankees starting catcher.

Geren showed surprising power in 1989. Buy his 1990 cards at a nickel and you could gain a decent yield. Our pick for his best 1990 card is Score.

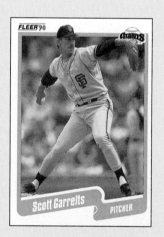
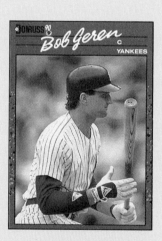

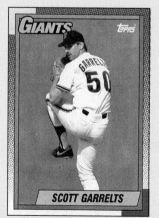

KIRK GIBSON

	BA	G	AB	R	H	2B	3B	HR	RBI	SB
1989	.213	71	253	35	54	8	2	9	28	12
Life	.274	1114	4005	669	1096	176	38	186	603	209

Position: Outfield
Team: Los Angeles Dodgers
Born: May 28, 1957 Pontiac, MI
Height: 6'3" **Weight:** 215 lbs.
Bats: Left **Throws:** Left
Acquired: Signed as a free agent, 2/88

Injuries kept Gibson, the 1988 National League MVP, from repeating that stellar performance in 1989. Both of his legs were troublesome. A hobbled Gibson slammed a heroic first-game home run in the 1988 World Series in his lone plate appearance. Hobbling triumphantly around the bases, he seemed certain to make a comeback. After all, he has five consecutive seasons of 25 or more homers. In 1989, he was a shadow of himself. He saw action in just 71 games, but still managed nine homers, 28 RBI, and 12 stolen bases. If he can perform like that hurt, imagine what Gibson could do if he becomes physically sound.

If Gibson doesn't retire early (as he's publicly considered), he has the chance for a resurgence. Investors who can find his 1990 card at 15 cents can get one of the season's biggest profits. Our pick for his best 1990 card is Fleer.

JOE GIRARDI

	BA	G	AB	R	H	2B	3B	HR	RBI	SB
1989	.248	59	157	15	39	10	0	1	14	2
Life	.248	59	157	15	39	10	0	1	14	2

Position: Catcher
Team: Chicago Cubs
Born: October 14, 1964 Peoria, IL
Height: 5'11" **Weight:** 195 lbs.
Bats: Right **Throws:** Right
Acquired: Fifth-round pick in 6/86
free-agent draft

After three years of minor league experience, Girardi skipped Triple-A and went to the 1989 Cubs. He worked as Damon Berryhill's backup in 1989 until Berryhill got hurt. Girardi batted in the .240s and helped the club defensively. He won a spot with Chicago on the basis of his 1988 season at Double-A Pittsfield. He displayed spectacular defensive abilities, throwing out 55 of 117 would-be basestealers for an Eastern League-leading success rate of 47 percent. Also, he outdid league catchers in fielding percentage, putouts, assists, and total chances. He hit a respectable .272 with seven homers and 41 RBI. Girardi had a 12-game hitting streak and an appearance in the league All-Star Game.

Girardi has to contend with Berryhill and Rick Wrona for a job. Girardi's 1990 cards are questionable investments for now. Our pick for his best 1990 card is Score.

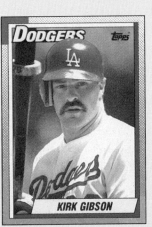
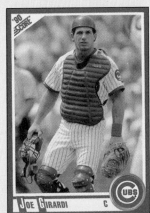

DAN GLADDEN

	BA	G	AB	R	H	2B	3B	HR	RBI	SB
1989	.295	121	461	69	136	23	3	8	46	23
Life	.276	731	2733	425	753	126	22	43	256	170

Position: Outfield
Team: Minnesota Twins
Born: July 7, 1957   San Jose, CA
Height: 5'11" **Weight:** 175 lbs.
Bats: Right **Throws:** Right
Acquired: Traded from Giants with David
         Blakley for Jose Dominguez,
         Bryan Hickerson, and Ray
         Velasquez, 3/87

Gladden is one of the hardest workers on the Twins. He even tackles mop-up relief-pitching assignments. Besides his better-than-expected pitching, his biggest contributions are his speed and defense. For the past six seasons, he has swiped 20 or more bases, twice surpassing 30. He slugged a grand slam in Game One of the 1987 World Series. In 1988, he tied for the team leads in triples (six) and outfield assists (12). He also had career highs with 91 runs scored, 62 RBI, and 11 homers. He tied Rickey Henderson and Kevin McReynolds for the major league lead in outfield double plays with five. Gladden's 1989 batting average was the highest since his 1984 rookie season with the Giants.

Gladden's platoon status keeps interest in his cards minimal. His 1990 commons would be a questionable purchase anywhere outside Minnesota. Our pick for his best 1990 card is Fleer.

TOM GLAVINE

	W	L	ERA	G	CG	IP	H	ER	BB	SO
1989	14	8	2.28	29	6	186	172	76	40	90
Life	23	29	4.30	72	7	431	428	206	136	194

Position: Pitcher
Team: Atlanta Braves
Born: March 25, 1966   Concord, MA
Height: 6' **Weight:** 175 lbs.
Bats: Left **Throws:** Left
Acquired: Second-round pick in 6/84
         free-agent draft

While many players suffer from the sophomore jinx, Glavine discovered a sophomore blessing in 1989. The lefty won a career-high 14 games to rank first on the Braves. Additionally, he led his team in complete games (six), shutouts (four), and innings pitched (186). He rebounded from a horrendous rookie season. Glavine's 1988 debut included a 7-17 mark and a 4.56 ERA (exactly double his 1989 total). He began his pro career in 1984, after starring both in baseball and hockey in high school. Glavine was a second-round draft selection by Atlanta and was a fourth-round pick by the Los Angeles Kings of the National Hockey League.

Glavine could help make Atlanta a winner again. Because most dealers overlook Braves cards, his 1990 cards will sell as commons. With even a little support, he could win 20 games. Our pick for his best 1990 card is Score.

GERMAN GONZALEZ

	W	L	ERA	G	SV	IP	H	ER	BB	SO
1989	3	2	4.66	22	1	29	32	15	11	25
Life	3	2	4.11	38	1	50	52	23	19	44

Position: Pitcher
Team: Minnesota Twins
Born: October 3, 1965
    Rio Caribe, Venezuela
Height: 6' **Weight:** 170 lbs.
Bats: Right **Throws:** Right
Acquired: Signed as a free agent, 12/86

Gonzalez had continued success with the Twins in 1989. He leapt from Double-A to the major leagues in 1988, with only two seasons worth of minor league experience. The undrafted free agent began his career at Class-A Kenosha in 1987, going 8-5 with 19 saves and 92 strikeouts in 82 innings. With Double-A Orlando in 1988, he had 31 saves, a 2-1 record, and a sterling 1.02 ERA in 50 appearances. He struck out 69 batters in 61 2/3 innings. Gonzalez split the 1989 season between the Twins and Triple-A Portland. He averaged nearly a strikeout for each inning pitched in 1989, giving the Twins another dependable arm in the bullpen. Gonzalez should play a large part in Minnesota's bullpen in 1990.

    As a middle reliever, Gonzalez isn't headed for immediate fame. Until he gets a starting or closing assignment, avoid his nickel-priced 1990 cards. Our pick for his best 1990 card is Topps.

JOSE GONZALEZ

	BA	G	AB	R	H	2B	3B	HR	RBI	SB
1989	.268	95	261	31	70	11	2	3	18	9
Life	.242	230	405	61	98	21	3	5	25	22

Position: Outfield
Team: Los Angeles Dodgers
Born: November 23, 1964
    Puerto Plata, Dominican Republic
Height: 6'2" **Weight:** 196 lbs.
Bats: Right **Throws:** Right
Acquired: Signed as a free agent, 12/80

One of the most frequent visitors to the Dodgers the past five seasons has been Gonzalez. Again in 1989, he reappeared from the minor leagues to fill a void in the Dodgers lineup. When center fielder John Shelby encountered an extended batting slump, the Dodgers gave the starting job to Gonzalez. As a result, he played in a career high of 95 games and set various career highs at the plate. His .268 batting average ranked fourth among Dodger regulars. He has an excellent reputation as a sure-handed fielder, and frequently gets summoned as a late-inning replacement. After nine pro seasons, Gonzalez seems to have proved everything at the minor league level.

    Gonzalez seems destined to be a fourth outfielder for Los Angeles. Unless he wins a starting job, overlook his 1990 commons. Our pick for his best 1990 card is Topps.

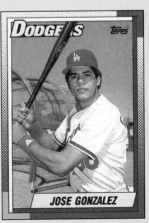

111

DWIGHT GOODEN

	W	L	ERA	G	CG	IP	H	ER	BB	SO
1989	9	4	2.89	19	0	118	93	38	47	101
Life	100	39	2.64	177	52	1291	1053	379	379	1168

Position: Pitcher
Team: New York Mets
Born: November 16, 1964   Tampa, FL
Height: 6'3"   **Weight:** 203 lbs.
Bats: Right   **Throws:** Right
Acquired: First-round pick in 6/82
free-agent draft

A sore arm derailed Gooden's chances to post another sensational season in 1989. He had a 9-4 record (achieving his 100th career victory) through June before problems with his right arm sidelined him on July 2. Understandably, the Mets had a tough time finding the win column in midseason without "Doc" in the lineup. In his 1984 debut, Gooden (with a 17-9 mark) was the N.L. Rookie of the Year, leading the league in strikeouts (with 276). He became the youngest pitcher to win a Cy Young when in 1985 he topped the league with 24 wins, a 1.53 ERA, 268 strikeouts, and 16 shutouts. In 1988, Gooden won his first six decisions and sailed to an 18-9 season.

Injuries may drop Gooden's 1990 cards as low as 35 cents, a great buy. Expect his cards to top 50 cents by the All-Star break. Our pick for his best 1990 card is Score.

TOM GORDON

	W	L	ERA	G	CG	IP	H	ER	BB	SO
1989	17	9	3.64	49	1	163	122	66	86	153
Life	17	11	3.78	54	1	179	138	75	93	171

Position: Pitcher
Team: Kansas City Royals
Born: November 18, 1967   Sebring, FL
Height: 5'9"   **Weight:** 160 lbs.
Bats: Right   **Throws:** Right
Acquired: Sixth-round pick in 6/86
free-agent draft

There's a reason why he is nicknamed "Flash." In 1988, Gordon shot from Class-A to the Royals in just one season. At stops in Class-A Appleton, Double-A Memphis, and Triple-A Omaha, he won 16 games and lost only five in 1988. For his efforts, he was named Minor League Player of the Year by *Baseball America*. In five late-season appearances with the Royals that season, he struck out 18 in 15 $^2/_3$ innings. During his entire season, he struck out 281 batters. In 1989, Gordon won ten games in middle relief before being moved to the starting rotation, and he averaged a strikeout per inning.

The hobby may love Gordon's 1990 cards for now. But wary investors will buy slowly at 50 cents, in fear that he may be a "Flash" in the pan. Our pick for his best 1990 card is Topps.

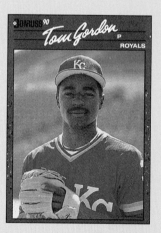

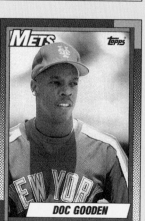

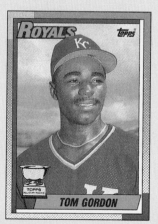

JIM GOTT

	W	L	ERA	G	SV	IP	H	ER	BB	SO
1989	0	0	0.00	1	0	1	1	0	1	1
Life	35	48	4.17	257	50	749	732	347	310	530

Position: Pitcher
Team: Pittsburgh Pirates
Born: August 3, 1959 Hollywood, CA
Height: 6'4" **Weight:** 220 lbs.
Bats: Right **Throws:** Right
Acquired: Signed as a free agent, 8/87

Gott's new-found success was short-lived. He injured his right elbow during his first outing of 1989 and was disabled for the entire season. The Pirates had hoped for another big year from him after 1988, when he earned a career-high 34 saves. His mark was a team record and was the second-highest total among N.L. relievers. He topped the club with 67 appearances and 59 games finished. Gott's major league debut came with the 1982 Blue Jays. He pitched for San Francisco in 1985 and 1986, but was released by the team in mid-1987. He was a bargain buy for Pittsburgh for just $50,000. If he regains his health, Gott will be a major force in the Pittsburgh pennant plans.

Gott's health is a question mark for now. Bypass his 1990 commons until he's back on track. Our pick for his best 1990 card is Donruss.

GOOSE GOZZO

	W	L	ERA	G	SV	IP	H	ER	BB	SO
89 AAA	5	1	2.76	12	2	62	56	19	19	34
89 Major	4	1	4.83	9	0	32	35	17	9	10

Position: Pitcher
Team: Toronto Blue Jays
Born: March 7, 1966 New Britain, CT
Height: 6'3" **Weight:** 212 lbs.
Bats: Right **Throws:** Right
Acquired: Drafted from Royals, 12/88

The Blue Jays found a gem when they acquired Gozzo prior to the 1989 season, after he spent five years in the Mets' and Royals' systems. Once the Blue Jays showed faith in him, he responded with a 12-1 combined minor league record. "Goose" racked up a 4-0 major league record in his first seven games with the '89 Blue Jays. His acquisition from Triple-A Syracuse gave Toronto a needed boost in its run for the pennant. He earned MVP honors in baseball, football, and basketball at his Connecticut high school. Gozzo's combined minor league record includes 30 saves and a 46-26 mark, with winning records for six of his seven teams.

Gozzo has some talent, but he still needs to come through with an entire good season before you should invest in his 15-cent 1990 cards. Our pick for his best 1990 card is Donruss.

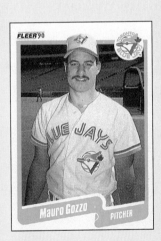

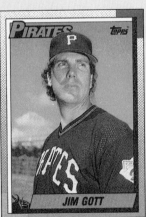

MARK GRACE

	BA	G	AB	R	H	2B	3B	HR	RBI	SB
1989	.314	142	510	74	160	28	3	13	79	14
Life	.305	276	996	139	304	51	7	20	136	17

Position: First base
Team: Chicago Cubs
Born: June 28, 1964   Winston-Salem, NC
Height: 6'2" **Weight:** 190 lbs.
Bats: Left **Throws:** Left
Acquired: 24th-round pick in 6/85
free-agent draft

Grace avoided the sophomore jinx by logging a solid 1989 season. The young first baseman topped the Cubbies in hitting in 1989, ranking among the N.L.'s top five hitters all season. After just two seasons in the minor leagues, the Cubs rushed Grace to Chicago's starting lineup in early 1988. He responded with seven homers, 57 RBI, and a .296 average. None of Grace's first-year blasts came in Wrigley Field. He distinguished himself in his minor league career by winning the league batting title with a .342 mark during his 1986 debut in Peoria. In 1987, Grace captured the Double-A Eastern League MVP with a .333 average and a league-best 101 RBI.

With the 1989 pennant hoopla, Grace's 1990 cards may be overpriced at more than $1. Those prices won't bring any quick earnings, so let the buyer beware. Our pick for his best 1990 card is Donruss.

MARK GRANT

	W	L	ERA	G	SV	IP	H	ER	BB	SO
1989	8	2	3.33	50	2	116	105	43	32	69
Life	18	24	4.12	131	4	441	434	202	165	257

Position: Pitcher
Team: San Diego Padres
Born: October 24, 1963   Aurora, IL
Height: 6'2" **Weight:** 205 lbs.
Bats: Right **Throws:** Right
Acquired: Traded from Giants with Chris
Brown, Mark Davis, and Keith
Comstock for Dave Dravecky,
Craig Lefferts,and Kevin Mitchell,
7/87

After a five-year wait, Grant earned his first winning record with the Padres in 1989. He found his niche in relief, a role he's assumed with the Padres since 1988. He set career highs in various categories, including wins, games, innings pitched, and ERA. He has shown impressive durability in his more than two years with San Diego. In 1988, he made 11 starts and 22 relief appearances for the Padres, going 2-8 in 97 innings. He toiled for parts of six seasons in the Giants' organization. San Francisco juggled him between the bullpen and the starting rotation. The Padres seem content with Grant's new prominence in the club's relief corps.

Grant has a so-so lifetime record. Also, he'll be taken for granted as a middle reliever. His 1990 commons are risky investments. Our pick for his best 1990 card is Fleer.

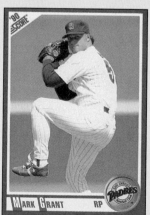
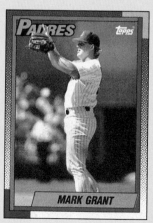

TOMMY GREENE

	W	L	ERA	G	CG	IP	H	ER	BB	SO
89 AAA	9	12	3.61	26	2	152	136	61	50	125
89 Major	1	2	4.10	4	1	26	22	12	6	17

Position: Pitcher
Team: Atlanta Braves
Born: April 6, 1967   Lumberton, NC
Height: 6'5"   **Weight:** 225 lbs.
Bats: Right   **Throws:** Right
Acquired: First-round pick in 6/85
　　　　　free-agent draft

Greene rang up more than 100 strikeouts for the fourth straight season in 1989. Pitching for Triple-A Richmond, he continued to be one of the team's most durable hurlers when it comes to starts, innings pitched, and strikeouts. Despite a 7-17 losing record in 1988, his first season in Triple-A, he paced Richmond in starts, Ks, and innings pitched. Greene had a one-hit shutout in his pro debut on August 27, 1985. In 1986, he was named Braves' Minor League Pitcher of the Year. If the 1990 Braves are looking for a tireless performer for their pitching staff, Greene could be their man.

Greene looks to have a bright future. Look for his 1990 issues for less than 15 cents. If he breaks out of the gate strongly, his card prices could double. Our pick for his best 1990 card is Score.

MIKE GREENWELL

	BA	G	AB	R	H	2B	3B	HR	RBI	SB
1989	.308	145	578	87	178	36	0	14	95	13
Life	.319	476	1646	255	526	109	14	59	315	35

Position: Outfield
Team: Boston Red Sox
Born: July 18, 1963   Louisville, KY
Height: 6'   **Weight:** 195 lbs.
Bats: Left   **Throws:** Right
Acquired: Sixth-round pick in 6/82
　　　　　free-agent draft

Although Boston legend Wade Boggs is a perennial team leader in batting average, Greenwell is keeping pace in numerous offensive categories. In four major league seasons, he has yet to bat below .300. He shared Boston's Rookie of the Year honors in 1987, his first full season. In 1988, Greenwell set an A.L. record with 23 game-winning RBI, he was second in the league in on-base percentage, and he was third in average, hits, and RBI. In his second full season, he was named an A.L. All-Star, pacing the Sox to an A.L. East championship. Greenwell should be a fixture in Boston's left field for years to come.

Greenwell has quietly become a star. Invest in his 1990 cards at 50 cents. His issues will attain Don Mattingly-like popularity. Our pick for his best 1990 card is Donruss.

TOMMY GREGG

	BA	G	AB	R	H	2B	3B	HR	RBI	SB
1989	.243	102	276	24	67	8	0	6	23	3
Life	.250	137	328	32	82	13	0	7	30	3

Position: Outfield
Team: Atlanta Braves
Born: July 29, 1963 Boone, NC
Height: 6'1" **Weight:** 190 lbs.
Bats: Left **Throws:** Left
Acquired: Traded from Pirates for
　　Ken Oberkfell, 8/88

Gregg had a top-notch season with the 1989 Atlanta Braves, marking his first full season in the major leagues. He never got much of a chance in the Pittsburgh organization, playing in just 14 games after more than three minor league seasons. After going to Atlanta in August 1988, he joined the Braves for 11 games. He was an instant hit, batting .345. In 1989, Gregg was one of the top reserves for the Braves. He was one of just seven Braves to appear in more than 100 games. Before signing with Pittsburgh as a seventh-round pick in the 1985 free-agent draft, Gregg earned all-conference honors in college ball at Wake Forest.

　　Gregg's 1990 cards will be hot commodities and affordable at 15 cents or less. He could be a significant bat for the Braves. Our pick for his best 1990 card is Topps.

KEN GRIFFEY Jr.

	BA	G	AB	R	H	2B	3B	HR	RBI	SB
88 A	.338	58	219	49	74	13	3	11	42	32
89 Major	.264	127	455	61	120	23	0	16	61	16

Position: Outfield
Team: Seattle Mariners
Born: November 21, 1969 Donora, PA
Height: 6'3" **Weight:** 195 lbs.
Bats: Left **Throws:** Left
Acquired: First-round pick in 6/87
　　free-agent draft

Even before he played one inning, Griffey was the talk of fans everywhere. He was the youngest player in the major leagues at the beginning of 1989. With only two years of minor league experience, Griffey was installed as the Mariners center fielder. He made it big immediately, hitting .287 with 13 homers and 45 RBI before slipping in a bathtub in August. The slip cost him a few weeks on the disabled list. With his father Ken Sr. active with the Reds, 1989 marked the first time that a father and son were in the big leagues at the same time. Ken Jr. was *Baseball America's* 1988 Class-A Player of the Year.

　　Everyone wants Griffey's 1990 cards. To miss getting left out of the gold rush, buy his cards quickly. With a banner sophomore year, his cards could reach $1. Our pick for his best 1990 card is Donruss.

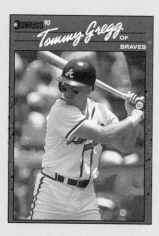

KEN GRIFFEY Sr.

	BA	G	AB	R	H	2B	3B	HR	RBI	SB
1989	.263	106	236	26	62	8	3	8	30	4
Life	.297	2000	7004	1100	2077	353	77	147	824	198

Position: Outfield
Team: Cincinnati Reds
Born: April 10, 1950 Donora, PA
Height: 6' **Weight:** 210 lbs.
Bats: Left **Throws:** Left
Acquired: Signed as a free agent, 8/88

While the baseball world was focused upon the 1989 exploits of Ken Griffey Jr., Ken Sr. was still a productive member of the Reds. Griffey celebrated his 17th major league season as a pinch-hitter and reserve outfielder for Cincinnati, the team he enjoyed his major league debut with in 1973. After an absence of more than six seasons, he proved he could still fuel Cincinnati's offense. His finest seasons came with the Reds, a team he played with from 1973 to 1981. He surpassed the .300 mark six times. In 1980, he achieved career highs with 13 homers and 85 RBI. Griffey stole a career-high 34 bases in 1976 and could top the 200-steals plateau in 1990.

Griffey's 1990 cards are common-priced. Due to the popularity of his son, cards of Ken Sr. might increase in value, too. Our pick for his best 1990 card is Topps.

ALFREDO GRIFFIN

	BA	G	AB	R	H	2B	3B	HR	RBI	SB
1989	.247	136	506	49	125	27	2	0	29	10
Life	.253	1603	5723	658	1451	218	73	23	452	178

Position: Shortstop
Team: Los Angeles Dodgers
Born: March 6, 1957
Santo Domingo,
Dominican Republic
Height: 5'11" **Weight:** 165 lbs.
Bats: Both **Throws:** Right
Acquired: Traded from Athletics with Jay Howell and Jesse Orosco for Bob Welch, Charlie Spikes, and Jack Savage, 12/87

Griffin recovered from a broken right hand to make a comeback with the 1989 Dodgers. After playing just 94 games in 1988 and hitting a career-low .199, he seemed more like his old self in 1989. He stole ten bases last season, marking the seventh time he'd reached double figures in steals. Griffin's lifetime high was 33 swipes with the 1986 Athletics. His best offensive effort came in his first full major league season with the 1979 Blue Jays. He batted .287 in 153 games. He notched a personal-high 64 RBI with the 1985 A's. Griffin started his pro career in 1974 after signing with the Indians as a 16-year-old free agent.

Griffin's 1990 cards are commons. Based on his problems during the last two seasons, he seems on the downside of his career. Our pick for his best 1990 card is Fleer.

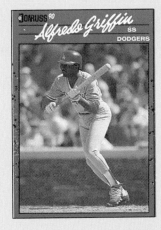

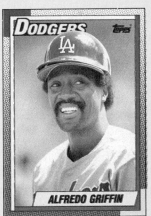

MARQUIS GRISSOM

	BA	G	AB	R	H	2B	3B	HR	RBI	SB
89 AA	.299	78	278	43	83	15	4	3	31	24
89 Major	.257	26	74	16	19	2	0	1	2	1

Position: Outfield
Team: Montreal Expos
Born: April 17, 1967   Atlanta, GA
Height: 5'11"   **Weight:** 190 lbs.
Bats: Right   **Throws:** Right
Acquired: Third-round pick in 6/88
                    free-agent draft

Grissom's second solid season in the Expos' farm system carved out a chance for stardom with the parent club. He began his pro career in 1988 at Class-A Jamestown. He topped his club in several offensive categories. He hit .323 with eight homers, 39 RBI, and 23 stolen bases. He paced the loop with 69 runs scored and 146 total bases. Managers in the circuit ranked Grissom as the top prospect in *Baseball America*. In 1989, he advanced to Double-A Jacksonville, batting near .300 and ranking among league leaders in steals throughout the season. Playing at Florida A&M in 1988, Grissom as a sophomore won nine games while pitching and batted .448 with 12 homers while playing the outfield.

Grissom seems capable of challenging for a starting spot. His 1990 cards may hit the jackpot if purchased for 15 cents or less. Our pick for his best 1990 card is Fleer.

KEVIN GROSS

	W	L	ERA	G	CG	IP	H	ER	BB	SO
1989	11	12	4.38	31	4	201	188	98	88	158
Life	71	78	3.95	234	27	1306	1276	573	518	885

Position: Pitcher
Team: Montreal Expos
Born: June 8, 1961   Downey, CA
Height: 6'5"   **Weight:** 215 lbs.
Bats: Right   **Throws:** Right
Acquired: Traded from Phillies for Floyd
                    Youmans and Jeff Parrett, 12/88

Gross registered his fourth season of double-digit wins in the last five years in 1989. He had a losing record, but his 11 wins ranked second on the Expos. He was second on the club in starts, complete games, innings pitched, and strikeouts. He pitched in the minors for three seasons before debuting with the 1983 Phillies. His most prosperous season came in 1985, when Gross was 15-13. One of the low points of his career came on August 10, 1987, when umpires found sandpaper in his glove. He was suspended for ten days. Gross redeemed himself in 1988, when he gained his first All-Star nomination and pitched one scoreless inning.

Being a .500 pitcher isn't a fast track to fame. Gross needs to gain his first 20-win season before his 1990 cards will be worth more than 3 cents apiece. Our pick for his best 1990 card is Score.

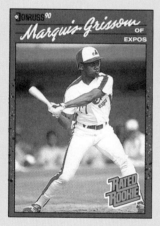

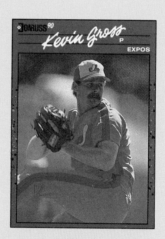

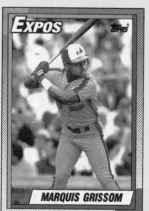

KELLY GRUBER

	BA	G	AB	R	H	2B	3B	HR	RBI	SB
1989	.290	135	545	83	158	24	4	14	73	10
Life	.263	438	1627	229	428	75	13	48	208	47

Position: Infield
Team: Toronto Blue Jays
Born: February 26, 1962   Bellaire, TX
Height: 6'   **Weight:** 185 lbs.
Bats: Right   **Throws:** Right
Acquired: Drafted from Indians, 12/83

Gruber continued to shine as Toronto's starting third base-man in 1989, gaining his first All-Star berth. He gained acclaim by hitting a career-high .290, adding 14 home runs and 73 RBI. In 1988, he set a Toronto team record for third basemen by driving in 81 runs. His first season as a starting third sacker was highlighted by a .278 batting average with 16 home runs. He had the unique distinction of batting in all nine spots in the batting order that year. His 1987 season was limited to 138 games, due to a variety of injuries. Toronto drafted Gruber from the Indians and promoted him to the majors in 1984.

Gruber's 1990 cards will cost a nickel or less. His cards are a low-cost investment that could pay off if he continues his yearly improvement. Our pick for his best 1990 card is Score.

MARK GUBICZA

	W	L	ERA	G	CG	IP	H	ER	BB	SO
1989	15	11	3.04	36	8	255	252	86	63	173
Life	84	67	3.51	199	33	1313	1207	512	502	850

Position: Pitcher
Team: Kansas City Royals
Born: August 14, 1962   Philadelphia, PA
Height: 6'5"   **Weight:** 210 lbs.
Bats: Right   **Throws:** Right
Acquired: Second-round pick in 6/81
　　　　　　free-agent draft

Gubicza fell short of his attempts to repeat his 20-win success with the 1989 Kansas City Royals. He was the third-leading winner with the Royals, trailing Bret Saberhagen and Tom Gordon in victories. Most importantly, Gubicza reached double figures in wins for the sixth straight season. His career high for triumphs came in 1988, when his 20-8 season gained him his first All-Star nomination. Gubicza spun two two-hitters in 1988 and set a team record by striking out 14 in one game against Minnesota. He finished third in A.L. Cy Young Award balloting. Gubicza began his pro career in 1981 and made his major league debut in 1984.

Gubicza's 1990 cards could sell for a nickel or less. He's young, talented, and plays for a strong team, all of which makes his cards appealing investments. Our pick for his best 1990 card is Score.

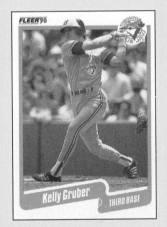

PEDRO GUERRERO

	BA	G	AB	R	H	2B	3B	HR	RBI	SB
1989	.311	162	570	60	177	42	1	17	117	2
Life	.308	1242	4321	637	1330	218	26	193	732	90

Position: First base
Team: St. Louis Cardinals
Born: June 29, 1956
    San Pedro de Macoris,
    Dominican Republic
Height: 6' **Weight:** 197 lbs.
Bats: Right **Throws:** Right
Acquired: Traded from Dodgers for
    John Tudor, 9/88

Guerrero's first full season with the Cardinals was a memorable one in 1989. He kept his average at .300 for most of 1989. His batting mark was a welcome surprise after the .268 he hit in 44 games after joining the Redbirds in '88. He starred with the Dodgers for eight seasons, earning spots on four All-Star teams. Only once did Guerrero hit less than .298 with the Dodgers, where he played first base, third base, and outfield. In 1981, his .333 average in the World Series won him MVP honors. Prior to 1989, he had exceeded 30 homers three times and 100 RBI twice. After signing with the Indians, Guerrero toiled in the minors for six seasons before getting his major league debut in 1978.

Guerrero still has the stuff to be a future MVP. Stockpile his 1990 cards at a dime or less. Our pick for his best 1990 card is Topps.

LEE GUETTERMAN

	W	L	ERA	G	SV	IP	H	ER	BB	SO
1989	5	5	2.45	70	13	103	98	28	26	51
Life	17	15	4.30	159	13	337	381	161	107	148

Position: Pitcher
Team: New York Yankees
Born: November 22, 1958
    Chattanooga, TN
Height: 6'8" **Weight:** 225 lbs.
Bats: Left **Throws:** Left
Acquired: Traded from Mariners with Clay
    Parker and Wade Taylor for Steve
    Trout and Henry Cotto, 12/87

Guetterman had spent three years in the major leagues as a reliever, but his 1989 season with the Yankees was his first chance to work as a closer. He appeared in a personal-best 70 games in 1989, earning the first 13 saves of his career. He had divided his time between starting and long relief. His first full major league season came in 1986 with the Mariners. He was 0-4 with a 7.34 ERA in 41 games. In 1987, Guetterman started for the M's, compiling an 11-4 record. He spent four seasons in the Mariners' minor league chain. Guetterman played his college baseball at Liberty Baptist and was Sid Bream's teammate.

Guetterman had an admirable season as a short reliever. To make sure that he isn't too good to be true, wait a year before investing in his common-priced 1990 cards. Our pick for his best 1990 card is Fleer.

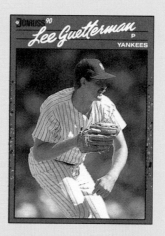

OZZIE GUILLEN

	BA	G	AB	R	H	2B	3B	HR	RBI	SB
1989	.253	155	597	63	151	20	8	1	54	36
Life	.263	769	2761	314	726	98	35	6	224	101

Position: Shortstop
Team: Chicago White Sox
Born: January 20, 1964
  Ocumare del Tuy, Venezuela
Height: 6'1" **Weight:** 150 lbs.
Bats: Left **Throws:** Right
Acquired: Traded from Padres with Bill
  Long, Luis Salazar, and Tom
  Lollar for LaMarr Hoyt, Todd
  Simmons, and Kevin Kristan,
  12/84

Guillen continued to make offensive improvements with the White Sox in 1989, racking up career highs in RBI and stolen bases. The starting shortstop for the ChiSox since 1985, he drove in more than 50 RBI for the second time in his career in 1989. He had stolen 25 bases in 1987 and 1988, his previous highs. Guillen was Chicago's sole representative on the 1988 All-Star team, although he couldn't participate in the game due to a leg injury. He won A.L. Rookie of the Year honors in 1985 by hitting .273 with one homer and 33 RBI. Chicago discovered Guillen in the Padres' system, where he worked for four years.

Guillen is a good shortstop but is far from stardom. His 1990 cards will be a nickel or less, a price unlikely to increase until he becomes a .300 hitter. Our pick for his best 1990 card is Score.

MARK GUTHRIE

	W	L	ERA	G	CG	IP	H	ER	BB	SO
89 AAA	3	4	3.65	7	1	44	45	18	16	35
89 Major	2	4	4.55	13	0	57	66	29	21	38

Position: Pitcher
Team: Minnesota Twins
Born: September 22, 1965 Buffalo, NY
Height: 6'4" **Weight:** 202 lbs.
Bats: Left **Throws:** Left
Acquired: Seventh-round pick in 6/87
  free-agent draft

The Twins in 1989 summoned Guthrie from the minors after just seven games at Triple-A. In his major league debut against the Orioles, he threw one and two-thirds innings of scoreless relief, striking out three and walking none. He was 2-4 in 13 appearances for Minnesota, and started in eight games. The Louisiana State University product began his pro career in 1987, pitching in just four games due to injury. Guthrie's best success came in 1988, his first full season with Class-A Visalia. He was 12-9, and his 182 Ks were third in the California League. Prior to his promotion in 1989, Guthrie was 8-3 with a 1.97 ERA at Double-A Orlando.

Guthrie doesn't have that much professional experience. However, the Twins want the lefty as a starter, which makes his 15-cent rookie cards promising. Our pick for his best 1990 card is Topps.

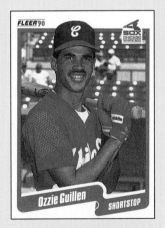

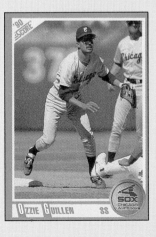
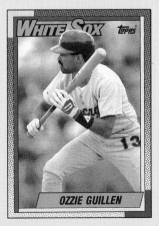

CHRIS GWYNN

	BA	G	AB	R	H	2B	3B	HR	RBI	SB
1989	.235	32	68	8	16	4	1	0	7	1
Life	.225	61	111	11	25	5	1	0	9	1

Position: Outfield
Team: Los Angeles Dodgers
Born: October 13, 1964   Los Angeles, CA
Height: 6'   **Weight:** 200 lbs.
Bats: Left   **Throws:** Left
Acquired: First-round pick in 6/85
　　　　　　free-agent draft

A broken foot replaced a lucky break for Gwynn in 1989. He got a midseason call-up from Triple-A Albuquerque but saw his time in the majors curtailed by a stress fracture of the right foot. He was sent to the minors on a rehabilitation assignment and banged up his knee in a home plate collision during his return, effectively ending his season. The younger brother of Padres star Tony Gwynn, Chris had his most prosperous season in Triple-A in 1988. His stats included 123 hits, five homers, 61 RBI, and a .299 average. Prior to his 1985 pro debut, he had a sterling three-year collegiate baseball career at San Diego State, being an All-American in 1984.

Injuries unfairly blighted Gwynn's 1989 stats. Still, see if he can bounce back before pursuing his 1990 cards. Our pick for his best 1990 card is Topps.

TONY GWYNN

	BA	G	AB	R	H	2B	3B	HR	RBI	SB
1989	.336	158	604	82	203	27	7	4	62	40
Life	.332	1060	4078	617	1354	192	51	45	416	221

Position: Outfield
Team: San Diego Padres
Born: May 9, 1960   Los Angeles, CA
Height: 5'11"   **Weight:** 205 lbs.
Bats: Left   **Throws:** Left
Acquired: Third-round pick in 6/81
　　　　　　free-agent draft

One of the safest assumptions in baseball today is that Gwynn will post an annual average of .300 or better. He stayed true to form in 1989, leading the league in batting. He is a yearly N.L. hit leader as well, with past league leads in 1984, 1986, and 1987. In fact, he's only one of four major leaguers who registered more than 1,000 hits from 1984 to 1988. He hit a career-high .370 in 1984 to win his second batting crown. The average was the N.L.'s highest since Stan Musial hit .376 in 1948. Gwynn's 1988 batting title came despite missing 29 games with an injured thumb. Each year, Gwynn claims more of the Padres' team records.

Gwynn can't be overlooked by the hobby forever. Even at 50 cents, his 1990 cards have unbelievable investment promise. Our pick for his best 1990 card is Donruss.

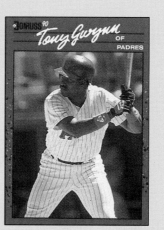

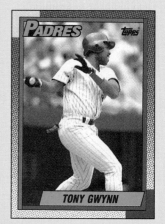

CHIP HALE

	BA	G	AB	R	H	2B	3B	HR	RBI	SB
89 AAA	.273	108	411	49	112	16	9	2	34	3
89 Major	.208	28	67	6	14	3	0	0	4	0

Position: Infield
Team: Minnesota Twins
Born: December 2, 1964   Santa Clara, CA
Height: 5'11" **Weight:** 180 lbs.
Bats: Left **Throws:** Right
Acquired: 17th-round pick in 6/87
free-agent draft

Hale is one of the biggest surprises in the Minnesota farm system. He has made steady progress in the Twins' organization during his three-year career. When Gary Gaetti was disabled in August, Hale was summoned to assist with infield chores. Before getting his call-up, he was the starting second baseman for Triple-A Portland, where he was batting .273. In 1988 at Double-A Orlando, he was second on the team in homers (11) and RBI (65). Hale's .345 average in his first pro season at Class-A Kenosha in 1987 was tops in the Midwest League, making him the first Twins June draftee to win a league batting title in his first year.

Hale has an excellent shot at the Twins second base job. Pursue his rookie 1990 cards at 10 cents or less. Our pick for his best 1990 card is Donruss.

MEL HALL

	BA	G	AB	R	H	2B	3B	HR	RBI	SB
1989	.260	113	361	54	94	9	0	17	58	0
Life	.280	845	2777	390	772	147	18	88	408	27

Position: Outfield
Team: New York Yankees
Born: September 16, 1960   Lyons, NY
Height: 6'1" **Weight:** 205 lbs.
Bats: Left **Throws:** Left
Acquired: Traded from Indians for
Joel Skinner and Turner Ward,
3/89

When the Indians felt that signing Hall to a free agent contract in 1989 seemed impossible, they dispatched him to the Yankees. He fit in well with the Bronx bombers, launching 17 homers. Hall's highest total in the majors is 18 dingers, a total he reached both in 1986 and 1987. At Triple-A Iowa in 1983, he slammed 32 homers and drove in 126 runs, which when combined with his .329 batting average gained him American Association Rookie of the Year honors and a spot on the league All-Star team. Hall began his pro career in 1978 and first reached the Chicago Cubs in 1981, after four minor league seasons.

If Hall plays with a team that will use him full-time, he has a chance to redeem himself with card collectors. For now, his 1990 commons are risky investments. Our pick for his best 1990 card is Donruss.

JEFF HAMILTON

	BA	G	AB	R	H	2B	3B	HR	RBI	SB
1989	.245	151	548	45	134	35	1	12	56	0
Life	.237	368	1087	106	258	57	3	23	109	0

Position: Third base
Team: Los Angeles Dodgers
Born: March 19, 1964 Flint, MI
Height: 6'3" **Weight:** 207 lbs.
Bats: Right **Throws:** Right
Acquired: 29th-round pick in 6/82
free-agent draft

Hamilton will try to keep the third base position for Los Angeles. He spent his second full season as the Dodgers third baseman and established career highs in numerous offensive categories. His 151 games were the most of his seven years in pro baseball, as were his 35 doubles. He had a mediocre rookie season in 1988. He batted just .236 in 111 games, hitting six homers and 33 RBI. In postseason play, Hamilton batted .217 in the N.L.C.S. and .105 in the World Series. But in 1989, he led the Dodgers in two-base hits, while his homers and RBI trailed only Eddie Murray.

Hamilton's production is only adequate for a third baseman. He needs to become more offensively dominant before his 1990 cards rise from their price of 3 cents or less. Our pick for his best 1990 card is Fleer.

ATLEE HAMMAKER

	W	L	ERA	G	SV	IP	H	ER	BB	SO
1989	6	6	3.76	28	0	76	78	32	23	30
Life	55	57	3.54	199	5	979	946	385	249	566

Position: Pitcher
Team: San Francisco Giants
Born: January 24, 1958 Carmel, CA
Height: 6'2" **Weight:** 200 lbs.
Bats: Both **Throws:** Left
Acquired: Traded from Royals with
Renie Martin, Craig Chamberlain,
and Brad Wellman for Vida Blue
and Bob Tufts, 3/82

Hammaker was a reliever and spot starter for the 1989 Giants, pitching in a variety of situations. This marked his second straight season as a swing man for San Francisco. He hasn't remained in the team's starting rotation due to his constant health problems. Since he began his pro career in 1979, he has been on the disabled list eight times. His worst disability came in 1986, when he missed the entire season due to rotator cuff surgery. He underwent arm surgery twice in 1984, then reinjured his shoulder in spring training. Hammaker returned to the majors on May 1, 1987, posting a 10-10 record that year.

Hammaker hurls in whatever role he's assigned, but he isn't a main priority of the Giant pitching staff. Don't expect his common-priced 1990 cards to gain much in value. Our pick for his best 1990 card is Score.

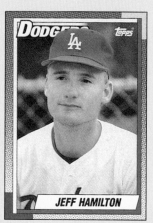

CHRIS HAMMOND

	W	L	ERA	G	CG	IP	H	ER	BB	SO
89 AAA	11	7	3.38	24	3	157	144	59	96	142
88 AA	16	5	1.72	26	4	183	127	35	77	127

Position: Pitcher
Team: Cincinnati Reds
Born: January 21, 1966 Atlanta, GA
Height: 6'1" **Weight:** 190 lbs.
Bats: Left **Throws:** Left
Acquired: Sixth-round pick in 1/86
   free-agent draft

Hammond first got the attention of Reds fans in 1988 when he helped Double-A Chattanooga to a Southern League championship. He led the league with a 16-5 record and a 1.72 ERA. His season was highlighted by a 36-inning scoreless streak, and he struck out 127 batters in 183 innings. Hammond was Chattanooga's MVP and a Southern League All-Star that year. At Class-A Tampa in 1987, he was 11-11 with six complete games in 24 starts. He whiffed 126 batsmen in 170 innings. Hammond was 6-0 with 82 strikeouts in 41 innings as a high school senior in Birmingham.

Wait for Hammond to win a Reds roster spot before purchasing his rookie 1990 cards. He needs to have a taste of the majors before his first-year cards will be worth more than a dime apiece. Our pick for his best 1990 card is Fleer.

ERIK HANSON

	W	L	ERA	G	CG	IP	H	ER	BB	SO
1989	9	5	3.18	17	1	113	103	40	32	75
Life	11	8	3.19	23	1	155	138	55	44	111

Position: Pitcher
Team: Seattle Mariners
Born: May 18, 1965 Kinnelon, NJ
Height: 6'6" **Weight:** 205 lbs.
Bats: Right **Throws:** Right
Acquired: Second-round pick in 6/86
   free-agent draft

Hanson's first full season with the Mariners in 1989 was ravaged by injury, sidelining hopes that he could become one of the A.L.'s best young pitchers. His potential was accented by the Triple-A Pacific Coast League strikeout crown he won in 1988. At Calgary that year, he fanned 154 batters in 161 innings. When he was promoted to Seattle in September, Hanson was 2-3 with a respectable 3.24 ERA. After winning a spot in the Mariners rotation prior to the 1989 season, he was plagued by tendinitis in his right shoulder and other arm problems. He recuperated back at Calgary before having an abbreviated season with the Mariners. Hanson has a chance of becoming a mainstay in Seattle.

The M's still have unlimited faith in Hanson. His 1990 cards would be impressive investments at 15 cents or less. Our pick for his best 1990 card is Donruss.

PETE HARNISCH

	W	L	ERA	G	CG	IP	H	ER	BB	SO
1989	5	9	4.62	18	2	103	97	53	64	70
Life	5	11	4.73	20	2	116	110	61	73	80

Position: Pitcher
Team: Baltimore Orioles
Born: September 23, 1966   Commack, NY
Height: 6'   **Weight:** 195 lbs.
Bats: Right   **Throws:** Right
Acquired: Third-round pick in 6/87
           free-agent draft

Harnisch got a second chance at the major leagues with the 1989 Orioles. In his first ten games, he was 2-5 with one complete-game shutout to his credit. In only his third professional season, he had shot quickly through the Baltimore organization. In 1988 at Double-A Charlotte, he went 7-6 in 20 starts. When promoted to Triple-A Rochester, he earned a 4-1 mark with three complete games in seven starts. Despite losing to the Yankees in one late-season appearance in 1988, he displayed his mettle by striking out Dave Winfield, Mike Pagliarulo, and Willie Randolph to escape a bases-loaded jam. Harnisch could see increased action with the O's in 1990.

Despite his so-so record, Baltimore stuck with Harnisch. He may get better with age, but his common-priced 1990 cards are questionable investments for now. Our pick for his best 1990 card is Topps.

BRIAN HARPER

	BA	G	AB	R	H	2B	3B	HR	RBI	SB
1989	.325	126	385	43	125	24	0	8	57	2
Life	.281	391	941	91	265	50	2	22	127	3

Position: Catcher; outfield
Team: Minnesota Twins
Born: October 16, 1959   Los Angeles, CA
Height: 6'2"   **Weight:** 195 lbs.
Bats: Right   **Throws:** Right
Acquired: Signed as a free agent, 12/87

Harper had the season of his dreams with the Minnesota Twins in 1989. He appeared in 126 games, more than twice the amount of any year he spent in the majors, and he established single-season highs in every offensive category in 1989. Most importantly, he spent the entire season in the big leagues. Harper hadn't accomplished this feat since his pro career began in 1977. He first reached the majors in 1979 for one game for the Angels. At Triple-A Salt Lake City in 1981, he hit a career-best 28 homers, 122 RBI, and .350 average in 134 games. Harper bounced around for several years with the Pirates, Cardinals, Tigers, and A's before settling with Minnesota.

Harper will log a lot of playing time again in '90, but he won't start. This makes investing in his 1990 commons a futile proposition. Our pick for his best 1990 card is Score.

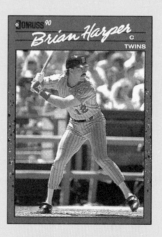
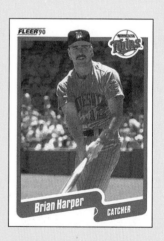

GENE HARRIS

	W	L	ERA	G	SV	IP	H	ER	BB	SO
89 AL	1	4	6.48	10	1	33	47	24	15	14
Life	2	5	5.91	21	0	53	63	35	25	25

Position: Pitcher
Team: Seattle Mariners
Born: December 5, 1964   Sebring, FL
Height: 5'11" **Weight:** 190 lbs.
Bats: Right **Throws:** Right
Acquired: Traded from Expos with
      Brian Holman and
      Randy Johnson for
      Mark Langston and
      Mike Campbell, 5/89

Just when Harris appeared ready to ensure a spot on the Mariners pitching staff in 1989, a muscle pull placed him on the disabled list. He pitched in just ten games for Seattle before getting injured, going 1-4 with one save. This was the second mishap in three years to sidetrack his career. In 1988, Harris missed nearly two months after having a cyst removed from his back. Before joining Seattle, he appeared in 11 games for the 1989 Expos. He was 1-1 in 11 relief appearances. A starter at Double-A Jacksonville in 1988, he was 9-5 with a 2.56 ERA and seven complete games. Harris will be a major part of the 1990 M's.

Give Harris another chance before deciding about investing in his 1990 cards. If he gets a full season with the Mariners, he may establish his full ability. Our pick for his best 1990 card is Donruss.

GREG HARRIS

	W	L	ERA	G	SV	IP	H	ER	BB	SO
1989	8	9	2.60	56	6	135	106	39	52	106
Life	10	9	2.47	59	6	153	119	42	55	121

Position: Pitcher
Team: San Diego Padres
Born: December 1, 1963   Greensboro, NC
Height: 6'2" **Weight:** 190 lbs.
Bats: Right **Throws:** Right
Acquired: Tenth-round pick in 6/85
      free-agent draft

In his first full season with San Diego, Harris became a workhorse. Throughout four seasons in the minor leagues, he had worked almost exclusively as a starter. However, he found full-time work in the majors by moving to the Padres bullpen. He provided the perfect complement for lefthanded stopper Mark Davis in 1989. In 1986, Harris was 13-7 with eight complete games at Class-A Charleston. He was named the Padre organization's Pitcher of the Year for the second straight season after going 12-11 at Double-A Wichita in 1987. After making the conversion from starter to reliever, Harris may have found the secret to a long career in the majors.

Harris may become the Padres closer if Davis slips away. Harris's 1990 cards would be suitable buys at a dime or less. Our pick for his best 1990 card is Topps.

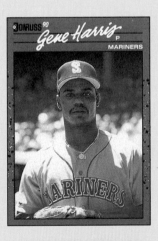
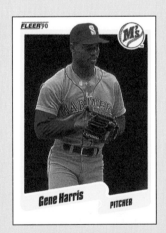

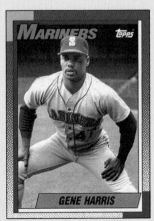
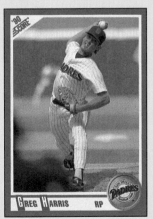

LENNY HARRIS

	BA	G	AB	R	H	2B	3B	HR	RBI	SB
1989	.236	115	335	36	79	10	1	3	26	14
Life	.251	131	378	43	95	11	1	3	34	18

Position: Infield
Team: Los Angeles Dodgers
Born: October 28, 1964   Miami, FL
Height: 5'10"   **Weight:** 200 lbs.
Bats: Left   **Throws:** Right
Acquired: Traded from Reds with
Kal Daniels for Mariano Duncan
and Tim Leary, 7/89

Harris became a key utility player for Los Angeles in 1989, giving the team a much-needed hitter and fielder off the bench. The Dodgers were persuaded to obtain him by his 1988 performance with Cincinnati. After six seasons in the minors, Harris made the most of his 16-game stay, batting .372 with eight RBI. He got a promotion to the majors after a first-rate season at Triple-A Nashville in 1988. In 107 games, Harris batted .277 with a league-leading 45 steals. In 1987 with Nashville, he hit .248 with two homers and 30 stolen bases in 120 games. His ability to perform a variety of tasks makes Harris a key addition to Los Angeles.

Harris was relatively successful but didn't land a starting position. If he remains a utility player, his 1990 commons won't gain in price. Our pick for his best 1990 card is Fleer.

BRYAN HARVEY

	W	L	ERA	G	SV	IP	H	ER	BB	SO
1989	3	3	3.44	51	25	55	36	21	41	78
Life	10	8	2.58	104	42	136	101	39	63	148

Position: Pitcher
Team: California Angels
Born: June 2, 1963   Chattanooga, TN
Height: 6'2"   **Weight:** 212 lbs.
Bats: Right   **Throws:** Right
Acquired: Signed as a free agent, 8/84

Harvey's accented his fine 1988 rookie debut with a strong sophomore performance for the 1989 California Angels. He finished second in A.L. Rookie of the Year balloting in 1988, when he was 7-5 with 17 saves and a 2.13 ERA in 50 games. He didn't give up a homer until his 32nd appearance, ending a streak of 49 2/3 innings. In 1989, Harvey assumed a bigger share of the bullpen work. He topped the Halos with 51 appearances, 42 games finished, and a career-high 25 saves. He notched 41 saves in his minor league career. Before he was signed as an undrafted free agent, Harvey played for a nationally known slow pitch softball team with his father.

Harvey could become one of the league's top relief aces if his success continues. His 1990 cards will be common-priced, an enticing price for investments. Our pick for his best 1990 card is Score.

RON HASSEY

	BA	G	AB	R	H	2B	3B	HR	RBI	SB
1989	.228	97	268	29	61	12	0	5	23	1
Life	.272	1046	3067	325	833	157	7	65	402	13

Position: Catcher
Team: Oakland Athletics
Born: February 27, 1953 Tucson, AZ
Height: 6'2" **Weight:** 195 lbs.
Bats: Left **Throws:** Right
Acquired: Signed as a free agent, 1/88

Hassey's 12th major league season was in a reserve role with the 1989 Athletics. He joined the A's in 1988 as a free agent, and he is relief ace Dennis Eckersley's exclusive catcher. Because Eckersley has preferred pitching to Hassey, both men were late-inning additions during crucial games in the last two years. He produced a .500 batting average in the 1988 A.L.C.S. In the third game, he provided a double, homer, and three RBI, including the game-winning hit. Hassey has been a substitute for most of his career. His finest major league season came with the 1985 Yankees, when he smacked 13 homers and 42 RBI in just 267 at-bats.

Because he's spent his time as a part-timer, Hassey's cards have never been big sellers. His 1990 commons aren't good investments. Our pick for his best 1990 card is Fleer.

BILLY HATCHER

	BA	G	AB	R	H	2B	3B	HR	RBI	SB
1989	.251	135	481	59	111	19	3	4	51	24
Life	.263	609	2166	314	569	99	15	30	212	151

Position: Outfield
Team: Pittsburgh Pirates
Born: October 4, 1960 Williams, AZ
Height: 5'9" **Weight:** 175 lbs.
Bats: Right **Throws:** Right
Acquired: Traded from Astros for
　　　　　Glenn Wilson, 8/89

Hatcher struggled in 1989 with the lowest batting average of his four-year major league career, a slump that got him traded to the Pirates. But after joining the Bucs on August 18, he had two hits (one a home run) and two runs scored to lead his new club to a 7-6 win over Atlanta. Hatcher had his biggest year in 1987, when he hit .296 with 11 homers, 63 RBI, and 53 stolen bases for the Astros. However, he was suspended for ten days that year when umpires caught him using an illegally corked bat. In the 1986 National League Championship Series against the Mets, Hatcher's 14th-inning homer off Jesse Orosco tied the game at 4-4.

Hatcher isn't a power hitter and has never hit .300 in the majors. His modest lifetime record doesn't justify investing in his 1990 commons. Our pick for his best 1990 card is Topps.

MICKEY HATCHER

	BA	G	AB	R	H	2B	3B	HR	RBI	SB
1989	.295	94	224	18	66	9	2	2	25	1
Life	.283	1045	3245	336	918	169	19	38	362	11

Position: Outfield; infield
Team: Los Angeles Dodgers
Born: March 15, 1955 Cleveland, OH
Height: 6'2" **Weight:** 200 lbs.
Bats: Right **Throws:** Right
Acquired: Signed as a free agent, 4/87

Hatcher bolstered the Los Angeles bench for a second straight season in 1989. He is the unofficial leader of the "Stuntmen," the Dodgers reserve corps. He remained one of the National League's top pinch-hitters in 1989. He hit .295 in 94 games, the third-highest average of his ten-year major league career. He played with the Minnesota Twins from 1981 to 1986, batting over .300 twice. The Dodgers signed Hatcher as a free agent and collected dividends in the 1988 World Series. He batted .368 and his two-run homer in Game Five provided the winning RBI.

Hatcher has modest lifetime statistics that don't merit investing in his 1990 commons. However, his cards could have some long-term value if he has a post-baseball career in broadcasting, much like Bob Uecker or Joe Garagiola. Our pick for his best 1990 card is Donruss.

ANDY HAWKINS

	W	L	ERA	G	CG	IP	H	ER	BB	SO
1989	15	15	4.80	34	5	208	238	111	76	98
Life	75	73	4.00	233	24	1311	1327	582	488	587

Position: Pitcher
Team: New York Yankees
Born: January 21, 1960 Waco, TX
Height: 6'3" **Weight:** 215 lbs.
Bats: Right **Throws:** Right
Acquired: Signed as a free agent, 12/88

Hawkins was the leading winner for the 1989 Yankees. After seven years with the Padres, he signed a hefty free-agent contract with New York. He led the Yanks in wins, starts, complete games, innings pitched, shutouts, and strikeouts. His career-best record came in 1985 with San Diego, when he was 18-8 in 33 starts. In 1984, Hawkins was 8-9 as a starter and a reliever. He gave up just one run in 12 innings of relief during the 1984 World Series against Detroit. He earned San Diego's only Series win with one-hit relief over five and one-third innings. Hawkins could help the Yankees contend for a pennant.

Hawkins basically is a .500 pitcher without 100 career wins. His 1990 commons won't bring any long-term gains and will be neglected investments. Our pick for his best 1990 card is Fleer.

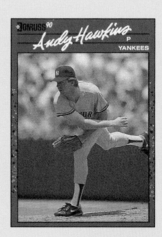

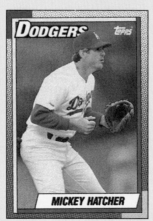

CHARLIE HAYES

	BA	G	AB	R	H	2B	3B	HR	RBI	SB
1989	.257	87	304	26	78	15	1	8	43	3
Life	.251	94	315	26	79	15	1	8	43	3

Position: Third base
Team: Philadelphia Phillies
Born: May 29, 1965 Hattiesburg, MS
Height: 6' **Weight:** 190 lbs.
Bats: Right **Throws:** Right
Acquired: Traded from Giants with
　　　　Terry Mulholland and
　　　　Dennis Cook for Steve Bedrosian,
　　　　7/89

Hayes acquired the lofty responsibility of taking over the Phillies third base job following Mike Schmidt's retirement in mid-1989. After six minor league seasons in the Giants' farm system, Hayes got a second chance at the majors when acquired by the Phillies. He batted only in the .230s through his first month as a starter, but the Phillies management showed ample patience in giving him a chance to succeed. He came into his own as a hitter beginning in 1987 with Double-A Shreveport. There, Hayes batted .304 with 14 homers and 75 RBI. He topped Texas League third basemen in games, total chances, and fielding percentage. In 1988 at Triple-A Phoenix, Hayes hit .307 in 131 games.

Hayes hits well but his defense remains dubious. At a nickel or less, his 1990 cards will be long-shot investments. Our pick for his best 1990 card is Donruss.

VON HAYES

	BA	G	AB	R	H	2B	3B	HR	RBI	SB
1989	.259	154	540	93	140	27	2	26	78	28
Life	.274	1195	4191	619	1147	236	31	122	573	217

Position: Outfield
Team: Philadelphia Phillies
Born: August 31, 1958 Stockton, CA
Height: 6'5" **Weight:** 185 lbs.
Bats: Left **Throws:** Right
Acquired: Traded from Indians for
　　　　Manny Trillo, George Vuckovich,
　　　　Jerry Willard, Jay Baller, and
　　　　Julio Franco, 12/82

Hayes enjoyed a comeback with the Phillies in 1989. After missing six weeks of the 1988 season due to injury, he surpassed his 1988 power totals by the All-Star break. He was a member of the N.L. All-Star team for the first time in 1989. With Mike Schmidt's midseason retirement, Hayes was forced to carry the power burden for Philadelphia's offense. Such tasks were no problems to Hayes in the past, as he had notched double-digit homer totals from 1984 through 1987. In 1988, he assisted the team by playing first base, third base, and two outfield positions. The Phillies coveted his services so much that they gave up five players to obtain Hayes in 1983.

Hayes is an All-Star caliber player. His 1990 cards will bring a profit when bought at less than a dime. Our pick for his best 1990 card is Topps.

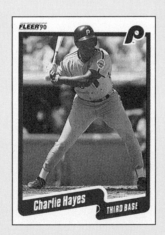

MIKE HEATH

	BA	G	AB	R	H	2B	3B	HR	RBI	SB
1989	.263	122	396	38	104	16	2	10	43	7
Life	.252	1154	3703	412	932	152	24	78	419	47

Position: Catcher
Team: Detroit Tigers
Born: February 5, 1955 Tampa, FL
Height: 5'11" **Weight:** 180 lbs.
Bats: Right **Throws:** Right
Acquired: Traded from Cardinals for
　　　　　Mike Laga and Ken Hill, 8/86

Although Heath was considered a reserve catcher for the 1989 Tigers, he was kept busy all year while starting back-stop Matt Nokes nursed his injured knees. Heath's 122 games marked the third-highest total of his 17-year career. He hadn't seen so much action since his 1985 campaign with the A's. Additionally, his homers, RBI and total hits were the third-best he'd achieved in the majors. His top offensive season came with Oakland in 1984. He hit 13 round-trippers and 64 RBI. He played his first pro season in 1973. He had his major league debut with the 1978 Yankees. Seven seasons with the A's and one with St. Louis preceded Heath's arrival in Detroit.

Heath hasn't been a starting catcher for four years. Because he's nearing the last years of his career, his 1990 commons are unwise investments. Our pick for his best 1990 card is Score.

NEAL HEATON

	W	L	ERA	G	CG	IP	H	ER	BB	SO
1989	6	7	3.05	42	5	147	127	50	55	67
Life	61	83	4.46	260	23	1223	1297	606	431	551

Position: Pitcher
Team: Pittsburgh Pirates
Born: March 3, 1960 Jamaica, NY
Height: 6'1" **Weight:** 195 lbs.
Bats: Left **Throws:** Left
Acquired: Traded from Expos for
　　　　　Brett Gideon, 3/89

Although his record didn't show it, Heaton had a modestly successful season with the 1989 Pirates. He rebounded from a horrible slump he endured with the 1988 Expos, which included a 3-10 record and a 4.99 ERA. His 1989 ERA was the lowest of his nine-year career, a real switch from his lifetime 4.65 ERA (prior to 1989). Heaton had won in double figures three times in his career, most recently a career-high 13-10 result with the 1987 Expos. Although he had spent more than four seasons in the American League without batting, he rapped out 14 base hits. Only hurlers Orel Hershiser and Bob Forsch had better seasons at the plate than did Heaton.

Heaton needs to even his career record at .500 before card investors will take him seriously. For now, don't consider his 1990 commons. Our pick for his best 1990 card is Fleer.

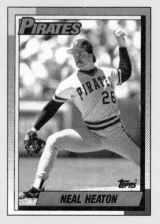

DANNY HEEP

	BA	G	AB	R	H	2B	3B	HR	RBI	SB
1989	.300	113	320	36	96	17	0	5	49	0
Life	.259	828	1880	201	486	94	5	30	218	12

Position: First base; outfield
Team: Boston Red Sox
Born: July 3, 1957 San Antonio, TX
Height: 5'11" **Weight:** 185 lbs.
Bats: Left **Throws:** Left
Acquired: Signed as a free agent, 2/89

Read off the list of .300 hitters for the 1989 Red Sox and Heep's name jumps off the page. Right along with Wade Boggs, Mike Greenwell, and Ellis Burks is Heep, a scrappy reserve who's played for four different organizations in 12 years. He had career highs in average, hits, and RBI for the '89 BoSox. Heep has made a career as a pinch-hitter and defensive replacement. His pro career began in 1978, and he got his major league debut with the 1979 Astros. He has played in three League Championship Series and two World Series. One of his career highlights came in 1980 with Triple-A Tucson. Heep hit .343 in 96 games to win the Pacific Coast League batting crown.

Heep is a capable reserve, but cards of reserves don't make good investment vehicles. Don't pursue his 1990 commons. Our pick for his best 1990 card is Donruss.

DAVE HENDERSON

	BA	G	AB	R	H	2B	3B	HR	RBI	SB
1989	.250	152	579	77	145	24	3	15	80	8
Life	.260	1078	3465	494	902	191	16	127	474	39

Position: Outfield
Team: Oakland Athletics
Born: July 21, 1958 Dos Palos, CA
Height: 6'2" **Weight:** 210 lbs.
Bats: Right **Throws:** Right
Acquired: Signed as a free agent, 12/87

Anyone who didn't appreciate Henderson's offensive contributions to the 1989 Athletics didn't see his power display in Game Three of the World Series. In a wild 13-7 Oakland win, he smashed a two-run double off the top of the right field fence and added two homers to give him four RBI for the night. For Henderson, it was a moral victory. With the 1986 Red Sox and 1988 A's, he had played for World Series losers. For those two Series, however, he had a .356 average with 16 hits, two homers, and six RBI. Henderson had a career year in 1988, with 24 homers, 97 RBI, and a .304 average.

Henderson will never be a Hall of Famer, but he could achieve some impressive totals before he's done. His 1990 cards, at a nickel or less, could bring tidy short-term profits. Our pick for his best 1990 card is Topps.

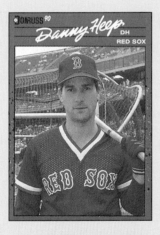
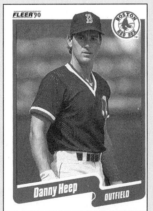

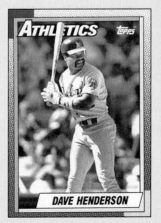

RICKEY HENDERSON

	BA	G	AB	R	H	2B	3B	HR	RBI	SB
1989	.274	150	541	113	148	26	3	12	57	77
Life	.290	1472	5524	1171	1603	261	47	138	561	871

Position: Outfield
Team: Oakland Athletics
Born: December 25, 1958 Chicago, IL
Height: 5'10" **Weight:** 195 lbs.
Bats: Right **Throws:** Right
Acquired: Traded from Yankees for
      Eric Plunk, Luis Polonia, and
      Greg Cadaret, 6/89

The most prolific basestealer of the 1980s, Henderson returned to Oakland in 1989, the site where his career began ten years previously. He helped to make the offensively robust A's even stronger with his midseason return. He scored 100-plus runs for the eighth season. He also continued on an incredible stolen base pace, racking up his 800th career steal in 1989. Barring injury, he will eclipse Ty Cobb's 892 career swipes in 1990, before his 31st birthday. Lou Brock's record 938 steals is within easy reach for Henderson, who set a single-season record with 130 pilfers in 1982. Henderson's first homer in 1989 gave him a record 36 career round-trippers as a leadoff man.

Oakland's postseason star, Henderson will have one of the hottest 1990 cards. To guarantee quick profits, try to pay less than 50 cents for his issues. Our pick for his best 1990 card is Topps.

TOM HENKE

	W	L	ERA	G	SV	IP	H	ER	BB	SO
1989	8	3	1.92	64	20	89	66	19	25	116
Life	27	22	2.81	320	122	442	346	138	146	521

Position: Pitcher
Team: Toronto Blue Jays
Born: December 21, 1957 Kansas City, MO
Height: 6'5" **Weight:** 225 lbs.
Bats: Right **Throws:** Right
Acquired: Selected in the player
      compensation pool draft, 1/85

The Toronto all-time saves leader, Henke bolstered his records with another sterling season in 1989. He led the club in appearances and saves, and finished 56 of his 64 appearances. His 1.92 ERA was the best in his career. In the last five years, his ERA has inched above 3.00 just once. He earned double-digit save totals for the sixth straight season. In 1987, he saved a career-high 34 games and made his first All-Star Game appearance. He hurled two and two-thirds innings of scoreless, two-hit relief. Henke is best known for his low-slung sidearm motion and his incredible strikeout-to-innings pitched ratios.

Henke's 1990 cards will cost a nickel or less. Due to the glut of quality relievers in the '80s, don't expect his cards to increase in value quickly. Our pick for his best 1990 card is Donruss.

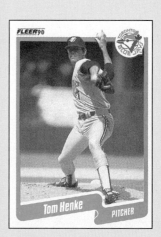

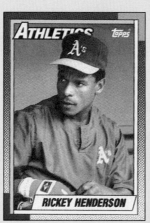

MIKE HENNEMAN

	W	L	ERA	G	SV	IP	H	ER	BB	SO
1989	11	4	3.70	60	8	90	84	37	51	69
Life	31	13	2.85	180	37	278	242	88	105	202

Position: Pitcher
Team: Detroit Tigers
Born: December 11, 1961 St. Charles, MO
Height: 6'4" **Weight:** 195 lbs.
Bats: Right **Throws:** Right
Acquired: Third-round pick in 6/84
  free-agent draft

Despite the 1989 Tiger record, Henneman emerged unscathed with one of his best marks ever. His 11 victories were tops on the 1989 club. He also led the team in appearances and games finished. After pitching in three minor league campaigns, his 1987 rookie season consisted of an 11-3 record with seven saves in 55 games. He won his first eight decisions and wound up on various All-Rookie team lists. In 1988, he had career highs of 65 appearances and a 1.87 ERA. His nine wins and 22 saves made him the top member of the Tigers bullpen. Henneman converted all but seven save opportunities in 1988.

Henneman's 1990 cards will be priced at a nickel or less. While he's one of the best hurlers the Tigers have, he's not likely to pitch enough to make his cards more valuable. Our pick for his best 1990 card is Donruss.

GUILLERMO HERNANDEZ

	W	L	ERA	G	SV	IP	H	ER	BB	SO
1989	2	2	5.74	32	15	31	36	20	16	30
Life	70	63	3.37	744	147	1045	952	392	349	788

Position: Pitcher
Team: Detroit Tigers
Born: November 14, 1954
  Aguada, Puerto Rico
Height: 6'2" **Weight:** 185 lbs.
Bats: Left **Throws:** Left
Acquired: Traded from Phillies with
  Dave Bergman for Glenn Wilson
  and John Wockenfuss, 3/84

Hernandez moved closer to becoming Detroit's top reliever in history with 15 saves in 1989. In just five seasons with the Bengals, he has registered 120 saves. He's just six saves away from breaking John Hiller's all-time record of 125 saves. Hernandez's abbreviated 1989 season didn't compare to some of his feats with the Tigers. In 1984, his first season with the Tigers, he was 9-3 with a league-leading 80 appearances, 32 saves, and a 1.92 ERA. He earned his first of three straight All-Star Game nominations, and he was named the A.L. MVP and Cy Young Award winner. He then saved games that clinched the division pennant, A.L. pennant, and World Championship.

Hernandez will have 1990 cards available at a nickel or less. Due to his decline over the last two years, his cards are chancy investments. Our pick for his best 1990 card is Score.

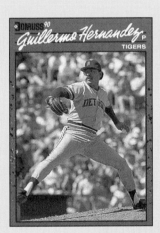
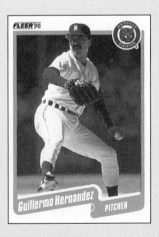

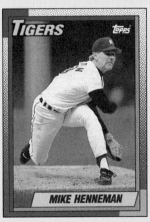
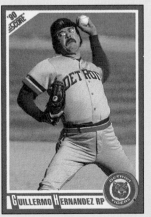

KEITH HERNANDEZ

	BA	G	AB	R	H	2B	3B	HR	RBI	SB
1989	.233	75	215	18	50	8	0	4	19	0
Life	.298	2045	7240	1117	2156	424	60	161	1063	98

Position: First base
Team: New York Mets
Born: October 20, 1953 San Francisco, CA
Height: 6' **Weight:** 205 lbs.
Bats: Left **Throws:** Left
Acquired: Traded from Cardinals for
  Neil Allen and Rick Ownbey, 6/83

For the second consecutive year, injuries haunted Hernandez. Even while disabled, he was a valuable asset as a pinch-hitter. In 1987, he hit .290 with a career-high 18 home runs and 89 RBI. That season marked his fifth All-Star Game appearance, in which he holds a cumulative .300 average. Hernandez set a major league record with 24 game-winning RBI. His dazzling fielding resulted in a streak of 11 consecutive Gold Gloves. In postseason play, he has hit .281 through three League Championship Series. In the 1982 World Series with the Cardinals, Hernandez had one homer and eight RBI.

Even if Hernandez retires before the season, his 1990 cards will remain valuable. Invest at 25 cents or less each. He has an outside chance at the Hall of Fame, his cards will be choice property if he heads to Cooperstown. Our pick for his best 1990 card is Donruss.

TOM HERR

	BA	G	AB	R	H	2B	3B	HR	RBI	SB
1989	.287	151	561	65	161	25	6	2	37	10
Life	.275	1266	4587	605	1262	220	37	22	493	172

Position: Second base
Team: Philadelphia Phillies
Born: April 4, 1956 Lancaster, PA
Height: 6' **Weight:** 185 lbs.
Bats: Both **Throws:** Right
Acquired: Traded from Twins with
  Tom Nieto and Eric Bullock for
  Shane Rawley, 10/88

Herr got a homecoming when the Twins included him in a 1988 trade to the Phillies, a team near his home. Back in the N.L. in 1989 after a half-season with Minnesota, he exceeded his 1988 totals in hits and RBI by the 1989 All-Star break. Herr's 1988 season was blighted by two stints on the disabled list, which kept him to 101 total games. His greatest season to date has been in 1985 with St. Louis, when he batted .302 with eight home runs and 110 RBI. He became the seventh second baseman in modern N.L. history to top 100 RBI, and the first player since George Kell in 1950 to drive in 100 runs with less than ten homers.

Because Herr isn't a perennial .300 hitter, his common-priced 1990 cards aren't worthy investments. Our pick for his best 1990 card is Fleer.

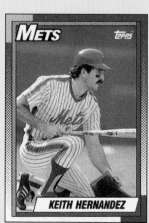

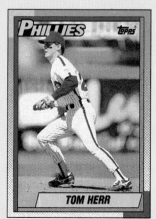

OREL HERSHISER

	W	L	ERA	G	CG	IP	H	ER	BB	SO
1989	15	15	2.31	35	8	257	226	66	77	178
Life	98	64	2.69	231	58	1457	1240	435	434	1011

Position: Pitcher
Team: Los Angeles Dodgers
Born: September 16, 1958 Buffalo, NY
Height: 6'3" **Weight:** 190 lbs.
Bats: Right **Throws:** Right
Acquired: 17th-round pick in 6/79
　　　　　free-agent draft

Hershiser couldn't duplicate his award-winning season of 1988, but he continued to be the ace of the Dodgers in 1989. Fans are still talking about his 1988 season, a 23-8 campaign. He achieved an incredible milestone when he hurled 59 consecutive scoreless innings, breaking Don Drysdale's record, which had stood for 20 years. Following four postseason victories, Hershiser was named Most Valuable Player both for the N.L.C.S. and World Series, and was named the league's Cy Young recipient. In 1989, Hershiser was ranked among the top league pitchers in victories, ERA, complete games, strikeouts, shutouts, and innings pitched.

Don't be fooled by the Dodger slumps. Hershiser would have been a 20-game winner with even minimal support. Snatch up his 1990 cards at a quarter, then count your loot when he heads for another Cy Young. Our pick for his best 1990 card is Score.

ERIC HETZEL

	W	L	ERA	G	CG	IP	H	ER	BB	SO
89 AAA	4	4	2.48	12	4	80	65	22	32	79
89 Major	2	3	6.26	12	0	50	61	35	28	33

Position: Pitcher
Team: Boston Red Sox
Born: September 25, 1963 Crowley, LA
Height: 6'3" **Weight:** 175 lbs.
Bats: Right **Throws:** Right
Acquired: First-round pick in 6/85
　　　　　free-agent draft

A sore arm sidelined Hetzel in August 1989, effectively deflating his chances for a solid rookie season. Hetzel was placed on the 21-day disabled list on August 3 after appearing in just seven games for the BoSox. Before the injury, his record was 1-2 with a 5.17 ERA, including 18 walks and 21 strikeouts in 31 1/3 innings. Injuries are nothing new to Hetzel. In 1986, after just one year of minor league experience, he suffered a slipped disc in his back. Once recovered, he went on to post a 6-10 record at Triple-A Pawtucket. However, his team scored only 19 runs in his ten losses, three of which were shutouts. Hetzel posted a 10-4 record with Louisiana State in 1985.

Hetzel fared poorly with Boston in 1989. Don't invest in his 1990 cards, even at 3 cents apiece, until he has some success in the bigs. Our pick for his best 1990 card is Donruss.

GREG HIBBARD

	W	L	ERA	G	CG	IP	H	ER	BB	SO
89 AAA	2	3	2.64	9	2	58	47	17	11	45
89 Major	6	7	3.21	23	2	137	142	49	41	55

Position: Pitcher
Team: Chicago White Sox
Born: September 13, 1964
New Orleans, LA
Height: 6' **Weight:** 180 lbs.
Bats: Left **Throws:** Left
Acquired: Traded from Royals with
Melido Perez and Chuck Mount
for Floyd Bannister, 12/87

Hibbard's performance with the 1989 White Sox caused fans to reevaluate the team's 1987 trade of veteran pitcher Floyd Bannister. Hibbard equaled Bannister's numbers through most of the '89 season, giving the White Sox a needed lefty in the starting rotation. One of Hibbard's finest outings with the Sox came on September 13, his 25th birthday. He allowed just four hits over eight and one-third innings to beat the Orioles. He reached Chicago on the strength of his 1988 season at Triple-A Vancouver, where he won a career-high 11 games. He began his pro career in the Royals' organization in 1986, working solely in relief. In 1987, Hibbard played for three teams as a starter, advancing to Double-A before being traded.

Hibbard looks like a major winner for future ChiSox teams. Buy his 1990 cards at a dime or less. Our pick for his best 1990 card is Fleer.

KEVIN HICKEY

	W	L	ERA	G	SV	IP	H	ER	BB	SO
1989	2	3	2.92	51	2	49	38	16	23	28
Life	7	11	3.19	175	16	192	172	68	82	91

Position: Pitcher
Team: Baltimore Orioles
Born: February 25, 1956 Chicago, IL
Height: 6'1" **Weight:** 195 lbs.
Bats: Left **Throws:** Left
Acquired: Signed as a free agent, 12/87

Just like a cat with nine lives, Hickey was reincarnated by yet another team in 1989. After a five-year absence from the majors, he returned to become a productive member of the Orioles. While he wasn't used as a closer, he finished 17 games. He landed with the Baltimore organization after being released by the White Sox (twice), Yankees, and Phillies. When he made the Baltimore roster in 1989, he was pitching for his 14th team in 12 seasons. Before he began his pro career in 1978, he was discovered by scouts as a member of a world championship 16-inch softball team; Hickey never played baseball at the high school level.

Hickey has a rags-to-riches story, but he doesn't have the lifetime record to make his 1990 commons worthy investments. Our pick for his best 1990 card is Fleer.

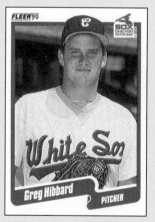

TED HIGUERA

	W	L	ERA	G	CG	IP	H	ER	BB	SO
1989	9	6	3.46	22	2	135	125	52	48	91
Life	78	44	3.28	154	46	1085	941	395	331	857

Position: Pitcher
Team: Milwaukee Brewers
Born: November 9, 1958
　　　　 Los Mochis, Mexico
Height: 5'10"　**Weight:** 178 lbs.
Bats: Both　**Throws:** Left
Acquired: Purchased from Juarez in
　　　　 Mexican League, 9/83

Preseason back surgery got Brewers hurler Higuera off to a late start in 1989, limiting him to his fewest appearances in five seasons. The disability kept him idle until May, allowing him just 22 games pitched. He won in double digits from 1985 to 1988, making at least 30 starts and pitching 200-plus innings. Higuera's strikeout totals in 1986 to 1988 ranged from 192 to a career-high 240 in 1987. Other highlights of his 1987 season included an 18-11 record and 261 innings pitched. He earned his first All-Star appearance in 1986, throwing three innings of scoreless, one-hit relief. Higuera's 1986 record was 20-11, which earned him a second-place spot in Cy Young balloting.

　Higuera could be a Cy Young winner if he's healthy. Smart investors, however, will wait on his nickel-priced 1990 cards until he proves that he's physically sound. Our pick for his best 1990 card is Donruss.

KEN HILL

	W	L	ERA	G	CG	IP	H	ER	BB	SO
1989	7	15	3.80	33	2	196	186	83	99	112
Life	7	16	3.90	37	2	210	202	91	105	118

Position: Pitcher
Team: St. Louis Cardinals
Born: December 14, 1965　Lynn, MA
Height: 6'2"　**Weight:** 175 lbs.
Bats: Right　**Throws:** Right
Acquired: Traded from Tigers with
　　　　 Mike Laga for Mike Heath, 8/86

In less than one year, Hill jumped from Double-A Arkansas to the 1989 Cardinals starting rotation. In his four-game 1988 call-up with St. Louis, he was 0-1 with a 5.14 ERA. He was 9-9 in 1988 with Arkansas, striking out 107 batters in 115 innings. The Cardinals' farm system experimented with converting Hill to a reliever in 1987. At Arkansas, he was 3-5 with two saves in 18 games. After being transferred to Class-A St. Petersburg that year, he had a win and two saves. When the Cardinals acquired Hill in a 1986 trade with the Tigers, the media considered him an afterthought to the transaction. Now, Hill might turn out to be the bargain in the trade.

　Hill's record bodes ill for card investors. Cautious investors won't spend anything on his 10-cent 1990 cards until he shakes his slump. Our pick for his best 1990 card is Topps.

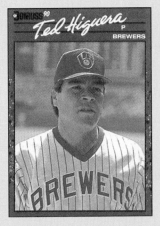

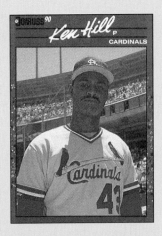

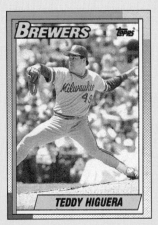

SHAWN HILLEGAS

	W	L	ERA	G	SV	IP	H	ER	BB	SO
1989	7	11	4.74	50	3	119	132	63	51	76
Life	17	20	4.14	79	3	274	268	126	117	183

Position: Pitcher
Team: Chicago White Sox
Born: August 21, 1964   Dos Palos, CA
Height: 6'2" **Weight:** 208 lbs.
Bats: Right **Throws:** Right
Acquired: Traded from Dodgers for
　　　　Ricky Horton, 10/88

Though Hillegas is a pitcher, not a batter, his career has comprised a series of near misses. After three years in the minors, he was Los Angeles' final cut in 1988 spring training. Late in June, he saw a reprieve and managed a 3-4 mark in ten starts before being traded to the ChiSox, missing out on World Series action. Hillegas's record was 3-2 with a 3.15 ERA in six starts with Chicago. Despite his relative inexperience, he has flirted with more than one no-hitter, holding opponents hitless for as long as six innings. Hillegas led Middle Georgia Junior College to a second-place finish at the National JUCO Tournament in 1983.

Hillegas's 1990 cards will cost 3 cents. Since his part-time bullpen work and his so-so lifetime stats are two strikes against him, don't invest. Our pick for his best 1990 card is Score.

BRIAN HOLMAN

	W	L	ERA	G	CG	IP	H	ER	BB	SO
1989	8	10	3.44	23	6	159	160	61	62	82
Life	12	18	3.36	41	7	260	261	97	96	140

Position: Pitcher
Team: Seattle Mariners
Born: January 25, 1965   Denver, CO
Height: 6'4" **Weight:** 185 lbs.
Bats: Right **Throws:** Right
Acquired: Traded from Expos with
　　　　Gene Harris and Randy Johnson
　　　　for Mike Campbell and
　　　　Mark Langston, 5/89

After five quiet years in the minors, Holman has hummed like a fastball. The Mariners obtained him as one of three rookies for Mark Langston. Holman had the best record of the three ex-Expos and was third-highest in wins with Seattle. In the minors since age 18, he started 1988 at Triple-A Indianapolis, notching an 8-1 record in 13 starts. He was called up to Montreal June 25. Although his first outing was a loss, he avenged himself with a shutout in his second start. Holman ended the '88 season with 18 games for Montreal, including 16 starts, a 4-8 record, and a 3.23 ERA.

The M's are counting on Holman for big things. With a full season to pitch in the A.L., he may grant their wishes. Buy his 1990 cards at a nickel. Our pick for his best 1990 card is Fleer.

SHAWN HOLMAN

	W	L	ERA	G	SV	IP	H	ER	BB	SO
89 AAA	3	1	1.91	51	11	90	74	19	36	38
89 Major	0	0	1.80	5	0	10	8	2	11	9

Position: Pitcher
Team: Detroit Tigers
Born: November 10, 1964 Sewickley, PA
Height: 6'2" **Weight:** 186 lbs.
Bats: Right **Throws:** Right
Acquired: Traded from Pirates with
　　　Pete Rice for Terry Harper, 6/87

Holman climbed to Triple-A Toledo in 1989, growing into a respectable reliever. His career didn't start to take off until he converted to relief work in 1987. In 1988, Holman was 8-3 with a 1.87 ERA and ten saves at Class-A Glens Falls. An eight-year minor league veteran, his top winning season came in 1985, as a member of the Pirates' organization. At Class-A Prince William, he went 10-11 with four complete games and two shutouts. The Tigers considered him for major league duty beginning in 1988, when he held a spot on the parent club's roster until March 20. The pitching-hungry Tigers club will likely give Holman an ample chance at the majors in 1990.

Holman was one of the brightest of Detroit's freshman pitchers. His rookie 1990 cards are inviting purchases at 15 cents or less. Our pick for his best 1990 card is Score.

BRIAN HOLTON

	W	L	ERA	G	SV	IP	H	ER	BB	SO
1989	5	7	4.02	39	0	116	140	52	39	51
Life	18	16	3.46	152	3	312	333	120	104	183

Position: Pitcher
Team: Baltimore Orioles
Born: November 29, 1959 McKeesport, PA
Height: 6' **Weight:** 193 lbs.
Bats: Right **Throws:** Right
Acquired: Traded from Dodgers with
　　　Ken Howell and Juan Bell for
　　　Eddie Murray, 12/88

Holton had something of an identity crisis in 1989. He had been a Dodger for all ten years of his pro career, serving since his '87 rookie season as a set-up man. His contributions to Los Angeles' 1988 World Championship include holding the team's best ERA (1.70, second-lowest in the majors) and second-best winning percentage. After pitching his last 34 innings of the regular season allowing only one run, Holton held Oakland scoreless for two innings in the first game of the Series, helping to set the stage for the Dodgers' dramatic comeback.

No stranger to hard work, Holton still had trouble shifting to his role as part-time starter. Wait for Holton adapt to his new responsibilities before socking more than 3 cents apiece into his 1990 cards. Our pick for his best 1990 card is Fleer.

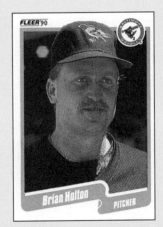

RICK HONEYCUTT

	W	L	ERA	G	SV	IP	H	ER	BB	SO
1989	2	2	2.35	64	12	76	56	20	26	52
Life	95	125	3.76	428	20	1858	1906	777	558	850

Position: Pitcher
Team: Oakland Athletics
Born: June 29, 1954 Chattanooga, TN
Height: 6'1" **Weight:** 190 lbs.
Bats: Left **Throws:** Left
Acquired: Traded from Dodgers for
　　　Tim Belcher, 8/87

Honeycutt's 13th season was a lucky one in the 1989 Oakland bullpen. He achieved career highs in appearances, saves, games finished, and ERA. His ERA was the lowest of his pro career, dating back to 1976. Ever since he broke into the majors with Seattle in 1978, he had been used primarily as a starter. However, Oakland manager Tony LaRussa, inspired by the successful conversion of Dennis Eckersley from starting to relief, did the same for Honeycutt in 1988. He answered the challenge with a 3-2 record with seven saves in 55 appearances. Honeycutt earned Oakland's only World Series win against the Dodgers in 1988 by pitching three and one-third innings of hitless relief.

Honeycutt will never unseat Eckersley's as Oakland's star reliever. He did his job well in 1989 but without fanfare. His 1990 commons are suspect investments. Our pick for his best 1990 card is Topps.

CHARLIE HOUGH

	W	L	ERA	G	CG	IP	H	ER	BB	SO
1989	10	13	4.35	30	5	182	168	88	95	94
Life	174	157	3.60	713	93	2888	2446	1155	1263	1874

Position: Pitcher
Team: Texas Rangers
Born: January 5, 1948 Honolulu, HI
Height: 6'2" **Weight:** 190 lbs.
Bats: Right **Throws:** Right
Acquired: Purchased from Dodgers, 7/80

Hough will celebrate his silver anniversary as a pro player in 1990. The ageless knuckleballer ranked third on the 1989 Rangers with ten wins. His wins gave him double-digit victory totals for the eighth straight season. Hough was the team's leading winner from 1982 to 1988. In 1987, he had career highs with an 18-13 record and 223 strikeouts. He began his pro career in 1966 and reached the majors with the 1970 Dodgers. He was a reliever for most of the 1970s, starting just 18 games in a decade. Hough owns 61 lifetime saves in addition to his Ranger record of 127 career wins.

Hough's many years in the bullpen limited his lifetime wins. However, he's had a hand in 235 wins in his career, giving him a modest shot at Cooperstown. His 1990 commons are uncertain investments but may produce long-term profits. Our pick for his best 1990 card is Donruss.

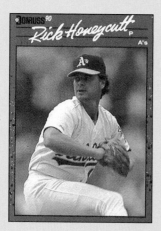

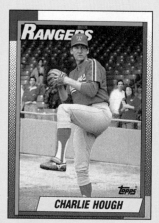

JACK HOWELL

	BA	G	AB	R	H	2B	3B	HR	RBI	SB
1989	.228	144	474	56	108	19	4	20	52	0
Life	.241	542	1711	224	413	87	13	68	218	9

Position: Third base
Team: California Angels
Born: August 18, 1961 Tucson, AZ
Height: 6' **Weight:** 185 lbs.
Bats: Left **Throws:** Right
Acquired: Signed as a free agent, 6/83

Howell was the second-leading home run swatter on the 1989 Angels. He homered in double figures for the third consecutive season, although his average was the lowest of his seven-year career. He broke in with California after two minor league seasons. During his minor league career, Howell averaged more than one RBI for every two games played. With the 1985 Halos, he hit a paltry .197. However, his five homers and 18 RBI in just 43 games was impressive enough to get a midseason call-up again the next season. Howell's top season came in 1987, when he hit 23 homers and knocked in 64 runs.

Howell's 1990 cards will cost a nickel. Even if he does hit 20 homers a year, he needs to drive in more runs or have a higher average before he's considered a star. Our pick for his best 1990 card is Fleer.

JAY HOWELL

	W	L	ERA	G	SV	IP	H	ER	BB	SO
1989	5	3	1.58	56	28	79	60	14	22	55
Life	39	36	3.58	344	111	579	551	230	210	472

Position: Pitcher
Team: Los Angeles Dodgers
Born: November 26, 1955 Miami, FL
Height: 6'3" **Weight:** 205 lbs.
Bats: Right **Throws:** Right
Acquired: Traded from Athletics with
    Jesse Orosco and Alfredo Griffin
    for Bob Welch, Jack Savage, and
    Matt Young, 12/87

Howell had the second-best save total of his career with the 1989 Dodgers. He led Los Angeles with 28 saves and a career-low 1.58 ERA in 1989. He paced the team in appearances and games finished (41). He earned his third All-Star team appearance in 1989. Fans forgot his 1988 accomplishments when he was caught with pine tar in his glove during the '88 N.L.C.S. He was ejected from the game and suspended for two games. Before the controversy, he had ended the regular season with a 5-3 record, 21 saves, and a 2.08 ERA in 50 games. Howell's career high for saves is 29, earned with the 1985 Athletics.

Even though Howell is one of baseball's best relievers, it's unlikely that he'll register Hall of Fame-caliber stats. His nickel-priced 1990 cards have limited long-term appeal. Our pick for his best 1990 card is Score.

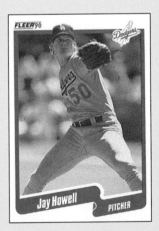

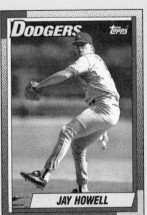

KEN HOWELL

	W	L	ERA	G	CG	IP	H	ER	BB	SO
1989	12	12	3.44	33	1	204	155	78	86	164
Life	30	41	3.81	227	1	506	428	214	226	479

Position: Pitcher
Team: Philadelphia Phillies
Born: October 28, 1960 Detroit, MI
Height: 6'3" **Weight:** 228 lbs.
Bats: Right **Throws:** Right
Acquired: Traded from Orioles for
 Phil Bradley and Gordon Dillard,
 12/88

Howell was an immediate hit with the 1989 Phillies, earning a career-high 12 victories and 164 strikeouts. In his first year of starting, he tied for the team lead in wins and posted his lowest ERA since his 3.33 debut with the 1984 Dodgers. Howell enjoyed a fine rookie season in 1984, going 5-5 with six saves, but losing records and growing ERAs filled the next three seasons. He was optioned back to the minors in 1987 and faced rehabilitation from shoulder surgery in 1988. The Dodgers traded him to Baltimore for Eddie Murray, but the O's returned Howell to the National League less than a week later.

Howell was a commendable first-year starter for the Phils. However, investors would be smart to wait for a second year of success from him before buying his 1990 commons. Our pick for his best 1990 card is Fleer.

KENT HRBEK

	BA	G	AB	R	H	2B	3B	HR	RBI	SB
1989	.272	109	375	59	102	17	0	25	84	3
Life	.290	1156	4178	624	1212	224	16	201	724	19

Position: First base
Team: Minnesota Twins
Born: May 21, 1960 Minneapolis, MN
Height: 6'4" **Weight:** 235 lbs.
Bats: Left **Throws:** Right
Acquired: 17th-round pick in 6/78
 free-agent draft

Hrbek posted his sixth-straight season of 20-plus homers while slugging for the 1989 Minnesota Twins. He led the Twins in round-trippers in 1989, his ninth season in the majors. Going into the 1989 season, "Herbie" had homered 100 times in Minnesota's Metrodome, making him baseball's all-time indoor home run champion. He had reached the second deck of the Metrodome 21 times, a stadium record. Hrbek was a vital part of the 1987 World Championship team, hitting .285 with 34 homers and 90 RBI. His World Series grand slam clinched Game Six. He broke in with the Twins in 1982. He was the only rookie named to the All-Star team. Hrbek's first-season stats included 23 homers, 92 RBI, and a .301 average.

Hrbek's 1990 cards will start at 15 cents. He's already surpassed the 200-homer level. His cards are lucrative buys. Our pick for his best 1990 card is Topps.

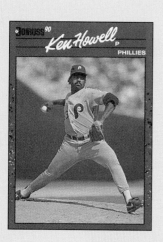

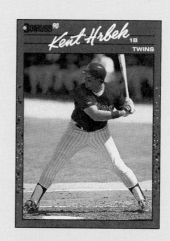

REX HUDLER

	BA	G	AB	R	H	2B	3B	HR	RBI	SB
1989	.245	92	155	21	38	7	0	6	13	15
Life	.247	212	430	66	106	22	3	10	28	45

Position: Infield
Team: Montreal Expos
Born: September 2, 1960   Tempe, AZ
Height: 6'   **Weight:** 180 lbs.
Bats: Right   **Throws:** Right
Acquired: Purchased from Orioles, 6/88

Hudler saw more action during his first season with the Montreal Expos in 1989 than he had in his three previous call-ups with the New York Yankees and Baltimore Orioles combined. The Yankees' top pick of the 1978 draft spent six full seasons in the minors, debuting as a Yankee pinch-runner in 1984. Bought by Montreal early in 1988, Hudler hit the bigs to stay by swiping 19 bases in a row without being nabbed. Of his 29 steals that season, ten were of third; he was caught just seven times overall. He maintained hitting streaks just as impressive, making his offensive value obvious. Defensively, Hudler has split time between second base and short.

Hudler should be a reserve infielder with the Expos. Until he becomes a starter somewhere, his 1990 commons won't gain any value. Our pick for his best 1990 card is Score.

BRUCE HURST

	W	L	ERA	G	CG	IP	H	ER	BB	SO
1989	15	11	2.69	33	10	244	214	73	66	179
Life	103	84	4.00	270	64	1704	1783	759	545	1222

Position: Pitcher
Team: San Diego Padres
Born: March 24, 1958   St. George, UT
Height: 6'3"   **Weight:** 215 lbs.
Bats: Left   **Throws:** Left
Acquired: Signed as a free agent, 12/88

Although Hurst wasn't the instant ticket to a pennant the Padres wanted, he did tally a double-digit win total for the seventh consecutive season. After pitching for the Red Sox from 1980 through 1988, he was pursued by numerous teams when he declared free agency. He signed a three-year contract with San Diego, who made several personnel moves in hopes for a divisional title. The veteran lefty did lead the Padres in strikeouts and was among league leaders in innings pitched and complete games. The Padres hope that Hurst can soon duplicate his 1988 success with the Red Sox, when he was 18-6 in 33 games.

After a year's adjustment to a new league, Hurst should be a solid winner with the Padres. Buy his 1990 cards at 10 cents or less for a quick profit. Our pick for his best 1990 card is Fleer.

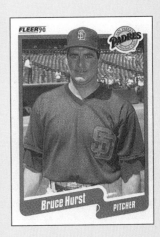

JEFF HUSON

	BA	G	AB	R	H	2B	3B	HR	RBI	SB
1989	.162	32	74	1	12	5	0	0	2	3
Life	.216	52	116	8	25	7	0	0	5	5

Position: Shortstop
Team: Montreal Expos
Born: August 15, 1964 Scottsdale, AZ
Height: 6'3" **Weight:** 170 lbs.
Bats: Left **Throws:** Right
Acquired: Signed as a free agent, 8/85

While waiting at Triple-A Indianapolis in 1989 for a chance at the majors, Huson was making headlines in the American Association. In a poll conducted by *Baseball America,* league managers ranked him as the circuit's best defensive shortstop and most exciting player. An off-season weight-lifting program helped beef Huson up for the 1989 season, allowing him to acquire batches of extra-base hits. In 1986 at Class-A Burlington, his pro debut, he batted .289 with 16 home runs and 72 RBI. With Double-A Jacksonville in 1988, he claimed the Southern League basestealing title with 56 pilfers. The Expos gave Huson a 20-game trial in September 1988, when he batted .310.

Huson's rookie 1990 cards will start at around 15 cents. That price is too high, considering that he may not even gain a roster spot. Our pick for his best 1990 card is Score.

PETE INCAVIGLIA

	BA	G	AB	R	H	2B	3B	HR	RBI	SB
1989	.236	133	453	48	107	27	4	21	81	5
Life	.252	541	1920	274	484	93	13	100	303	23

Position: Designated hitter; outfield
Team: Texas Rangers
Born: April 2, 1964 Pebble Beach, CA
Height: 6'1" **Weight:** 220 lbs.
Bats: Right **Throws:** Right
Acquired: Traded from Montreal for Bob
    Sebra and Jim Anderson, 11/85

In 1989, Incaviglia exceeded 20 homers and 80 RBI for the third time in four seasons. Although his batting average was the lowest of his career, his RBI were just under the 88 he tallied during his 1986 rookie season. That year he banged out 30 homers, his major league best. He went directly to the majors without any minor league experience. Since the start of the free-agent draft in 1965, only 13 other players have managed the transition. Incaviglia came to the majors after a distinguished career at Oklahoma State from 1983 to 1985, where he set an NCAA record with 100 career homers.

Incaviglia's 1990 cards will be a nickel or less. He's streaky but has the ability to win a league homer crown. Buy a few dollar's worth then sell for a short-term gain when he leads the league. Our pick for his best 1990 card is Fleer.

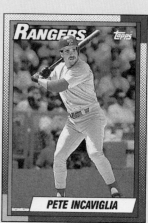

JEFF INNIS

	W	L	ERA	G	SV	IP	H	ER	BB	SO
1989	0	1	3.18	29	0	39	38	14	8	16
Life	1	3	2.89	58	0	84	86	27	14	58

Position: Pitcher
Team: New York Mets
Born: July 5, 1962 Decatur, IL
Height: 6' **Weight:** 170 lbs.
Bats: Right **Throws:** Right
Acquired: 13th-round pick in 6/83
free-agent draft

Innis battled back from the minors to appear with the New York Mets for a third consecutive season in 1989. He earned three wins and ten saves in Triple-A Tidewater before joining New York. He gained his first and only major league victory in 1988 against the Chicago Cubs. He threw 13 scoreless innings in 1988 spring training, and the Mets kept Innis on the roster from mid-April through mid-June. Before he returned to Triple-A, he had a sparkling 1.89 ERA from 17 appearances. He had his best season in 1986 with Double-A Jackson. Innis was 4-5 with 25 saves, leading the Texas League and setting a team record.

Innis's 1990 cards will be 3 cents or less in 1990. Because he seems destined for middle relief with the Mets, his cards don't seem worthy of investment. Our pick for his best 1990 card is Topps.

BO JACKSON

	BA	G	AB	R	H	2B	3B	HR	RBI	SB
1989	.256	135	515	86	132	15	6	32	105	26
Life	.244	400	1432	204	350	50	13	81	235	66

Position: Outfield
Team: Kansas City Royals
Born: November 30, 1962 Bessemer, AL
Height: 6'1" **Weight:** 225 lbs.
Bats: Right **Throws:** Right
Acquired: Fourth-round pick in 6/86 free-agent draft

In 1989, Jackson joined Willie Mays as the only players to hit a homer and steal a base in an All-Star Game. Jackson's first-inning leadoff home run, two hits, and two RBI earned him MVP honors. In 1989, he was among league leaders in home runs and RBI. He became the first Royals "25/25" man with 25 homers and 27 stolen bases in 1988. That effort bested his 1987 rookie performance of 22 homers. He has made constant improvements, including a yearly inflation of his .207 average in 1986. Jackson, a star running back for the Raiders, is the first player in NFL history to have two 90-plus-yards runs from scrimmage.

Jackson's 1990 cards may be up to 75 cents. That's a tough price to stock up on, but they are headed for the $1 barrier so buy while you can. Our pick for his best 1990 card is Score.

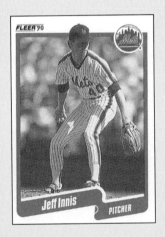

DANNY JACKSON

	W	L	ERA	G	CG	IP	H	ER	BB	SO
1989	6	11	5.60	20	1	115	122	72	57	70
Life	66	66	3.66	174	16	1089	1043	443	433	661

Position: Pitcher
Team: Cincinnati Reds
Born: January 5, 1962 San Antonio, TX
Height: 6' **Weight:** 205 lbs.
Bats: Right **Throws:** Left
Acquired: Traded from Royals with Angel
　　　　　　Salazar for Ted Power and Kurt
　　　　　　Stillwell, 11/87

After narrowly missing the Cy Young Award in 1988, Jackson was sidelined with shoulder problems in 1989. His injury-plagued campaign was his least productive since his 1984 rookie season with the Royals, when he was 2-6 in 15 games. He had a fantasy season in 1988, his first in the N.L. He was 23-6 with 15 complete games, tying Orel Hershiser for league highs in both categories. Hershiser narrowly beat Jackson for the Cy Young, partially because the Dodgers beat the Reds for the division title. Jackson's career-high victory mark was a big improvement from his best in Kansas City, a 14-12 record in 1985.

Smart investors will avoid paying more than 3 cents each for Jackson's 1990 cards before knowing if he's physically fit for 1990. If he wins again, sell quick for short-term gains. Our pick for his best 1990 card is Score.

DARRIN JACKSON

	BA	G	AB	R	H	2B	3B	HR	RBI	SB
1989	.218	70	170	17	37	7	0	4	20	1
Life	.246	182	374	48	92	19	3	10	40	5

Position: Outfield
Team: San Diego Padres
Born: August 22, 1963   Los Angeles, CA
Height: 6' **Weight:** 185 lbs.
Bats: Right **Throws:** Right
Acquired: Traded from Cubs with Calvin
　　　　　　Schiraldi and Phil Stephenson for
　　　　　　Luis Salazar and Marvelle
　　　　　　Wynne, 8/89

After Jackson staged a successful recovery from cancer surgery, he missed going to the 1989 N.L.C.S. with the Cubs by less than one month. He finished the season by tying his career high in RBI with 20. He looked like a phenom in 1987, before his surgery. He hit .274 with 23 homers, 81 RBI, and 13 stolen bases at Triple-A Iowa that year. He had 15 assists and six double plays from center field. *Baseball America* touted his throwing arm as the best in the American Association. In 1988, his first full season with Chicago, Jackson hit .266 with six homers and 20 RBI in 100 games.

With the bevy of outfielders in San Diego, it's unlikely that Jackson will start for the Padres. His common-priced 1990 cards aren't useful investments until he gets a starting assignment somewhere. Our pick for his best 1990 card is Fleer.

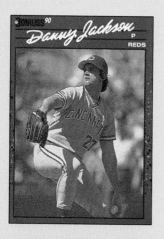

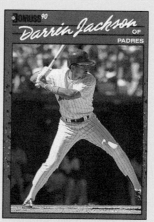

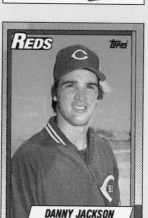

MIKE JACKSON

	W	L	ERA	G	SV	IP	H	ER	BB	SO
1989	4	6	3.17	65	7	99	81	35	54	94
Life	13	21	3.36	191	12	321	255	120	157	266

Position: Pitcher
Team: Seattle Mariners
Born: December 22, 1964 Houston, TX
Height: 6' **Weight:** 185 lbs.
Bats: Right **Throws:** Right
Acquired: Traded from Phillies with Glenn
Wilson and Dave Grundage for
Phil Bradley and John Fortungo,
12/87

Although Mike Jackson hasn't achieved the fame of the rock singer who shares his name, he's becoming known as one of the toughest pitchers in the Seattle bullpen. In 1989, team announcers called him "The Thriller," and he gave M's fans their share of thrills. He was second to Mike Schooler in saves, games, and games finished for the Mariners. With a fastball in the mid-90s, Jackson averaged nearly a strikeout per inning in 1989. He pitched in more than 60 games for the second straight year. During 1987, his first full season in the majors, Jackson pitched in 55 games for the Phillies.

On the chance that Jackson becomes a starter, pick up a few of his 1990 cards for 3 cents or less. If the M's support him offensively, he could be a major winner. Our pick for his best 1990 card is Fleer.

BROOK JACOBY

	BA	G	AB	R	H	2B	3B	HR	RBI	SB
1989	.272	147	519	49	141	26	5	13	64	2
Life	.273	914	3257	400	888	152	19	98	390	13

Position: Third base
Team: Cleveland Indians
Born: November 23, 1959 Philadelphia, PA
Height: 5'11" **Weight:** 195 lbs.
Bats: Right **Throws:** Right
Acquired: Traded from Braves with Brett
Butler and Rick Behenna for Len
Barker, 8/83

After a year of aberration, Jacoby seems to be back on track for the Indians. His offensive marks faltered in 1988, while his fielding shone as never before. Third in the A.L. with a career-best .975 fielding percentage, his ten errors in 407 chances were a career low in 1988. He didn't match this splendor in the grass in 1989, making 17 mishaps. However, his batting average was closer to par and his homers were back in double digits. He began his career in the Atlanta organization in 1979. A perennial All-Star in the minors, he was frequently a top contender in power stats. In 1987, Jacoby hit a career-high 32 homers with Cleveland, getting the Tribe's MVP.

Jacoby needs to have strong offensive seasons back-to-back. Until he looks more consistent at the plate, bypass his 1990 commons. Our pick for his best 1990 card is Fleer.

CHRIS JAMES

	BA	G	AB	R	H	2B	3B	HR	RBI	SB
1989	.243	132	482	55	117	17	2	13	65	5
Life	.256	413	1452	165	372	64	9	50	190	15

Position: Third base; outfield
Team: San Diego Padres
Born: October 4, 1962 Rusk, TX
Height: 6'1" **Weight:** 190 lbs.
Bats: Right **Throws:** Right
Acquired: Traded from Phillies for Randy
　　　　　Ready and John Kruk, 6/89

Once thought of as the successor to Phillies third baseman Mike Schmidt, James got a new start on his career when he was shipped to the Padres. Originally an outfielder, Philadelphia converted him into a third sacker. His power has always been his strongest point, however. His average remained low in 1989, but he topped double digits in homers for the third straight year. James's rookie year with Philadelphia in 1987 was his best in the majors. He batted .293 with 17 homers and 54 RBI in 115 games. He had recovered from a broken left ankle in 1986. Although his average dipped to .242 in 1988, James blasted a personal best of 19 homers and 66 RBI.

James may be a starter for the Padres again in 1990. He's ripe for a rebound, so take a gamble on his common-priced 1990 cards. Our pick for his best 1990 card is Donruss.

DION JAMES

	BA	G	AB	R	H	2B	3B	HR	RBI	SB
89 AL	.306	71	245	26	75	11	0	4	29	1
Life	.285	567	1751	225	499	92	16	19	165	32

Position: Outfield
Team: Cleveland Indians
Born: November 9, 1962 Philadelphia, PA
Height: 6'1" **Weight:** 170 lbs.
Bats: Left **Throws:** Left
Acquired: Traded from Braves for Oddibe
　　　　　McDowell, 7/89

James returned to the American League via Cleveland in 1989, after a three-year absence. The Braves traded him in mid-1989 to the Indians for outfielder Oddibe McDowell. While James didn't match McDowell's power production, James hit a team-leading .306 in his 71 games with the Tribe. He first became a starter with the 1987 Braves, where he posted better marks than he had accumulated in three call-ups with the Brewers. He got his major league debut with the Brewers in late 1983, after four years in the minors. He batted .295 in 128 games in Milwaukee in 1984, but the Brewers wanted more than one homer and 30 RBI from an outfield starter.

James doesn't hit high enough or for sufficient power to be star material. His 1990 commons will probably stay at that value for years. Our pick for his best 1990 card is Donruss.

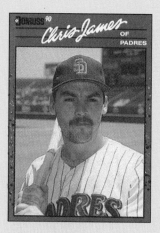
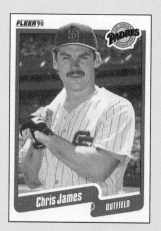

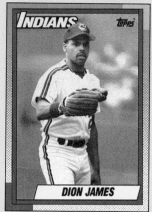

STAN JAVIER

	BA	G	AB	R	H	2B	3B	HR	RBI	SB
1989	.248	112	310	42	77	12	3	1	28	12
Life	.236	384	979	127	455	36	7	5	80	43

Position: Outfield
Team: Oakland Athletics
Born: January 9, 1965   San Francisco de
         Macoris, Dominican Republic
Height: 6'   **Weight:** 185 lbs.
Bats: Both   **Throws:** Right
Acquired: Traded from Yankees with Jay
         Howell, Tim Birtsas, Jose Rijo,
         and Eric Plunk for Rickey
         Henderson and Bert Bradley,
         12/84

Son of long-time Cardinals infielder Julian Javier and name-sake of dad's teammate Stan "The Man" Musial, Stan Javier began his career in the Redbirds flock at age 16. His career took several turns before he wound up as a reserve outfielder for the Oakland Athletics. He was part of a 1982 trade with the Yankees' organization. He climbed the minor league ladder to get a seven-game debut with the 1984 Yanks. The best year of his career came at Double-A Huntsville in 1985. He hit .284 with nine homers, 64 RBI, and 61 stolen bases. Less than a year later, Javier was serving Oakland as a fine baserunner and defensive replacement.

With the A's, Javier is resigned to part-time work. His 1990 cards will sell as commons and won't gain value until he starts. Our pick for his best 1990 card is Fleer.

MIKE JEFFCOAT

	W	L	ERA	G	CG	IP	H	ER	BB	SO
1989	9	6	3.58	22	2	130	139	52	33	64
Life	15	16	4.01	131	2	287	318	128	91	134

Position: Pitcher
Team: Texas Rangers
Born: August 3, 1959   Pine Bluff, AR
Height: 6'2"   **Weight:** 197 lbs.
Bats: Left   **Throws:** Left
Acquired: Signed as a free agent, 11/86

After bouncing around for five years, Jeffcoat got his first real chance at success in 1989. With 156 innings to his credit spread over five seasons, his 130 innings of work in 1989 seemed like a bonanza. His nine wins set a career-high and marked his best record since his 5-2 effort with the 1984 Indians. He had relieved in all but eight of his first 109 games in the majors. He proved his ability as a starter with Triple-A Oklahoma City in 1988. He went 9-5 with six complete games and two shutouts in 22 starts. Jeffcoat was invited to 1989 spring training by Texas as a nonroster player and earned a spot on the big league team.

Jeffcoat needs to have a solid winning season as a starter to get the hobby excited about his 1990 commons. Our pick for his best 1990 card is Score.

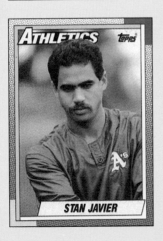

151

GREGG JEFFERIES

	BA	G	AB	R	H	2B	3B	HR	RBI	SB
1989	.258	141	508	72	131	28	2	12	56	21
Life	.271	176	623	91	169	37	4	18	75	26

Position: Second base
Team: New York Mets
Born: August 1, 1967 Burlingame, CA
Height: 5'10" **Weight:** 175 lbs.
Bats: Both **Throws:** Right
Acquired: First-round pick in 6/85 free-
agent draft

In 1989, Jefferies had problems living up to expectations placed on him after his glorious minor league career. He batted .321 in a 29-game trial with the Mets in 1988, but saw his average dip in 1989 when he was struggling to become a second baseman. In '88, he helped the Mets win the N.L. East. Jefferies established a rookie N.L.C.S. record with nine hits against the Dodgers. In 1986, he hit .354 with 11 home runs and 80 RBI in 95 games for Class-A Lynchburg. He hit .367 with 20 homers and 101 RBI at Double-A Jackson in 1987. *Baseball America* then named Jefferies the Minor League Player of the Year for a second straight season.

Jefferies's 1990 card prices will quell. He's still adored by Mets fans, so buying his 1990 cards at 50 cents will pay off fast if he rebounds. Our pick for his best 1990 card is Score.

STEVE JELTZ

	BA	G	AB	R	H	2B	3B	HR	RBI	SB
1989	.243	116	263	28	64	7	3	4	25	4
Life	.213	653	1646	172	351	42	20	5	120	17

Position: Shortstop
Team: Philadelphia Phillies
Born: May 29, 1959 Paris, France
Height: 5'11" **Weight:** 180 lbs.
Bats: Both **Throws:** Right
Acquired: Ninth-round pick in 6/80 free-
agent draft

Jeltz faced one of the biggest challenges of his career in 1989, and he responded with his best offensive season. The Phillies had tried to cure his ailments at the plate. The solution was competition. Shortstop Dickie Thon was signed as a free agent, and Jeltz no longer had a guaranteed job. The struggle for survival helped him amass a career-high batting average 60 points higher than his 1988 effort. He is a self-taught switch-hitter who won a full-time job in 1986. Jeltz, who had hit his only home run in 1984, tallied four round-trippers in 1989. He is best known for his fielding; Jeltz's errorless streaks had been as long as 46 games.

Because of Jeltz's constant batting woes, he's lucky to remain on the Phillies roster. His 1990 commons are undesirable investment choices. Our pick for his best 1990 card is Fleer.

DAVE JOHNSON

	W	L	ERA	G	CG	IP	H	ER	BB	SO
89 AAA	7	6	3.26	18	2	105	104	38	31	60
89 Major	4	7	4.23	14	4	89	90	42	28	26

Position: Pitcher
Team: Baltimore Orioles
Born: October 24, 1959 Baltimore, MD
Height: 5'10" **Weight:** 180 lbs.
Bats: Right **Throws:** Right
Acquired: Traded from Astros with Victor
    Hithe for Carl Nichols, 3/89

Hard work and patience finally paid off for Johnson in 1989. After eight seasons down under and a forgettable five-game debut with the Pirates in 1987, he finally arrived in the majors to stay on August 1, 1989, with the Orioles. The Baltimore native quickly established himself as a fan favorite with the O's, carving out a 4-4 record (with three complete games) in his first nine starts. The Birds promoted Johnson on the merits of his 7-6 mark and 3.26 ERA he notched with Triple-A Rochester in 1989. The best season of his career came in 1988 at Triple-A Buffalo. Johnson led the American Association with 15 victories, nine complete games, and 29 starts.

Johnson's age and his late-season slump detract from his card values. His 1990 commons are questionable buys. Our pick for his best 1990 card is Topps.

HOWARD JOHNSON

	BA	G	AB	R	H	2B	3B	HR	RBI	SB
1989	.287	153	571	104	164	41	3	36	101	41
Life	.258	869	2805	427	724	135	10	136	422	127

Position: Third base
Team: New York Mets
Born: November 29, 1960 Clearwater, FL
Height: 5'10" **Weight:** 195 lbs.
Bats: Both **Throws:** Right
Acquired: Traded from Tigers for Walt Terrell,
    12/84

One of the best trades never made for the 1989 season involved New York Mets third baseman Johnson. The Mets never went through with rumored trades that might have sent him packing. Keeping Johnson helped the Mets throughout the season. "HoJo" was the foundation of the Mets' offense, pacing the team in homers and RBI through most of 1989. Surprisingly, Johnson's batting average remained above .300 past the 1989 All-Star break. In his past four seasons in the Big Apple, his average never climbed above .265. Johnson first gained national attention in 1987, when he slugged 36 homers and notched 99 RBI. He hit .230 with 24 homers and 68 RBI in 1988.

Try to buy Johnson's 1990 cards at 35 cents. Successful Mets usually have exorbitant card prices, so you'll soon be looking at prices near $1 if he can retrace his 1989 achievements. Our pick for his best 1990 card is Score.

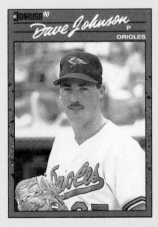

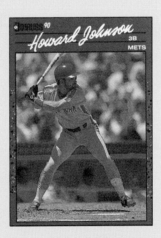

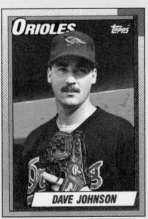

LANCE JOHNSON

	BA	G	AB	R	H	2B	3B	HR	RBI	SB
1989	.300	50	180	28	54	8	2	0	16	16
Life	.248	116	363	43	90	14	4	0	29	28

Position: Outfield
Team: Chicago White Sox
Born: July 7, 1963 Cincinnati, OH
Height: 5'11" **Weight:** 155 lbs.
Bats: Left **Throws:** Left
Acquired: Traded from Cardinals with Ricky
Horton for Jose DeLeon, 2/88

Johnson got closer to cracking the White Sox outfield with a banner season at Triple-A Vancouver in 1989, batting .304 with 33 stolen bases. The White Sox gave him an early call-up, and he appeared in a career-high 50 games. He tied fellow rookie Carlos Martinez for third on Chicago with a .300 average, while Johnson's 16 stolen bases ranked second on the ChiSox. He has hit .300 or better in four of his five minor league seasons, and he's swiped 40-plus bases the last four seasons in a row. With the '87 Cardinals, Johnson became the first pinch-runner in N.L.C.S. history to steal a base.

If Johnson gets the chance to start, he should produce lots of steals and a high batting average. His 1990 cards are good investments at a nickel apiece. Our pick for his best 1990 card is Fleer.

RANDY JOHNSON

	W	L	ERA	G	CG	IP	H	ER	BB	SO
89 AL	7	9	4.40	22	2	131	118	64	70	114
Life	10	13	4.48	33	3	187	170	93	103	155

Position: Pitcher
Team: Seattle Mariners
Born: September 10, 1963 Walnut Creek,
CA
Height: 6'10" **Weight:** 225 lbs.
Bats: Right **Throws:** Left
Acquired: Traded from Expos with Brian
Holman and Gene Harris for Mike
Campbell and Mark Langston,
5/89

The tall order of replacing superstar Mark Langston in the Mariners starting rotation became the responsibility of Johnson, the tallest player in major league history. Upon joining the M's, he responded with three straight victories before losing a 1-0 complete-game decision on July 1. After four seasons in the Montreal farm system, Johnson only received limited opportunities to prove himself on the big league level. In 1988, he was 3-0 in his first four games with the Expos. During three of his four minor league seasons, Johnson struck out more than 100 batters (averaging better than one strikeout per inning).

Johnson's first full season in the majors in 1989 looked hopeful. Experience (and a few more Mariner runs) will improve his marks. Purchase his 1990 cards at a dime or less. Our pick for his best 1990 card is Score.

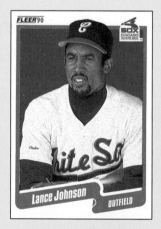
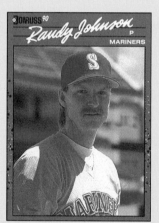
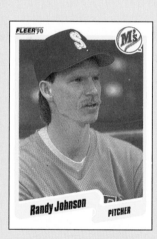

WALLACE JOHNSON

	BA	G	AB	R	H	2B	3B	HR	RBI	SB
1989	.272	85	114	9	31	3	1	2	17	1
Life	.263	381	520	46	137	16	6	4	54	18

Position: Infield
Team: Montreal Expos
Born: December 25, 1956 Gary, IN
Height: 5'11" **Weight:** 185 lbs.
Bats: Both **Throws:** Right
Acquired: Signed as a free agent, 4/84

In 3,332 professional plate appearances, Johnson has struck out just 213 times, an average of just once for every 16 at-bats. This uncanny knack for getting the bat on the ball has earned "the Hit Man" numerous nicknames and a spot as the Expos top pinch-hitter. Entering the 1989 season, his lifetime pinch-hitting average was a hefty .344. He was a league leader in pinch hits in both 1987 and 1988, acquiring higher numbers in a shorter time than any Expo in history. In 1981 during an 11-game call-up, "Magic" helped the Expos snag their first division title. Johnson's three timely hits helped make the difference, including a key triple in the division-clinching game.

Pinch-hitters are important players, but they seldom rise to stardom. From a financial standpoint, Johnson's 1990 cards aren't profitable investments. Our pick for his best 1990 card is Fleer.

DOUG JONES

	W	L	ERA	G	SV	IP	H	ER	BB	SO
1989	7	10	2.34	59	32	80	76	21	13	65
Life	17	19	2.67	174	78	276	269	82	60	237

Position: Pitcher
Team: Cleveland Indians
Born: June 24, 1957 Covina, CA
Height: 6'2" **Weight:** 195 lbs.
Bats: Right **Throws:** Right
Acquired: Signed as a free agent, 4/85

Jones needed a long time to get to the majors. Now that he's there, he's making his mark using indelible ink. In 1989, he provided 32 out of 36 total saves for the Indians. His total was fourth in A.L. save leaders. After only three full seasons in Cleveland, he is first on the Tribe's all-time save list, with 78. In 1988, he broke Cleveland's record for most saves in one season (37) and for most consecutive saves (15), the latter a major league mark. He's appeared in the last two All-Star games. Jones picked up the save in the '89 All-Star Game by hurling one and one-third innings of scoreless relief.

Jones's 1990 cards sell for the bargain of 3 cents or less. His card prices could triple by pitching Cleveland to a winning season. Our pick for his best 1990 card is Donruss.

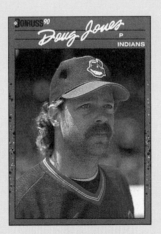

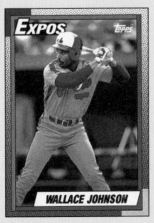

RON JONES

	BA	G	AB	R	H	2B	3B	HR	RBI	SB
1989	.290	12	31	7	9	0	0	2	4	1
Life	.290	45	155	22	45	6	1	10	30	1

Position: Outfield
Team: Philadelphia Phillies
Born: June 11, 1964 Seguin, TX
Height: 5'10" **Weight:** 200 lbs.
Bats: Left **Throws:** Right
Acquired: Signed as a free agent, 10/84

After an impressive 1988 debut with the Phillies, Jones was derailed by a torn tendon in his right knee in 1989. He had a .290 average with two homers and four RBI in 12 games before going on the disabled list. He was first called up by the Phillies in August 1988 and homered for his first major league hit. Jones's short season in the majors was highlighted by four three-hit games and four three-RBI outings. When he was called up, he was leading the Triple-A International League with 75 RBI, which held up as a league best. In 1986, Jones won the Class-A Florida State League batting crown with a mammoth .371 mark.

Jones will have ample opportunity to win an outfield position. His 1990 cards, at a nickel or less, could be a bargain investment. Our pick for his best 1990 card is Topps.

TIM JONES

	BA	G	AB	R	H	2B	3B	HR	RBI	SB
1989	.293	42	75	11	22	6	0	0	7	1
Life	.283	73	127	12	36	6	0	0	10	5

Position: Infield
Team: St. Louis Cardinals
Born: December 1, 1962 Sumter, SC
Height: 5'10" **Weight:** 175 lbs.
Bats: Left **Throws:** Right
Acquired: Third-round pick in 6/85 free-agent draft

When Jose Oquendo claimed the Cardinals second base job, Jones became the team's utility player. After four seasons in the minor leagues, he was called up to the Cardinals in 1988. He saw action in 31 games, hitting .269. In 1988, he was voted best defensive shortstop and best baserunner in a poll taken among Triple-A American Association managers. Jones posted career bests with 95 hits, six home runs, 63 runs scored, and 39 stolen bases. Before being promoted to Triple-A Louisville in 1987, he was hitting a personal best of .330 in 61 games at Double-A Arkansas. After the 1988 season, Jones played winter baseball to polish his skills as a catcher.

Jones will not displace Ozzie Smith, Oquendo, or Terry Pendleton from their jobs. For now, Jones remains a backup infielder. His 1990 commons aren't good investments. Our pick for his best 1990 card is Topps.

RICKY JORDAN

	BA	G	AB	R	H	2B	3B	HR	RBI	SB
1989	.285	144	523	63	149	22	3	12	75	4
Life	.293	213	796	104	233	37	4	23	118	5

Position: First base
Team: Philadelphia Phillies
Born: May 26, 1965 Richmond, CA
Height: 6'5" **Weight:** 210 lbs.
Bats: Right **Throws:** Right
Acquired: First-round pick in 6/83
free-agent draft

Jordan was a bright spot for the 1989 Phillies. He batted .285 in 144 games, with 12 homers and 75 RBI. He logged his sophomore season with the Phils in 1989. His 1988 debut with the team was an auspicious one. He became just the fourth Philly (and 31st player in National League history) to homer in his first at-bat. His home run came on July 7 against Houston's Bob Knepper. Jordan's rookie season was highlighted by an 18-game hitting streak, fifth-longest of the N.L. season. He finished his rookie campaign with 11 homers, 43 RBI, and a .308 average in 69 games. Jordan had five and a half years of minor league experience dating back to 1983.

Jordan's 1989 rookie cards have sold for as much as $2 apiece. Expect his 1990 editions to start at 50 cents, a decent price for investors. Our pick for his best 1990 card is Donruss.

FELIX JOSE

	BA	G	AB	R	H	2B	3B	HR	RBI	SB
89 AAA	.287	103	383	58	110	25	0	14	62	11
89 Major	.193	20	57	3	11	2	0	0	5	0

Position: Outfield
Team: Oakland Athletics
Born: May 8, 1965 Santo Domingo,
Dominican Republic
Height: 6'1" **Weight:** 190 lbs.
Bats: Both **Throws:** Right
Acquired: Signed as a free agent, 1/84

Jose is one of the top prospects in the A's farm system. He made waves for a second straight year at Triple-A Tacoma in 1989. He batted near .300 the whole season, despite making two brief appearances with Oakland before call-ups. Oakland kept him on the roster at the beginning of the season as insurance when Jose Canseco was injured. Felix was compared to Canseco in 1988, when Felix batted .317 with 12 home runs and 83 RBI for Tacoma. He even racked up 16 stolen bases in 24 attempts. In 1985, he batted .285 for Class-A Modesto, with a career-high 14 homers. If the A's need another bat, Jose will be the first called.

After repeated chances, Jose hasn't won a job with the A's. Unless he joins another team, don't pay more than a nickel for his 1990 cards. Our pick for his best 1990 card is Fleer.

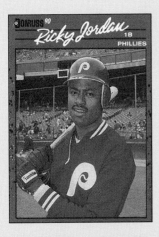

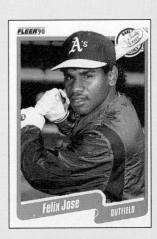

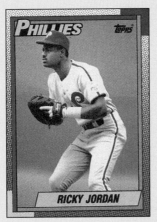

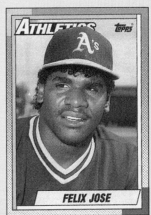

WALLY JOYNER

	BA	G	AB	R	H	2B	3B	HR	RBI	SB
1989	.282	159	593	78	167	30	2	16	79	3
Life	.288	620	2347	341	676	121	8	85	381	24

Position: First base
Team: California Angels
Born: June 16, 1962   Atlanta, GA
Height: 6'2" **Weight:** 198 lbs.
Bats: Left **Throws:** Left
Acquired: Third-round pick in 6/83 free-
agent draft

If Joyner had hit the baseball world at any other time, he would have been an overnight superstar. Jose Canseco narrowly snatched Rookie of the Year honors from Joyner in 1986. Joyner, however, became the first rookie voted to the All-Star lineup since fans began selecting players in 1970. He slugged 22 homers and had 100 RBI in '86. The following year, his teammates voted him California's MVP, as he registered 34 homers, 100 runs scored, and 117 RBI. In 1988, he logged a career-high .295 batting average, with only 51 whiffs in 597 at-bats. That still was an off year for Joyner, who totaled only 13 home runs and 85 RBI.

The Angels and Joyner gained a new wave of popularity in 1989. Joyner's 1990 card could be a big seller. Currently, it's a good buy at around a quarter. Our pick for his best 1990 card is Fleer.

DAVE JUSTICE

	BA	G	AB	R	H	2B	3B	HR	RBI	SB
89 AAA	.261	115	391	47	102	24	3	12	58	12
89 Major	.235	16	51	7	12	3	0	1	3	2

Position: Outfield
Team: Atlanta Braves
Born: April 14, 1966   Cincinnati, OH
Height: 6'3" **Weight:** 195 lbs.
Bats: Left **Throws:** Left
Acquired: Fourth-round pick in 6/85 free-
agent draft

Justice distinguished himself as one of Atlanta's top prospects in 1989. After being demoted from Triple-A Richmond in 1988 when he hit .203 in 70 games, he stuck with the club all year in 1989. He surpassed the double digit mark in homers for the third time in his five-year pro career. In 1987, he was plagued by a broken wrist. At Class-A in 1986, he hit a combined .290 with 22 home runs and 105 RBI with both Sumter and Durham. With Pulaski of the Appalachian League in 1985, Justice tied for the league lead in homers with ten and had 46 RBI in 66 games, earning a spot on the league All-Star Team.

Justice will start if he can supply the Braves with a little punch. But for now, his rookie 1990 cards are long-shot investments at 15 cents. Our pick for his best 1990 card is Fleer.

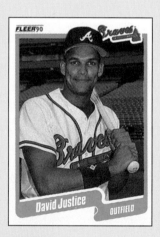

RON KARKOVICE

	BA	G	AB	R	H	2B	3B	HR	RBI	SB
1989	.264	71	182	21	48	9	2	3	24	0
Life	.205	193	479	51	98	20	2	12	53	8

Position: Catcher
Team: Chicago White Sox
Born: August 8, 1963   Union, NJ
Height: 6'1"   **Weight:** 215 lbs.
Bats: Right   **Throws:** Right
Acquired: First-round pick in 6/82
           free-agent draft

Karkovice's season totals prove that there has been no such thing as a second-string catcher with the White Sox. Because starter Carlton Fisk has been injury-prone over recent years, Karkovice has seen more duty than the average substitute. He played in a career high of 71 games in 1989 and achieved personal major league bests in most offensive categories. His greatest offensive season was in 1986 at Double-A Birmingham. He clubbed 20 home runs and 53 RBI while batting .282. He began his career in 1982, and spent parts of his first seven seasons in the minor leagues. But Karkovice remained in the majors through 1989, valued for his top-notch defense and his strong throwing ability, both considered among the best in baseball.

Cards of part-time catchers aren't good card buys. Avoid Karkovice's 1990 commons. Our pick for his best 1990 card is Score.

ROBERTO KELLY

	BA	G	AB	R	H	2B	3B	HR	RBI	SB
1989	.302	137	441	65	133	18	3	9	48	35
Life	.291	198	570	86	166	25	4	11	62	49

Position: Outfield
Team: New York Yankees
Born: October 1, 1964   Panama City,
           Panama
Height: 6'4"   **Weight:** 185 lbs.
Bats: Right   **Throws:** Right
Acquired: Signed as a free agent, 2/82

After five full seasons in the minors and a lengthy injury, Kelly finally played a full major league season. What a season it was, as he attained a .300-plus batting average and 30-plus stolen bases. Previously, he had his best average in 1986, batting .291 in Double-A ball. In 1987, he led the Triple-A International League with 51 stolen bases in 61 attempts. In 1988, he banged into an outfield wall, resulting in wrist and knee injuries. As a consequence, Kelly appeared in just 38 games. He started his career with the Yankee organization in 1982. Kelly's 1989 offensive showing and future promise are important to a team looking to recapture its glory.

Kelly's 1990 cards may be highly overpriced at close to $1. Give him another year to prove himself before you sink that much money into his cards. Our pick for his best 1990 card is Score.

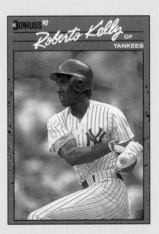

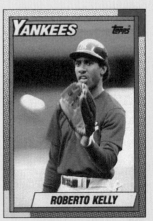

TERRY KENNEDY

	BA	G	AB	R	H	2B	3B	HR	RBI	SB
1989	.239	125	355	19	85	15	0	5	34	1
Life	.264	1315	4505	437	1189	215	11	108	589	5

Position: Catcher
Team: San Francisco Giants
Born: June 4, 1956   Euclid, OH
Height: 6'4" **Weight:** 230 lbs.
Bats: Left   **Throws:** Right
Acquired: Traded from Orioles for Bob
Melvin, 1/89

Kennedy caught in more than 100 games in 1989, marking the eighth time he surpassed that total. He was the third most active catcher of the 1980s, with only Gary Carter and Bob Boone catching more games. Kennedy's batting totals have slipped considerably over the last two seasons. From 1982 to 1987, he had double-digit homer totals each year. His biggest production came with the 1982 Padres, when he batted .293 with 21 homers and 97 RBI in a career-high 153 games. The son of Giants executive Bob Kennedy, Terry has been active in pro baseball since 1977. After just two minor league seasons, he earned his first major league appearance, with the 1978 Cardinals.

Kennedy's age and the rigors of his position may work against him in the future. His lifetime totals make his 1990 commons uncertain investments. Our pick for his best 1990 card is Score.

JIMMY KEY

	W	L	ERA	G	CG	IP	H	ER	BB	SO
1989	13	14	3.88	33	5	216	226	93	27	118
Life	74	79	3.36	224	20	1115	1043	416	279	614

Position: Pitcher
Team: Toronto Blue Jays
Born: April 22, 1961   Huntsville, AL
Height: 6'1" **Weight:** 190 lbs.
Bats: Right   **Throws:** Left
Acquired: Third-round pick in 6/82
free-agent draft

Even though he had a losing record in 1989, Key was the second-highest winner on the Blue Jays. He marked his fifth straight double-digit winning season in 1989 with a 13-14 record. He first rose to prominence as a starter in 1985, his second season in the majors. His sophomore record was 14-6, good enough to get him an appearance in the All-Star game. He achieved a career high in 1987, when he posted a 17-8 record. He leads all lefthanders in Blue Jays history in career wins. When he won his first game as a starter on May 1, 1985, it became the first time in 614 games that a Blue Jays lefthanded starter won a game.

Key has a lifetime losing record. He needs to register a 20-win season before investors will take his 1990 commons seriously. Our pick for his best 1990 card is Fleer.

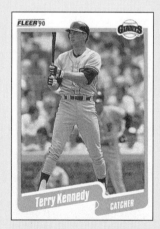

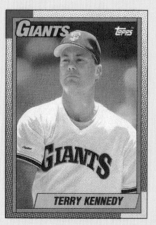

ERIC KING

	W	L	ERA	G	CG	IP	H	ER	BB	SO
1989	9	10	3.39	25	1	159	144	60	64	72
Life	30	24	3.36	224	4	482	423	203	221	285

Position: Pitcher
Team: Chicago White Sox
Born: April 10, 1964 Oxnard, CA
Height: 6'2" **Weight:** 180 lbs.
Bats: Right **Throws:** Right
Acquired: Traded from Detroit for Kenny
Williams, 4/89

While a 9-10 record might seem like a disappointing season to some, to King it meant being the second-leading winner of the 1989 Chicago White Sox. He also notched the lowest ERA (3.39) and pitched the most innings (159) of his four-year career. After he fell from favor with Tigers manager Sparky Anderson, King was moved to the White Sox. His nine wins were the second highest total of his career. After spending four years in the Giants' farm system, he went to the Bengals in a six-player trade after the 1985 season. In 1986, King rewarded Detroit with an 11-4 record, three saves, and three complete games.

King is one of the best pitching hopes the ChiSox have in 1990. However, wait until he has one big winning season before investing in his common-priced 1990 cards. Our pick for his best 1990 card is Topps.

JEFF KING

	BA	G	AB	R	H	2B	3B	HR	RBI	SB
89 AAA	.254	51	169	25	43	5	2	6	29	7
89 Major	.195	75	215	31	42	13	3	5	19	4

Position: Infield
Team: Pittsburgh Pirates
Born: December 26, 1964 Marion, IN
Height: 6'1" **Weight:** 180 lbs.
Bats: Right **Throws:** Right
Acquired: First-round pick in 6/86
free-agent draft

When Pirates first baseman Sid Bream went down with an injury in early 1989, King was called up to fill in at first base and then at third base. He spent the 1988 season at Double-A Harrisburg, hitting .255 with 14 homers and 66 RBI. An 11-game hitting streak and a fourth-best mark for homers highlighted his season. King first displayed power potential in 1987 at Class-A Salem; his 26 homers were second best in the Carolina League. He was named College Player of the Year by *The Sporting News* in 1986 after a fantastic career at Arkansas. King may win a spot at either third base or first base for the Pirates.

King needs to pump up his average, but his five homers makes the Pirates hopeful. Spend a nickel apiece on his 1990 cards. Our pick for his best 1990 card is Donruss.

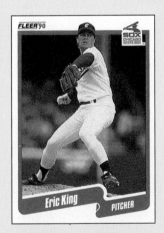

BOB KIPPER

	W	L	ERA	G	SV	IP	H	ER	BB	SO
1989	3	4	2.93	52	4	83	55	27	33	58
Life	17	30	4.50	153	4	401	377	200	155	274

Position: Pitcher
Team: Pittsburgh Pirates
Born: July 8, 1964 Aurora, IL
Height: 6'2" **Weight:** 175 lbs.
Bats: Right **Throws:** Left
Acquired: Traded from Angels with Mike
        Brown and Pat Clements for
        John Candelaria, George
        Hendrick, and Al Holland, 8/85

Kipper got the hang of relief pitching in 1989 and was one of the most important members of the Pirate bullpen. He earned the first four major league saves of his career in 1989, and his career-low 2.93 ERA was the fifth-best among the Bucs. He finished 15 games that season. Kipper faced his first major league season as a reliever in 1988, after working as a starter in 1986 and 1987. He debuted with the Angels in 1985. His most successful season as a starter was in 1986, when he won six, lost eight, and had only 34 walks in 114 innings. His first relief season, 1988, was moderately successful as he became a middle reliever. Kipper appeared in 50 contests, finishing 15 of them.

   Kipper's middle relief role with Pittsburgh limits his chances for fame. His 1990 commons are mediocre investments. Our pick for his best 1990 card is Topps.

RON KITTLE

	BA	G	AB	R	H	2B	3B	HR	RBI	SB
1989	.302	51	169	26	51	10	0	11	37	0
Life	.241	721	2323	316	561	84	3	156	407	16

Position: Designated hitter; outfield
Team: Chicago White Sox
Born: January 5, 1958 Gary, IN
Height: 6'4" **Weight:** 220 lbs.
Bats: Right **Throws:** Right
Acquired: Signed as a free agent, 11/88

Nostalgia and disappointment greeted Kittle upon his return to the White Sox in 1989. Fans remembered the Kittle of old, the 1983 A.L. Rookie of the Year who hit 35 homers and 100 RBI in his first season. Those memories were rekindled when he posted the highest batting average of any 1989 White Sox regular. However, the same back problems that have haunted the Gary, Indiana, native throughout his career reappeared in 1989. His participation was limited to 51 games. In 1988 with the Indians, he smashed 18 home runs in 225 at-bats, for a career-high 8.0 home run percentage. Kittle's best pro year came when he had 50 homers, 144 RBI, and .345 batting average at Triple-A Edmonton in 1982.

   Kittle can still hit with power. But because the next injury could end his career, his 1990 commons seem like risky investments. Our pick for his best 1990 card is Donruss.

  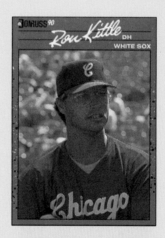 

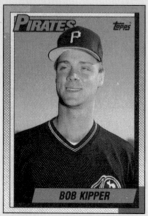  

MARK KNUDSON

	W	L	ERA	G	CG	IP	H	ER	BB	SO
1989	8	5	3.35	40	1	123	110	46	29	47
Life	13	17	4.32	75	2	273	306	131	68	113

Position: Pitcher
Team: Milwaukee Brewers
Born: October 28, 1960   Denver, CO
Height: 6'5"   **Weight:** 215 lbs.
Bats: Right   **Throws:** Right
Acquired: Traded from Astros with Don
    August for Danny Darwin, 8/86

After parts of four major league seasons with a grand total of five victories, Knudson blossomed for the 1989 Brewers. Working both as a starter and reliever, he achieved career highs in wins, games, innings pitched, and strikeouts. His ERA was the fifth lowest on the 1989 Brewers staff, and he finished 16 games. Perhaps Knudson's biggest victory simply was remaining with a major league team for an entire season. In 1988 at Triple-A Denver, he was 11-8 with 3.40 ERA and just 33 walks in 164 innings pitched. He was a third-round selection in the 1982 draft for the Astros. Knudson worked as a starter through parts of seven minor league seasons through 1988.

Knudson plays a minor role in the Brewers' pitching plans. Unless he breaks into the starting rotation, his 1990 commons won't be worthwhile investments. Our pick for his best 1990 card is Fleer.

BRAD KOMMINSK

	BA	G	AB	R	H	2B	3B	HR	RBI	SB
1989	.237	71	198	27	47	8	2	8	33	8
Life	.219	298	855	119	187	32	5	20	95	37

Position: Outfield
Team: Cleveland Indians
Born: April 4, 1961   Lima, OH
Height: 6'3"   **Weight:** 187 lbs.
Bats: Right   **Throws:** Right
Acquired: Signed as a free agent, 12/88

Komminsk returned from a two-year exile in the minors to land a part-time job with the 1989 Indians. The once-revered Braves prospect fell on hard times beginning in 1987. After Milwaukee obtained him in an even-up trade for Dion James, Komminsk appeared in just seven games for the Brew Crew. He was sent back to the minors to rekindle his offense. In 1988 at Triple-A Denver, he hit .239 with 16 homers and 57 RBI. At Denver in 1987, he hit .298 with 110 runs, 31 doubles, 32 homers, 96 RBI, and 18 stolen bases. The Indians took a chance on him in 1989, using him in 71 games. He played 196 games for Atlanta in 1983 and '84 but hit just 12 homers.

Komminsk probably will not start for the Tribe. His common-priced 1990 cards are inadvisable purchases, unless he finds a spot. Our pick for his best 1990 card is Donruss.

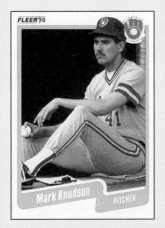

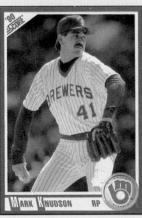

RANDY KRAMER

	W	L	ERA	G	SV	IP	H	ER	BB	SO
1989	5	9	3.96	35	2	111	90	49	61	52
Life	6	11	4.08	40	2	121	102	55	62	59

Position: Pitcher
Team: Pittsburgh Pirates
Born: September 20, 1960 Palo Alto, CA
Height: 6'2" **Weight:** 180 lbs.
Bats: Right **Throws:** Right
Acquired: Traded from Rangers for Jeff
  Zaske, 9/86

When the 1989 Pirates pitching staff was haunted by injuries, one of the new faces the team turned to was Kramer. In five appearances during 1988 at Pittsburgh, he was 1-2. He stuck with the Pirates in 1989, seeing action both as a starter and reliever and keeping his ERA at the 4.00 level. In 1988 with the Triple-A Buffalo Bisons, Kramer was 10-8 as a starter with six complete games. His 198 innings pitched topped the American Association, while his 28 starts and 120 strikeouts were third best in the circuit. He recorded six no-hitters during his high school and college career. One of Kramer's high school teammates was Toronto hurler Dave Steib.

Being both a starter and a reliever is a strain on any pitcher's career. For now, Kramer's 1990 cards aren't worth more than a nickel apiece. Our pick for his best 1990 card is Fleer.

CHAD KREUTER

	BA	G	AB	R	H	2B	3B	HR	RBI	SB
1989	.152	87	158	16	24	3	0	5	9	0
Life	.182	103	209	19	38	5	1	6	14	0

Position: Catcher
Team: Texas Rangers
Born: August 26, 1964 Marin County, CA
Height: 6'2" **Weight:** 190 lbs.
Bats: Both **Throws:** Right
Acquired: Fifth-round pick in 6/85
  free-agent draft

Kreuter was one of four catchers to see substantial duty behind the plate for the Rangers in 1989. Although he had rookie difficulties hitting major league pitching, he showed defensive promise, which convinced the Rangers to give him a fair chance to prove himself. He had a successful debut in 1988 when he hit .275 with one homer in 16 games for the Rangers. The Rangers called Kreuter up after his 1988 effort at Double-A Tulsa. He had a .265 average with three homers and 51 RBI, and he played in the Texas League All-Star Game. If his hitting improves, Kreuter could wind up as the Rangers full-time backstop.

The Rangers have stayed with Kreuter's catching, despite his sickly batting average. Until he lifts his lowly average, don't pay more than 3 cents each for his 1990 cards. Our pick for his best 1990 card is Donruss.

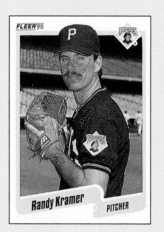

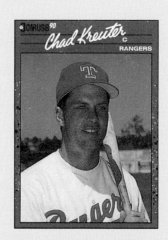

BILL KRUEGER

	W	L	ERA	G	SV	IP	H	ER	BB	SO
1989	3	2	3.84	34	3	93	96	40	33	72
Life	30	33	4.44	132	4	541	577	267	264	262

Position: Pitcher
Team: Milwaukee Brewers
Born: April 24, 1958
      Waukegan, IL
Height: 6'5" **Weight:** 210 lbs.
Bats: Left **Throws:** Left
Acquired: Signed as a free agent, 4/89

Krueger had a busy year for the 1989 Brewers, setting a new career high for appearances. Active in professional baseball since 1980, he appeared in 34 games for the Brew Crew. He worked mostly in relief, drawing just five starting assignments. His three saves ranked third on the team. Krueger first made the majors with the 1983 A's. In 1984, he won a career-high ten games. After a 9-10 record in 1985, he started to have elbow problems. Acquired by the Dodgers in 1987, he had his best professional season to date with the 1988 Triple-A Albuquerque Dukes. Krueger led the Pacific Coast League in wins (15), ERA (3.01), and shutouts (four), and he was named to the league All-Star Team.

Krueger seems destined for relief work throughout his career. His so-so lifetime record dictates avoiding his 1990 commons as investments. Our pick for his best 1990 card is Fleer.

JOHN KRUK

	BA	G	AB	R	H	2B	3B	HR	RBI	SB
1989	.300	112	357	53	107	13	6	8	44	3
Life	.290	492	1460	212	424	60	11	41	217	28

Position: Outfield
Team: Philadelphia Phillies
Born: February 9, 1961 Charleston, WV
Height: 5'10" **Weight:** 195 lbs.
Bats: Left **Throws:** Left
Acquired: Traded from Padres with Randy
      Ready for Chris James, 6/89

A change of scenery helped Kruk reach the .300 mark for the third time in four major league seasons. After falling to an all-time low of .241 with the 1988 Padres, he was traded to Philadelphia in June. A wounded left knee, an injured shoulder, and a jammed thumb slowed Kruk in 1988. He seemed on the verge of stardom after his 1987 season in San Diego. He batted .313 and smacked career highs of 20 homers and 91 RBI. He was named the Padre Rookie of the Year in 1986, thanks to a .309 average in 122 games. Kruk climaxed a five-year career in the minors in 1985, when he won the Pacific Coast League batting crown with a .351 average.

If Kruk stays healthy, he could recapture the offensive magic he knew in 1987. His 1990 commons seem like a reasonable gamble. Our pick for his best 1990 card is Topps.

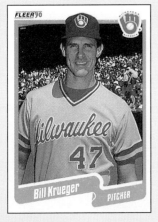

MIKE KRUKOW

	W	L	ERA	G	CG	IP	H	ER	BB	SO
1989	4	3	3.98	8	0	43	37	19	18	18
Life	124	117	3.90	369	41	2190	2188	949	767	1478

Position: Pitcher
Team: San Francisco Giants
Born: January 31, 1952 Long Beach, CA
Height: 6'4" **Weight:** 205 lbs.
Bats: Right **Throws:** Right
Acquired: Traded from Phillies with Mark
    Davis and C. L. Penigar for Jose
    Morgan and Al Holland, 12/82

A rotator cuff injury kept Krukow on the disabled list for all but eight games in 1989, threatening the career of one of San Francisco's most productive hurlers. He was placed on the 60-day disabled list on June 5. His shoulder miseries began in 1988, when he pitched in just 20 games, the previous low of his career. His shoulder caused a three-week disability in 1987, the year he was 5-6. His record fails to show that he had 17 no-decisions in 28 starts, the second highest in baseball history. His greatest season occurred in 1986, when he was 20-9. Krukow ranked third in the Cy Young balloting, and made his first All-Star game appearance that year.

Sadly, Krukow's career seems all but over, due to constant shoulder problems. His 1990 commons have little investment potential. Our pick for his best 1990 card is Topps.

JEFF KUNKEL

	BA	G	AB	R	H	2B	3B	HR	RBI	SB
1989	.270	108	293	39	79	21	2	8	29	3
Life	.241	438	638	71	154	31	8	15	55	7

Position: Infield
Team: Texas Rangers
Born: March 25, 1962
    West Palm Beach, FL
Height: 6'2" **Weight:** 190 lbs.
Bats: Right **Throws:** Right
Acquired: First-round pick in 6/83
    free-agent draft

When the Rangers traded shortstop Scott Fletcher in 1989, Kunkel saw his playing time multiply. He appeared in a career-high 108 games, and established personal bests in several offensive departments. After hitting just seven home runs in parts of five major league seasons, Kunkel belted eight round-trippers in 1989. For the second straight season, he served as a mop-up relief pitcher. He made just one pitching appearance in 1989, giving up four runs in one and two-thirds innings. When Kunkel tossed one scoreless inning against the Twins in 1988, it marked the first time in franchise history (since 1961) that a nonpitcher pitched in a regular-season game.

Kunkel will battle for the starting shortstop job in 1990. However, don't invest in his 1990 commons before he gets a full-time position. Our pick for his best 1990 card is Fleer.

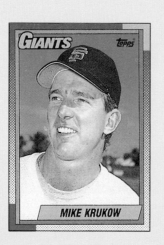

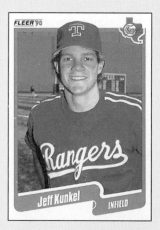

RANDY KUTCHER

	BA	G	AB	R	H	2B	3B	HR	RBI	SB
1989	.225	77	160	28	36	10	3	2	18	3
Life	.227	181	374	65	86	21	5	9	35	10

Position: Outfield; infield
Team: Boston Red Sox
Born: April 20, 1960 Anchorage, AK
Height: 5'11" **Weight:** 175 lbs.
Bats: Right **Throws:** Right
Acquired: Traded from Giants for Dave
        Henderson, 12/87

Kutcher served as the Boston Red Sox' top reserve in 1989, filling in wherever needed. His 77 games played marked his major league career high. Most importantly, 1989 was the first season in his 11-year pro career in which he remained with a major league team for an entire season. He has stayed in the majors by playing a variety of positions. Pitcher and catcher are the only two spots Kutcher hasn't tackled yet. He finally won a major league spot with the San Francisco Giants in 1986 after a stunning start at Triple-A Phoenix, getting a .346 average, 11 homers, and 39 RBI in 55 games.

Kutcher's prime value to Boston is as a pinch-runner, pinch-hitter, and defensive replacement. With those limited roles, it's unlikely that investors could profit from his 1990 commons. Our pick for his best 1990 card is Topps.

MIKE LaCOSS

	W	L	ERA	G	SV	IP	H	ER	BB	SO
1989	10	10	3.17	45	6	150	143	53	65	78
Life	91	94	3.93	384	12	1614	1650	705	662	714

Position: Pitcher
Team: San Francisco Giants
Born: May 30, 1956 Glendale, CA
Height: 6'4" **Weight:** 200 lbs.
Bats: Right **Throws:** Right
Acquired: Signed as a free agent, 3/86

LaCoss won in double figures for the fifth time in his major league career in 1989. He was 10-10 for the San Francisco Giants. He pitched in 45 games for the Giants, the most ever in his 16 professional seasons. He racked up six saves, one complete game, 18 starts, and 16 finished games. LaCoss started 19 times in 1988, going 7-7 with a 3.62 ERA. He was at his best in 1979, when he won a career-high 14 games for the Cincinnati Reds. He also landed his first and only All-Star nomination that year, pitching one scoreless inning. It took him five minor league seasons before he debuted with the Reds in 1978. Of LaCoss's 384 major league appearances, 226 have been as a starter.

LaCoss spends too much time in the bullpen to be considered star material. His 1990 commons are marginal investments. Our pick for his best 1990 card is Score.

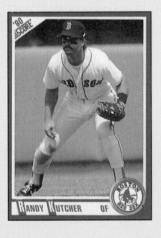

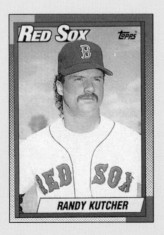

STEVE LAKE

	BA	G	AB	R	H	2B	3B	HR	RBI	SB
1989	.252	58	155	9	39	5	1	2	14	0
Life	.239	325	714	59	171	27	4	11	76	1

Position: Catcher
Team: Philadelphia Phillies
Born: March 14, 1957   Inglewood, CA
Height: 6'1"   **Weight:** 190 lbs.
Bats: Right   **Throws:** Right
Acquired: Traded from Cardinals with
      Curt Ford for Milt Thompson,
      12/88

Lake spent his seventh year in the majors with the 1989 Phillies. He was a third-round pick by the Orioles in 1975. He premiered in the majors with the 1983 Cubs. Since then, he has been used by three major league teams strictly as a reserve catcher. His busiest season came in 1987, when he caught in 74 games for the Cardinals. He notched career highs with two homers and 19 RBI that season. In 1988, he hit .278, and he hit in the .250s in '89. Still, Lake has remained active in pro baseball mainly due to his defensive ability.

A lifetime substitute, Lake isn't a household name with baseball fans. Even if he gets more playing time due to the lack of high-quality competition in the Phillies catching corps, his 1990 commons are ill-advised investments. Our pick for his best 1990 card is Score.

DENNIS LAMP

	W	L	ERA	G	SV	IP	H	ER	BB	SO
1989	4	2	2.32	42	2	112	96	29	27	61
Life	86	87	3.81	520	35	1605	1728	680	479	736

Position: Pitcher
Team: Boston Red Sox
Born: September 23, 1952
      Los Angeles, CA
Height: 6'3"   **Weight:** 215 lbs.
Bats: Right   **Throws:** Right
Acquired: Signed as a free agent, 1/87

Lamp earned the lowest ERA of his career with the 1989 Red Sox. He had a 2.32 ERA in 112 innings, the best of the BoSox. He also saved two games and finished 14 in 42 appearances, all in relief. He hadn't been so active since 1985. With Toronto, Lamp posted an 11-0 record, just one short of the consecutive win record for A.L. relievers. In three relief appearances during the 1985 A.L.C.S., he limited Kansas City to just two hits and no runs in nine and one-third innings (striking out ten). Debuting in the majors with the 1977 Cubs, Lamp began his six-year minor league career as a starter.

Lamp's modest career record is due to years of long and middle relief. His statistics don't merit investment in his 1990 commons. Our pick for his best 1990 card is Fleer.

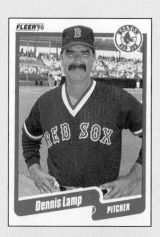

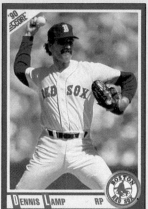

LES LANCASTER

	W	L	ERA	G	SV	IP	H	ER	BB	SO
1989	4	2	1.36	42	8	73	60	11	15	56
Life	16	11	3.68	113	13	291	287	119	100	170

Position: Pitcher
Team: Chicago Cubs
Born: April 21, 1962   Dallas, TX
Height: 6'2"   **Weight:** 200 lbs.
Bats: Right   **Throws:** Right
Acquired: Signed as a free agent, 6/85

Lancaster found needed relief in 1989 in the team's bullpen. He became a top-notch middle reliever, as evidenced by his team-leading, career-best 1.36 ERA. In 42 games, he gave up just 11 earned runs and finished 15 games, earning eight saves. He yielded only two homers and 15 walks through the season. Lancaster debuted with the Cubs as a starter in 1987, going 8-3 in 27 games. His record dropped to 4-6 (with five saves) in 1988. The Cubs demoted him to Triple-A Iowa in 1989, where he was 5-7 in 17 games before getting a midseason call-up. With his newly discovered control, Lancaster should be guaranteed an entire season in the majors in 1990.

Lancaster's surprising season makes investors think twice about his 1990 cards. He could land a starting role or close more games. His common-priced cards are tempting investments. Our pick for his best 1990 card is Donruss.

BILL LANDRUM

	W	L	ERA	G	SV	IP	H	ER	BB	SO
1989	2	3	1.67	56	26	81	60	15	28	51
Life	6	5	3.53	117	28	171	170	67	69	113

Position: Pitcher
Team: Pittsburgh Pirates
Born: August 17, 1958   Columbia, SC
Height: 6'2"   **Weight:** 205 lbs.
Bats: Right   **Throws:** Right
Acquired: Signed as a free agent, 1/89

When reliever Jim Gott was disabled during the first month of the 1989 season, the Pirates were in dire need of relief. The man they chose as their hero was Landrum, a journeyman hurler who's never logged an entire major league season in ten years. But he led the team in saves, games, ERA, and games finished (50). He had survived in the minors for seven seasons before debuting with the 1986 Reds. The White Sox had drafted him in 1984 but returned him to the Reds. He was traded to the Cubs in the 1988 season, but Pittsburgh was the only team willing to sign Landrum as a free agent in 1989.

Landrum had a great season in 1989. But, it was his first full season in the bigs. Check out his performance before investing anything in his 1990 cards. Our pick for his best 1990 card is Donruss.

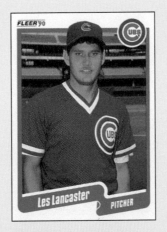

MARK LANGSTON

	W	L	ERA	G	CG	IP	H	ER	BB	SO
89 NL	12	9	2.39	24	6	177	138	47	93	175
Life	86	76	3.80	200	47	1374	1206	580	668	1253

Position: Pitcher
Team: Montreal Expos
Born: August 20, 1960   San Diego, CA
Height: 6'2" **Weight:** 185 lbs.
Bats: Right **Throws:** Left
Acquired: Traded from Mariners with Mike
Campbell for Brian Holman,
Randy Johnson, and Gene
Harris, 5/89

Since his full-season debut with the 1984 Mariners, Langston has paced a losing team to new levels of respect in the eyes of baseball watchers. His trade to the Expos gave him a chance to pitch with a winner. He has a fastball that is hard to beat. In four of his five major league seasons before 1989, he struck out at least 200 batters a year, snagging three strikeout titles. After an injury-plagued '85 season left Langston with a 7-14 record, he regained his strikeout title in 1986, registered 19 wins against 13 losses in 1987, and dropped his ERA to 3.34 in 1988.

Langston is poised for a strong showing after landing a free-agent contract. Buy his 1990 card for a quarter, then double your money in less than a year. Our pick for his best 1990 card is Donruss.

CARNEY LANSFORD

	BA	G	AB	R	H	2B	3B	HR	RBI	SB
1989	.336	148	551	81	185	28	2	2	52	37
Life	.294	1588	6139	884	1807	287	38	141	748	201

Position: Third base
Team: Oakland Athletics
Born: February 7, 1957   San Jose, CA
Height: 6'2" **Weight:** 195 lbs.
Bats: Right **Throws:** Right
Acquired: Traded from Red Sox with
Garry Hancock and Jerry King
for Tony Armas and Jeff
Newman, 12/82

Lansford has served the A's as a voice of experience. In 1989, he shook himself out of a 1988 slump to lead the A's with his first .300 average in five years. He stayed in the batting race throughout 1989, posting his first challenge for a batting title since his 1981 crown. With the Red Sox that year, he hit .336. He was second on the 1989 A's in stolen bases, trailing only Rickey Henderson. Injuries had hampered Lansford at the plate, but he maintained a reputation as a solid third baseman. He played three minor league seasons before getting his debut with the 1978 Angels. Lansford's sophomore season consisted of a career-high 19 homers, a mark he's reached three times.

Lansford's 1990 cards will cost less than a dime, a decent investment price for a perennial batting leader. Our pick for his best 1990 card is Score.

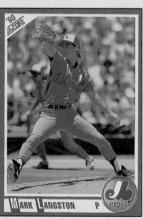

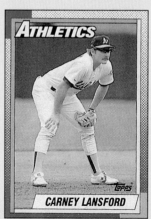

DAVE LaPOINT

	W	L	ERA	G	CG	IP	H	ER	BB	SO
1989	6	9	5.62	20	0	113	146	71	45	51
Life	73	75	3.96	264	9	1324	1408	583	496	732

Position: Pitcher
Team: New York Yankees
Born: July 29, 1959 Glens Falls, NY
Height: 6'3" **Weight:** 231 lbs.
Bats: Left **Throws:** Left
Acquired: Signed as a free agent, 12/88

LaPoint continued his North American tour during the 1989 season. The veteran lefty pitched for the Yankees, his eighth different major league team in ten seasons. The stress of regularly changing employers showed on his record. His 1989 miseries contrasted his 1988 success. Splitting his time between the White Sox and Pirates, he had overall stats of 14 wins, 13 losses, and a 3.25 ERA. In his eight starts for Pittsburgh, he was 4-2 with a 2.77 ERA. He made his first and only World Series appearance for the 1982 Cardinals, pitching in two games without gaining a decision. Before he began team hopping, LaPoint toiled in the minors from 1977 to 1980.

If LaPoint can't win with the hard-hitting Yankees, his career is in trouble. At this point, his lifetime stats and 1989 slump makes his common-priced 1990 cards unappealing. Our pick for his best 1990 card is Donruss.

BARRY LARKIN

	BA	G	AB	R	H	2B	3B	HR	RBI	SB
1989	.342	97	325	47	111	14	4	4	36	10
Life	.289	414	1511	229	437	66	14	31	154	79

Position: Shortstop
Team: Cincinnati Reds
Born: April 28, 1964 Cincinnati, OH
Height: 6' **Weight:** 185 lbs.
Bats: Right **Throws:** Right
Acquired: First-round pick in 6/85
free-agent draft

A troublesome right elbow limited Larkin to just 97 games with the 1989 Reds, curtailing what might have been his best season ever. Like most of his Cincinnati teammates, he was sidelined in 1989. Despite his injury, he hit a sparkling .342 with four homers, 36 RBI, and ten stolen bases. He won his second straight All-Star nomination, but he was injured and failed to appear. A speedy contact hitter, he is respected as one of the toughest strikeouts in the N.L. In 1988, he won a spot on the Silver Slugger team. Before he became a first-round draft choice for the Reds in 1985, Larkin was a member of the 1984 U.S. Olympic baseball team.

Larkin's 1990 cards will be inexpensive, because he missed considerable action in 1989. At 15 cents or less, they are good risks. Our pick for his best 1990 card is Topps.

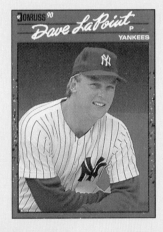

GENE LARKIN

	BA	G	AB	R	H	2B	3B	HR	RBI	SB
1989	.267	136	446	61	119	25	1	6	46	5
Life	.267	370	1184	140	316	66	5	18	144	9

Position: First base; designated hitter
Team: Minnesota Twins
Born: October 24, 1962 Astoria, NY
Height: 6'3" **Weight:** 212 lbs.
Bats: Both **Throws:** Right
Acquired: 20th-round pick in 6/84
　　　　　free-agent draft

Working both as a designated hitter and Kent Hrbek's back-up at first base, Larkin suffered a slight power loss, seeing his homers and RBI drop from eight and 70 in 1988 to six and 46 in '89. However, he remained consistent in batting average. He hit .267 for the second consecutive season, as compared to a .266 average during his 1987 rookie campaign. He was promoted to Minnesota after four consecutive seasons of .300-plus hitting in the minors. He became the first Columbia University player to advance to the majors since Hall of Famer Lou Gehrig. Larkin hit .450 during his senior season and went on to break all of Gehrig's college team records.

　Until Larkin pumps up his average or increases his homers, his 1990 cards will not climb beyond a nickel or less. Our pick for his best 1990 card is Fleer.

TIM LAUDNER

	BA	G	AB	R	H	2B	3B	HR	RBI	SB
1989	.222	100	239	24	53	11	1	6	27	1
Life	.225	734	2038	221	458	97	5	77	263	3

Position: Catcher
Team: Minnesota Twins
Born: June 7, 1958 Mason City, IA
Height: 6'3" **Weight:** 214 lbs.
Bats: Right **Throws:** Right
Acquired: Third-round pick in 6/79
　　　　　free-agent draft

Laudner is a slick-fielding, durable backstop with a knack for clutch hitting. His 1989 dip in stats marked the second of the last six seasons that he has not homered in double figures. Twins fans hoped that he might be on the brink of new offensive success after his .251 average in 1988, Laudner's highest effort since the .255 clip he hit during his 1982 rookie season. He has hit in pressure situations, as evidenced by his .318 average (with one homer and four RBI) in the 1987 World Series. He had his best hitting success in 1981. Laudner set a Double-A Southern League record with 42 round-trippers, with 104 RBI and a .284 batting average.

　Laudner needs to hit for a better average if he hopes to maintain his roster spot with Minnesota. His 1990 commons are poor investments. Our pick for his best 1990 card is Topps.

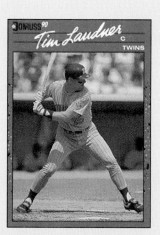

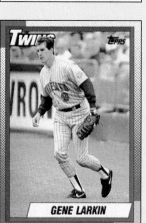
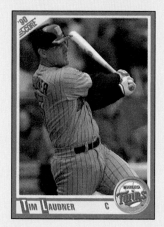
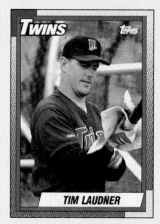

MIKE LaVALLIERE

	BA	G	AB	R	H	2B	3B	HR	RBI	SB
1989	.316	68	190	15	60	10	0	2	23	0
Life	.269	437	1226	92	330	58	2	8	142	3

Position: Catcher
Team: Pittsburgh Pirates
Born: August 18, 1960 Charlotte, NC
Height: 5'10" **Weight:** 190 lbs.
Bats: Left **Throws:** Right
Acquired: Traded from Cardinals with
    Andy Van Slyke and Mike
    Dunne for Tony Pena, 4/87

LaValliere had everything but his health with the 1989 Pittsburgh Pirates. He batted a career-high .316, but was limited to just 68 games. The season was his shortest since his 12-game debut with the 1985 St. Louis Cardinals. He faced a tough battle when he joined Pittsburgh in 1987. He had been traded (along with Andy Van Slyke and Mike Dunne) for catcher Tony Pena. Replacing a fan favorite and annual All-Star like Pena seemed like a huge chore for anyone, especially a rookie. LaValliere, however, made success seem easy. He hit .300 in 121 games, and he won an N.L. Gold Glove.

LaValliere is underrated both as a fielder and a hitter. He doesn't hit for power, but he handles all other tasks well. His 1990 commons could bring long-term profits. Our pick for his best 1990 card is Score.

VANCE LAW

	BA	G	AB	R	H	2B	3B	HR	RBI	SB
1989	.235	130	408	38	96	22	3	7	42	2
Life	.257	1138	3668	442	944	186	25	71	433	34

Position: Third base
Team: Chicago Cubs
Born: October 1, 1956 Boise, ID
Height: 6'1" **Weight:** 190 lbs.
Bats: Right **Throws:** Right
Acquired: Signed as a free agent, 12/87

Missing more than 30 games of the 1989 season had a damaging effect on Law's stats. The Chicago Cubs third baseman saw his batting average drop to its second-lowest in his eight-year career. His woes were a stark contrast from his 1988 success with the Cubs. He opened the season with a 16-game hitting streak and proceeded to hit a career-high .293 for the season, eighth-best in the National League. His 78 RBI were a personal best in a pro career that began in 1978. After making a 1980 major league debut with the Pittsburgh Pirates, Law went on to spend three seasons with the White Sox and three with the Montreal Expos.

Law's 1990 commons are inferior investments. He needs to rekindle his 1988 success before investors might change their minds. Our pick for his best 1990 card is Topps.

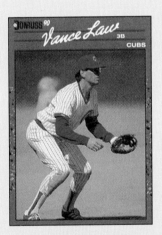
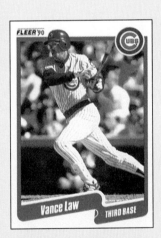

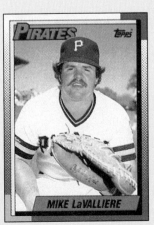

RICK LEACH

	BA	G	AB	R	H	2B	3B	HR	RBI	SB
1989	.272	110	239	32	65	14	1	1	23	2
Life	.265	721	1545	181	409	87	10	16	167	8

Position: Outfield; designated hitter
Team: Texas Rangers
Born: May 4, 1957 Ann Arbor, MI
Height: 6' **Weight:** 195 lbs.
Bats: Left **Throws:** Left
Acquired: Signed as a free agent, 1/89

Leach played in 110 games in 1989, tying a career high. He had a characteristic year, serving the team as a pinch-hitter and spot starter. Such second-string duty has been the story of his major league life. He was a highly touted rookie back in 1979, when he was a first-round draft pick for the Tigers. In less than two minor league seasons, Leach was a major leaguer. However, he never won a starting spot with Detroit and was released prior to the 1984 campaign. Toronto signed him, and he stayed with the Blue Jays through 1988. Leach's best season came in Toronto in 1986, when he hit .309 with five homers and 39 RBI.

Part-timers seldom have investment-worthy baseball cards, as is the case with Leach. Don't invest in his 1990 commons. Our pick for his best 1990 card is Score.

TERRY LEACH

	W	L	ERA	G	SV	IP	H	ER	BB	SO
89 AL	5	6	4.15	30	0	73	78	34	36	34
Life	29	15	3.24	196	7	439	431	158	136	226

Position: Pitcher
Team: Kansas City Royals
Born: March 13, 1954 Selma, AL
Height: 6' **Weight:** 191 lbs.
Bats: Right **Throws:** Right
Acquired: Traded from Mets for
   Ajuedo Vasquez, 6/89

When the Kansas City Royals acquired Leach in 1989, they obtained one of baseball's most experienced pitchers. Although he had less than four years' worth of major league tenure going into 1989, he had been active in pro baseball since 1976. He spent parts of his first 11 seasons in the minors before spending the whole season with the Mets in 1986. Leach's best season came with the 1987 Mets, when he chalked up an 11-1 record in 44 games. His ten-game winning streak led the majors that year and set a Mets record. Leach appeared in 30 games for the Royals in 1989, starting three, winning five, and finishing six.

Leach, a middle reliever, will play a minor part for Royals, so his common-priced 1990 cards will not bring any short-term yields. Our pick for his best 1990 card is Score.

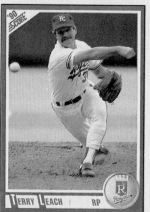

TIM LEARY

	W	L	ERA	G	CG	IP	H	ER	BB	SO
1989	8	14	3.52	33	2	207	205	81	68	123
Life	45	56	3.71	168	15	831	859	348	244	544

Position: Pitcher
Team: Cincinnati Reds
Born: December 23, 1958
Santa Monica, CA
Height: 6'3" **Weight:** 205 lbs.
Bats: Right **Throws:** Right
Acquired: Traded from Dodgers with
Mariano Duncan for Kal Daniels
and Lenny Harris, 7/89

Leary, the National League Comeback Player of the Year in 1988, had a disappointing 1989 season with the Reds. He won a career-high 17 games in 1988, but he slumped to 8-14 in 1989, though he had a 3.52 ERA. The Dodgers had demoted him to their bullpen when it looked like he lost the zip off his fastball. Cincinnati, struggling to replace injured pitching ace Danny Jackson, hoped that Leary could stage another comeback in a new uniform. His pro career began in 1980. He premiered with the Mets just one year later. In 1985, Leary was shipped to Milwaukee, where he tallied a 12-12 effort in 1986.

Leary has been streaky throughout the 1980s. He may have one or two more successful seasons. However, his age and his often-sore arm work against him. Avoid his 1990 commons. Our pick for his best 1990 card is Score.

MANNY LEE

	BA	G	AB	R	H	2B	3B	HR	RBI	SB
1989	.260	99	300	27	78	9	2	3	34	4
Life	.265	370	920	96	244	27	9	7	90	10

Position: Infield
Team: Toronto Blue Jays
Born: June 17, 1965 San Pedro
de Macoris, Dominican Republic
Height: 5'9" **Weight:** 161 lbs.
Bats: Both **Throws:** Right
Acquired: Drafted from Astros, 12/84

Despite frequent injuries, Lee put in more appearances in 1989 than he had before. Although he enjoyed good health, he couldn't match his 1988 major league career highs in average (.291), games (116), at-bats (381), runs (38), hits (111), doubles (16), and RBI (38). He worked as an infield reserve in 1989 and showed flashes of excellence. In 1984, he led the Class-A South Atlantic League with a .329 batting average. He was once considered Toronto's second baseman of the future, before the emergence of Nelson Liriano. Lee has been involved in professional baseball since age 17. As a child in the Dominican Republic, he grew up on the same street near Cardinal slugger Pedro Guerrero.

Lee has youth, enthusiasm, and strong fielding ability. He could challenge for a starting spot. Currently, however, his common-priced 1990 cards are mediocre investments. Our pick for his best 1990 card is Donruss.

CRAIG LEFFERTS

	W	L	ERA	G	SV	IP	H	ER	BB	SO
1989	2	4	2.69	70	20	107	93	32	22	71
Life	32	39	3.00	472	54	683	600	228	205	422

Position: Pitcher
Team: San Francisco Giants
Born: September 29, 1957
    Munich, West Germany
Height: 6'1" **Weight:** 210 lbs.
Bats: Left **Throws:** Left
Acquired: Traded from Padres with Dave
    Dravecky and Kevin Mitchell for
    ChrisBrown, Keith Comstock,
    Mark Davis, and Mark Grant,
    7/87

Before the 1989 Giants obtained stopper Steve Bedrosian, they depended on Lefferts for relief. He notched a career-high 20 saves. He finished 32 games for the Giants, pacing the team to its second division title in the last three seasons. He was part of the multiplayer trade that sent Kevin Mitchell to San Francisco. Lefferts premiered with the 1983 Cubs. Traded to the 1984 Padres, he helped the team to the N.L. West crown with three wins, ten saves, and a 2.13 ERA in 62 games. Lefferts won the last two games of the N.L.C.S. and saved the Padres only World Series win that year.

Lefferts will be overshadowed by Bedrosian. For this reason, and for the unsure investment potential of reliever cards, buying Lefferts's 1990 commons isn't advised. Our pick for his best 1990 card is Topps.

CHARLIE LEIBRANDT

	W	L	ERA	G	CG	IP	H	ER	BB	SO
1989	5	11	5.14	33	3	161	196	92	54	73
Life	92	78	3.77	276	40	1573	1654	658	478	724

Position: Pitcher
Team: Kansas City Royals
Born: October 4, 1956 Chicago, IL
Height: 6'3" **Weight:** 200 lbs.
Bats: Right **Throws:** Left
Acquired: Traded from Reds for
    Bob Tufts, 5/83

Leibrandt struggled through the 1989 season, setting career lows in many categories. He earned just five victories in a disappointing year, his worst in the majors since 1982 (his last year as a Cincinnati reliever). The Royals, in an effort to revive his proficiency, demoted him to the bullpen for the first time since he left the Reds. The Reds gave up on Leibrandt after 1982 and traded him to Kansas City. After a promising year and a half in Triple-A, the Royals recalled him in May 1984. He carved out an 11-7 record that season, then won a career-high 17 games for the 1985 World Championship club. Leibrandt's 1989 slide marked the first time in six years that he hadn't won in double figures.

See if Leibrandt rebounds from his slump before considering one of his 1990 commons. Our pick for his best 1990 card is Fleer.

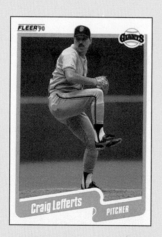

AL LEITER

	W	L	ERA	G	CG	IP	H	ER	BB	SO
1989	1	2	5.67	5	0	33	32	21	23	26
Life	7	8	3.77	23	0	113	105	62	71	114

Position: Pitcher
Team: Toronto Blue Jays
Born: October 23, 1965   Toms River, NJ
Height: 6'3"   **Weight:** 210 lbs.
Bats: Left   **Throws:** Left
Acquired: Traded from Yankees for
Jesse Barfield, 5/89

A sore shoulder shelved Leiter less than two months after the 1989 season began. On May 21, he was placed on the 21-day disabled list with tendinitis in his left shoulder. He had pitched in just five games before getting sidelined. The Yankees parted with him in 1989 after he gave New York two promising performances in 1987 and '88. Although Leiter wound up with a 6-6 record and a fat ERA after 18 total games, his two-season total of 88 strikeouts in 80 innings was most impressive. Active in pro baseball since 1984, he obviously has major league promise. Leiter's only challenge is staying healthy.

Leiter wouldn't be the first pitcher to be prematurely finished by injuries. His 1990 cards will be a nickel or less, still risky for a pitcher who's physically questionable. Our pick for his best 1990 card is Donruss.

MARK LEMKE

	BA	G	AB	R	H	2B	3B	HR	RBI	SB
1989	.182	14	55	4	10	2	1	2	10	0
Life	.204	30	113	12	23	6	1	2	12	0

Position: Infield
Team: Atlanta Braves
Born: August 13, 1965   Utica, NY
Height: 5'9"   **Weight:** 167 lbs.
Bats: Both   **Throws:** Right
Acquired: 27th-round pick in 6/83
free-agent draft

Lemke spent his first full season as the starting second baseman at Triple-A Richmond in 1989, proving he's a worthy challenger for an infield job with the Atlanta Braves. He was the first player on his team to surpass 100 hits and 50 RBI. He got his first shot at the Atlanta infield in 1988, after spending most of the season at Double-A Greenville. With the Braves, Lemke batted .224 in 16 games, .350 against righthanded pitching. For his Greenville feats—including .270 with 16 homers, 80 RBI, 81 runs scored, and 18 stolen bases—Lemke was second in the Southern League Player of the Year voting. The slugger has deceptive power, as evidenced by his career-high 20 homers at Durham in 1987.

Lemke has a chance of winning a starting job with the Braves, making his common-priced 1990 cards worthwhile buys. Our pick for his best 1990 card is Topps.

JEFFREY LEONARD

	BA	G	AB	R	H	2B	3B	HR	RBI	SB
1989	.254	150	566	69	144	20	1	24	93	6
Life	.268	1281	4567	575	1222	203	37	134	648	159

Position: Outfield; designated hitter
Team: Seattle Mariners
Born: September 22, 1955
      Philadelphia, PA
Height: 6'4" **Weight:** 200 lbs.
Bats: Right **Throws:** Right
Acquired: Signed as a free agent, 12/88

Leonard made believers out of Seattle fans with a sparkling 1989 season. After a so-so 1988 showing with the Brewers, the M's raised some eyebrows by signing him to a two-year deal. But, with more than a decade of big league experience, Leonard proved he still had offensive punch. He battled Alvin Davis for the club lead in homers, RBI, and total bases all season. Leonard was selected for the 1989 A.L. All-Star team. He is known for his "one-flap-down" home run trot. Leonard's clutch hitting for the '87 Giants in the N.L.C.S. against St. Louis (four homers and .417 average) won him the series MVP Award.

Because Leonard has streaky career stats, his nickel-priced 1990 cards have inadequate long-term investment chances. Our pick for his best 1990 card is Fleer.

DEREK LILLIQUIST

	W	L	ERA	G	CG	IP	H	ER	BB	SO
88 AAA	10	12	3.38	28	2	171	179	64	36	80
89 Major	8	10	3.97	32	0	165	202	73	34	79

Position: Pitcher
Team: Atlanta Braves
Born: February 20, 1966 Winter Park, FL
Height: 6' **Weight:** 210 lbs.
Bats: Left **Throws:** Left
Acquired: First-round pick in 6/87
      free-agent draft

A nonroster invitee to spring training in 1989, Lilliquist earned a job with the Braves after just two minor league seasons. In 1988 at Triple-A Richmond, he was 10-12 with a 3.38 ERA. He struck out 80, but walked only 36 (less than two per nine innings). At Class-A Bradenton in 1987, he allowed no runs and only three hits while striking out 18 in 16 innings. With Class-A Durham that year, he was 2-1 with two complete games (and 29 strikeouts in 25 innings). Lilliquist hurled the University of Georgia to the 1987 College World Series and was named the College Pitcher of the Year by *Baseball America.*

Lilliquist will get his first regular card in several 1990 sets. Pay less than a quarter for his rookie cards, then get ready for some price increases if he has a good April. Our pick for his best 1990 card is Donruss.

JOSE LIND

	BA	G	AB	R	H	2B	3B	HR	RBI	SB
1989	.232	153	578	52	134	21	3	2	48	15
Life	.255	342	1332	155	340	53	11	4	108	32

Position: Second base
Team: Pittsburgh Pirates
Born: May 1, 1964   Toabaja, Puerto Rico
Height: 5'11"   **Weight:** 170 lbs.
Bats: Right   **Throws:** Right
Acquired: Signed as a free agent, 12/82

Lind suffered a sophomore letdown in 1989. His average slipped 30 points from his .262 average in 1988. He had 26 fewer hits in 1989, and he scored 30 less runs. His biggest accomplishments in '89 were his 48 RBI and 15 stolen bases. The Pirates hoped that he could repeat his first-season performance of 1987, when he was .322 in 35 games. He inherited the job when Johnny Ray was traded to the Angels in midseason. Lind is prized by the Pirates as a slick fielder and agile athlete. He's demonstrated his jumping ability by hurdling over the heads of standing players. Lind has enough talent to be one of the league's best second basemen.

Lind needs to hit for a higher average before investors will profit from his cards. For now, his 1990 issues will remain at 3 cents or less, not a bad buy. Our pick for his best 1990 card is Donruss.

NELSON LIRIANO

	BA	G	AB	R	H	2B	3B	HR	RBI	SB
1989	.263	132	418	51	110	26	3	5	53	16
Life	.259	268	852	116	221	38	7	10	86	41

Position: Second base
Team: Toronto Blue Jays
Born: June 3, 1964   Puerto Plata, Dominican Republic
Height: 5'10"   **Weight:** 165 lbs.
Bats: Both   **Throws:** Right
Acquired: Signed as a free agent, 11/82

Although Liriano had 110 hits for the Toronto Blue Jays in 1989, he got the most attention for just one single. On April 22, 1989, he had a ninth-inning single off Nolan Ryan, spoiling a no-hit bid by the legendary hurler. Liriano's hit was one of the first times he was acclaimed for his hitting. After failing to top .300 in his seven professional seasons, he has gained a reputation for his fine fielding. However, he hit well enough to keep a Toronto roster spot for the entire season in 1989. It took Liriano five seasons to reach the majors, before premiering with Toronto in late 1987.

Liriano needs to hit more consistently before he can consider his second base job safe from Manny Lee. Because of his job instability, Liriano's 1990 commons are shaky investments. Our pick for his best 1990 card is Score.

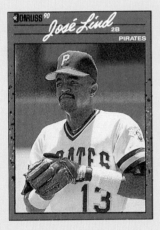

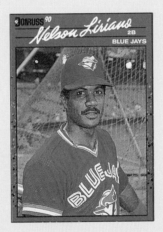

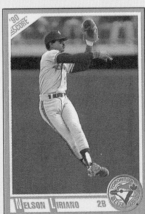

GREG LITTON

	BA	G	AB	R	H	2B	3B	HR	RBI	SB
89 AAA	.180	30	89	6	16	4	2	2	6	1
89 Major	.252	71	143	12	36	5	3	4	17	0

Position: Third base
Team: San Francisco Giants
Born: July 13, 1964 Pensacola, FL
Height: 6' **Weight:** 175 lbs.
Bats: Right **Throws:** Right
Acquired: First-round pick in 1/84
free-agent draft

Litton briefly occupied the starting third baseman's job for the 1989 Giants before losing the spot to Matt Williams. Litton earned the team's starting spot through a solid batting average and tidy defensive work. In his first 50 games with the Giants, he batted a solid .277 with four homers and 13 RBI. His modest power put him on the bench in favor of the power-hitting Williams. Litton had five years of minor league experience going into 1989, with his best offensive season coming with 1985 Class-A Fresno. He hit .266 with 12 homers and 103 RBI. Litton was a Class-A Northwest League All-Star in 1984, his first pro season.

Giant fans loved Litton for his World Series homer, but he might wind up as a second-stringer. Unless he is starting, decline investing in his 10-cent 1990 cards. Our pick for his best 1990 card is Donruss.

BILL LONG

	W	L	ERA	G	SV	IP	H	ER	BB	SO
1989	5	5	3.92	30	1	98	101	43	37	51
Life	21	25	4.33	110	4	455	492	219	113	213

Position: Pitcher
Team: Chicago White Sox
Born: February 29, 1960 Cincinnati, OH
Height: 6' **Weight:** 185 lbs.
Bats: Right **Throws:** Right
Acquired: Traded from Padres with
Luis Salazar, Ozzie Guillen,
and Tim Lollar for LaMarr
Hoyt, Todd Simmons, and
Kevin Kristan, 12/84

Long worked both as a starter and reliever for the 1989 Chicago White Sox, tallying his lowest ERA in his three-year major league career. He had won eight games a season in both 1987 and 1988, working primarily in a starting capacity. In 1989, he made just eight starts in 30 appearances. Long polished his skills with four years in the San Diego Padres' minor league system from 1981 to 1984. The White Sox became interested in him after he was 14-5 at Double-A Beaumont in 1984, leading the Texas League in victories. Long topped the Triple-A American Association with 13 wins in 1985, which led to his major league debut by season's end.

Long has a subpar lifetime record. His questionable stats, and his undefined role with the 1990 ChiSox, makes his 1990 commons inferior investment choices. Our pick for his best 1990 card is Topps.

RICK LUECKEN

	W	L	ERA	G	SV	IP	H	ER	BB	SO
89 AAA	4	1	2.31	36	16	47	33	12	22	39
89 Major	2	1	3.42	19	1	23	23	9	13	16

Position: Pitcher
Team: Kansas City Royals
Born: November 15, 1960 McAllen, TX
Height: 6'6" **Weight:** 210 lbs.
Bats: Right **Throws:** Right
Acquired: Signed as a free agent, 12/87

Luecken rebounded from an injury in 1988 to have a fantastic 1989 season and to show a lot of promise. At Triple-A Omaha, he led the American Association with 16 saves. He also won four games, lost one, and had a 2.31 earned run average. He pitched one inning of scoreless relief in the 1989 Triple-A All-Star Game, striking out one batter. The Royals called him up in September, and he appeared in 19 games—all in relief. Luecken was 2-1 with a 3.42 ERA, with 12 games finished and one save. In 1988 at Omaha, he was 5-0 with a 2.03 ERA and nine saves. Luecken gained five saves that season at Double-A Memphis, going 4-1 with a 2.19 ERA.

Luecken is old for a rookie and probably will not be the Kansas City stopper. Decline investing in his 10-cent 1990 cards. Our pick for his best 1990 card is Donruss.

SCOTT LUSADER

	BA	G	AB	R	H	2B	3B	HR	RBI	SB
1989	.252	40	103	15	26	4	0	1	8	3
Life	.253	79	166	26	42	7	1	3	19	4

Position: Outfield
Team: Detroit Tigers
Born: September 30, 1964 Chicago, IL
Height: 5'10" **Weight:** 165 lbs.
Bats: Left **Throws:** Left
Acquired: Sixth-round pick in 6/85
free-agent draft

In 1989, after a third year at the Triple-A level, Lusader got his third shot at the majors when late-season call-ups came. He was one of the finest September hitters for Detroit, giving him a chance at making the 1990 squad. To find adequate playing time for Lusader in 1989, the Tigers loaned him to Houston's Triple-A affiliate. He began his pro career in 1985. He progressed to Triple-A Toledo in 1987, where he set personal highs in homers (17) and RBI (80). In his 1987 major league debut, he batted .319 in 23 games for Detroit. Lusader was returned to the minors in 1988, and he led Toledo with a .261 average.

Lusader didn't stick in the majors for an entire season in 1989. See if he gets more playing time before buying his 1990 commons. Our pick for his best 1990 card is Score.

FRED LYNN

	BA	G	AB	R	H	2B	3B	HR	RBI	SB
1989	.241	117	353	44	85	11	1	11	46	1
Life	.284	1879	6729	1045	1913	385	42	300	1088	70

Position: Outfield
Team: Detroit Tigers
Born: February 3, 1952 Chicago, IL
Height: 6'1" **Weight:** 190 lbs.
Bats: Left **Throws:** Left
Acquired: Traded from Orioles for
Cesar Jejia, Robinson Garces,
and Chris Hoiles, 8/88

Lynn achieved an important milestone with the 1989 Tigers. Although the 16-year veteran hit a modest .241 with 11 homers and 46 RBI, it was enough to push him past the 300-homer plateau. He cleared a smaller hurdle, playing in 117 games, the most activity he endured since 1985. Lynn's reckless style made him a regular on the disabled list through the years. He has played in more than 140 games just four times in his career. Immediate fame awaited him during his 1975 debut season with the Red Sox. Lynn won both the A.L. MVP and Rookie of the Year awards, becoming the first double-dipper in history.

The injury-plagued Lynn has missed out on greatness due to numerous disabilities. Because his career is quietly winding down, his 1990 commons are marginal investments. Our pick for his best 1990 card is Fleer.

BARRY LYONS

	BA	G	AB	R	H	2B	3B	HR	RBI	SB
1989	.247	79	235	15	58	13	0	3	27	0
Life	.241	188	465	36	112	24	2	7	64	0

Position: Catcher
Team: New York Mets
Born: June 30, 1960 Biloxi, MS
Height: 6'1" **Weight:** 202 lbs.
Bats: Right **Throws:** Right
Acquired: 15th-round pick in 6/82
free-agent draft

Lyons, a backup catcher for the Mets, got some hope for the future when the team announced that Gary Carter wouldn't be offered a new contract. That meant that Lyons will get more playing time. It's been a long wait for him; he has been active in pro baseball since 1982. His 79 games with the 1989 Mets marked the most action he had seen in any of his first four major league seasons. He earned his first major league grand slam on August 20, 1987. His blast was the team's 149th homer of the year, a club record. Lyons had his best offensive season with Double-A Jackson in 1985, when he hit .307 with 11 homers and 108 RBI.

Lyons will play a larger role for the 1990 Mets. However, his statistics don't justify investment in his 1990 commons. Our pick for his best 1990 card is Score.

STEVE LYONS

	BA	G	AB	R	H	2B	3B	HR	RBI	SB
1989	.264	140	443	51	117	21	3	2	50	9
Life	.262	596	1726	218	452	83	13	14	164	29

Position: Infield
Team: Chicago White Sox
Born: June 3, 1960 Tacoma, WA
Height: 6'3" **Weight:** 192 lbs.
Bats: Left **Throws:** Right
Acquired: Traded from Red Sox for
     Tom Seaver, 6/86

Even though he doesn't have a full-time position, Lyons continues to be one of the most active members of the Chicago White Sox. After playing more than 100 games at third base in 1988, he filled in at numerous locations for the 1989 squad. After debuting as a backup catcher in 1988, his only untried position is pitcher (which he has attempted in exhibition games). He is the next candidate for playing all nine positions in one game, a feat accomplished only twice in the majors. Lyons achieved a career high with 50 RBI in 1989 and is one of the team's top pinch-hitters.

Being a utility player rules out investment in Lyons' 1990 cards, which are priced at 3 cents or less. He will have to win one position to see any value increase in his cards. Our pick for his best 1990 card is Score.

MIKE MACFARLANE

	BA	G	AB	R	H	2B	3B	HR	RBI	SB
1989	.223	69	157	13	35	6	0	2	19	0
Life	.245	147	387	38	95	22	0	6	48	0

Position: Catcher
Team: Kansas City Royals
Born: April 12, 1964 Stockton, CA
Height: 6'1" **Weight:** 200 lbs.
Bats: Right **Throws:** Right
Acquired: Fourth-round pick in 6/85
     free-agent draft

Macfarlane proved in 1989 that he could handle the defensive chores that the full-time job behind the plate require. He made just one error in 69 games, making him the leading candidate to replace perennial Gold Glove catcher Bob Boone. In 1988, Macfarlane showed his worth by throwing out 11 baserunners, including Rickey Henderson on two occasions. Macfarlane saw his batting decline from his 1988 effort of four homers, 26 RBI, and a .265 average. But he has hit well before. In 1987, with Triple-A Omaha, he slugged 13 home runs, 50 RBI, and a .262 average in 87 games. He has to show that he can hit before he will be the Kansas City catching heir apparent.

Macfarlane doesn't have a starting job yet. Smart investors will see how he responds to full-time duty before spending anything on his 1990 commons. Our pick for his best 1990 card is Donruss.

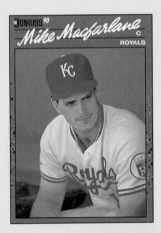

JULIO MACHADO

	W	L	ERA	G	SV	IP	H	ER	BB	SO
89 AAA	1	2	0.62	14	5	29	16	2	17	37
89 Major	0	1	3.27	10	0	11	9	4	3	14

Position: Pitcher
Team: New York Mets
Born: December 1, 1965 Zulia, Venezuela
Height: 5'9" **Weight:** 160 lbs.
Bats: Right **Throws:** Right
Acquired: Signed as a free agent, 4/89

Machado made news in 1989, both for his impressive pitching debut and for his colorful personality. The New York press dubbed him "Iguana Man," because he enjoys eating the small reptiles. But he gained the most attention for his pitching performance. During his 1989 rookie season, he struck out 14 in just 11 innings. In his first major league appearance, he brushed back Terry Pendleton with a fastball. Machado boldly admitted to the press afterward that he purposely buzzed Pendleton to keep him from crowding the plate. Machado pitched in the Phillies' farm system from 1985 to 1988 but was released. But Machado soared through the Mets' organization in just one year.

Machado is brash and talented. Playing with the Mets will give him maximum visibility. His rookie 1990 cards are good investments at 15 cents or less. Our pick for his best 1990 card is Donruss.

GREG MADDUX

	W	L	ERA	G	CG	IP	H	ER	BB	SO
1989	19	12	2.95	35	7	238	222	78	82	135
Life	45	38	3.77	105	18	674	677	282	248	396

Position: Pitcher
Team: Chicago Cubs
Born: April 14, 1966 San Angelo, TX
Height: 6' **Weight:** 170 lbs.
Bats: Right **Throws:** Right
Acquired: Second-round pick in 6/84
    free-agent draft

Maddux achieved a new career high for wins in 1989, but he missed the elusive 20-game circle for the second straight year. He notched a team-leading 19-12 record (second highest in the N.L.) to pace the Cubs to a division crown. He also had seven complete games. In 1988, he seemed ready to win 20 games, especially after he earned a record-setting 15-3 mark before the All-Star break. However, Maddux slumped to a 3-5 mark (with seven no-decisions) after the break, ending the year at 18-8. He spent his first season with the Cubs in 1987, but labored through a 6-14 year. In 1987, he was the youngest player in the league. Now, Maddux ranks as Chicago's pitching ace.

Maddux, the new Cubs ace, is a great investment. At 15 cents or less, his 1990 cards are excellent bargains. Our pick for his best 1990 card is Donruss.

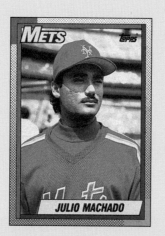

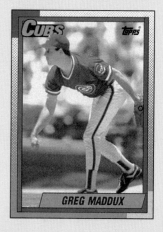

DAVE MAGADAN

	BA	G	AB	R	H	2B	3B	HR	RBI	SB
1989	.286	127	374	47	107	22	3	4	41	1
Life	.293	334	898	110	263	50	4	8	103	1

Position: First base
Team: New York Mets
Born: September 30, 1962 Tampa, FL
Height: 6'3" **Weight:** 195 lbs.
Bats: Left **Throws:** Right
Acquired: Second-round pick in 6/83
   free-agent draft

After three full seasons with the Mets, Magadan should see more playing time. With first baseman Keith Hernandez not getting a new contract offer from the team for 1990, it looks like Magadan may become a starter. In 1988, he filled in for two months when Hernandez suffered a pulled hamstring. Magadan continued at first base in 1989 when Hernandez remained injured. Magadan's .286 batting average was the second-highest among Mets starters in 1989. He earned career highs in most offensive categories in his second year of 100-plus appearances. Although he had batted above .300 from 1983 to 1987, Magadan had never hit more than three homers before 1989.

Investors know that Magadan's career could bloom in 1990. Also, Mets cards always sell well. This means that anyone who gets his 1990 issues for a nickel will have made a good investment. Our pick for his best 1990 card is Fleer.

JOE MAGRANE

	W	L	ERA	G	CG	IP	H	ER	BB	SO
1989	18	9	2.91	34	9	234	219	76	72	127
Life	32	25	2.89	428	17	570	509	183	183	328

Position: Pitcher
Team: St. Louis Cardinals
Born: July 2, 1964 Des Moines, IA
Height: 6'6" **Weight:** 230 lbs.
Bats: Right **Throws:** Left
Acquired: First-round pick in 6/85
   free-agent draft

Magrane was better than ever with the 1989 Cardinals, tallying a team-leading 18 victories. His career-high win total was third-best in the National League. In 1988, his 2.18 ERA topped the senior circuit (although he had a 5-9 record). He became the first Cardinal in 40 years to win an ERA title. His best record in St. Louis had been a 9-7 mark that he posted in his 1987 rookie season. That year, he wound up third in N.L. Rookie of the Year balloting. He soared through the St. Louis minor league system after being the 18th player chosen in the 1985 free-agent draft. Magrane played his college ball at the University of Arizona.

Magrane is headed for the 20-win circle. Get his 1990 cards for 15 cents or less, before he gets the attention he deserves. Our pick for his best 1990 card is Fleer.

RICK MAHLER

	W	L	ERA	G	CG	IP	H	ER	BB	SO
1989	9	13	3.83	40	5	220	242	94	51	102
Life	87	101	3.95	334	41	1750	1865	768	539	857

Position: Pitcher
Team: Cincinnati Reds
Born: August 5, 1953 Austin, TX
Height: 6'1" **Weight:** 202 lbs.
Bats: Right **Throws:** Right
Acquired: Signed as a free agent, 12/88

Mahler joined the Reds as a free agent to start the 1989 season, freeing himself from the Braves. His change of employment did him limited good. His nine wins ranked third among the 1989 Reds. Of his 40 appearances, only nine came in relief. Despite his losing record, he was one of Cincinnati's most dependable pitchers. His 220 innings pitched trailed only starter Tom Browning. For Mahler, it was the sixth time in his major league career that he topped 200 innings in a season. He spent the first ten seasons of his career with Atlanta, winning a high of 17 games in 1985.

Mahler's lifetime record is below average, partially due to the lack of offense the Braves offered him. Nonetheless, his age will hamper his future progress. Pass on his 1990 commons. Our pick for his best 1990 card is Topps.

CANDY MALDONADO

	BA	G	AB	R	H	2B	3B	HR	RBI	SB
1989	.217	129	345	39	75	23	0	9	41	4
Life	.251	818	2236	260	562	127	10	70	332	23

Position: Outfield
Team: Cleveland Indians
Born: September 5, 1960
   Humacao, Puerto Rico
Height: 6' **Weight:** 195 lbs.
Bats: Right **Throws:** Right
Acquired: Signed as a free agent, 11/89

Maldonado moves to the Indians in search of a starting spot. He suffered through the worst slump of his career with the 1989 Giants. He watched his once-healthy average continue its downward spiral of 75 points over the last two seasons. His tribulations were a far cry from 1987, when Maldonado powered the Giants to a division pennant. Despite missing six weeks, he established career highs by hitting .292 with 20 homers and 85 RBI. He was voted team MVP in 1986 when he socked 18 home runs and 85 RBI for a .252 average. Maldonado that year established a Giants record with 17 pinch-hits in one season, including a record-tying four homers.

Maldonado may have a shot at a starting position. But his unimpressive career totals will reduce the demand for his 1990 cards, even at 3 cents or less. Our pick for his best 1990 card is Fleer.

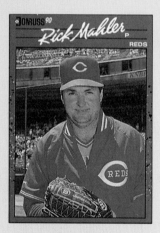

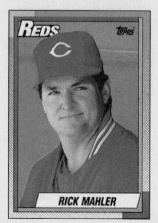

KELLY MANN

	BA	G	AB	R	H	2B	3B	HR	RBI	SB
89 AAA	.246	117	345	37	85	14	1	8	56	1
89 Major	.208	7	24	1	5	2	0	0	1	0

Position: Catcher
Team: Atlanta Braves
Born: August 17, 1967   Santa Monica, CA
Height: 6'3"   **Weight:** 215 lbs.
Bats: Right   **Throws:** Right
Acquired: Traded from Cubs with
         Pat Gomez for Paul
         Assenmacher, 8/89

Atlanta needed catching help, which bodes well for Mann, a scrappy young catcher bred in the Cubs' farm system. He has always been respected for his receiving abilities. With Double-A Charlotte in 1989, he was rated by *Baseball America* as the best defensive catcher in the Southern League. Mann received the same honor in 1988, playing with Winston-Salem of the Class-A Carolina League. At the plate with Charlotte, he set career highs in both homers and RBI. In September 1989, he bypassed Triple-A and advanced to the majors following his acquisition by the Braves. Mann's promotion to the bigs capped a five-year pro career that began with Wytheville in 1985.

The Braves badly need a catcher. Mann may be the man. Gamble on his rookie 1990 cards at a dime or less. Our pick for his best 1990 card is Fleer.

FRED MANRIQUE

	BA	G	AB	R	H	2B	3B	HR	RBI	SB
1989	.294	119	378	46	111	25	1	4	52	4
Life	.260	420	1088	127	283	49	11	15	122	16

Position: Infield
Team: Texas Rangers
Born: November 5, 1961
         Bolivar, Venezuela
Height: 6'1"   **Weight:** 175 lbs.
Bats: Right   **Throws:** Right
Acquired: Traded from White Sox with
         Harold Baines for Scott Fletcher,
         Sam Sosa, and Wilson Alvarez,
         7/89

Manrique was one of the keys to the deal that sent Harold Baines to Texas in 1989. The Rangers wanted the veteran infielder to fill the gap left by departing Scott Fletcher. Manrique complied, hitting a career-high .294 and filling in around the Texas infield. His 52 RBI in 1989 tied his professional best, which he first reached back in 1981 in the Double-A Southern League. He was a starting second baseman for the White Sox in 1987 and 1988, his first two full seasons in the majors. Before the White Sox, he made brief appearances with the 1986 Cardinals, the 1985 Expos, and the 1984 and 1981 Blue Jays.

Manrique will have to battle for the starting shortstop job with the 1990 Rangers. Investors should skip his common-priced 1990 cards, due to the possibility that he'll be kept on the bench. Our pick for his best 1990 card is Topps.

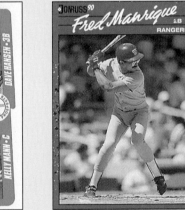

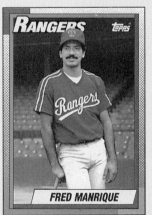

KIRT MANWARING

	BA	G	AB	R	H	2B	3B	HR	RBI	SB
1989	.210	85	200	14	42	4	2	0	18	2
Life	.223	131	323	26	72	11	2	1	33	2

Position: Catcher
Team: San Francisco Giants
Born: July 15, 1965 Elmira, NY
Height: 5'11" **Weight:** 185 lbs.
Bats: Right **Throws:** Right
Acquired: Second-round pick in 6/86
　　　　　free-agent draft

Manwaring more than doubled his major league game appearances in 1989 with the Giants. A rookie in 1988, he hit .294 during his first 16 games with the Giants that year, finishing the season with 17 major league starts. He spent seven games in the bigs in 1987. He got his first big league hit off Rick Mahler that year, then collected his first homer in the majors one year later against the same pitcher. Manwaring developed a strong defensive reputation in three minor league seasons. With Double-A Shreveport in 1987, he gunned down 33 percent of would-be basestealers. His behind-the-plate guidance was credited for Shreveport's league-leading team ERA. Manwaring stands as the heir apparent to Terry Kennedy's catching job.

　Manwaring gets better with experience. His 1990 cards, at a nickel or less, are suitable investments. Our pick for his best 1990 card is Score.

MIKE MARSHALL

	BA	G	AB	R	H	2B	3B	HR	RBI	SB
1989	.260	105	377	41	98	21	1	11	42	2
Life	.271	928	3249	395	882	155	6	137	484	26

Position: Outfield
Team: Los Angeles Dodgers
Born: January 12, 1960 Libertyville, IL
Height: 6'5" **Weight:** 215 lbs.
Bats: Right **Throws:** Right
Acquired: Sixth-round pick in 6/78
　　　　　free-agent draft

Marshall was limited to only 11 dingers in 1989, his lowest total in the last seven seasons. His limited appearances (105 games) reduced his total power output. Despite the drop-off, he reached double figures in round-trippers for the seventh consecutive season. His best offensive display came in 1985, when he blasted 28 homers and 93 RBI. In 1988, he had a .277 average, 20 home runs, and 82 runs batted in. Unlike other free-swinging power men, he has topped 100 strikeouts only once (in 1985). He's divided his career between first base and the outfield, but Marshall has preferred the outfield in recent years to relieve stress on his bad back.

　Marshall's power has been overlooked in the past. A reduction in homers and playing time will lessen the appeal of his 1990 cards. At 3 cents or less, they are solid investments. Our pick for his best 1990 card is Donruss.

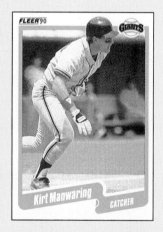
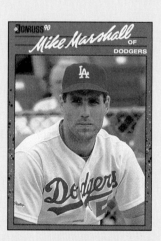

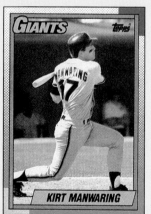

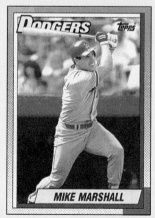

CARLOS MARTINEZ

	BA	G	AB	R	H	2B	3B	HR	RBI	SB
1989	.300	109	350	44	105	22	0	5	32	4
Life	.281	126	405	49	114	23	0	5	32	5

Position: First base; third base
Team: Chicago White Sox
Born: August 11, 1965
      LaGuaira, Venezuela
Height: 6'5" **Weight:** 175 lbs.
Bats: Right **Throws:** Right
Acquired: Traded from Yankees with Ron
      Hassey and Bill Lindsey for Ron
      Kittle, Joel Skinner, and Wayne
      Tolleson, 9/85

Once a promising Yankee farmhand, Martinez has found more opportunities as a member of the White Sox. He quickly advanced through the Chicago system, making a 1988 appearance in Chicago on September 2. After getting a hit in his first big league game, he finished his 17-game debut with a .164 average. In 1989, Martinez became Chicago's primary third baseman. He was one of the best hitters on the ChiSox, and he proved capable of handling the defensive chores around third base. He jumped from Double-A Birmingham to the majors in 1988. Martinez batted .277 with 14 homers and 73 RBI for Birmingham, and he was named team MVP after leading it in nine offensive categories.

Martinez will probably be the ChiSox starting first baseman. Feel lucky if you can get his 1990 cards for 15 cents or less. Our pick for his best 1990 card is Topps.

CARMELO MARTINEZ

	BA	G	AB	R	H	2B	3B	HR	RBI	SB
1989	.221	111	267	23	59	12	2	6	39	0
Life	.249	812	2414	294	600	114	7	88	353	8

Position: Outfield
Team: San Diego Padres
Born: July 28, 1960 Dorado, Puerto Rico
Height: 6'2" **Weight:** 220 lbs.
Bats: Right **Throws:** Right
Acquired: Traded from Cubs with Craig
      Lefferts and Fritz Connally for
      Scott Sanderson, 12/83

Martinez, frustrated with his inability to land a starting role with the 1989 Padres, declared his free agency at season's end. He didn't have much chance to display his talents last season, when he was used as a backup first baseman and outfielder. He came to the Padres prior to 1984 season, and helped the team win the National League pennant during his first year. His top major league stats occurred in 1985, when he batted .253 with 21 homers and 72 RBI. A natural first baseman, he was converted into a left fielder when he joined the Padres. Due first to the presence of Steve Garvey and then Jack Clark, Martinez has been given little chance to play at his best position.

Don't invest in Martinez's 1990 commons before he lands a starting job somewhere. Our pick for his best 1990 card is Topps.

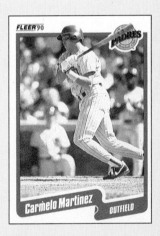

DAVE MARTINEZ

	BA	G	AB	R	H	2B	3B	HR	RBI	SB
1989	.274	126	361	41	99	16	7	3	27	23
Life	.263	459	1375	175	362	48	22	18	116	66

Position: Outfield
Team: Montreal Expos
Born: September 26, 1964   New York, NY
Height: 5'10"   **Weight:** 170 lbs.
Bats: Left   **Throws:** Left
Acquired: Traded from Cubs for
　　　　Mitch Webster, 7/88

Martinez was a part-time center fielder for the 1989 Montreal Expos, a role that limited his offensive accomplishments. He stole 23 bases for the second consecutive year, which ranked third on the team behind Tim Raines and Otis Nixon. Martinez had an impressive 1987 outing with the Chicago Cubs, highlighting his first full season in the majors. He batted .292 with 70 runs scored, eight homers, and 36 RBI, working mostly as a leadoff hitter. In 1988, dividing his time between the Cubs and the Expos, he drove in a career-high 46 runs. Martinez's three-year minor league career is best remembered for his .342 average in 1985, which won him the Class-A Carolina League batting title.

Unless Martinez is a full-timer with the 1990 Expos, there won't be any demand for his common-priced 1990 cards. Our pick for his best 1990 card is Fleer.

DENNIS MARTINEZ

	W	L	ERA	G	CG	IP	H	ER	BB	SO
1989	16	7	3.18	34	5	232	227	82	49	142
Life	153	123	3.90	428	86	2485	2500	1076	755	1267

Position: Pitcher
Team: Montreal Expos
Born: May 14, 1955   Granada, Nicaragua
Height: 6'1"   **Weight:** 183 lbs.
Bats: Right   **Throws:** Right
Acquired: Traded from Orioles for
　　　　Rene Gonzales, 6/86

Martinez tied his career highs in both wins and strikeouts in a banner season with the 1989 Expos. His team-leading 16 wins matched his personal bests achieved in 1978 and 1982 with the Orioles. His 142 strikeouts were the most since his 1978 success. He pitched with the Orioles for ten seasons before being traded for a minor leaguer. He had a 108-93 A.L. record. Through the years, he has shown remarkable fielding ability and a deceptive pickoff move. He earned a bit of baseball history during his debut on September 14, 1976. Martinez was the first Nicaragua-born player to appear in the major leagues.

Martinez won't be a Hall of Famer. But don't count out his cards yet. He is a Cy Young candidate. His nickel-priced 1990 cards are decent gambles to be sold for short-term gains. Our pick for his best 1990 card is Donruss.

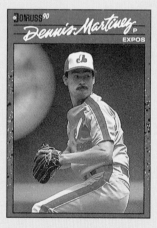

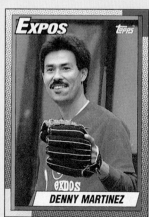

EDGAR MARTINEZ

	BA	G	AB	R	H	2B	3B	HR	RBI	SB
1989	.240	65	171	20	41	5	0	2	20	2
Life	.268	92	246	26	66	14	2	2	30	2

Position: Third base
Team: Seattle Mariners
Born: January 2, 1963   New York, NY
Height: 5'11"   **Weight:** 175 lbs.
Bats: Right   **Throws:** Right
Acquired: Signed as a free agent, 12/82

Martinez shared the Mariners third baseman's job with Jim Presley in 1989 before being returned to Triple-A Calgary. Martinez couldn't seem to earn full control of the job from Presley. After winning the Pacific Coast League batting title in 1988 with a .363 average, Martinez had the inside track as an M's starter. It's been a long climb to the majors for him, since he began his pro career in 1983. His first successful season was with Class-A Wausau in 1983, hitting .303 with 15 homers and 66 RBI. In 1987, he batted .329 at Calgary with ten homers and 66 RBI before getting a 13-game trial with Seattle. Martinez batted .372 during his debut period.

Martinez will battle for the third base job. He could be a notable player if he gets a chance. Invest a few bucks in his 1990 commons. Our pick for his best 1990 card is Topps.

RAMON MARTINEZ

	W	L	ERA	G	CG	IP	H	ER	BB	SO
1989	6	4	3.19	15	2	98	79	35	41	89
Life	7	7	3.36	24	2	134	106	50	63	112

Position: Pitcher
Team: Los Angeles Dodgers
Born: March 22, 1968   Santo Domingo,
   Dominican Republic
Height: 6'4"   **Weight:** 172 lbs.
Bats: Right   **Throws:** Right
Acquired: Signed as a free agent, 9/84

Martinez proved that the Dodgers couldn't keep him in the minor leagues forever. He was called up for just a single game in early 1989, and he spun a shutout against the Braves. Despite his initial success, the Dodgers demoted him. However, Martinez kept piling up accomplishments in Triple-A. He notched a 10-2 record and a Pacific Coast League-leading 127 strikeouts. Possibly the Dodgers heard the cheers of league managers, who voted Martinez the circuit's best pitching prospect and finest fastballer, and recalled him following the All-Star break. After five starts in Los Angeles, he was 3-0 with 29 strikeouts in 32 innings. Martinez could become one of the senior circuit's toughest competitors.

If the Dodgers have a sure thing in 1990, it's Martinez. His sophomore-season 1990 cards are great buys at 15 cents or less. Our pick for his best 1990 card is Donruss.

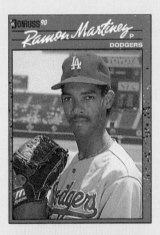

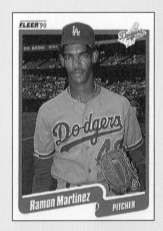

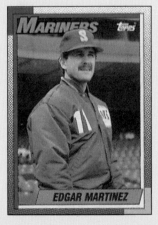

GREG MATHEWS

	W	L	ERA	G	CG	IP	H	ER	BB	SO
1989				Did not play						
Life	26	35	3.79	68	4	411	384	173	148	206

Position: Pitcher
Team: St. Louis Cardinals
Born: May 17, 1962   Harbor City, CA
Height: 6'2"   **Weight:** 180 lbs.
Bats: Right   **Throws:** Left
Acquired: Tenth-round pick in 6/84
　　　　　free-agent draft

Tendinitis in his left elbow kept Mathews from pitching an inning for the 1989 Cardinals. He first had health problems in 1988, when he spent two months on the disabled list. His 1988 season was limited to a 4-6 record in 13 games. He posted an 11-11 record with the 1987 Redbirds, his second full season in the majors. He was a starter in the opener of the N.L.C.S., winning with seven and one-third innings of four-hit work. He followed up an 11-win season he enjoyed in 1986, making him the first Cardinals hurler in 11 years to earn ten-plus wins in his first two years. Mathews made the Cardinals roster in just over two minor league seasons.

Constant ailments cast doubts on Mathews' future. Until he appears fully recovered, his 1990 commons are dangerous investments. Our pick for his best 1990 card is Topps.

DON MATTINGLY

	BA	G	AB	R	H	2B	3B	HR	RBI	SB
1989	.303	158	631	79	191	37	2	23	113	3
Life	.323	1015	4022	615	1300	272	15	164	717	8

Position: First base
Team: New York Yankees
Born: April 20, 1961   Evansville, IN
Height: 6'   **Weight:** 175 lbs.
Bats: Left   **Throws:** Left
Acquired: 19th-round pick in 6/79
　　　　　free-agent draft

After five of the most spectacular seasons anyone could wish for, Mattingly came down to earth. As usual, a Mattingly slump produces stats other players would die for. He bagged 18 round-trippers in '88, the first season since his 1983 debut that the slugger did not claim 30 homers or more. His homer pace in 1989 was similar to '88. He has rightfully earned a faithful following. He entered 1989 as the five-year leader in RBI, placing second in hits, and third in batting average. He also broke or tied records in smacking extra-base hits in ten consecutive games, homering in six consecutive games, and notching six grand slams in a single season.

Mattingly's 1990 cards are some of the most expensive, selling for $1 to $1.50. That's a bit too stiff for investors wanting any short-term profits. Our pick for his best 1990 card is Donruss.

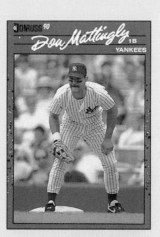

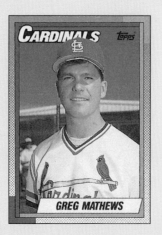

TOM McCARTHY

	W	L	ERA	G	SV	IP	H	ER	BB	SO
1989	1	2	3.51	31	0	66	72	26	20	27
Life	3	2	3.64	40	1	84	88	34	26	34

Position: Pitcher
Team: Chicago White Sox
Born: June 18, 1961
      Lundstahl, West Germany
Height: 6' **Weight:** 180 lbs.
Bats: Right **Throws:** Right
Acquired: Traded from Mets with Steve
      Springer for Vince Maksudian
      and Vince Harris, 8/88

McCarthy joined the 1989 White Sox for six games in late 1988, after spending nearly a decade in the Red Sox' and Mets' organizations. Up with the White Sox for the first time in 1988, he posted a 2-0 mark with one save and a 1.38 ERA in six relief appearances. McCarthy continued his success with the White Sox in 1989, providing vital righthanded relief for the Chicago bullpen. His only prior major league experience came with the Red Sox in July 1985. With Double-A Jackson in 1987, McCarthy collected a career-high 21 saves.

McCarthy's age and previous failures work against him. In an ordinary middle relief role, he's unlikely become a star, so decline investing in his 10-cent 1990 cards. Our pick for his best 1990 card is Topps.

KIRK McCASKILL

	W	L	ERA	G	CG	IP	H	ER	BB	SO
1989	15	10	2.93	32	6	212	202	69	59	107
Life	56	44	3.90	133	27	869	837	377	310	565

Position: Pitcher
Team: California Angels
Born: April 9, 1961 Kapuskasing, Ontario
Height: 6'1" **Weight:** 196 lbs.
Bats: Right **Throws:** Right
Acquired: Fourth-round pick in 6/82
      free-agent draft

When McCaskill reached his ninth victory in 1989 by the middle of July, he topped his production of both 1987 and 1988. His biggest victory in 1989 was remaining free of injuries. His recovery helped the Angels contend in the A.L. West race. The first injury to haunt McCaskill was bone spurs in his pitching elbow in 1987, limiting him to just 14 games. In 1988, a radical nerve irritation of the right arm ended his season at 8-6. He enjoyed his best success in his sophomore campaign of 1986, going 17-10 with ten complete games and 202 strikeouts. McCaskill's arm ailments have forced the one-time power pitcher to sharpen his off-speed deliveries.

Due to McCaskill's age, past arm problems, and unspectacular lifetime record, his cards aren't high-priority buys. Don't pay more than a nickel for his 1990 issues. Our pick for his best 1990 card is Donruss.

LLOYD McCLENDON

	BA	G	AB	R	H	2B	3B	HR	RBI	SB
1989	.286	92	259	47	74	12	1	12	40	6
Life	.254	209	468	64	115	21	1	17	67	11

Position: Outfield; catcher
Team: Chicago Cubs
Born: January 11, 1959 Gary, IN
Height: 5'11" **Weight:** 195 lbs.
Bats: Right **Throws:** Right
Acquired: Traded from Reds for
Rolando Roomes, 12/88

McClendon shared the starting left fielder's job on the Cubs in 1989, working as a catcher when needed. Appearing in 92 games, he split time in the outfield with rookie Dwight Smith. The Cubs wanted to give McClendon a chance to recover from a back injury. Recover he did, registering a career-high 12 homers, 40 RBI, and a batting average boosted from .219 to .286. In 1988 with the Reds, he played in left and right field, first base, third base, and catcher. He began his pro career in the Mets' organization in 1980 and moved to the Reds in 1982, when McClendon was one of three players dealt for Tom Seaver.

McClendon may hit lots of homers in Wrigley, but he won't get any respect from investors until he wins a job. This makes his 1990 commons expendable. Our pick for his best 1990 card is Fleer.

BOB McCLURE

	W	L	ERA	G	SV	IP	H	ER	BB	SO
1989	6	1	1.55	48	3	52	39	9	15	36
Life	62	53	3.77	557	52	1058	1016	443	451	645

Position: Pitcher
Team: California Angels
Born: April 29, 1953 Oakland, CA
Height: 5'11" **Weight:** 175 lbs.
Bats: Right **Throws:** Left
Acquired: Signed as a free agent, 1/89

After three seasons of agonizing over an obese ERA, Angels reliever McClure went on a crash diet. His stunning 1.55 mark over 48 games was the second-lowest in the American League and a personal best that was 12 years in the making. His lowest ERA had been with the 1977 Brewers, when he totaled a 2.54 in 68 games. Although used as a starter by the Brewers for three seasons beginning in 1982, his 1989 stats seem to indicate a real talent for middle relief. Before beginning his pro career in 1973, he was a Little League teammate of Keith Hernandez. Besides Milwaukee, McClure has made major league appearances with the Royals, Expos, and Mets.

McClure's age limits his future in the majors. Because he's nearing the end of his career, it's a bad idea to invest in his 1990 commons. Our pick for his best 1990 card is Topps.

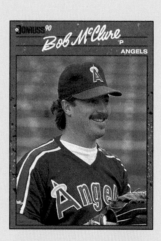

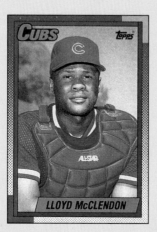

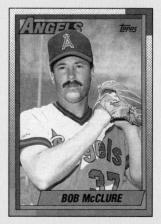

LANCE McCULLERS

	W	L	ERA	G	SV	IP	H	ER	BB	SO
1989	4	3	4.57	52	3	84	83	43	37	82
Life	25	31	3.25	281	39	476	394	172	225	408

Position: Pitcher
Team: New York Yankees
Born: March 8, 1964 Tampa, FL
Height: 6'1" **Weight:** 215 lbs.
Bats: Both **Throws:** Right
Acquired: Traded from Padres with Jimmy
 Jones and Stan Jefferson for
 Jack Clark and Pat Clements,
 10/88

Even though his ERA obviously suffered in 1989, McCullers enjoyed his first winning mark in more than four seasons of major league ball. The Yankees reliever maintained his ratio of nearly one strikeout per inning in 1989 and picked up three saves and 20 games finished. He marked his eighth professional season in 1989, spanning a career that began at age 18. McCullers debuted with the Padres at age 21 in 1985, picking up five saves in his first 21 appearances. He grabbed a career high of ten wins in 1986. He enjoyed the most success in 1987, when he was 8-10 with 16 saves in 78 appearances. In 1988, McCullers won three games and saved ten, getting a 2.49 ERA in 60 appearances.

Due to his inconsistency, McCullers hasn't been a popular card investment subject. Even though he is a Yankee, his 1990 commons are risky ventures. Our pick for his best 1990 card is Score.

BEN McDONALD

	W	L	ERA	G	CG	IP	H	ER	BB	SO
89 A	0	0	2.00	2	0	9	10	2	0	9
89 Major	1	0	8.59	6	0	7	8	7	4	3

Position: Pitcher
Team: Baltimore Orioles
Born: November 24, 1967
 Baton Rouge, LA
Height: 6'7" **Weight:** 212 lbs.
Bats: Right **Throws:** Right
Acquired: First-round pick in 6/89
 free-agent draft

After the Orioles finally signed McDonald to a two-year contract, the famed collegiate star reached the major leagues during his first professional season. He made his professional debut with Class-A Frederick Keys on August 23, 1989, drawing more than 6,500 to the game. He first gained national attention in 1988 as a member of Team USA. His two complete-game wins helped the Americans to an Olympic gold medal. During his three years at Louisiana State, he was 29-14 with six saves and 373 strikeouts in 308 innings. McDonald was named College Player of the Year by *Baseball America* in 1988.

Watch for McDonald's rookie 1990 cards to start at 75 cents, an outrageous price. He'll need at least a year of minor league seasoning, so wait until after he gets sent down and the price falls to buy. Our pick for his best 1990 card is Score.

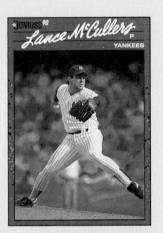

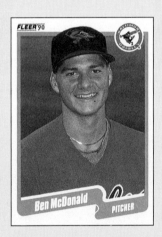

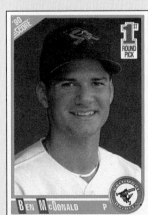

ODDIBE McDOWELL

	BA	G	AB	R	H	2B	3B	HR	RBI	SB
89 NL	.304	76	280	56	85	18	4	7	24	15
Life	.257	589	2102	244	540	101	25	63	204	130

Position: Outfield
Team: Atlanta Braves
Born: August 25, 1962   Hollywood, FL
Height: 5'9" **Weight:** 160 lbs.
Bats: Left **Throws:** Left
Acquired: Traded from Indians for
         Dion James, 7/89

McDowell didn't last a season with the 1989 Indians before getting traded. He was part of the trade that sent Julio Franco to Texas in 1988. McDowell's success with the Tribe was limited, as illustrated by his .222 average, three homers, and 22 RBI in 69 games. Cleveland swapped him in mid-season to the Braves and his spark returned. His .304 average was second on the club. He first reached the majors in 1985, after only 31 games in the minors. He hit 18 homers and 42 RBI in his first 111 games. His sophomore totals included a .266 average, 18 homers, 49 RBI, and 33 stolen bases. Before signing with the Rangers in 1984, McDowell was on the US Olympic baseball team.

McDowell's 1990 cards are long-shot investments, but he may get new life in Atlanta. At a nickel or less, his new cards are reasonable investments. Our pick for his best 1990 card is Fleer.

ROGER McDOWELL

	W	L	ERA	G	SV	IP	H	ER	BB	SO
1989	4	8	1.96	69	23	92	79	20	38	47
Life	36	32	2.91	324	103	525	469	170	176	260

Position: Pitcher
Team: Philadelphia Phillies
Born: December 21, 1960   Cincinnati, OH
Height: 6'1" **Weight:** 185 lbs.
Bats: Right **Throws:** Right
Acquired: Traded from Mets with Len
         Dykstra for Juan Samuel, 6/89

McDowell went from first to worst when he was traded from the Mets to the Phillies in 1989. The June trade ended a six-and-a-half-year association between the Mets organization and McDowell. He took the trade in stride and set about stabilizing the Phils pitching staff. His 23 saves were the second-best total of his career. In 1987, he achieved a personal-high of 25 saves. He was unstoppable in 1986, when he helped the Mets to a World Championship. He went 14-9 with 22 saves, including a victory in the seventh game of the World Series. McDowell could be a long-term solution to the team's bullpen needs.

The truth is that cards of few relievers ever have great resale value. If you invest in McDowell's 1990 commons, don't expect any short-term returns. Our pick for his best 1990 card is Topps.

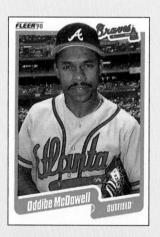

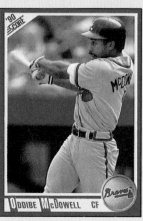

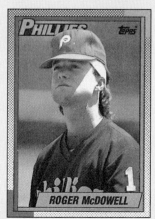

CHUCK McELROY

	W	L	ERA	G	SV	IP	H	ER	BB	SO
89 AAA	1	2	2.93	14	3	15	13	5	11	11
89 Major	0	0	1.74	11	0	10	12	2	4	8

Position: Pitcher
Team: Philadelphia Phillies
Born: October 1, 1967 Galveston, TX
Height: 6' **Weight:** 160 lbs.
Bats: Left **Throws:** Left
Acquired: Eighth-round pick in 6/86
        free-agent draft

McElroy was one of the hoard of rookie pitchers auditioning for the 1989 Phillies. After spending three seasons in the minors as a starter, with a 28-22 cumulative mark, he turned to relief. He began the 1989 season at Double-A Reading, going 3-1 with 12 saves in 32 appearances. He spent just 14 games at Triple-A before getting his call-up to Philadelphia. With the Phils, he finished four of his 11 games. His ERA was the lowest of any Phillies rookie. He has refined his breaking pitches, showcasing his above-average fastball. The Phillies will give McElroy a long look in 1990 spring training.

  McElroy may be sent for a season of Triple-A ball. If he's sent down, his rookie 1990 cards may dip to a dime or less. When the price drops, investors should move quickly. Our pick for his best 1990 card is Fleer.

WILLIE McGEE

	BA	G	AB	R	H	2B	3B	HR	RBI	SB
1989	.236	58	199	23	47	10	2	3	17	8
Life	.292	1039	4084	551	1194	172	71	49	483	246

Position: Outfield
Team: St. Louis Cardinals
Born: November 2, 1958
        San Francisco, CA
Height: 6'1" **Weight:** 176 lbs.
Bats: Both **Throws:** Right
Acquired: Traded from Yankees for
        Bob Sykes, 10/81

After serving as the starting center fielder for the St. Louis Cardinals for seven seasons, McGee lost his job in 1989. He appeared in just 58 games due to numerous injuries and the emergence of Milt Thompson as an outfielder starter. McGee's .236 batting average tied his professional worst, a low he reached during his first minor league season in 1977. He had a distinguished seven years as a Redbirds starter. A four-time All-Star, he won the 1985 National League MVP award. He won his first batting title with a .353 mark, and he led the senior circuit with 216 hits and 18 triples. McGee's 56 stolen bases marked another personal best.

  McGee's 1990 cards will be a nickel or less. Due to the career setback he suffered in 1989, his new cards will generate little interest in the hobby. Our pick for his best 1990 card is Fleer.

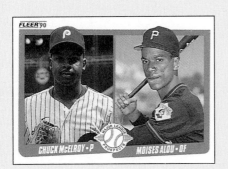

FRED McGRIFF

	BA	G	AB	R	H	2B	3B	HR	RBI	SB
1989	.269	161	551	98	148	27	3	36	92	7
Life	.269	425	1387	257	373	78	7	90	217	16

Position: First base
Team: Toronto Blue Jays
Born: October 31, 1963   Tampa, FL
Height: 6'3"   **Weight:** 215 lbs.
Bats: Left   **Throws:** Left
Acquired: Traded from Yankees with
Dave Collins, Mike Morgan, and
cash for Dale Murray and
Tom Dodd, 12/82

After only two full seasons, McGriff has become Toronto's most valuable asset. His exploits in 1989 placed him at or near league leads in homers, slugging percentage, runs, and total bases. He rises to challenges. His 1981 minor league debut produced a dismal .148 batting average. The following year he was named an All-Star first baseman in the Gulf Coast League by virtue of his circuit-pacing totals in home runs, RBI, and bases on balls. By 1988, his second major league season, McGriff led A.L. first basemen in fielding. It was his first year as an infield starter, after starting out as a designated hitter in '87.

McGriff is better known now that he won the A.L. home run championship. His 1990 cards are selling for a quarter. Paying more for his cards is risky. Our pick for his best 1990 card is Fleer.

MARK McGWIRE

	BA	G	AB	R	H	2B	3B	HR	RBI	SB
1989	.231	143	490	74	113	17	0	33	95	1
Life	.259	467	1650	268	427	68	5	117	321	2

Position: First base
Team: Oakland Athletics
Born: October 1, 1963   Pomona, CA
Height: 6'5"   **Weight:** 225 lbs.
Bats: Right   **Throws:** Right
Acquired: First-round pick in 6/84
free-agent draft

A back injury gave McGwire a late start in 1989, but he still topped the team in home runs. He was second in a line of Oakland Rookie of the Years, following Jose Canseco (1986) and preceding Walt Weiss (1988), marking the first time an A.L. team won the award for three straight seasons. McGwire was a member of the 1984 U.S. Olympic team. After a two-year stint in the minors, he advanced to Oakland. In his first season in 1987, he batted .289 and bashed 49 home runs (a major league rookie record). McGwire's most memorable homer in 1988 gave the A's their only World Series victory.

Despite his low batting average, McGwire remains one of the A.L.'s finest long-ball threats. Feel lucky if you can buy his 1990 cards at 50 cents or less. Our pick for his best 1990 card is Donruss.

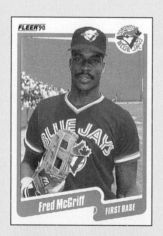

KEVIN McREYNOLDS

	BA	G	AB	R	H	2B	3B	HR	RBI	SB
1989	.272	148	545	74	148	25	3	22	85	15
Life	.270	942	3476	475	940	171	27	143	539	67

Position: Outfield
Team: New York Mets
Born: October 16, 1959 Little Rock, AR
Height: 6'1" **Weight:** 215 lbs.
Bats: Right **Throws:** Right
Acquired: Traded from Padres with
　　Gene Walter and Adam Ging for
　　Shawn Abner, Stanley Jefferson,
　　Kevin Mitchell, Kevin Armstrong,
　　and Kevin Brown, 12/86

A top-notch season to many players was a slump to Mets outfielder McReynolds. Although he hit .272 with 22 homers and 85 RBI, it was his lowest output since 1985. Since he was obtained from the San Diego Padres in December 1986, he's been an offensive and defensive team leader for the Mets. He set career highs with 29 homers (in 1987) and 99 RBI (in 1988). He was a first-round selection by the Padres in 1981, and needed less than two minor league seasons to reach the majors. His rookie-season totals of 20 homers and 75 RBI helped the Padres to their first National League title.

　McReynolds refused to appear on baseball cards early in his career, making his current issues more appealing. He also is a successful member of a prosperous team, which makes his 15-cent 1990 cards blue-chip investments. Our pick for his best 1990 card is Donruss.

BOB MELVIN

	BA	G	AB	R	H	2B	3B	HR	RBI	SB
1989	.241	85	278	22	67	10	1	1	32	1
Life	.225	391	1147	110	258	49	5	25	119	4

Position: Catcher
Team: Baltimore Orioles
Born: October 28, 1961 Palo Alto, CA
Height: 6'4" **Weight:** 205 lbs.
Bats: Right **Throws:** Right
Acquired: Traded from Giants for
　　Terry Kennedy, 1/89

Melvin's first year as an Oriole saw him smack more hits than ever before. He set career highs in hits and his .241 batting average. He's been improving his offensive numbers every year since his big league debut with the Tigers in 1985. The next three years were spent with the Giants, where Melvin threw out 35 percent of would-be basestealers (5 percent better than fellow N.L. catchers). He contributed to the Giants' 1987 division title by clubbing seven homers in April alone and batting .348 during the deciding two weeks of the season. Melvin started two games of the N.L.C.S., batting .429 over three games.

　As long as starting catcher Mickey Tettleton keeps clouting homers, Melvin will be warming the bench. Such part-time status spells doom for investors who purchase his 1990 commons. Our pick for his best 1990 card is Topps.

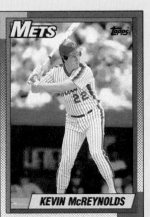

HENSLEY MEULENS

	BA	G	AB	R	H	2B	3B	HR	RBI	SB
89 AAA	.257	95	335	55	86	8	2	11	45	3
89 Major	.179	8	28	2	5	0	0	0	1	0

Position: Third base
Team: New York Yankees
Born: June 23, 1967
      Curacao, Netherlands Antilles
Height: 6'3" **Weight:** 190 lbs.
Bats: Right **Throws:** Right
Acquired: Signed as a free agent, 10/85

When the Yankees traded third baseman Mike Pagliarulo in mid-1989, it left a possible job opening for Meulens. He was one of the top power hitters in the Yankee farm system. "Bam Bam" spent most of 1989 as the starting third baseman for Double-A Albany. He has become a minor league star, landing league All-Star Team memberships on an annual basis. His first honor was on the Gulf Coast League All-Stars in 1986. In 1987, he starred in the Carolina League. With Class-A Prince William, he hit .300 with a league-leading 28 homers and 103 RBI. His season was blighted by 37 errors and 124 strikeouts, however. Meulens combined for 19 homers and 62 RBI in 1988.

Meulens will have to fight for a spot on the Yankees. His 1990 cards are fair investments at a dime or less. Our pick for his best 1990 card is Score.

BRIAN MEYER

	W	L	ERA	G	SV	IP	H	ER	BB	SO
89 AAA	5	4	2.80	58	15	80	81	25	33	56
89 Major	0	1	4.50	12	1	18	16	9	13	13

Position: Pitcher
Team: Houston Astros
Born: January 29, 1963 Camden, NJ
Height: 6'1" **Weight:** 190 lbs.
Bats: Right **Throws:** Right
Acquired: 16th-round pick in 6/86
      free-agent draft

Meyer continued his climb to the majors with another fine season in his four-year career. Spending his fourth year in the minors in 1989, he was the leading reliever for Triple-A Tucson. He reached double digits in saves for the fourth straight season. In eight relief outings with the '88 Astros, Meyer was 0-0 with a 1.46 ERA. He struck out ten and walked just four in 12 1/3 innings. His only two runs allowed were due to two solo home runs. Meyer's promotion was based on his stellar 1988 performance with Double-A Columbus, where he netted a club-record 25 saves (third best in Double-A in '88). Meyer's save total was the highest among all Astros pitchers for a second straight season.

Few rookie relievers become stars with expensive cards. Meyer's 10-cent 1990 issues are forgettable. Our pick for his best 1990 card is Donruss.

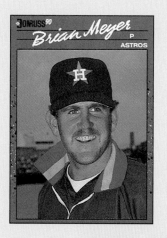

BOB MILACKI

	W	L	ERA	G	SV	IP	H	ER	BB	SO
1989	14	12	3.74	37	3	243	233	101	88	113
Life	16	12	3.46	40	4	268	242	103	97	131

Position: Pitcher
Team: Baltimore Orioles
Born: July 28, 1964   Trenton, NJ
Height: 6'4" **Weight:** 220 lbs.
Bats: Right **Throws:** Right
Acquired: Second-round pick in 6/83
free-agent draft

After five seasons of patience, Milacki got his long-awaited chance to join the Baltimore starting rotation in 1989. He was one of the four Oriole pitchers to win in double figures during the season. He emerged as the chief strikeout artist of the starting staff, erasing his previous career high of 103 Ks with Triple-A Rochester in 1988. He was 12-8 with a 2.70 ERA with Rochester that year. Baltimore gave Milacki his major league debut in 1988, using him in three games. He went 2-0 with a sparkling 0.72 ERA. Of the only three games won by the Orioles after September 11, Milacki started all three. With more experience, expect Milacki's accomplishments to grow in 1990.

Milacki's 14 wins made him one of baseball's hottest young pitchers in 1989. At a dime or less, his 1990 cards are banner investments. Our pick for his best 1990 card is Donruss.

KEITH MILLER

	BA	G	AB	R	H	2B	3B	HR	RBI	SB
1989	.231	57	143	15	33	7	0	1	7	6
Life	.254	122	264	38	67	10	3	2	13	14

Position: Infield
Team: New York Mets
Born: June 12, 1963   Midland, MI
Height: 5'11" **Weight:** 180 lbs.
Bats: Right **Throws:** Right
Acquired: Signed as a free agent, 9/84

In 1989, for the third year running, Miller was on call as a reserve infielder for the Mets. Although he couldn't uncover a starting job, he appeared in a career-high 57 games. He was a second-round draft pick of the Yankees in 1984, but the club voided his contract because he was injured. The Mets signed him that fall as a free agent. He needed just three minor league seasons to reach the majors in 1987. He hit .373 in his 25-game audition. He batted .329 at Double-A Jackson in 1986, only five months after undergoing wrist surgery. Miller refined his skills playing college baseball at Oral Roberts.

Miller looks like the team's top reserve. Reserves, however, don't have investment-worthy baseball cards. Avoid his 1990 commons until he wins a full-time job. Our pick for his best 1990 card is Donruss.

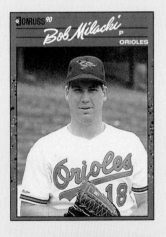

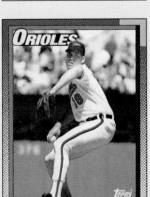

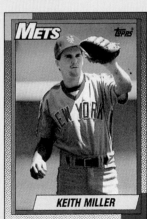

RANDY MILLIGAN

	BA	G	AB	R	H	2B	3B	HR	RBI	SB
1989	.268	124	365	56	98	23	5	12	45	9
Life	.259	167	448	66	116	28	5	15	53	10

Position: First base
Team: Baltimore Orioles
Born: November 27, 1961   San Diego, CA
Height: 6'2" **Weight:** 225 lbs.
Bats: Right **Throws:** Right
Acquired: Traded from Pittsburgh for
　　　Peter Blohm, 11/88

A full season in the majors did wonders for Milligan. After three games with the 1987 Mets and 40 games with the 1988 Pirates, he settled into place as the Orioles' starting first sacker in 1989. In 124 games, he improved 1988's .220 batting average, increased his major league homers by 75 percent, and drove in 45 runs. He labored for seven minor league seasons before getting his first shot at the bigs. He proved his ability in 1987 at Triple-A Tidewater. He led the International League with a .326 average, 99 runs scored, 91 walks, and 103 RBI. Milligan slammed 29 homers, just two behind the league leader, narrowly stopping him from a minor league triple crown.

Milligan is getting a late start on a starting career. Give him one more season to establish his ability, then decide if his 1990 commons are reasonable investments. Our pick for his best 1990 card is Topps.

GREG MINTON

	W	L	ERA	G	SV	IP	H	ER	BB	SO
1989	4	3	2.20	62	8	90	76	22	37	42
Life	58	64	3.11	699	150	1115	1071	385	476	475

Position: Pitcher
Team: California Angeles
Born: July 29, 1951   Lubbock, TX
Height: 6'2" **Weight:** 207 lbs.
Bats: Both **Throws:** Right
Acquired: Signed as a free agent, 6/87

Even at age 38, Minton held his own as a reliever. He appeared in 62 games, his highest total since 1985. He registered a sparkling 2.20 ERA, second-lowest on the Angels. He hadn't earned such a small ERA since 1982, when he had a 1.83 mark. Minton earned his only All-Star nomination in 1982, when he tallied a career-best 30 saves. He pitched for San Francisco from 1976 through 1987, when the Giants released him after just 15 appearances. With the Giants, he earned 19 saves for five consecutive seasons from 1980 to 1984. Minton began his pro career in 1970 and pitched in the minors for parts of his first nine seasons.

Minton's 1990 commons won't bring any short-term gains. But he's participated in 208 victories in his career, a fact that baseball history may smile on favorably. Our pick for his best 1990 card is Fleer.

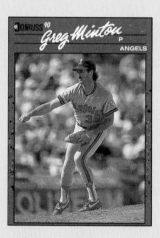
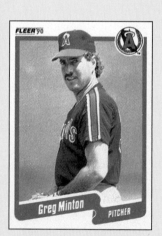

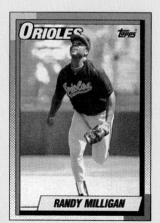
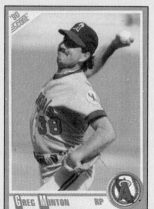

KEVIN MITCHELL

	BA	G	AB	R	H	2B	3B	HR	RBI	SB
1989	.291	154	543	100	158	34	6	47	125	3
Life	.175	548	1854	279	509	101	17	100	319	20

Position: Outfield
Team: San Francisco Giants
Born: January 13, 1962 San Diego, CA
Height: 5'11" **Weight:** 210 lbs.
Bats: Right **Throws:** Right
Acquired: Traded from Padres with Dave
　　　　　Dravecky and Craig Lefferts for
　　　　　Chris Brown, Keith Comstock,
　　　　　Mark Davis, and Mark Grant,
　　　　　7/87

One of the greatest first-half starts of the decade was
recorded in 1989 by Mitchell. He went on a home run tear,
at one point setting a pace that threatened Roger Maris's
single-season homer record of 61. Fans were ready to
award Mitchell both the N.L. home run and RBI titles by the
All-Star break, when he was elected as a starting outfielder.
Before 1989, his top totals were 22 homers in 1987 and 80
RBI in 1988. The Mets called him up to the big leagues in
1986, but the team couldn't find him a starting position.
Mitchell played six different positions with the Mets.

　Mitchell's 1990 cards, at 50 to 75 cents, are too expensive for investment. If he can repeat his success, then it's
safe to jump on the bandwagon. Our pick for his best 1990
card is Topps.

DALE MOHORCIC

	W	L	ERA	G	SV	IP	H	ER	BB	SO
1989	2	1	4.99	32	2	58	65	32	18	24
Life	15	19	3.53	220	31	311	322	122	81	145

Position: Pitcher
Team: New York Yankees
Born: January 25, 1956 Cleveland, OH
Height: 6'3" **Weight:** 220 lbs.
Bats: Right **Throws:** Right
Acquired: Traded from Rangers for
　　　　　Cecilio Guante, 8/88

Mohorcic saw his pitching opportunities cut almost in half for
the 1989 Yankees. He pitched in 32 games, down from the
56 he pitched for both New York and Texas in 1988, and
down from the career-high 74 games he received with the
1987 Rangers. In 1986, he was one of the oldest rookies in
baseball history at age 30. He set an A.L. record that year
by appearing in 13 straight games. He saved 16 with a 2.99
ERA in 1987. Mohorcic's ERA climbed to 4.22 in 1988 and
4.99 in '89. He pitched for Triple-A Columbus in 1989,
notching three saves and a 1.69 ERA in 16 games. Mohorcic could still find a spot on the Yankees.

　Mohorcic had a bad year and got a late start on his career
stats. Investing in his 1990 cards would be a bad move. Our
pick for his best 1990 card is Fleer.

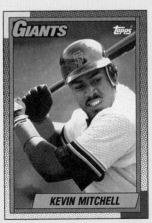

PAUL MOLITOR

	BA	G	AB	R	H	2B	3B	HR	RBI	SB
1989	.315	155	615	84	194	35	4	11	56	27
Life	.300	1437	5828	989	1751	310	60	119	581	344

Position: Third base; designated hitter
Team: Milwaukee Brewers
Born: August 22, 1956 St. Paul, MN
Height: 6' **Weight:** 185 lbs.
Bats: Right **Throws:** Right
Acquired: First-round pick in 6/77
    free-agent draft

Like Robin Yount, Molitor has devoted his career to the Brewers. And like Yount, Molitor has turned on the gas after age 30. He has been effective in the infield, the outfield, and at designated hitter. He has managed to stay off the disabled list for most of the past three seasons, a problem that had plagued him earlier. In 1987, he posted career highs in batting average (.353), RBI (75), and stolen bases (45), and led the league with 114 runs and 41 doubles. In 1982, he led the A.L. with 136 runs. Molitor, like Yount, needed only 64 games in the minors before hitting the bigs. Molitor's greatest feat was a 39-game hitting streak in 1987.

He's a legend in Milwaukee but unknown in other cities. Until Molitor can gain fame, his 1990 cards will not rise beyond the 15-cent mark. Our pick for his best 1990 card is Fleer.

JEFF MONTGOMERY

	W	L	ERA	G	SV	IP	H	ER	BB	SO
1989	7	3	1.37	63	18	92	66	14	25	94
Life	16	7	2.69	122	19	174	145	52	64	154

Position: Pitcher
Team: Kansas City Royals
Born: January 7, 1962 Wellston, OH
Height: 5'11" **Weight:** 180 lbs.
Bats: Right **Throws:** Right
Acquired: Traded from Reds for Van Snider,
    2/88

Despite having less than a year's worth of major league experience, Montgomery became the Royals relief ace in 1989. He led all A.L. relievers with a 1.37 ERA (allowing just 14 runs in 63 appearances). He tied Steve Farr for the team lead with 18 saves in 1989. Montgomery started 1988 at Triple-A Omaha, where he was 1-2 with 13 saves and a 1.91 ERA in 20 appearances. He joined the Royals on June 3, becoming a middle reliever. He ended the year 7-2 in 45 games. He was a ninth-round draft pick by Cincinnati in 1983. Montgomery finally made it to the bigs in 1987, after five seasons in the Reds' minor league system.

The American League is brimming with talented relievers, which makes cards of capable pitchers like Montgomery of secondary interest. His 1990 commons are questionable investments until he has more experience. Our pick for his best 1990 card is Fleer.

MIKE MOORE

	W	L	ERA	G	CG	IP	H	ER	BB	SO
1989	19	11	2.61	35	6	241	193	70	83	172
Life	85	107	4.13	262	62	1698	1691	779	618	1109

Position: Pitcher
Team: Oakland Athletics
Born: November 26, 1959 Eakly, OK
Height: 6'4" **Weight:** 205 lbs.
Bats: Right **Throws:** Right
Acquired: Signed as a free agent, 11/88

In more than six seasons with the Mariners, Moore registered only one winning mark and never saw an ERA anywhere close to 3.00. Those who assumed he would do better with a better offense were proved right in 1989. Signing on with Oakland, Moore saw his ERA plummet close to two points with an extremely healthy winning percentage and a strikeout total that placed him near the top of the league. He has pitched more than 210 innings annually since 1984, and he has struck out at least 150 batters in four of his eight seasons. Moore was the nation's top selection in the 1981 free-agent draft, a first for a righthander.

Moore can be a consistent winner if he plays with a contender. Invest in his 1990 cards at a quarter to bring the best returns. Our pick for his best 1990 card is Score.

KEITH MORELAND

	BA	G	AB	R	H	2B	3B	HR	RBI	SB
1989	.278	123	425	45	118	20	0	6	45	3
Life	.279	1306	4581	511	1279	214	14	121	674	28

Position: Infield; outfield; designated hitter
Team: Baltimore Orioles
Born: May 2, 1954 Dallas, TX
Height: 6' **Weight:** 200 lbs.
Bats: Right **Throws:** Right
Acquired: Traded from Tigers for
  Brian Dubois, 9/89

Moreland escaped the 1989 Tigers when he was sent to Baltimore in a late-season trade. He moved from the Padres to the Tigers prior to the start of the 1989 season. That trade gave him his first taste of the American League, after ten years in the National League. The Orioles gave up a promising rookie to get the immediate benefit of Moreland's talent and experience. His past accomplishments include six double-digit homer seasons with the Cubs from 1982 to 1987. He reached a personal high of 106 RBI in 1985 (batting a career-best .307). Moreland's top homer production came in 1987, when he pounded 27 four-baggers.

Moreland will be a utility player for Baltimore in 1990, playing first, third, the outfield, designated hitter, and possibly catcher. His part-time status rules out investment in his 1990 commons. Our pick for his best 1990 card is Score.

MIKE MORGAN

	W	L	ERA	G	CG	IP	H	ER	BB	SO
1989	8	11	2.53	40	0	152	130	43	33	72
Life	42	79	4.51	197	24	938	1035	470	346	414

Position: Pitcher
Team: Los Angeles Dodgers
Born: October 8, 1959 Tulare, CA
Height: 6'2" **Weight:** 215 lbs.
Bats: Right **Throws:** Right
Acquired: Traded from Orioles for
       Mike Devereaux, 3/89

Morgan's bad luck lessened only a bit after joining the 1989 Dodgers. He looked incredible after his first nine appearances in the National League, going 3-1 with a league-leading 0.77 ERA. But his luck faded fast, and he ended up with yet another losing season. He did finish the season with a career-best 2.53 ERA, however. He was signed out of high school in 1978 by Oakland, going straight to the majors. He lost his first three starts before being demoted to Triple-A. He pitched with Yankees and Toronto before joining the Mariners in 1985. In 1987, he won a career-high 12 games with the M's. Morgan's .347 lifetime winning percentage tells the story of his decade of struggling.

Morgan will have to work miracles simply to even his lifetime record. His 1990 commons are bad investment ideas. Our pick for his best 1990 card is Fleer.

HAL MORRIS

	BA	G	AB	R	H	2B	3B	HR	RBI	SB
89 AAA	.326	111	417	70	136	24	1	17	66	5
89 Major	.278	15	18	2	5	0	0	0	4	0

Position: Outfield; first base
Team: New York Yankees
Born: April 9, 1965 Fort Rucker, AL
Height: 6'3" **Weight:** 200 lbs.
Bats: Left **Throws:** Left
Acquired: Eighth-round pick in 6/86
       free-agent draft

Morris takes off like a shot each season, and the Yankees have kept pace with their prospect's talent with frequent promotions. The Yankees placed him on the big league roster in mid-1989. After spending early 1989 at Triple-A Columbus, International League managers rated Morris as the best defensive first baseman in the circuit. At the time of his promotion, he had a .320-plus average. His first season was in 1986, when he played 36 games at Class-A Oneonta with three homers, 36 RBI, and a .378 average. Morris was not only a New York-Penn League All-Star, but the circuit's Rookie of the Year as well.

Morris will have his first baseball cards in 1990. Avoid investing more than a dime in his 1990 issues until the Yankees give him a starting job. Our pick for his best 1990 card is Topps.

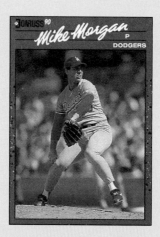

JACK MORRIS

	W	L	ERA	G	CG	IP	H	ER	BB	SO
1989	6	14	4.86	24	10	170	189	92	59	115
Life	183	132	3.66	394	143	2794	2536	1137	989	1818

Position: Pitcher
Team: Detroit Tigers
Born: May 16, 1955 St. Paul, MN
Height: 6'3" **Weight:** 200 lbs.
Bats: Right **Throws:** Right
Acquired: Fifth-round pick in 6/76
free-agent draft

Morris suffered through an injury-filled, slump-cursed 1989 season. His 6-14 record was his worst outcome in the last 11 years. Prior 1989, he had posted consecutive winning records of 14 or more victories a season. He seemed jinxed when he began 1989 with six straight losses. However, skeptics realized the veteran righty wasn't himself when he went on the 21-day disabled list in May due to elbow problems. Morris worked as a reliever during 1978, his first full season in Detroit. He became a permanent starter in 1979, earning two 20-game wins and four All-Star nominations. Morris starred in the 1984 World Series, earning complete-game wins in the first and fourth games.

Morris should shake his slump. His 1990 cards at a dime or less are good, but not great, long-term investments. Our pick for his best 1990 card is Score.

LLOYD MOSEBY

	BA	G	AB	R	H	2B	3B	HR	RBI	SB
1989	.221	135	502	72	111	25	3	11	43	24
Life	.257	1292	5124	768	1319	242	60	149	651	255

Position: Outfield
Team: Toronto Blue Jays
Born: November 5, 1959 Portland, OR
Height: 6'3" **Weight:** 200 lbs.
Bats: Left **Throws:** Right
Acquired: First-round pick in 6/78
free-agent draft

For the second straight season, Moseby struggled with a low batting average. His batting average plummeted from .282 in 1987 to an all-time low of .221 in 1989. But his power has remained through the years. In seven seasons, he has reached double figures in home runs. In 1987, he powered 26 homers and 96 RBI, both career highs. His highest batting average, .315, came in 1983. He ranks as Toronto's all-time leader in 11 different offensive categories. While Moseby was named an All-American at Oakland High School, baseball wasn't always easy for him. As a Little Leaguer, he played catcher, only to be cut from his team.

Moseby could be ready for a rebound. His 1990 cards will sell for a nickel or less, a price that may allow for some short-term profits if Moseby helps Toronto repeat. Our pick for his best 1990 card is Donruss.

JOHN MOSES

	BA	G	AB	R	H	2B	3B	HR	RBI	SB
1989	.281	129	242	33	68	12	3	1	31	14
Life	.263	620	1508	213	396	67	16	10	129	95

Position: Outfield
Team: Minnesota Twins
Born: August 9, 1957   Los Angeles, CA
Height: 5'10"   **Weight:** 170 lbs.
Bats: Both   **Throws:** Left
Acquired: Signed as a free agent, 4/88

Moses closed out the 1980s by playing in a career-high 129 games with the 1989 Twins. Ever since he began his pro career in 1980, he hadn't seen as much action in a single season. The Twins used him as a backup outfielder and defensive replacement in 1989. His speed made him a much-used player, letting him rank third on the club in stolen bases. He made an early major league debut after just three years in the minors. With the 1982 Mariners, Moses hit .318 in 22 games. In 1987, he spent his first full season in the majors. He provided the M's with three homers and a career-high 38 RBI. In 1988, Moses hit .316 with 33 runs scored and 11 stolen bases for Minnesota.

Moses doesn't have a starting job with the Twins, which makes his 1990 commons unappealing investments. Our pick for his best 1990 card is Score.

TERRY MULHOLLAND

	W	L	ERA	G	CG	IP	H	ER	BB	SO
1989	4	7	4.92	25	2	115	137	63	36	66
Life	7	15	4.66	49	4	216	238	112	78	111

Position: Pitcher
Team: Philadelphia Phillies
Born: March 9, 1963   Uniontown, PA
Height: 6'3"   **Weight:** 200 lbs.
Bats: Right   **Throws:** Left
Acquired: Traded from Giants with Charlie Hayes and Dennis Cook for Steve Bedrosian, 6/89

After failing to win a major league job in five pro seasons, Mulholland was given a spot in the 1989 Phillies starting rotation. The Phils knew that he was a durable hurler, having pitched more than 140 innings in each of the prior four seasons. Before being traded, he was shuttled between San Francisco and Triple-A Phoenix in 1989. At Phoenix, he was 4-5 with a 2.99 ERA and three complete games. Before he began his pro career, he starred at Marietta College. He was a first-round selection by the Giants in 1984. After just two years, Mulholland reached Triple-A, where he pitched for parts of the next four seasons.

Mulholland's 1990 cards will start at a nickel. After three shots in the majors, he hasn't shown any outstanding talent. Postpone investing in his cards. Our pick for his best 1990 card is Topps.

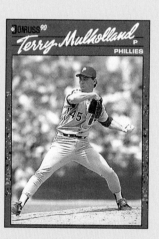
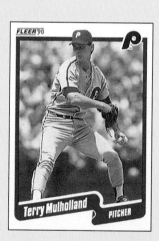

DALE MURPHY

	BA	G	AB	R	H	2B	3B	HR	RBI	SB
1989	.228	154	574	60	131	16	0	20	84	3
Life	.270	1829	6749	1065	1820	292	37	354	1088	151

Position: Outfield
Team: Atlanta Braves
Born: March 12, 1956 Portland, OR
Height: 6'4" **Weight:** 215 lbs.
Bats: Right **Throws:** Right
Acquired: First-round pick in 6/74
free-agent draft

Bad luck plagued Murphy for the second straight year in 1989. He continued his batting slump, but he still was a leading RBI man for Atlanta. In 1988, despite a .226 average, the seven-time All-Star clobbered 24 home runs. Murphy hit a personal best of 44 round-trippers in 1987. He's hit more than 30 homers in six seasons. He smashed 36 home runs and drove in a league-leading 109 runs in 1982 to win his first N.L. MVP. In 1983, he batted .302 with 36 homers and 121 RBI to win his second straight N.L. MVP Award, becoming the youngest player ever to attain such a feat. Murphy led the N.L. in home runs in 1984 and '85.

Collectors have little faith in Murphy's 1990 cards. Dealers may ask 35 cents for his cards, an exorbitant price. Our pick for his best 1990 card is Fleer.

ROB MURPHY

	W	L	ERA	G	SV	IP	H	ER	BB	SO
1989	5	7	2.74	74	9	105	97	32	41	107
Life	19	18	2.64	273	16	344	285	101	134	317

Position: Pitcher
Team: Boston Red Sox
Born: May 26, 1960 Miami, FL
Height: 6'2" **Weight:** 205 lbs.
Bats: Left **Throws:** Left
Acquired: Traded from Reds with Nick
Esasky for Todd Benzinger, Jeff
Sellers, and Luis Vasquez, 12/88

Murphy was a bonus in the 1989 trade that sent Nick Esasky to Boston. While Esasky led the BoSox in homers, Murphy was pacing the pitching staff in appearances. He pitched in 74 games in 1989, second best in the American League. However, it was his lowest total in the last three seasons. He worked in 87 games in 1987, then topped the National League with 76 appearances in 1988. He was Cincinnati's first-round selection in the 1981 free-agent draft, the third pick overall. Five years later, Murphy repaid the Reds' faith with an incredible 34-game rookie season, including a 6-0 record and a 0.72 ERA in 50 innings.

Murphy isn't likely to get lots of acclaim from the bullpen with stopper Lee Smith stealing the show. Regardless of his performance, Murphy's 1990 commons may not be good investments. Our pick for his best 1990 card is Topps.

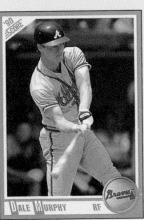

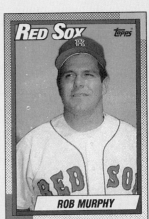

EDDIE MURRAY

	BA	G	AB	R	H	2B	3B	HR	RBI	SB
1989	.247	160	594	66	147	29	1	20	88	7
Life	.291	1980	7439	1114	2168	380	26	353	1278	68

Position: First base
Team: Los Angeles Dodgers
Born: February 24, 1956 Los Angeles, CA
Height: 6'2" **Weight:** 225 lbs.
Bats: Both **Throws:** Right
Acquired: Traded from Orioles for Brian
    Holton, Ken Howell, and Juan
    Bell, 12/88

A new league caused few problems for Murray in 1989, during his first year with the Dodgers. He supplied some vital spark to Los Angeles. His 20 homers and 88 RBI were team highs. The Los Angeles native's .247 average was the lowest of his 13-year career. Unlike many long-ball hitters, he has batted .290 or better eight times. Beginning with his A.L. Rookie of the Year season in 1977, Murray was one of the most potent hitters in Baltimore history. The seven-time All-Star has surpassed the 20-homer mark 12 times and has surpassed 100 RBI on five occasions. Among switch-hitters, only Mickey Mantle has hit more home runs.

Murray still hits with considerable power. His 1990 cards are a bargain at a quarter or less. They could leap in value if the Dodgers start winning. Our pick for his best 1990 card is Score.

JEFF MUSSELMAN

	W	L	ERA	G	SV	IP	H	ER	BB	SO
89 NL	3	2	3.08	20	0	26	27	9	14	11
Life	23	12	3.78	109	3	205	200	86	103	108

Position: Pitcher
Team: New York Mets
Born: June 21, 1963 Doylestown, PA
Height: 6' **Weight:** 185 lbs.
Bats: Left **Throws:** Left
Acquired: Traded from Blue Jays for
    Mookie Wilson, 8/89

Musselman was the prize lefty that the Mets landed in a trade for fan favorite Mookie Wilson. Musselman worked in short relief in his first 20 games with New York. He had owned two seasons of experience with the Blue Jays before coming to the Big Apple. He was a sixth-round selection in the 1985 draft. By the end of 1986, he had pitched in six games for Toronto. In 1987, he appeared in a career-high 68 games (fifth-best in history for a rookie). He earned a 12-5 record with five saves, winning Toronto's Rookie of the Year award. Musselman was 8-5 as a starter in 1988 although he spent almost three months on the disabled list.

Musselman will get little attention in the talent-heavy Mets pitching staff. His 1990 commons are mediocre investments. Our pick for his best 1990 card is Donruss.

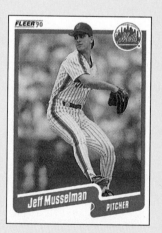

RANDY MYERS

	W	L	ERA	G	SV	IP	H	ER	BB	SO
1989	7	4	2.35	65	24	84	62	22	40	88
Life	17	13	2.74	185	56	240	179	73	97	264

Position: Pitcher
Team: New York Mets
Born: September 19, 1962 Vancouver, WA
Height: 6'1" **Weight:** 208 lbs.
Bats: Left **Throws:** Left
Acquired: First-round pick in the secondary
phase of 6/82 free-agent draft

A player like Myers on a team like the Mets is as close to a sure hit as baseball gets. As a community college All-State pitcher, he had hurled fewer than 20 games but had a no-hitter. The Mets wisely allowed him time to develop slowly in the minors. He had an excellent strikeout ratio (one per inning) and low number of walks, with faith that his up-and-down ERA would stabilize itself. In at least 50 games pitched per season, he had ERAs of 3.97 in 1987, 1.72 in '88, and 2.35 in 1989. His assignment as a saver has grown over the past two seasons, with "Macho Man" converting 26 of 29 opportunities in 1988.

Myers is an integral part of the Mets. Even though he's a reliever, his 1990 cards are good investments at 10 cents. Our pick for his best 1990 card is Donruss.

CHARLES NAGY

	W	L	ERA	G	CG	IP	H	ER	BB	SO
89 A	8	4	1.51	13	6	95	69	16	24	99
89 AA	4	5	3.35	15	2	94	102	35	32	65

Position: Pitcher
Team: Cleveland Indians
Born: May 5, 1967 Fairfield, CT
Height: 6'3" **Weight:** 200 lbs.
Bats: Left **Throws:** Right
Acquired: First-round pick in 6/88
free-agent draft

After being a member of the gold medal-winning 1988 U.S. Olympic baseball team, Nagy played his first year in the Indians' farm system in 1989. He reached the Double-A Canton by August. He was 1-1 with one complete game in his first four starts there. He led Team USA with a 1.05 ERA during the club's summer schedule, going 3-1 with six saves. Nagy then made two Olympic appearances, recording one save. He had a top-notch career pitching at the University of Connecticut. He was 10-7 with five saves and a 2.59 ERA in 29 games (19 being starts). Nagy's honors included two selections as All-Big East Pitcher of the Year.

Investors need time before discerning Nagy's true potential. His Olympian status gives him high visibility and makes his rookie 1990 cards tempting at 10 cents. Our pick for his best 1990 card is Score.

JAIME NAVARRO

	W	L	ERA	G	CG	IP	H	ER	BB	SO
89 AA	5	2	2.47	11	1	77	61	21	35	78
89 Major	7	8	3.12	19	1	109	119	38	32	56

Position: Pitcher
Team: Milwaukee Brewers
Born: March 27, 1967 Bayamon,
    Puerto Rico
Height: 6'4" **Weight:** 210 lbs.
Bats: Right **Throws:** Right
Acquired: Third-round pick in 6/87
    free-agent draft

In less than one year, Navarro moved from Class-A to the rotation of the 1989 Brewers. In his first eight major league starts, he was 3-3. He posted a healthy 2.59 ERA and struck out 26 batters in his first 48 innings. At Double-A El Paso in 1989, he was 5-2 with a 2.47 ERA and 78 Ks in 77 innings. In 1988, he was 15-4 in 27 appearances for Class-A Stockton. *Baseball America* ranked Navarro as the second-best prospect in the California League. He started his career in 1987 at Helena, notching a 4-3 record in 13 starts. He whiffed 95 batters in 85 innings. Navarro has been a pleasant surprise to the Brewers with his steady progress to the majors.

Navarro can be a pitching mainstay with the Brewers. For a healthy investment, spend a dime or less on his 1990 cards. Our pick for his best 1990 card is Fleer.

GENE NELSON

	W	L	ERA	G	SV	IP	H	ER	BB	SO
1989	3	5	3.26	50	3	80	60	29	30	70
Life	46	50	4.14	318	18	844	818	388	332	536

Position: Pitcher
Team: Oakland Athletics
Born: December 3, 1960 Tampa, FL
Height: 6' **Weight:** 175 lbs.
Bats: Right **Throws:** Right
Acquired: Traded from White Sox with
    Bruce Tanner for Donnie Hill,
    12/86

Nelson maintained his large workload for the Oakland A's in 1989, pitching in 50-plus games for the fourth straight season. Ever since 1987, he has been the perfect reliever and set-up man for stoppers like Dennis Eckersley. Nelson played for A's manager Tony LaRussa in Chicago, which convinced the skipper to bring the tireless righty to the West Coast. The 1981 New York Yankees were Nelson's first team in the majors. He was promoted after going 20-3 in the Florida State League in 1980. He pitched with Seattle in 1982 and 1983, but worked just as a part-time reliever. With the White Sox in 1985, Nelson won a personal high of ten games.

As a middle reliever, Nelson gets little acclaim. Because of his obscure job, his 1990 commons shouldn't be invested in. Our pick for his best 1990 card is Donruss.

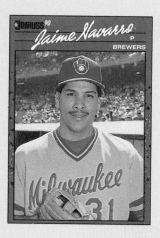

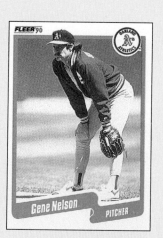

AL NEWMAN

	BA	G	AB	R	H	2B	3B	HR	RBI	SB
1989	.253	141	446	62	113	18	2	0	38	25
Life	.229	476	1227	171	281	44	7	1	95	65

Position: Infield
Team: Minnesota Twins
Born: June 30, 1960   Kansas City, MO
Height: 5'9"   **Weight:** 183 lbs.
Bats: Both   **Throws:** Right
Acquired: Traded from Expos for
　　　　　Mike Shade, 2/87

The Twins gave Newman a shot at the second baseman's job in 1989. He played in a career-high 141 games last season, posting personal bests in most offensive categories. His season was highlighted by a team-leading 25 stolen bases. The Twins acquired the versatile infielder in 1987, using him at various positions. Newman played in more than 100 games again in 1988, becoming one of the team's top reserves. He was a first-round selection by the Expos in 1981. He began his career the next year, and spent nearly four seasons in the minors before getting his major league debut. Newman hit his only major league homer on July 6, 1986, against Atlanta's Zane Smith.

Because Newman hasn't started, there won't be significant interest in his 1990 commons. Don't invest in them until he is assured of a job. Our pick for his best 1990 card is Score.

ROD NICHOLS

	W	L	ERA	G	CG	IP	H	ER	BB	SO
1989	4	6	4.40	15	0	71	81	35	24	42
Life	5	13	4.72	26	0	141	154	74	47	73

Position: Pitcher
Team: Cleveland Indians
Born: December 29, 1964   Burlington, IA
Height: 6'2"   **Weight:** 190 lbs.
Bats: Right   **Throws:** Right
Acquired: Fifth-round pick in 6/85
　　　　　free-agent draft

Nichols moved closer to landing a full-time position with the Indians during a 15-game audition in 1989. He returned to the Tribe after a stellar season at Triple-A Colorado Springs, including an 8-1 record in ten starts. With Cleveland, he made 11 starts and four relief appearances. He debuted with the Indians in 1988, pitching in 11 games. His only win (in ten starts) came versus Yankee Tommy John. Nichols had started the 1988 season in Class-A and climbed to the majors by the end of July. He began his pro career in 1985, after lettering in baseball for three years at the University of New Mexico.

The Indians should give Nichols another extended shot. This is a make-or-break year for the pitcher. See how he does before investing anything in his 1990 commons. Our pick for his best 1990 card is Donruss.

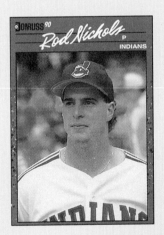

MATT NOKES

	BA	G	AB	R	H	2B	3B	HR	RBI	SB
1989	.250	87	268	15	67	10	0	9	39	1
Life	.278	370	1188	142	315	33	2	60	186	3

Position: Catcher
Team: Detroit Tigers
Born: October 31, 1963   San Diego, CA
Height: 6'1" **Weight:** 185 lbs.
Bats: Left **Throws:** Right
Acquired: Traded from Giants with
        Dave LaPoint and Eric King for
        Juan Berenguer, Bob Melvin, and
        Scott Medvin, 10/85

Nokes saw his shaky health decline more with the 1989 Tigers. He appeared in just 87 games, partially due to a torn knee ligament suffered in a June collision at home plate. His stats suffered from the layoff, as he hit less than ten homers for the third time in his nine-year professional career. The Tigers hoped that he could return to the rookie season form he displayed in 1987. He batted .289 with 32 homers and 87 RBI. He was named the team's Rookie of the Year, and he earned an All-Star appearance for his efforts. Nokes's sophomore season in 1988 showed a modest dip (.251 average, 16 homers, and 53 RBI).

Nokes's 1990 cards will be 10 to 15 cents each. Judging from his weak knees, he needs to play a full season to convince investors to pursue his cards again. Our pick for his best 1990 card is Score.

KEN OBERKFELL

	BA	G	AB	R	H	2B	3B	HR	RBI	SB
1989	.269	97	156	19	42	6	1	2	17	0
Life	.281	1431	4563	535	1283	226	43	28	410	61

Position: Infield
Team: San Francisco Giants
Born: May 4, 1956   Maryville, IL
Height: 6'1" **Weight:** 210 lbs.
Bats: Left **Throws:** Right
Acquired: Traded from Pirates for
        Roger Samuels, 5/89

Oberkfell's 1989 statistics with the Giants don't adequately reflect the contributions he made to the N.L. champs. When he was acquired in early May, he became the team's top pinch-hitter. Coming off the bench, he hit an impressive .375 (18 for 48). His 18 pinch-hits set a new club record. During the last two games of the World Series, he started at third base to give the Giants more offense. San Francisco wanted Oberkfell for his clutch hitting and sure defense as an infield backup. He played second base with the Cardinals from 1977 to 1980. "Obie" moved to third base in 1981. He played with the Braves from 1984 to 1987. In 1986 and 1987, he knocked in a career-high 48 runs each season.

Because Oberkfell won't be starting in 1990, his cards won't command any premiums. Overlook his 1990 commons. Our pick for his best 1990 card is Topps.

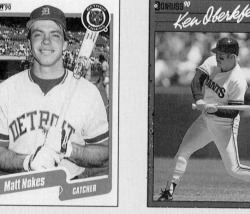

CHARLIE O'BRIEN

	BA	G	AB	R	H	2B	3B	HR	RBI	SB
1989	.234	62	188	22	44	10	0	6	35	0
Life	.227	128	352	39	80	20	1	8	45	0

Position: Catcher
Team: Milwaukee Brewers
Born: May 1, 1961 Tulsa, OK
Height: 6'2" **Weight:** 190 lbs.
Bats: Right **Throws:** Right
Acquired: Traded from A's with Steve Keifer,
   Pete Kendrick, and Mike Fulmer
   for Moose Haas, 3/86

O'Brien played in 62 games for the 1989 Milwaukee Brewers, reaching new highs in most offensive categories. He belted six homers and 35 RBI, far exceeding his career totals of two home runs and ten RBI. He has never been a starter in the major leagues, although he had a promising debut with the 1985 Oakland Athletics. He batted .273 in his 16-game debut. It took four minor league seasons for him to climb up the minor league ladder. Before his pro career started, he was a college star at Wichita State. O'Brien won All-American honors in 1982 when he led the team to a second-place finish in the College World Series.

O'Brien's chief value to Milwaukee is defensive. Because of his limited hitting ability, his future is cloudy. Avoid his 1990 commons. Our pick for his best 1990 card is Donruss.

PETE O'BRIEN

	BA	G	AB	R	H	2B	3B	HR	RBI	SB
1989	.259	155	555	75	144	24	1	12	55	3
Life	.271	1101	3906	494	1058	185	17	126	542	22

Position: First base
Team: Cleveland Indians
Born: February 9, 1958 Santa Monica, CA
Height: 6'2" **Weight:** 205 lbs.
Bats: Left **Throws:** Left
Acquired: Traded from Rangers with
   Oddibe McDowell and Jerry
   Browne for Julio Franco, 12/88

O'Brien brought some early excitement to the 1989 Indians. He hit better than .400 for the first month of the season, far outdistancing any other American Leaguers. A dreadful mid-season slump brought him back to reality, reducing his average to its lowest since 1983. While his 12 homers marked the sixth straight year he topped double figures, his dozen dingers were his lowest total since 1983. Active in the majors since 1982, he had established a reputation as a slick-fielding first baseman and decent power hitter. Both in 1986 and 1987, he pounded a high of 23 homers. In 1987, he registered a 15-game hitting streak. O'Brien can serve the Tribe for years to come.

O'Brien's 1990 cards will be 3 cents or less. Pick up a few now. If he slugs the Indians into contention, that price could triple fast. Our pick for his best 1990 card is Topps.

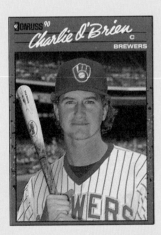

RON OESTER

	BA	G	AB	R	H	2B	3B	HR	RBI	SB
1989	.246	109	305	23	75	15	0	1	14	1
Life	.264	1212	4060	448	1072	180	32	42	331	39

Position: Second base
Team: Cincinnati Reds
Born: May 5, 1956 Cincinnati, OH
Height: 6'2" **Weight:** 195 lbs.
Bats: Both **Throws:** Right
Acquired: Ninth-round pick in 6/74
    free-agent draft

Oester played his tenth full season with the Reds in 1989, refusing to succumb to an injury-plagued career. The Cincinnati native batted a modest .246, his lowest since 1984, but his 109 games were the most he participated in since 1986. In 1987, he suffered a career-threatening knee injury. He returned to action just eight months after complete reconstructive surgery, which included a rehabilitation in the minors. Oester played six seasons in the minors before becoming a Reds starter in 1980. His best season was in 1983, when he had 11 homers, 63 runs scored, and 58 RBI. By teaming with shortstop Barry Larkin, Oester has given the Reds baseball's only current hometown-born keystone combo.

Oester has unremarkable lifetime hitting stats. He also may not have a starting job for too much longer. Don't invest in his 1990 commons. Our pick for his best 1990 card is Topps.

BOB OJEDA

	W	L	ERA	G	CG	IP	H	ER	BB	SO
1989	13	11	3.47	31	5	192	179	74	78	95
Life	88	73	3.65	242	37	1364	1301	553	458	822

Position: Pitcher
Team: New York Mets
Born: December 17, 1957 Los Angeles, CA
Height: 6'1" **Weight:** 195 lbs.
Bats: Left **Throws:** Left
Acquired: Traded from Red Sox with
    John Mitchell, Tom McCarthy,
    and Chris Bayer for Calvin
    Schiraldi, Wes Gardner,
    John Christensen, and LaSchelle
    Tarver, 11/85

While Ojeda didn't set any records with the 1989 Mets, his biggest accomplishment was simply being able to pitch. On September 21, 1988, he was injured using an electric hedge clipper. Extensive surgery saved the index finger on his pitching hand. The upper portion of the finger was almost completely severed before surgery. His recuperation was proven by his 13 wins in 1989, his second-highest total in ten major league campaigns. After four minor league seasons, Ojeda won a starting spot with the Red Sox. He won 12 games for the BoSox both in 1983 and 1984. His best-ever season came with the 1986 Mets. He was 18-5 and had a win in Game Three of the World Series.

The best investors could hope for from Ojeda would be consecutive 20-win seasons. His 1990 commons are dark-horse investments. Our pick for his best 1990 card is Score.

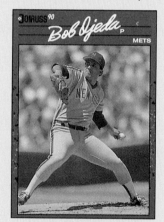

JOHN OLERUD

	BA	G	AB	R	H	2B	3B	HR	RBI	SB
1989	.375	6	8	2	3	0	0	0	0	0
Life	.375	6	8	2	3	0	0	0	0	0

Position: First base; pitcher
Team: Toronto Blue Jays
Born: August 5, 1968   Seattle, WA
Height: 6'5"   **Weight:** 205 lbs.
Bats: Left   **Throws:** Left
Acquired: Third-round pick in 6/89
　　　　　　free-agent draft

Olerud represented a gamble to major league teams. Once thought a top prize in the 1989 draft due to his career at Washington State, he was overlooked until the third round by the Blue Jays. His 1988 stats, including a 15-0 pitching record and a .464-average, 23-homer, and 81-RBI batting record, transformed Olerud into rookie gold. But in January 1989, he collapsed after a workout. He underwent surgery for an aneurysm of the brain the following month. Still, he appeared in 27 games, hitting .359 and posting a 3-2 pitching mark. Part of Olerud's first contract included a $25,000 donation to the medical facility that treated his aneurysm.

Olerud's promise as a pitcher and hitting makes him an exciting card investment prospect. His rookie 1990 cards are excellent buys at 15 cents a card. Our pick for his best 1990 card is Donruss.

STEVE OLIN

	W	L	ERA	G	SV	IP	H	ER	BB	SO
89 AAA	4	1	3.22	42	24	50	34	18	15	46
89 Major	1	4	3.75	25	1	36	35	15	14	24

Position: Pitcher
Team: Cleveland Indians
Born: October 10, 1965   Portland, OR
Height: 6'2"   **Weight:** 185 lbs.
Bats: Right   **Throws:** Right
Acquired: 16th-round pick in 6/87 draft

Olin needed just three seasons to cruise through the Cleveland Indians' minor league system and land a big league job. A submarine-type pitcher, the young reliever was called up by Cleveland in 1989 after he earned a Pacific Coast League-leading 24 saves with Colorado Springs. In Triple-A, he was 4-1 in 42 games, including 46 strikeouts in 50 innings. His success might seem surprising, considering that he wasn't drafted until the 16th round in 1987. In his first full minor league season, 1988, he had a combined 8-2 record with 23 saves in 62 games in Class-A ball. Olin played at Portland State University for four years before he began his pro career.

Expect Olin's rookie 1990 cards to go for at least 15 cents each. Give him a full season in the majors before passing judgment on his cards. Our pick for his best 1990 card is Donruss.

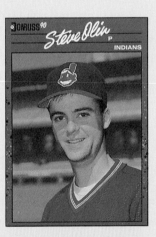

JOE OLIVER

	BA	G	AB	R	H	2B	3B	HR	RBI	SB
89 AAA	.292	71	233	22	68	13	0	6	31	0
89 Major	.272	49	151	13	41	8	0	3	23	0

Position: Catcher
Team: Cincinnati Reds
Born: July 24, 1965 Memphis, TN
Height: 6'3" **Weight:** 210 lbs.
Bats: Right **Throws:** Right
Acquired: Second-round pick in 6/83
   free-agent draft

After nearly seven minor league seasons, Oliver wound up 1989 sharing the catching duties with the Reds. He had one of his finest major league outings on August 23 against the Cubs. He collected four hits (one of them a two-run homer) and a total of four RBI to pace the Reds to an 8-5 triumph. After handling full-time catching duties, Oliver was derailed by a September 12 home plate collision that broke a bone in his lower spine. Strong defense has always been Oliver's trademark. In 1983, he led the Pioneer League in fielding percentage. Midwest League managers ranked his arm the best in the circuit in 1984.

Oliver has the inside track on the starting catcher position for Cincinnati. Buy his 1990 cards at 15 cents or less for a sturdy profit. Our pick for his best 1990 card is Fleer.

GREGG OLSON

	W	L	ERA	G	SV	IP	H	ER	BB	SO
1989	5	2	1.69	64	27	85	57	16	46	90
Life	6	3	1.88	74	27	96	67	20	56	99

Position: Pitcher
Team: Baltimore Orioles
Born: October 11, 1966 Omaha, NE
Height: 6'4" **Weight:** 211 lbs.
Bats: Right **Throws:** Right
Acquired: First-round pick in 6/88
   free-agent draft

Olson became one of the A.L.'s hottest rookies in 1989. He went 15-for-15 in his first save opportunities as he became the Orioles stopper. He was elected to the 1988 U.S. Olympic baseball squad, but he decided to start his pro career early instead. He was the fourth player selected in the nation in the June 1988 draft. He pitched in just 16 minor league games that season in both Class-A and Double-A. Promoted to Baltimore, he was 1-1 in ten relief outings in 1988. He was a two-time All-American with Auburn. Olson's emergence was a major factor in Baltimore's winning record in 1989.

Olson set a record for single-season rookie saves in 1989. Paying a quarter or less for his 1990 cards would be a slick move for investors. Our pick for his best 1990 card is Score.

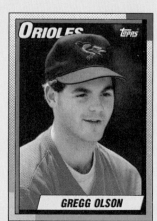

PAUL O'NEILL

	BA	G	AB	R	H	2B	3B	HR	RBI	SB
1989	.276	117	428	49	118	24	2	15	74	20
Life	.262	354	1087	132	285	64	6	38	176	30

Position: Outfield
Team: Cincinnati Reds
Born: February 25, 1963   Columbus, OH
Height: 6'4"   **Weight:** 210 lbs.
Bats: Left   **Throws:** Left
Acquired: Fourth-round pick in 6/81
free-agent draft

Cincinnati was treated to a banner season by O'Neill in 1989. He led the Triple-A American Association with 155 base hits and 32 doubles in 1985. After a five-year career in the Reds' farm system, O'Neill made his Cincinnati debut in 1985. He batted .333 in his five-game trial. He injured his thumb in 1986 and saw little playing time. In 1987, O'Neill was a part-time player for the Reds, hitting .256 in 84 games. He hit .252 with 73 RBI in 1988. Throughout 1989, O'Neill was among team leaders in batting, homers, RBI, and stolen bases. Although he was an all-state pitcher in high school, O'Neill has earned a starting spot in the Reds outfield.

A healthy O'Neill might duplicate the numbers of teammate Eric Davis. Dealers sell O'Neill's 1990 cards for as little as a nickel, an incredible investment possibility. Our pick for his best 1990 card is Donruss.

JOSE OQUENDO

	BA	G	AB	R	H	2B	3B	HR	RBI	SB
1989	.291	163	556	59	162	28	7	1	48	3
Life	.268	704	1910	210	511	63	9	10	158	31

Position: Second base
Team: St. Louis Cardinals
Born: July 4, 1963   Rio Peidras,
Puerto Rico
Height: 5'10"   **Weight:** 160 lbs.
Bats: Both   **Throws:** Right
Acquired: Traded from Mets with
Mark Davis for Angel Salazar and
John Young, 4/85

In his first full season as a starting player, Oquendo led the 1989 Cardinals and the National League in games played. Only Pittsburgh's Bobby Bonilla matched Oquendo's 163 appearances. He first gained the starting second baseman's job in July 1988. He set career highs in at-bats, runs, hits, doubles, triples, and RBI in 1989—tallying the second-best batting average of his six-year major league career. Oquendo was known as "the secret weapon" in St. Louis for his superb work as a utility player in 1986, his first year with the team. In 1988, he became the first Cardinal in 71 years to play all nine positions. He even pitched five innings of relief that season.

Oquendo's common-priced 1990 cards aren't good investments yet. If he has one incredible year, that status could change quickly. Our pick for his best 1990 card is Fleer.

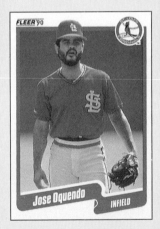

JESSE OROSCO

	W	L	ERA	G	SV	IP	H	ER	BB	SO
1989	3	4	2.08	69	3	78	54	18	26	79
Life	53	53	2.67	496	119	726	575	215	296	628

Position: Pitcher
Team: Cleveland Indians
Born: April 21, 1957   Santa Barbara, CA
Height: 6'2"   **Weight:** 185 lbs.
Bats: Right   **Throws:** Left
Acquired: Signed as a free agent, 12/88

Although he was no longer a closer, Orosco remained a valuable member of the bullpen for the 1989 Indians. A free-agent acquisition for the Tribe, he yielded his long-time closer role to Doug Jones. Instead, Orosco worked as a set-up man and middle reliever in a career-high 69 games. From 1983 to 1987, he was the bullpen star for the Mets, posting 16 or more saves each season. In 1983, he finished third in Cy Young balloting after going 13-7 with 17 saves and a 1.47 ERA. The next year, he collected 31 saves, his highest total ever. Orosco cemented New York's 1986 World Championship with three N.L.C.S. wins and two World Series saves (including the finale).

Pitching for the struggling Indians in a colorless relief role doesn't help the value of Orosco's cards. Avoid his 1990 commons. Our pick for his best 1990 card is Fleer.

JOE ORSULAK

	BA	G	AB	R	H	2B	3B	HR	RBI	SB
1989	.285	123	390	59	111	22	5	7	55	5
Life	.278	546	1645	233	458	77	22	17	126	65

Position: Outfield
Team: Baltimore Orioles
Born: May 31, 1962   Glen Ridge, NJ
Height: 6'1"   **Weight:** 185 lbs.
Bats: Left   **Throws:** Left
Acquired: Traded from Pirates for Terry Crowley and Rico Rossy, 11/87

Orsulak made the most of his limited playing time with the 1989 Orioles, driving in a career-high 55 runs. His RBI total was his best in seven major league seasons, surpassing his previous mark of 27 with the 1988 O's. He has enjoyed a new-found power stroke in his last two seasons. Before joining Baltimore, he had just three home runs in 1,127 at-bats with the Pirates (spread out over four seasons). In 1988, he stroked eight homers (including seven in a stretch of just 76 at-bats). He followed up with seven more dingers in 1989. At his New Jersey high school, Orsulak was an all-state soccer goalie.

Orsulak doesn't have the stats that could make him captivating to card collectors. His 1990 commons offer little excitement. Our pick for his best 1990 card is Score.

JOHN ORTON

	BA	G	AB	R	H	2B	3B	HR	RBI	SB
89 AA	.233	98	344	51	80	20	6	10	53	2
89 Major	.179	16	39	4	7	1	0	0	4	0

Position: Catcher
Team: California Angels
Born: December 8, 1965   Santa Cruz, CA
Height: 6'1"   **Weight:** 195 lbs.
Bats: Right   **Throws:** Right
Acquired: First-round pick in 6/87
         free-agent draft

Orton got an early chance at the limelight when Angels catcher Lance Parrish was injured in a home plate collision and backup backstop Bill Schroeder was lost to elbow surgery. Orton's rise to the majors has been a storybook climb. In his second major league start on September 25, 1989, Orton doubled, singled twice, and collected three RBI against the Royals. In his first pro season in 1987 at Salem, he batted .261 with eight homers and 36 RBI in 51 games. After a subpar offensive season in 1988 with Class-A Palm Springs, he still made the jump to the bigs the next year. Based on his success with the 1989 Angels, Orton could be in the majors to stay.

    Due to Orton's limited chance for full-time work, don't spend more than a nickel apiece on his 1990 cards. Our pick for his best 1990 card is Fleer.

SPIKE OWEN

	BA	G	AB	R	H	2B	3B	HR	RBI	SB
1989	.233	142	437	52	102	17	4	6	41	3
Life	.240	867	2847	353	682	111	36	25	253	55

Position: Shortstop
Team: Montreal Expos
Born: April 19, 1961   Cleburne, TX
Height: 5'10"   **Weight:** 170 lbs.
Bats: Both   **Throws:** Right
Acquired: Traded from Red Sox with
         Dan Gakeler for John Dopson
         and Luis Rivera, 12/88

Owen got his first taste of the N.L. when he joined the 1989 Expos. After losing the Boston shortstop job to rookie Jody Reed in 1988, Owen found happiness with Montreal, a team happy to get a veteran infielder with defensive skills. While he has never been an offensive powerhouse, he did tie his career high of six homers with Montreal. After being a first-round pick by the 1982 Mariners and playing a half-season at Double-A in 1983, the Mariners made Owen a major league starter. His greatest offensive success came in 1986 with the Red Sox. He batted .429 with nine hits in the A.L.C.S., then hit .300 in the World Series.

    Owen has passable lifetime statistics for a shortstop, but he's far from stardom. His 1990 commons have little profit potential. Our pick for his best 1990 card is Fleer.

MIKE PAGLIARULO

	BA	G	AB	R	H	2B	3B	HR	RBI	SB
89 NL	.196	50	148	12	29	7	0	3	14	2
Life	.230	679	2199	284	506	108	12	104	335	8

Position: Third base
Team: San Diego Padres
Born: March 15, 1960 Medford, MA
Height: 6'2" **Weight:** 195 lbs.
Bats: Left **Throws:** Right
Acquired: Traded from Yankees for
    Walt Terrell, 8/89

Pagliarulo, after watching his batting average erode for yet another season, found it hard to keep a starting job in 1989. The Yankees ended his four-year reign at third base by trading him to the Padres after the All-Star break. He had managed just four homers and 16 RBI in 74 games, and his batting average hung at .197. His luck was unchanged with San Diego, where his batting average remained under .200. He platooned at third with Bip Roberts. "Pags" had two notable offensive seasons with New York. In 1986, he hit 28 homers and 71 RBI. He increased those totals to 32 homers and 87 RBI the next year. But in 1988, Pagliarulo batted a paltry .216.

Pagliarulo may see his last chance in 1990. With his roster spot in jeopardy, his 1990 commons are poor investments. Our pick for his best 1990 card is Score.

DONN PALL

	W	L	ERA	G	SV	IP	H	ER	BB	SO
1989	4	5	3.31	53	6	87	90	32	19	58
Life	4	7	3.37	70	6	115	129	43	27	74

Position: Pitcher
Team: Chicago White Sox
Born: January 11, 1962 Chicago, IL
Height: 6'1" **Weight:** 180 lbs.
Bats: Right **Throws:** Right
Acquired: 23rd-round pick in 6/85
    free-agent draft

In 1989, his first full major league season, Pall emerged as a top righthanded reliever for the White Sox. He kept his ERA under 3.00 until September. His appearances and saves were second on the team behind ChiSox stopper Bobby Thigpen. In 17 appearances for the White Sox in 1988, Pall was 0-2 but had a 3.45 ERA. The White Sox promoted him after an accomplished 1988 season at Triple-A Vancouver. His ten saves earned him an appearance in the first Triple-A All-Star Game. During his first three pro seasons, he worked mostly as a starter. In 1987, Pall notched eight wins, three complete games, and a team-leading 139 strikeouts in 23 starts in Double-A.

A leading reliever for the 1989 ChiSox, Pall has a bright future with the Pale Hose. Buy his 1990 cards at 15 cents or less. Our pick for his best 1990 card is Donruss.

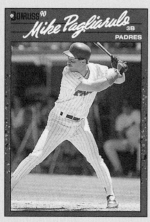
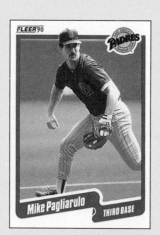
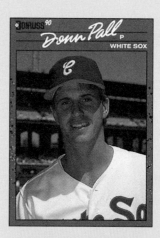

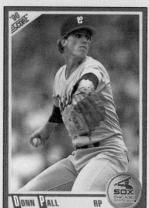

RAFAEL PALMEIRO

	BA	G	AB	R	H	2B	3B	HR	RBI	SB
1989	.275	156	559	76	154	23	4	8	64	4
Life	.287	414	1433	192	411	83	10	33	159	19

Position: First base
Team: Texas Rangers
Born: September 24, 1964   Havana, Cuba
Height: 6'   **Weight:** 180 lbs.
Bats: Left   **Throws:** Left
Acquired: Traded from Cubs with Jamie
Moyer and Drew Hall for Paul
Kilgus, Curtis Wilkerson, Mitch
Williams, Steve Wilson, Luis
Benitez, and Pablo Delgado,
12/88

In his first full season in the A.L., Palmeiro was a solid addition to the 1989 Rangers. He was given the Texas first baseman's job before the 1989 season, and he was one of the top RBI men on the club. Palmeiro spent just two seasons in the minors before making the jump in 1986 from Double-A (where he was the Eastern League MVP) to the Cubs. In 1987, he hit .276 with 14 homers and 30 RBI in just 84 games. He missed out on his first batting title by six points in 1988, hitting .307. Palmeiro was a three-time All-American at Mississippi State, where his teammates included Will Clark and Bobby Thigpen.

After a year's adjustment to a new league, Palmeiro could match his 1988 success. Buy his 1990 cards at a dime for your best investment chances. Our pick for his best 1990 card is Fleer.

DEAN PALMER

	BA	G	AB	R	H	2B	3B	HR	RBI	SB
89 AA	.296	133	498	82	125	31	5	25	90	15
89 Major	.105	16	19	0	2	2	0	0	1	0

Position: Third base
Team: Texas Rangers
Born: December 27, 1968   Tallahassee, FL
Height: 6'1"   **Weight:** 175 lbs.
Bats: Right   **Throws:** Right
Acquired: Third-round pick in 6/86
free-agent draft

Unlike most rookies, Palmer earned his major league debut in 1989 without serving time in Triple-A. He catapulted from Double-A Tulsa to the Rangers in late 1989. He sparked the Drillers with career highs in home runs and RBI. He hit homers in five consecutive games that year. Additionally, a *Baseball America* poll ranked Palmer as the best defensive third baseman in the Texas League. In 1988, he batted a career-high .266 with Class-A Port Charlotte, earning a spot in the Florida State League All-Star Game. Palmer's season was limited to 74 games, due to the discovery of bone chips in his wrist.

After an inconclusive debut with the 1989 Rangers, Palmer's future seems unpredictable. Play it safe and pay a nickel or less for his 1990 cards. Our pick for his best 1990 card is Donruss.

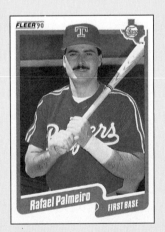

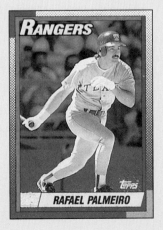

MARK PARENT

	BA	G	AB	R	H	2B	3B	HR	RBI	SB
1989	.191	52	141	12	27	4	0	7	21	1
Life	.181	113	298	22	54	7	0	13	29	1

Position: Catcher
Team: San Diego Padres
Born: September 16, 1961
Ashland, OR
Height: 6'5" **Weight:** 225 lbs.
Bats: Right **Throws:** Right
Acquired: Fourth-round pick in 6/79
free-agent draft

Parent worked as San Diego's second-string catcher for a second straight season in 1989. Active in professional baseball since 1979, he spent his first nine seasons in the minors, getting only the briefest call-ups with the Padres in 1986 and 1987. San Diego gave him a sufficient chance in 1988, using him in 41 games. He responded by hitting six homers and 15 RBI in just 118 at-bats. Three of those homers came in the last week of September. Parent has his work on the Padres cut out for him, considering that Benito Santiago and Sandy Alomar are two of the most highly regarded young backstops in the business.

Parent is a capable backup catcher, but his 1990 commons are questionable investments. If he wins a starting job somewhere, then they are potential buys. Our pick for his best 1990 card is Score.

CLAY PARKER

	W	L	ERA	G	CG	IP	H	ER	BB	SO
89 AAA	3	0	1.66	5	1	38	25	7	10	25
89 Major	4	5	3.68	22	2	120	123	49	31	53

Position: Pitcher
Team: New York Yankees
Born: December 19, 1962
Columbia, LA
Height: 6'1" **Weight:** 185 lbs.
Bats: Right **Throws:** Right
Acquired: Traded from Mariners with
Lee Guetterman and Wade
Taylor for Steve Trout and
Henry Cotto, 12/87

After beginning the 1989 season with Triple-A Columbus, Parker gained a position in the Yankees starting rotation. New York made him a nonroster invitee to 1989 spring training, in respect for his 1988 success at Columbus. He struck out 51 batters in 50 innings, giving up only nine walks that year. Parker began his pro career in 1985 after being drafted in the 15th round by the Mariners. In 1987 at Triple-A Calgary, he was 8-1 in 12 starts. Prior to the 1989 season, he had a cumulative 31-16 minor league record. Parker was a noted punter during his three-year college career at Louisiana State, refusing a deal with the Dallas Cowboys before signing a baseball contract.

Being a Yankee helps Parker get sizable attention. His 1990 issues will be enticing buys at 15 cents or less. Our pick for his best 1990 card is Donruss.

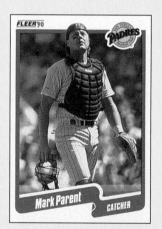
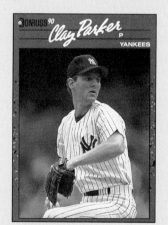
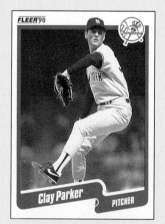

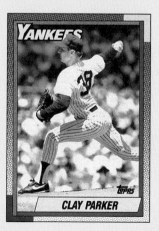

DAVE PARKER

	BA	G	AB	R	H	2B	3B	HR	RBI	SB
1989	.264	144	553	56	146	27	0	22	97	0
Life	.293	2177	8246	1154	2416	470	70	307	1242	147

Position: Outfield; designated hitter
Team: Oakland Athletics
Born: June 9, 1951 Jackson, MS
Height: 6'5" **Weight:** 230 lbs.
Bats: Left **Throws:** Right
Acquired: Traded from Reds for Jose
  Rijo and Tim Birtsas, 12/87

Parker mounted a comeback with the 1989 Athletics, helping the team to win a World Championship. His average ranked fourth on Oakland, while his homers were second. Parker's RBI total topped the Oakland offense and matched his number with the 1987 Reds. He surpassed the 90-RBI mark for the ninth time in his career. His round-trippers marked the eighth occasion he's exceeded 20 homers. His lifetime highs came with the 1985 Reds, when he tallied 34 homers and 125 RBI. The six-time All-Star debuted with the Pirates in 1973. Parker's legendary power should make him a popular free agent in the off-season.

Parker has a couple of seasons left. His 1990 cards, which will sell for 15 cents each, will generate few short-term profits. They'll appreciate if he gets a shot at the Hall of Fame. Our pick for his best 1990 card is Score.

JEFF PARRETT

	W	L	ERA	G	SV	IP	H	ER	BB	SO
1989	12	6	2.98	72	6	105	90	35	44	98
Life	31	17	3.29	190	18	279	228	102	132	237

Position: Pitcher
Team: Philadelphia Phillies
Born: August 26, 1961
  Indianapolis, IN
Height: 6'3" **Weight:** 200 lbs.
Bats: Right **Throws:** Right
Acquired: Traded from Expos with
  Floyd Youmans for Kevin
  Gross, 12/88

Parrett posted his second consecutive year of 12 wins in 1989, tying for the team lead on the Phillies. This third season of his major league career saw a number of to-date highs for him, including most games (72), innings (105), and strikeouts (98). For the third year running, he claimed six saves. He's struck out four consecutive batters on two occasions. He debuted with the Expos in 1986. He was at Triple-A Indianapolis before returning to Montreal in mid-1987. His 12-4, six-save 1988 campaign was curtailed by almost a month when he sliced open his finger on a bunt. Parrett won 12 games for a last-place team, and he may work wonders if the Phillies offense improves.

Parrett's 1990 cards will sell as commons. Relievers' cards seldom enjoy rapid price climbs, so investors should proceed with caution. Our pick for his best 1990 card is Topps.

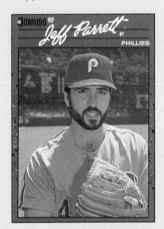

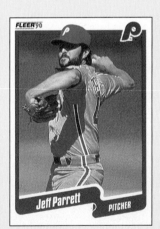

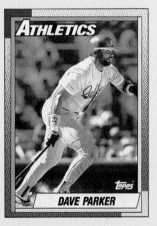

LANCE PARRISH

	BA	G	AB	R	H	2B	3B	HR	RBI	SB
1989	.238	124	433	48	103	12	1	17	50	1
Life	.256	1523	5596	711	1431	251	26	261	877	23

Position: Catcher
Team: California Angels
Born: June 15, 1956 Clairton, PA
Height: 6'3" **Weight:** 220 lbs.
Bats: Right **Throws:** Right
Acquired: Traded from Phillies for
David Holdridge, 10/88

Parrish continued his hard-hitting ways for the 1989 Angels. While he didn't have the healthiest batting average (.238), he hit 17 homers, third-highest on the Halos. His round-trippers marked the 12th straight year he's topped ten home runs. He exceeded 20 homers six times with Detroit, where he played from 1977 to 1986. Parrish's season high was 33, for the 1984 World Champions. A six-time All-Star, he began his professional career in 1974 and played in four minor league campaigns before reaching the majors in 1977. When he chose to sign with Detroit as a first-round pick in 1974, Parrish gave up a football scholarship to UCLA.

Parrish is on the downside of a distinguished career. He may not contend for the Hall of Fame, but his 1990 cards will be a decent buy at 3 cents or less. Our pick for his best 1990 card is Score.

DAN PASQUA

	BA	G	AB	R	H	2B	3B	HR	RBI	SB
1989	.248	73	246	26	61	9	1	11	47	1
Life	.243	477	1414	177	344	52	5	73	209	4

Position: Outfield; first base
Team: Chicago White Sox
Born: October 17, 1961 Yonkers, NY
Height: 6' **Weight:** 205 lbs.
Bats: Left **Throws:** Left
Acquired: Traded from the Yankees with
Mark Salas and Steve Rosenberg
for Richard Dotson and Scott
Nielsen, 11/87

Pasqua spent the last five weeks of 1989 benched with an injured knee. With his number of appearances cut almost in half from 1988, it's not surprising his power stats suffered, with only nine doubles and 11 homers, compared to 16 and 20 in 1988. It still was a good season overall for Pasqua, who raised his batting average from .227 to .259. These marks are closer to what he customarily achieved in the minors. With Triple-A Nashville in 1984, he racked up a league-best 33 homers. The following year, Pasqua's batting average peaked at .321, good enough to earn a call-up to the Yankees for 60 games.

Don't expect long-term gains from Pasqua's 1990 commons. But those investors who are willing to sell as soon as he has an All-Star season could make some profits. Our pick for his best 1990 card is Fleer.

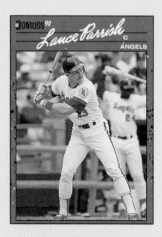

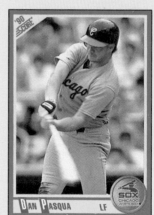

KEN PATTERSON

	W	L	ERA	G	SV	IP	H	ER	BB	SO
1989	6	1	4.52	50	0	65	64	33	28	43
Life	6	3	4.60	59	1	86	89	44	35	51

Position: Pitcher
Team: Chicago White Sox
Born: July 8, 1964   Costa Mesa, CA
Height: 6'4"   **Weight:** 210 lbs.
Bats: Left   **Throws:** Left
Acquired: Traded from Yankees with
Jeff Pries for Jerry Royster and
Mike Soper, 8/87

Patterson was one of the busiest members of the ChiSox pitching staff in 1989. He was only one of four White Sox pitchers to hurl in more than 40 games. Despite Chicago's losing record, he had one of the best win-loss ratios on the club. Hard work is nothing new to Patterson. He appeared in a career high of 55 games for Triple-A Vancouver in 1988, notching six wins and 12 saves. His conversion from the starting rotation to the bullpen came in early 1987. He began his pro career as a third-round selection by the Yankees in the 1985 free-agent draft. Patterson should help provide the White Sox with ample relief in 1990.

Patterson has to work harder for fame, due to his middle relief chores. His nickel-priced 1990 cards are borderline investments. Our pick for his best 1990 card is Score.

ALEJANDRO PENA

	W	L	ERA	G	SV	IP	H	ER	BB	SO
1989	4	3	2.13	53	5	76	62	18	18	75
Life	38	38	2.93	281	32	769	693	250	244	571

Position: Pitcher
Team: Los Angeles Dodgers
Born: June 25, 1959   Puerto Plata,
Dominican Republic
Height: 6'1"   **Weight:** 203 lbs.
Bats: Right   **Throws:** Right
Acquired: Signed as a free agent, 10/78

Pena backed up Jay Howell in the Los Angeles Dodgers' bullpen in 1989, ranking only behind Howell in games, ERA, saves, and games finished (28). Pena had the second-lowest ERA of his career, with 1988's 1.91 ERA being his major league-best. He has been a Dodgers bullpen stalwart for all but two years of his time in Los Angeles. In 1983 and 1984, he moved to the starting rotation and won 12 games each year. As a reliever, his season high for saves was 12 in 1988. Pena earned his 1981 debut in the majors with a career-high performance of 22 saves at Triple-A Albuquerque.

Pena doesn't have the lifetime wins or saves to make him a star reliever. In Howell's shadow, Pena has little chance of immediate stardom, which makes his 1990 commons unsavory investments. Our pick for his best 1990 card is Topps.

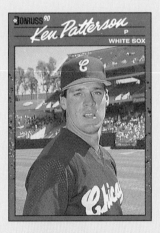

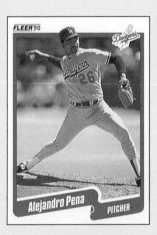

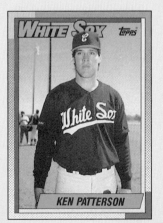

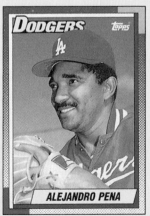

TONY PENA

	BA	G	AB	R	H	2B	3B	HR	RBI	SB
1989	.259	141	424	36	110	17	2	4	37	5
Life	.274	1207	4185	438	1146	193	22	82	472	59

Position: Catcher
Team: Boston Red Sox
Born: June 4, 1957 Monte Cristi,
Dominican Republic
Height: 6' **Weight:** 185 lbs.
Bats: Right **Throws:** Right
Acquired: Signed as a free agent, 11/89

Boston signed Pena to help remedy one of the team's long-standing flaws. He had held the starting backstop job with the Cardinals for the past two seasons. Nevertheless, Todd Zeile was starting by the season's end. Pena wasn't driving in enough runs to satisfy Cardinal management. But with the Red Sox offense, his production should be adequate. The four-time All-Star had his best year in St. Louis in 1988, when he hit .263 with ten homers and 51 RBI. He played in Pittsburgh from 1980 to '86. In 1984, he swatted 15 homers and 78 RBI. Pena batted .381 in the 1987 N.L.C.S. and .409 in the World Series during his only postseason experience.

Regardless of his defense, Pena has never hit forcefully enough to become immortal. His nickel-priced 1990 cards are unremarkable investments. Our pick for his best 1990 card is Donruss.

TERRY PENDLETON

	BA	G	AB	R	H	2B	3B	HR	RBI	SB
1989	.264	162	613	83	162	28	5	13	74	9
Life	.263	806	2986	358	785	135	22	38	384	92

Position: Third base
Team: St. Louis Cardinals
Born: July 16, 1960 Los Angeles, CA
Height: 5'9" **Weight:** 185 lbs.
Bats: Both **Throws:** Right
Acquired: Seventh-round pick in 6/82
free-agent draft

Pendleton's biggest accomplishment was staying healthy in 1989. He played in 162 games, setting career highs in games played, at-bats, doubles, triples, homers, and runs scored. Best of all, he seemed recovered from his 1988 injuries, which included a sore shoulder, a pulled hamstring, and torn cartilage in his knee. The Cardinals have felt that Pendleton would always hit if he could stay in the lineup. In 1987, he blossomed at the plate, hitting .286 with 12 homers and 96 RBI. He won his first Gold Glove award that year at third base. When Pendleton hit .324 in his 67-game debut in 1984, everyone knew that he was in the majors to stay.

Pendleton's penchant for injury is his only shortcoming. He needs another big offensive season before the hobby will be excited about his 1990 commons. Our pick for his best 1990 card is Donruss.

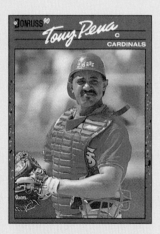

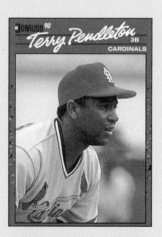

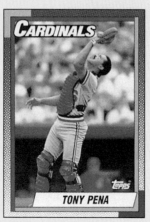

MELIDO PEREZ

	W	L	ERA	G	CG	IP	H	ER	BB	SO
1989	11	14	5.01	31	2	183	187	102	90	141
Life	24	25	4.48	66	5	390	391	194	167	284

Position: Pitcher
Team: Chicago White Sox
Born: February 15, 1966 San Cristobal,
          Dominican Republic
Height: 6'4" **Weight:** 180 lbs.
Bats: Right **Throws:** Right
Acquired: Traded from Royals with John
          Davis, Chuck Mount, and Greg
          Hibbard for Floyd Bannister and
          Dave Cochrane, 12/87

In 1988, Perez hit the majors running. Notching a 12-10 record, he also displayed remarkable stamina for a rookie. In 32 starts in 1988, he totaled 197 innings and 132 strike-outs, both of these Sox bests. In 1989, his 11-14 record still led his team. He topped the team in starts, innings pitched, and strikeouts. As a Sox rookie, he was the only starter on the staff to earn more than one complete game. Perhaps it's no surprise he has a knowledge of his craft that exceeds most youngsters. His older brother, Pascual, is a major league pitcher. In 1988, the Perez brothers led all major league siblings with a combined 24 wins.

Perez could be a major winner with some offensive support. His lifetime mark with the White Sox is misleading. Make a minor investment in his 1990 commons. Our pick for his best 1990 card is Fleer.

PASCUAL PEREZ

	W	L	ERA	G	CG	IP	H	ER	BB	SO
1989	9	13	3.31	33	2	198	178	73	45	152
Life	64	62	3.48	190	21	1156	1091	447	317	769

Position: Pitcher
Team: New York Yankees
Born: May 17, 1957 Haina,
          Dominican Republic
Height: 6'3" **Weight:** 175 lbs.
Bats: Right **Throws:** Right
Acquired: Signed as a free agent, 11/89

Perez struck it rich in the post-1989 free-agent sweep-stakes. He slumped for the 1989 Expos. After winning 12 games in 1988 (including a rain-shortened no-hitter), he endured a losing record for only the third time in his career. He's won in double figures three times in his career. In addition to throwing a normal selection of pitches, he throws the "Pascual Pitch," his own version of the blooper pitch. In a noted incident, in 1982 Perez had just received his first driver's license one morning and missed a start that day because he got lost coming to Atlanta's stadium.

It's unlikely, but if Perez repeats his early 1980s success with Atlanta (15 and 14 wins in two seasons) and leads the Yankees to a pennant, investors could gain large profits from his 1990 commons. Our pick for his best 1990 card is Topps.

GERALD PERRY

	BA	G	AB	R	H	2B	3B	HR	RBI	SB
1989	.252	72	266	24	67	11	0	4	21	10
Life	.270	643	2040	247	551	96	0	37	246	105

Position: Outfield; first base
Team: Atlanta Braves
Born: October 30, 1960 Savannah, GA
Height: 6' **Weight:** 190 lbs.
Bats: Left **Throws:** Right
Acquired: 11th-round pick in 6/78
    free-agent draft

Just when it seemed that Perry could be reaching stardom, a separated shoulder ended his 1989 season on July 10. The injury limited Perry to just 72 games, his lowest total since 1986. The Georgia native landed his first All-Star appearance in 1988, as a first baseman, when he batted a career-high .300 in 141 games. For two months, he led (or tied for) the National League batting lead before ending the year fifth in the race for the crown. In 1987, he hit .270, but he had career highs of 74 RBI and 42 steals. With Nick Esasky now a Brave, Perry will probably have to move to the outfield to find a starting spot in Atlanta.

Perry needs to get healthy before the hobby will even consider buying his cards. For now, his 1990 commons aren't promising investments. Our pick for his best 1990 card is Donruss.

GENO PETRALLI

	BA	G	AB	R	H	2B	3B	HR	RBI	SB
1989	.304	70	184	18	56	7	0	4	23	0
Life	.287	436	1025	108	294	45	7	20	120	5

Position: Catcher
Team: Texas Rangers
Born: September 25, 1959
    Sacramento, CA
Height: 6'1" **Weight:** 180 lbs.
Bats: Left **Throws:** Right
Acquired: Signed as a free agent, 5/85

Registering a career-best .304 batting average in 1989, Petralli cemented his position as the first Rangers catcher ever to bat .300. He first accomplished the feat in 1987. That year was his third on Texas and his sixth in the majors. Beginning in 1982, he was called up for partial seasons by the Jays. While doing well in the minors throughout, even being selected as the Triple-A International League's All-Star catcher before his 1983 call-up, Petralli seldom stayed in the bigs for more than six games. His first major league season came with the Rangers in 1986. In 1988, Petralli set career highs in doubles (14) and homers (seven) while playing in a career-high 129 games.

Petralli will remain a second-stringer in 1990. Cards of substitutes don't make good investments, so skip his 1990 commons. Our pick for his best 1990 card is Fleer.

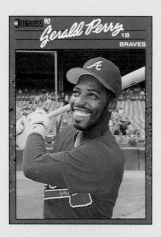
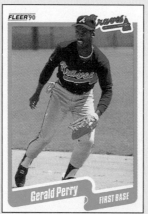

GARY PETTIS

	BA	G	AB	R	H	2B	3B	HR	RBI	SB
1989	.257	119	444	77	114	8	6	1	18	43
Life	.239	832	2765	438	661	81	33	17	197	273

Position: Outfield
Team: Texas Rangers
Born: April 3, 1958 Oakland, CA
Height: 6'1" **Weight:** 160 lbs.
Bats: Both **Throws:** Right
Acquired: Signed as a free agent,
          11/88

The Rangers signed Pettis for defense and speed. A sprained thumb limited him to just 119 games with the 1989 Detroit Tigers. The multiple Gold Glove winner provided the Tigers with significant outfield defense. His speed was a rare treat to Detroit's lead-footed lineup. But his offense is still a question mark. His .257 average was a dramatic improvement from 1988's .210 mark. But the Tigers were ready to give up on him in mid-1989. He has hit well in the past, as evidenced by his .346 average in the 1986 A.L.C.S. for the Angels. Pettis's best-ever marks of a .258 average, five homers, and 58 RBI came that year.

Pettis doesn't have the consistent offensive marks to make him a star. Until he hits with meaning, forget his 1990 commons. Our pick for his best 1990 card is Score.

KEN PHELPS

	BA	G	AB	R	H	2B	3B	HR	RBI	SB
1989	.242	97	194	26	47	4	0	7	29	0
Life	.245	705	1734	298	425	62	7	122	307	9

Position: Designated hitter
Team: Oakland Athletics
Born: August 6, 1954 Seattle, WA
Height: 6'1" **Weight:** 200 lbs.
Bats: Left **Throws:** Left
Acquired: Traded from Yankees for
          Scott Holcomb, 8/89

The Oakland Athletics guaranteed their 1989 pennant by making a late-season trade for Phelps. Although the A's didn't start him, they valued his pinch-hitting talents. If anyone can produce a homer on demand, he is a good bet. He debuted with the 1980 Royals. Going into 1989, he had a lifetime homer ratio of one for every 12.5 at-bats versus righthanders, the highest rate in the last 14 seasons. He slumped a bit from his 1988 accomplishments, when he slammed 23 homers as a designated hitter for the Mariners and Yankees, the league's second-highest for a DH. Phelps tallied a career high of 27 homers and 68 RBI with the 1987 Mariners.

Phelps will continue to work mostly as a pinch-hitter. Such limited work won't enhance the value of his common-priced 1990 cards. Our pick for his best 1990 card is Donruss.

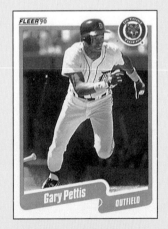
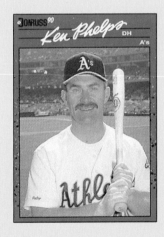

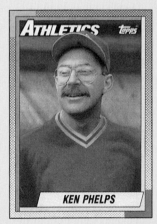

TONY PHILLIPS

	BA	G	AB	R	H	2B	3B	HR	RBI	SB
1989	.262	143	451	48	118	15	6	4	47	3
Life	.251	835	2588	354	649	107	25	33	259	56

Position: Second base
Team: Oakland Athletics
Born: April 25, 1959   Atlanta, GA
Height: 5'10"   **Weight:** 175 lbs.
Bats: Both   **Throws:** Right
Acquired: Traded from Padres with Kevin
　　　　Bell and Eric Mustard for Bob
　　　　Lacey and Roy Moretti, 3/81

For the first time since joining the Athletics in 1982, Phillips earned a spot in the starting lineup, at second base, and stayed there all season. In 1988 as the A's top utility player, he played every position save pitcher and catcher, even though injury caused him to sit out a good portion of the season. By 1989, his severely bruised leg was healed, and his 143 appearances were his most since 1984. All of his stats displayed improvements over his four seasons of part-time work, when repeated injuries forced rehabilitation assignments to the minors. Phillips learned versatility in high school, lettering in basketball, football, track, cross country, and baseball.

　Because of his lack of playing time, Phillips hasn't accumulated wondrous lifetime stats. Give him another year as a starter before considering his 1990 commons as investments. Our pick for his best 1990 card is Fleer.

JEFF PICO

	W	L	ERA	G	SV	IP	H	ER	BB	SO
1989	3	1	3.77	53	2	90	99	38	31	38
Life	9	8	3.99	82	3	203	207	90	68	95

Position: Pitcher
Team: Chicago Cubs
Born: February 12, 1966   Antioch, CA
Height: 6'2"   **Weight:** 170 lbs.
Bats: Right   **Throws:** Right
Acquired: 13th-round pick in 6/84
　　　　free-agent draft

Pico found better fortune as a full-time reliever with the 1989 Cubs. His 1988 rookie season was divided between the bullpen and starting rotation. Although he was 6-7 with two shutouts and three complete games, he had a fat 4.15 ERA. In 1989, he started just five out of 53 games. Pico's ERA dropped to 3.77, and his record was a tidy 3-1 with two saves. Relief is a new task for him. In 115 games during a five-year minor league career, he relieved in just two contests. When he tossed a scoreless four-hitter on May 31, 1988, Pico became the 37th pitcher in N.L. history to hurl a complete-game shutout in his major league debut.

　Wait a year before investing anything in Pico's nickel-priced 1990 cards. If he returns to starting, he'll have more investment-friendly cards. Our pick for his best 1990 card is Donruss.

DAN PLESAC

	W	L	ERA	G	SV	IP	H	ER	BB	SO
1989	3	4	2.35	52	33	61	47	16	17	52
Life	19	19	2.63	210	100	284	237	83	81	268

Position: Pitcher
Team: Milwaukee Brewers
Born: February 4, 1962 Gary, IN
Height: 6'5" **Weight:** 210 lbs.
Bats: Left **Throws:** Left
Acquired: First-round pick in 6/83
free-agent draft

Plesac was the Brewers only representative on the 1989 All-Star team. He led Milwaukee in ERA in 1989, keeping his earned run average below 3.00 for the third straight year. The former All-American suffered from injuries during both 1987 and 1988, but he posted incredible marks regardless. The 1988 season saw him striking out 52 batters in 52 innings 1/3, walking only 12. He reached 30 saves for the first time that season, all with only a fastball and slider, both clocking at well over 90 mph. He eventually may better his changeup. But for now, he intimidates batters with his power. Voted as an All-Star after his 1986 rookie season, Plesac has become a perennial choice for the game.

Plesac's 1990 cards will cost about a nickel apiece. That's a reasonable price for one of the A.L.'s top relief men. Our pick for his best 1990 card is Score.

ERIC PLUNK

	W	L	ERA	G	SV	IP	H	ER	BB	SO
1989	8	6	3.28	50	1	104	82	38	64	85
Life	23	21	4.19	157	8	397	326	185	267	352

Position: Pitcher
Team: New York Yankees
Born: September 3, 1963 Wilmington, CA
Height: 6'5" **Weight:** 210 lbs.
Bats: Right **Throws:** Right
Acquired: Traded from A's with Luis Polonia
and Greg Cadaret for Rickey
Henderson, 6/89

In his second full year in the majors (and first with the New York Yankees), Plunk notched another winning season. Though appearing in the same number of games in 1988 and '89, he increased his innings from 78 to 104. The extra work came once he proved he had conquered his 1988 bout with tendinitis. The tall righty became a reliever with the 1986 A's. After coming up through the New York Yankees' farm system, he was one of the five players traded to Oakland for Rickey Henderson. A near-instant replay ensued when Plunk and Henderson were returned to their original organizations in 1989.

Plunk's cards will never gain value if he remains a middle reliever and spot starter. Don't put any money into his 1990 commons, unless the Yankees make him a full-time starter or closer. Our pick for his best 1990 card is Topps.

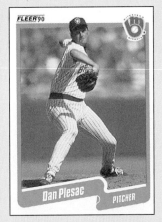
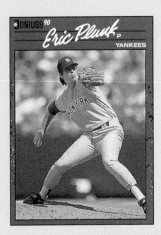

LUIS POLONIA

	BA	G	AB	R	H	2B	3B	HR	RBI	SB
1989	.300	125	433	70	130	17	6	3	46	22
Life	.293	334	1156	199	339	44	20	9	122	75

Position: Outfield
Team: New York Yankees
Born: October 12, 1964   Santiago City,
   Dominican Republic
Height: 5'8"   **Weight:** 155 lbs.
Bats: Left   **Throws:** Left
Acquired: Traded from A's with Greg
   Cadaret and Eric Plunk for
   Rickey Henderson, 6/89

Polonia's first season with the Yankees in 1989 was the best yet of his three stints in the bigs. His career-high .300 batting average ranked fourth among Yankees' regulars. Even so, his first two partial campaigns with Oakland were anything but inadequate. In 1987 with the A's, he batted .287 in 125 games. His ten triples were the second-best single-season total in Oakland history. He divided 1988 between Triple-A Tacoma and the A's. After a .292 effort in 84 games, he batted .400 in the American League Championship Series. Polonia's batting skills are obscured by his reputation as a defensive liability, which includes erratic throws from the outfield.

With Polonia's poor reputation in the outfield and team owner George Steinbrenner's lack of regard for him, he'll be sent packing. See where he lands before considering his 1990 commons. Our pick for his best 1990 card is Topps.

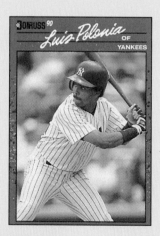

MARK PORTUGAL

	W	L	ERA	G	CG	IP	H	ER	BB	SO
1989	7	1	2.75	20	2	108	91	33	37	86
Life	18	19	4.40	92	5	346	345	169	142	224

Position: Pitcher
Team: Houston Astros
Born: October 30, 1962   Los Angeles, CA
Height: 6'   **Weight:** 200 lbs.
Bats: Right   **Throws:** Right
Acquired: Traded from Twins for
   Todd McClure, 12/88

Portugal got his first chance to pitch in the National League in 1989, and responded with a career-best 7-1 record for the Houston Astros. Among his seven victories (in 15 starts and five relief appearances) were two complete games and a shutout. He earned a chance with the Astros via a 7-5 record with a 3.78 ERA and five complete games at Triple-A Tucson in 1989. His best mark in the majors had come with the 1986 Minnesota Twins, a 6-10 record in 27 games. He spent parts of seasons with the Twins from 1985 to '88, pitching in 72 games. One of Portugal's most memorable outings with Minnesota came on September 21, 1986, when he fanned 13 Texas Rangers.

Portugal has mediocre lifetime statistics. See if he can remain in the majors for an entire season before buying his 1990 commons. Our pick for his best 1990 card is Score.

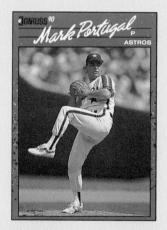

DENNIS POWELL

	W	L	ERA	G	SV	IP	H	ER	BB	SO
1989	2	2	5.00	43	2	45	49	25	21	27
Life	7	16	4.82	114	3	192	205	103	85	109

Position: Pitcher
Team: Seattle Mariners
Born: August 13, 1963   Moultrie, GA
Height: 6'3"   **Weight:** 200 lbs.
Bats: Right   **Throws:** Left
Acquired: Traded from Dodgers with Mike
　　　　　Watters for Matt Young, 12/86

The Seattle Mariners tested Powell as a reliever in 1989, using him in more games—though not necessarily in more innings—than in his four earlier half-seasons. Repeating the pattern that began in 1985 when he was first called up to the Los Angeles Dodgers, he split the 1989 season between the majors and minors. Powell posted a respectable 3-2 record with a 2.84 ERA in 18 games with Triple-A Calgary in 1989. Unfortunately, his success didn't translate to the majors. His 5.00 ERA was his lowest in his many major league trials, not a big achievement. The Mariners would love a hard-throwing lefty on the roster in 1990, but Powell is running out of chances to fill that spot.

Powell's 1990 commons are poor investments. He's had ample opportunities to succeed and hasn't cashed in yet. Our pick for his best 1990 card is Fleer.

TED POWER

	W	L	ERA	G	SV	IP	H	ER	BB	SO
1989	7	7	3.71	23	0	97	96	40	21	43
Life	57	56	4.15	347	41	876	877	404	352	530

Position: Pitcher
Team: Pittsburgh Pirates
Born: January 31, 1955   Guthrie, OK
Height: 6'4"   **Weight:** 220 lbs.
Bats: Right   **Throws:** Right
Acquired: Signed as a free agent, 11/89

Power signed with the Pirates as a swing man. He won seven games as a spot starter with the 1989 Cardinals. His presence benefited the Cardinals, which lost two starters to season-long injuries in spring training. Once a feared reliever with Cincinnati from 1983 to 1987, he led the league with 78 appearances in 1984, registering a 9-7 mark with 11 saves. The next year, he became the Reds closer with 27 saves (third-best in the N.L.) and eight wins. He earned a career-high ten wins both in 1986 and 1987. Power figured in the trade that sent pitcher Danny Jackson to Cincinnati in 1988. The Tigers obtained Power for the last month of the '88 season.

Power seems near the end of a long, checkered career. He'd need some incredible success to stimulate interest in his 1990 commons. Our pick for his best 1990 card is Fleer.

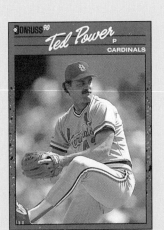

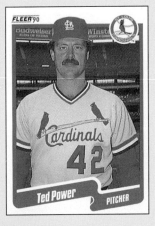

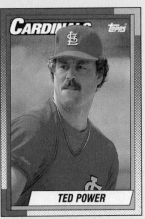

JIM PRESLEY

	BA	G	AB	R	H	2B	3B	HR	RBI	SB
1989	.236	117	390	42	92	20	1	12	41	0
Life	.250	799	2946	351	736	147	13	115	418	8

Position: Third base
Team: Seattle Mariners
Born: October 23, 1961   Pensacola, FL
Height: 6'1"   **Weight:** 190 lbs.
Bats: Right   **Throws:** Right
Acquired: Fourth-round pick in 6/79
         free-agent draft

Presley, once a bright hope for the Seattle Mariners, has been suffering through a three-year plague. He hit .275 with 28 homers in 1985, and complemented that with 27 homers, a career-best 104 RBI, and a .265 average in 1986. Such success seems like a thing of the past for him. His average has fallen into the .230s for 1988 and 1989. His once-healthy homer total withered to 14 in 1988 and 12 in '89. The impatient hitter has maintained his yearly strikeout totals. He has whiffed 720 times in the last five seasons. Presley has been in pro baseball since 1979 and has been a Mariner since mid-1984.

The M's have all but given up on Presley. Expect Darnell Coles and Edgar Martinez to share the M's third base job in 1990. Presley should wind up elsewhere, further devaluing his 1990 commons. Our pick for his best 1990 card is Fleer.

JOE PRICE

	W	L	ERA	G	SV	IP	H	ER	BB	SO
1989	2	5	4.35	31	0	70	71	34	30	52
Life	41	44	3.62	315	13	826	761	332	309	593

Position: Pitcher
Team: Boston Red Sox
Born: November 29, 1956   Inglewood, CA
Height: 6'4"   **Weight:** 215 lbs.
Bats: Right   **Throws:** Left
Acquired: Signed as a free agent, 5/89

After just seven games with the 1989 Giants, Price was cut loose. His ERA and his constant arm problems made him expendable. Boston grabbed him, hoping he could last one more season as a middle reliever. His shining moment with the Giants came in the fifth game of the 1987 National League Championship Series. He threw five innings of scoreless, one-hit relief to gain the win. Price began his pro career in 1977, and first reached the Reds in 1980. He remained with the team through 1986, working as a starter for three of his six seasons. In relief, he pitched in a career-high 59 games in 1982. As a starter, Price was 10-6 in 1983.

Price's fragile left arm may not last much longer. His common-priced 1990 cards are not good investments, considering his so-so lifetime totals. Our pick for his best 1990 card is Fleer.

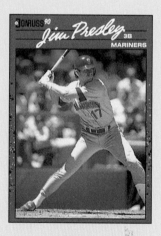

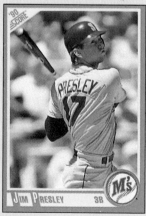

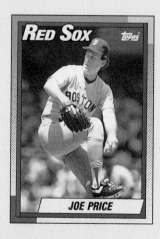

KIRBY PUCKETT

	BA	G	AB	R	H	2B	3B	HR	RBI	SB
1989	.339	159	635	75	215	45	4	9	85	11
Life	.323	924	3844	542	1243	197	38	96	506	84

Position: Outfield
Team: Minnesota Twins
Born: March 14, 1961   Chicago, IL
Height: 5'8"   **Weight:** 210 lbs.
Bats: Right   **Throws:** Right
Acquired: First-round pick in 1/82
　　　　　　free-agent draft

Puckett's services don't come cheap, but he had shown the Twins why he is a franchise player. He won the A.L. batting race in 1989 by three percentage points over rival Wade Boggs, and Puckett also led the league with 215 hits. In 1988, he batted .356, the highest mark for a righthanded batter since Joe DiMaggio batted .357 in 1941. Puckett led the A.L. with 234 base hits in '88. His RBI total reached a personal best of 121 in 1988, although his homers fell to 24 (down from the career-high 31 in 1986). Puckett became only the fourth player in history to reach 1,000 hits in only five years.

　　Collectors who spent a quarter for Puckett's 1988 cards collected when his first batting title arrived. His 1990 cards will be 50 cents or less. How much longer will you wait to cash in? Our pick for his best 1990 card is Topps.

TERRY PUHL

	BA	G	AB	R	H	2B	3B	HR	RBI	SB
1989	.271	121	354	41	96	25	4	0	27	9
Life	.280	1579	4796	671	1345	225	56	62	424	216

Position: Outfield
Team: Houston Astros
Born: July 8, 1956   Melville, Saskatchewan
Height: 6'2"   **Weight:** 200 lbs.
Bats: Left   **Throws:** Right
Acquired: Signed as a free agent, 9/73

Puhl ranks as the senior member of the Astros. He enters the 16th year of his professional career in 1990, which includes 13 seasons with Houston. He has never been a home run demon (especially in the canyonlike Astrodome). His best for round-trippers was 13 in 1980. Still, he's specialized in the two-base hit. Puhl reached his career high of 25 doubles for the third time in 1989. Speed has been one of his trademarks through the years. Although his stolen bases total was 32 in 1978, he stole in double digits for eight years running. Puhl now serves as Houston's top pinch-hitter.

　　Puhl has been a success in Houston for years. However, people outside Texas may not know about him. That obscurity is the main reason not to invest in Puhl's 1990 commons. Our pick for his best 1990 card is Fleer.

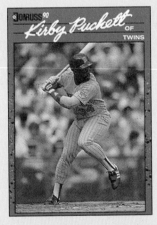
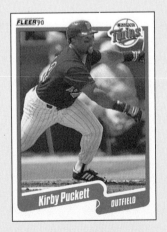
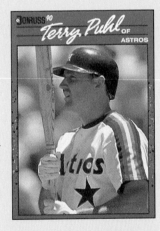

LUIS QUINONES

	BA	G	AB	R	H	2B	3B	HR	RBI	SB
1989	.244	97	340	43	83	13	4	12	34	2
Life	.225	259	641	77	144	25	8	13	68	7

Position: Second base
Team: Cincinnati Reds
Born: April 28, 1962 Ponce, Puerto Rico
Height: 5'11" **Weight:** 175 lbs.
Bats: Both **Throws:** Right
Acquired: Traded from Cubs for
Bill Landrum, 4/88

The power stats achieved by Quinones in 1989 may change the veteran's career course. First tasting the majors with the 1983 Athletics, he usually went through a team a year. For four seasons, he split his time between the majors and minors. In 1988, his first season with the Reds, he played in 23 games. While he had just one homer that season, he drove in 11 runs. In 1989, he didn't start the season on the Cincinnati roster. But batting coach Tony Perez gave Quinones career-saving batting tips that sparked his turnaround. His dozen homers in 1989 seem incredible, considering that he had just one in his first 162 games.

While some might regard Quinones a one-year wonder, he could be starting something big. His 1990 commons are attractive gambles but should be sold quickly for small gains. Our pick for his best 1990 card is Score.

CARLOS QUINTANA

	BA	G	AB	R	H	2B	3B	HR	RBI	SB
89 AAA	.287	82	272	45	78	11	2	11	52	6
89 Major	.208	34	77	6	16	5	0	0	6	0

Position: Outfield; first base
Team: Boston Red Sox
Born: August 26, 1965 Estado
Miranda, Venezuela
Height: 6'2" **Weight:** 195 lbs.
Bats: Right **Throws:** Right
Acquired: Signed as a free agent, 11/84

Quintana had a brief stay with Boston in 1989 before being shipped back to Triple-A Pawtucket for more seasoning. He had a .133 average in his first 14 games with Boston in 1989. In 1988, Quintana was Pawtucket's only International League All-Star after hitting .285 with 16 homers and 66 RBI. He topped the PawSox in 11 offensive categories. His homers tied him for the second-most in the league, while his .452 slugging percentage and 213 total bases were also second. On September 16, 1988, he made his big league debut, pinch-hitting for Jim Rice. At Double-A New Britain in 1987, Quintana hit .311 in 56 games before his season ended when he broke his right leg in a home plate collision.

Gamblers may want to pick up Quintana's second-year 1990 cards at a nickel apiece, in case he becomes the Red Sox first baseman. Our pick for his best 1990 card is Donruss.

DAN QUISENBERRY

	W	L	ERA	G	SV	IP	H	ER	BB	SO
1989	3	1	2.64	63	6	78	78	23	14	37
Life	56	45	2.69	669	244	1036	1051	310	159	377

Position: Pitcher
Team: St. Louis Cardinals
Born: February 7, 1953 Santa Monica, CA
Height: 6'2" **Weight:** 185 lbs.
Bats: Right **Throws:** Right
Acquired: Signed as a free agent, 7/88

Quisenberry, one of the most accomplished relievers of the 1980s, closed out the decade in fine style with the 1989 Cardinals. In his first full National League season, he was third on the Redbirds with six saves. His 2.64 ERA ranked second, as did his 35 games finished. The submarine-style reliever appeared in 63 games, his most active season since 1985, when he led the American League with 84 appearances. He had a distinguished ten-year career with the Royals, where he posted 238 saves and 51 wins. Quisenberry topped the league in saves in 1982 to '85, earning a lifetime-best 45 saves in 1983.

Scrap the policy of avoiding investments in relief pitcher cards. Quisenberry's combined total for wins and saves is 298. He may be a dark-horse candidate for the Hall of Fame, so take a chance on his 1990 commons. Our pick for his best 1990 card is Score.

TIM RAINES

	BA	G	AB	R	H	2B	3B	HR	RBI	SB
1989	.286	145	517	76	148	29	6	9	60	41
Life	.303	1275	4848	869	1467	262	76	87	490	585

Position: Outfield
Team: Montreal Expos
Born: September 16, 1959 Sanford, FL
Height: 5'8" **Weight:** 180 lbs.
Bats: Both **Throws:** Right
Acquired: Fifth-round pick in 6/77
    free-agent draft

Raines was among the batting leaders for the 1989 Expos. He had batted above .300 in five seasons in Montreal, the most notable year being 1986 when he won the N.L. batting title with a .334 mark. The winner of stolen base championships from 1981 through 1984, he is ranked among history's top ten base thieves. In 1987, Raines was named All-Star MVP for his three hits, the last being a game-winning triple in the 13th inning. He hit only .270 in an injury-plagued 1988, but he made a strong comeback in 1989. He performed in seven consecutive All-Star games from 1981 to 1987. Raines and Fred Lynn are the only players to be All-Stars during their first seven seasons.

"Rock" is a solid card investment. You can't go wrong if you pay a quarter for his 1990 cards. Our pick for his best 1990 card is Donruss.

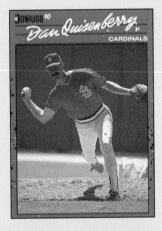

RAFAEL RAMIREZ

	BA	G	AB	R	H	2B	3B	HR	RBI	SB
1989	.246	151	537	46	132	20	2	6	54	3
Life	.262	1233	4640	484	1217	189	28	49	414	99

Position: Shortstop
Team: Houston Astros
Born: February 18, 1959   San Pedro
de Macoris, Dominican Republic
Height: 5'11"   **Weight:** 190 lbs.
Bats: Right   **Throws:** Right
Acquired: Traded from Braves for Mike
Stoker and Ed Whited, 12/87

Even though he's an Astro now, Ramirez is continuing the trail he blazed for himself with his 1980 major league debut in Atlanta. With a batting average usually in the .260s and a good number of doubles, "Raffy" had a reputation as a solid-hitting shortstop. In 1988, he hit .276 with 30 doubles, six homers, and 59 RBI. But the 13-year veteran endured a mediocre season with Houston in 1989. His tolerable fielding has eroded due to the artificial turf of the Astrodome. He illustrated this point with a league-leading 30 errors last season. So while he hits better than the average shortstop, Ramirez is an increasing liability in the infield.

Ramirez has passable batting stats. He hasn't shown consistency at the plate, though. Decline investing in his 1990 commons. Our pick for his best 1990 card is Donruss.

WILLIE RANDOLPH

	BA	G	AB	R	H	2B	3B	HR	RBI	SB
1989	.282	145	549	62	155	18	0	2	36	7
Life	.275	1869	6904	1098	1896	278	58	50	588	259

Position: Second base
Team: Los Angeles Dodgers
Born: July 6, 1954   Holly Hill, SC
Height: 5'11"   **Weight:** 170 lbs.
Bats: Right   **Throws:** Right
Acquired: Signed as a free agent, 12/88

Filling the shoes of Steve Sax wasn't an easy request, but Randolph fulfilled the task in 1989. He signed a free-agent deal with the Dodgers after spending the last 13 seasons with the Yankees, while Sax signed a free-agent pact with the Yankees. Randolph proved his worth immediately by winning a spot on the National League All-Star team (after being a member of five A.L. squads). In 1976, he was the first rookie ever listed on an All-Star fan ballot. His fielding in 1989 was the best the Dodgers had seen in years. Randolph, who broke into baseball with the 1975 Pirates, holds the Yankees record for most games played at second base (1,689).

Randolph doesn't generate the offense needed to make his nickel-priced 1990 cards profitable investments. Our pick for his best 1990 card is Donruss.

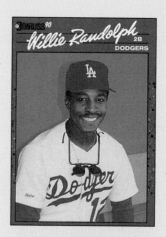

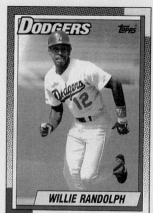

DENNIS RASMUSSEN

	W	L	ERA	G	CG	IP	H	ER	BB	SO
1989	10	10	4.26	33	1	183	190	87	72	87
Life	69	45	4.07	178	16	1044	967	472	381	644

Position: Pitcher
Team: San Diego Padres
Born: April 18, 1959 Los Angeles, CA
Height: 6'7" **Weight:** 225 lbs.
Bats: Left **Throws:** Left
Acquired: Traded from Reds for
    Candy Sierra, 6/88

Rasmussen is living proof that a change of scenery can do a pitcher wonders. The lefty started the 1988 season with the Cincinnati Reds, acquiring a nasty 2-6 record and a 5.75 ERA after only 11 games. Upon his midseason trade to the San Diego Padres, he regained mastery of the pitching mound in a 14-4 effort for his new employer. His 2.55 ERA was his lowest mark ever in the majors, while his six complete games were a team best. His double-digit winning season in 1989 continued his San Diego success. An excellent fielder with lots of stamina, Rasmussen frequently pitches into the seventh inning before needing relief.

    Rasmussen's 1990 cards will sell as commons. They're long-shot investments that will pay off only if he wins 20, or the Padres win their division. Our pick for his best 1990 card is Topps.

SHANE RAWLEY

	W	L	ERA	G	CG	IP	H	ER	BB	SO
1989	5	12	5.21	27	1	145	167	84	60	68
Life	111	118	4.02	469	41	1870	1934	836	734	991

Position: : Pitcher
Team: Minnesota Twins
Born: July 27, 1955 Racine, WI
Height: 6' **Weight:** 185 lbs.
Bats: Right **Throws:** Left
Acquired: Traded from Phillies for
    Tom Herr, Eric Bullock, and
    Tom Nieto, 10/88

Rawley became one of the first casualties of the 1989 youth movement of the Minnesota Twins. He seemed far from ancient. Nonetheless, the 16-year professional was enduring his least productive season since 1981. The Twins stated at season's end that he would not be offered a new contract for 1990. Looking for a new employer shouldn't be too difficult for him. He has worked for the Seattle Mariners, New York Yankees, and Philadelphia Phillies in his career. In 1980, he was a top reliever with Seattle, going 7-7 with 13 saves. With the 1987 Phillies, he posted a career-best 17-11 record, although his ERA was a 4.39. In 1988, Rawley was 8-16 with a 4.18 ERA for Philadelphia.

    Rawley's lifetime record is a step below average. Due to his unstable future in the majors, investing in his 1990 commons isn't recommended. Our pick for his best 1990 card is Donruss.

JOHNNY RAY

	BA	G	AB	R	H	2B	3B	HR	RBI	SB
1989	.289	134	530	52	153	16	3	5	62	6
Life	.291	1248	4784	557	1390	274	36	48	551	78

Position: Second base
Team: California Angels
Born: March 1, 1957   Chouteau, OK
Height: 5'11"   **Weight:** 185 lbs.
Bats: Both   **Throws:** Right
Acquired: Traded from Pirates for Miguel
  Garcia and Bill Merrifield, 8/87

Ray remained one of the unsung heroes for the Angels in 1989, leading the team in batting average for a second straight season. His .289 average didn't quite match his .306 effort in 1988, which marked his third .300-plus season in nine major league campaigns. He became the first switch-hitter in Angels history to top .300 with his 1988 mark, which was the sixth-highest in the team's existence. He has gained fame as a tough contact hitter. He struck out just 30 times in 1989. He took an instant liking to the A.L. when he was acquired from the Pirates. Ray hit .346 in his first 30 games with the Angels, becoming the team's regular second sacker.

The only way Ray will get his due is if he contends for a batting crown. For now, skip over his 1990 commons. Our pick for his best 1990 card is Score.

RANDY READY

	BA	G	AB	R	H	2B	3B	HR	RBI	SB
1989	.264	100	254	37	67	13	2	8	26	4
Life	.268	459	1358	207	364	77	18	33	163	19

Position: Infield
Team: Philadelphia Phillies
Born: January 8, 1960   San Mateo, CA
Height: 5'11"   **Weight:** 180 lbs.
Bats: Right   **Throws:** Right
Acquired: Traded from Padres with
  John Kruk for Chris James, 6/89

A talented utility player, Ready seldom knows what position he'll be playing a week down the road. Unfortunately, this uncertainty applies to his offensive efforts as well. Batting .309 in 1987 with 26 two-base hits, and 12 homers, 1988 found him with a .266 average, 16 doubles, and seven home runs. Ready's stats remained basically the same in 1989, despite changing teams. Happily, defense is another story altogether. In 1988, he became just the fifth third baseman in Padres history to tally eight assists in a single game. A three-sport high school letterman, he is the consummate team player. Not only is Ready able to play virtually any position, he can hit well, batting in any position in the lineup.

Unless Ready lands a full-time position with the Phillies, his 1990 commons won't be worthy investments. Our pick for his best 1990 card is Donruss.

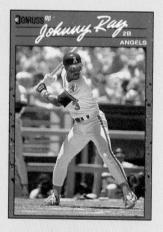

JEFF REARDON

	W	L	ERA	G	SV	IP	R	H	BB	SO
1989	5	4	4.07	65	31	73	33	68	12	46
Life	57	62	3.03	647	266	892	321	757	301	722

Position: Pitcher
Team: Minnesota Twins
Born: October 1, 1955 Dalton, MA
Height: 6' **Weight:** 200 lbs.
Bats: Right **Throws:** Right
Acquired: Traded from Expos with Tom
Neito for Al Cardwood, Jeff Reed,
Neal Heaton, and Yorkis Perez,
2/87

In 1989, Reardon didn't equal his earlier numbers, but he preserved his reputation as one of baseball's toughest stoppers. His ERA climbed to an uncharacteristic 4.07, but he collected 31 saves in 65 appearances. He finished all but four games as he surpassed the 30-save mark for the fifth consecutive season. He didn't come close to his 1988 stats, which included 42 saves and a 2.47 ERA. He joined the Twins in 1987 and helped bring Minnesota its first World Championship. He earned eight wins and 31 saves that year. Active in the majors since 1979, Reardon should be one of baseball's most-pursued free agents for the 1990 season.

Reardon is a famed reliever, but numerous other great stoppers have low-priced cards. His nickel-priced 1990 cards will only yield long-term profits if he gets a shot at the Hall of Fame. Our pick for his best 1990 card is Score.

GARY REDUS

	BA	G	AB	R	H	2B	3B	HR	RBI	SB
1989	.283	98	279	42	79	18	7	6	33	25
Life	.250	794	2603	458	650	136	39	68	260	279

Position: Outfield; first base
Team: Pittsburgh Pirates
Born: November 1, 1956 Athens, AL
Height: 6'1" **Weight:** 185 lbs.
Bats: Right **Throws:** Right
Acquired: Traded from White Sox for
Mike Diaz, 8/88

Redus was in the majors for six seasons before his batting average broke .260. The Pirates reserve outfielder reached a new career high in 1989, when he batted .283 in 98 games. Speed has always been his trademark, as evidenced by his 25 stolen bases. Although his total ranked second on the 1989 Bucs, it was one of the lowest totals of his eight-year major league career. In 1987, he stole 52 bases for the White Sox, third-highest in the A.L. Redus won two league stolen base titles while playing in the Reds' farm system from 1978 to 1982. He began as a second baseman, hitting .462 in his first minor league season. Redus was a NAIA All-American in college.

Redus is a capable substitute. However, he hasn't achieved the statistics needed to make his 1990 commons good investments. Our pick for his best 1990 card is Score.

JERRY REED

	W	L	ERA	G	SV	IP	H	ER	BB	SO
1989	7	7	3.19	52	0	101	89	36	43	50
Life	18	17	3.84	205	16	427	414	182	153	229

Position: Pitcher
Team: Seattle Mariners
Born: October 8, 1955, Bryson City, NC
Height: 6'1" **Weight:** 190 lbs.
Bats: Right **Throws:** Right
Acquired: Signed as a free agent, 4/86

Reed starred in middle relief for the Mariners again in 1989, posting career highs in wins, games, and innings pitched. After making late-season appearances with Seattle in 1986 and '87, he worked his second full season with the M's in 1989. As he's proven his worth to the team, his pitching opportunities have grown each year. He pitched in 46 games in 1988, accumulating a 3.96 ERA. He is a baseball veteran who started his pro career in 1977. After five minor league campaigns, he debuted with the 1981 Phillies. In 1982, he was obtained by the Indians, where he remained a short reliever. With the 1985 Tribe, Reed collected a career-high eight saves in 33 appearances.

Because he doesn't work as a stopper, Reed will get little attention in coming years. His modest lifetime totals don't merit investing in his 1990 commons. Our pick for his best 1990 card is Fleer.

JODY REED

	BA	G	AB	R	H	2B	3B	HR	RBI	SB
1989	.288	146	524	76	151	42	3	2	40	4
Life	.290	264	892	140	259	66	4	4	76	6

Position: Shortstop
Team: Boston Red Sox
Born: July 26, 1962 Tampa, FL
Height: 5'9" **Weight:** 160 lbs.
Bats: Right **Throws:** Right
Acquired: Eighth-round pick in 6/84
    free-agent draft

There was no sophomore slump for Reed in 1989. He finished third in 1988's American League Rookie of the Year balloting, buoyed by his .293 batting average with just 21 strikeouts in 338 at-bats. In 1989, he followed up with a minuscule 18 strikeouts in 524 plate appearances. His improving batting eye helped his fielding as well. The Red Sox shortstop shaved his 11 errors from 1988 down to seven in 1989. His hits increased by one-third, while his doubles nearly doubled. The Red Sox forgive his lack of homers due to his strong on-base ability. Reed shows team dedication by taking walks, bunts, or any other plus that helps the BoSox.

Reed has a healthy batting average and fine fielding ability. Buy his 1990 commons now, before he becomes the next "star" shortstop, similar to Ozzie Smith. Our pick for his best 1990 card is Score.

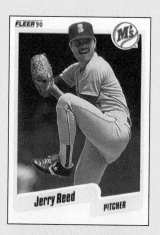

RICK REED

	W	L	ERA	G	CG	IP	H	ER	BB	SO
89 AAA	9	8	3.72	20	3	126	130	52	28	75
89 Major	1	4	5.60	15	0	54	62	34	11	34

Position: Pitcher
Team: Pittsburgh Pirates
Born: August 16, 1964   Huntington, WV
Height: 6'   **Weight:** 195 lbs.
Bats: Right   **Throws:** Right
Acquired: 26th-round pick in 6/86
free-agent draft

Although Reed was overlooked until the 26th round of the 1986 draft, he gained his due recognition as a member of the Pirates in 1989. He was back in the majors for a second year after becoming one of the top winners for Triple-A Buffalo. In 1988, he started the season pitching for Class-A Salem, and made brief stops at Double-A and Triple-A before joining the Pirates on August 4. He tallied a combined minor league record of 13-4 before making the majors. His first start was against the Mets. In his memorable big league debut, Reed allowed just three hits in eight innings to claim a 1-0 victory.

Reed's high ERA for the '89 Bucs decreases interest in his cards. Avoid his 1990 issues until he proves that he can pitch in the majors. Our pick for his best 1990 card is Donruss.

KEVIN REIMER

	BA	G	AB	R	H	2B	3B	HR	RBI	SB
89 AAA	.267	133	514	59	137	37	7	10	73	4
89 Major	.000	3	5	0	0	0	0	0	0	0

Position: Outfield; designated hitter
Team: Texas Rangers
Born: June 28, 1964   Macon, GA
Height: 6'2"   **Weight:** 215 lbs.
Bats: Left   **Throws:** Right
Acquired: 11th-round pick in 6/85
free-agent draft

Taking his career one step a season, Reimer reached the top of the minor league stairway as the designated hitter at Triple-A Oklahoma City in 1989. He was among team leaders in hits, average, and RBI. His efforts didn't match his 1988 production at Double-A Tulsa. He batted .302 with 21 homers and 76 RBI, all career highs. Reimer's 11 triples and 12 game-winning RBI were Texas League bests. He batted .400 during a 20-game hitting streak that year. His accomplishments earned him a September call-up to the majors. He earned his first major league homer off Chicago's Shawn Hillegas. Reimer's success continues his family's legacy in baseball. His father, Gerry, played 11 years in the Philadelphia organization.

Kevin is untested at the major league level. Don't spend anything on his 1990 cards until he establishes himself. Our pick for his best 1990 card is Fleer.

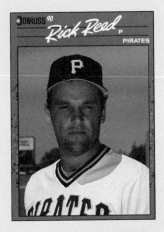

RICK REUSCHEL

	W	L	ERA	G	CG	IP	R	H	BB	SO
1989	17	11	2.94	32	2	208	75	195	54	111
Life	211	183	3.36	538	102	3451	1449	3469	897	1962

Position: Pitcher
Team: San Francisco Giants
Born: May 16, 1949 Quincy, IL
Height: 6'3" **Weight:** 240 lbs.
Bats: Right **Throws:** Right
Acquired: Traded from Pirates for Scott
    Medvin and Jeff Robinson, 8/87

"Big Daddy" earned one of his finest honors when he was selected as the N.L.'s starter for the 1989 All-Star Game. The tribute was well earned by the four-time All-Star, who secured his 200th career victory in 1989. The Giants 1987 acquisition of Reuschel helped guarantee a pennant for San Francisco. He won his second Gold Glove in 1987. In 1988, Reuschel went 19-11, the fourth-best N.L. win total. He made his debut with the Cubs in 1972 and won 20 games for Chicago in 1977. Following a 1981 trade to the Yankees, Reuschel suffered an injury and spent more than a year on the disabled list before working his way back to the bigs.

Reuschel gained considerable attention in postseason play. His 1990 cards will be underpriced at a nickel or less. Our pick for his best 1990 card is Donruss.

JERRY REUSS

	W	L	ERA	G	CG	IP	R	H	BB	SO
1989	9	9	5.13	30	1	140	88	171	34	40
Life	220	191	3.64	624	127	3660	1697	3726	1124	1906

Position: Pitcher
Team: Milwaukee Brewers
Born: June 19, 1949 St. Louis, MO
Height: 6'5" **Weight:** 225 lbs.
Bats: Left **Throws:** Left
Acquired: Traded from White Sox for
    Brian Drahman, 6/89

Reuss was swapped to the Brewers in mid-1989, the eighth team with which he's performed in his career. In his 21st major league season, he was 9-9, increasing his lifetime wins to 220. He has achieved the noteworthy career record without a single 20-win season. Reuss has won a career high of 18 games three times: with the 1975 Pirates and the 1980 and '82 Dodgers. It seemed like he was washed up prior to the 1988 season. He had been released by the Dodgers, Reds, and Angels. But Reuss made the 1988 White Sox as a nonroster player then led the team with a 13-9 record.

Reuss's career will achieve additional distinction by playing in 1990, celebrating his fourth decade in the majors. His 1990 commons are questionable investments that will pay off only if he lands in the Hall of Fame. Our pick for his best 1990 card is Donruss.

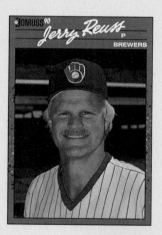

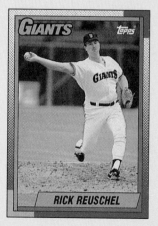
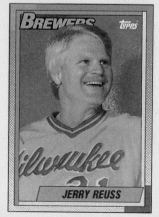

CRAIG REYNOLDS

	BA	G	AB	R	H	2B	3B	HR	RBI	SB
1989	.201	101	189	16	38	4	0	2	14	1
Life	.256	1491	4466	480	1142	143	65	42	377	58

Position: Infield
Team: Houston Astros
Born: December 27, 1952   Houston, TX
Height: 6'1"   **Weight:** 175 lbs.
Bats: Left   **Throws:** Right
Acquired: Traded from Mariners for
    Floyd Bannister, 12/78

Reynolds had his lowest average ever in 1989, his 11th year with the Astros. His career in Houston has seen numerous ups and downs. He was Houston's starting shortstop on an infrequent basis. Recently, he's been a valued backup infielder, due to his defensive skills. One of his notable accomplishments as a reserve was pitching an inning against the 1986 Mets. Although he gave up three runs on three hits, he struck out Howard Johnson. When Reynolds joined the Astros in 1979, he fulfilled a dream of playing for his hometown team. He grew up in the city and was named Houston's Top High School Athlete in 1971 before being a first-round draft choice of the Pirates.

    Reynolds, as a part-timer, commands no special attention among card collectors. His 1990 commons will be poor investments. Our pick for his best 1990 card is Topps.

HAROLD REYNOLDS

	BA	G	AB	R	H	2B	3B	HR	RBI	SB
1989	.300	153	613	87	184	24	9	0	43	25
Life	.266	694	2359	293	628	107	34	6	150	154

Position: Second base
Team: Seattle Mariners
Born: November 26, 1960   Eugene, OR
Height: 5'11"   **Weight:** 165 lbs.
Bats: Both   **Throws:** Right
Acquired: First-round pick in 6/80
    free-agent draft

After setting personal highs in six defensive categories in 1988, Reynolds set about to match these scores in 1989. After three false starts, he landed the starting position with the Mariners in 1986 at age 25. Given almost a full season, Reynolds adjusted and hefted his batting average closer to his minor league standard of .300. He is the Mariners first-ever two-time All-Star, and he was the recipient of the M's third Gold Glove. He was a two-sport All-State athlete in high school. One of Reynolds's best accomplishments was winning the 1987 A.L. stolen base crown with 60 swipes, overthrowing seven-season stolen base king Rickey Henderson.

    After having a .300 season in 1989, Reynolds looks promising as a card investment. His 1990 card is one of the year's biggest bargains at a nickel apiece. Our pick for his best 1990 card is Score.

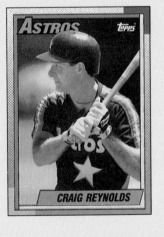

R.J. REYNOLDS

	BA	G	AB	R	H	2B	3B	HR	RBI	SB
1989	.270	125	363	45	98	16	2	6	48	22
Life	.264	691	2055	263	543	111	16	35	275	97

Position: Outfield
Team: Pittsburgh Pirates
Born: April 19, 1960 Sacramento, CA
Height: 6' **Weight:** 183 lbs.
Bats: Both **Throws:** Right
Acquired: Traded from Dodgers with
　　Sid Bream and Cecil Espy for
　　Bill Madlock, 9/85

Reynolds spent another busy season as a fourth outfielder with the Pittsburgh Pirates in 1989. In his last four seasons with the Bucs, his average has ranged from his career-best .270 in 1989 to a .248 mark in 1988. While playing in between 118 to 130 games a season, he's hit anywhere from six to nine homers a year, driving in between 48 to 51 runs. He improved his stolen bases to 22 in 1989, marking his sixth straight season of double-digit swipes. He began his career in the Los Angeles Dodgers' organization in 1980, and debuted with the Dodgers in 1983. Reynolds now serves the Bucs as a spot starter, pinch-hitter, and defensive replacement.

Reynolds's batting average and homers aren't high enough to gain him star billing. His 1990 commons are unlikely price gainers. Our pick for his best 1990 card is Topps.

RICK RHODEN

	W	L	ERA	G	CG	IP	H	ER	BB	SO
1989	2	6	4.28	20	0	96	108	46	41	41
Life	151	126	3.60	413	69	2589	2606	1036	801	1419

Position: Pitcher
Team: Houston Astros
Born: May 16, 1953 Boynton Beach, FL
Height: 6'4" **Weight:** 202 lbs.
Bats: Right **Throws:** Right
Acquired: Traded from Yankees for
　　John Fishel, Pedro DeLeon, and
　　Mike Hook, 1/89

Turning 36 in 1989 changed only one thing about Rhoden's game: He pitched fewer innings. In light of the work-horse habits he's kept in the past, fewer innings for him equals a normal season for any other pitcher. He had a shockingly bad adjustment back to the N.L. in 1989. His two wins were his lowest in 15 full major league seasons, a vast departure from ten seasons of double-digit wins (including seven in a row from 1982 to 1988). He has one of the most lethal pick-off moves in the majors and a proficient batting eye. In 1988, Rhoden became the first pitcher in A.L. history to start as a designated hitter since the rule was adopted in 1973.

Rhoden had above-average lifetime totals, but his slump killed nearly all interest in his 1990 commons. Our pick for his best 1990 card is Topps.

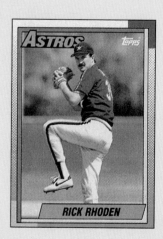

JIM RICE

	BA	G	AB	R	H	2B	3B	HR	RBI	SB
1989	.234	56	209	22	49	10	2	3	28	1
Life	.298	2089	8225	1249	2452	373	79	382	1451	58

Position: Outfield; designated hitter
Team: Boston Red Sox
Born: March 8, 1953 Anderson, SC
Height: 6'2" **Weight:** 216 lbs.
Bats: Right **Throws:** Right
Acquired: First-round pick in 6/71
free-agent draft

Red Sox fans were saddened when they learned that Rice would not be offered a contract for 1990. Everyone knew the end was near for the slugger who was reduced to just three homers, 28 RBI, and a .234 average in 56 games in 1989. Nevertheless, Rice symbolized a tradition with the Red Sox. He had joined the team as a rookie in 1974, after graduating through the Boston farm system. His 1975 rookie-season totals of 22 homers, 102 RBI, and a .309 average helped Boston to the A.L. pennant. In 1978, he had an MVP-winning season, including a .315 average with 46 homers and 139 RBI. He led the A.L. in six categories that year.

Rice is a future Hall of Famer, and investing up to a quarter in his 1990 issues will provide some sweet long-term profits. Our pick for his best 1990 card is Topps.

DAVE RIGHETTI

	W	L	ERA	G	SV	IP	H	ER	BB	SO
1989	2	6	3.00	55	25	69	32	73	26	51
Life	73	60	3.09	469	188	1083	424	951	447	897

Position: Pitcher
Team: New York Yankees
Born: November 28, 1958 San Jose, CA
Height: 6'4" **Weight:** 210 lbs.
Bats: Left **Throws:** Left
Acquired: Traded from Rangers with Mike
Griffin, Paul Mirabella, Juan
Beniquez, and Greg Jemison for
Sparky Lyle, Larry McCall, Dave
Rajsich, Mike Heath, Domingo
Ramos, and cash, 11/78

Righetti has led a double life during his nine seasons in the A.L. One of the league's most efficient relievers, "Rags" got a late start on setting relief records. During his first three seasons with the Yankees, he worked mainly as a starter. Righetti had his first real success in New York in 1981. In 15 starts, he went 8-4 with a 2.06 ERA. After winning 11 games in 1982, he claimed a 14-8 record in 1983. One of those victories was a July 4 no-hitter against Boston. As a reliever, Righetti was named A.L. Fireman of the Year in 1986, when he recorded eight wins and 46 saves, a major league record.

The Yankees are thinking about switching Righetti back to the starting rotation. Buy his 1990 cards at a dime, then sell when the Yankees become contenders again. Our pick for his best 1990 card is Donruss.

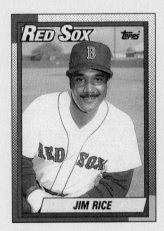

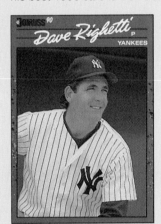

JOSE RIJO

	W	L	ERA	G	CG	IP	H	ER	BB	SO
1989	7	6	2.84	19	1	111	101	35	48	86
Life	39	44	3.86	164	6	675	630	290	321	601

Position: Pitcher
Team: Cincinnati Reds
Born: May 13, 1965 San Cristobal,
   Dominican Republic
Height: 6'2" **Weight:** 200 lbs.
Bats: Right **Throws:** Right
Acquired: Traded from A's with Tim Birtsas
   for Dave Parker, 12/87

Rijo seemed ready to repeat his 1988 success in 1989 for the Reds until back spasms limited his appearances and his effectiveness. He debuted with the Reds in 1988, registering a 13-8 record. It was the first winning mark in four major league seasons for him. Switching in midseason from relief to replace departed starter Dennis Rasmussen, Rijo notched his best-ever strikeouts-to-innings pitched ratio, with 160 Ks in 162 frames. His ERA came in at 2.39, far beating his previous low of 3.50. He debuted with the 1984 Yankees at age 19. He spent three years with the A's before moving to Cincinnati. With a nasty fastball and a smooth pickoff move, a healthy Rijo could be a major force with the 1990 Reds.

Wait until Rijo evens his career record before investing in his 1990 commons. Our pick for his best 1990 card is Donruss.

ERNEST RILES

	BA	G	AB	R	H	2B	3B	HR	RBI	SB
1989	.278	122	302	43	84	13	2	7	40	0
Life	.270	586	1864	237	503	73	15	29	207	15

Position: Infield
Team: San Francisco Giants
Born: October 2, 1960 Bainbridge, GA
Height: 6'1" **Weight:** 180 lbs.
Bats: Left **Throws:** Right
Acquired: Traded from Brewers for
   Jeffrey Leonard and cash, 6/88

When Riles was traded to San Francisco in mid-1988, it looked like someone had swindled the Giants. The Milwaukee Brewers were receiving noted slugger Jeffrey Leonard and cash for a backup infielder. However, by the end of the season, Leonard escaped Milwaukee via free agency. Riles, meanwhile, is still in San Francisco, contributing to the Giants in a multitude of ways. His .278 average was ordinary for Riles. It fell between his career-high .294 achieved with the 1988 Giants, and the low .252 tallied during his 1986 sophomore year in Milwaukee. San Francisco feels that any offense generated by Riles is a bonus to complement his defensive talents around the infield.

Because Riles is a utility player, his 1990 commons are poor investments. See if he can land a starting job before buying. Our pick for his best 1990 card is Topps.

BILLY RIPKEN

	BA	G	AB	R	H	2B	3B	HR	RBI	SB
1989	.239	115	318	31	76	11	2	2	26	1
Life	.239	323	1064	110	254	38	3	6	80	13

Position: Second base
Team: Baltimore Orioles
Born: December 16, 1964
　　　　Havre de Grace, MD
Height: 6'1" **Weight:** 180 lbs.
Bats: Right **Throws:** Right
Acquired: 11th-round pick in 6/82
　　　　free-agent draft

In his third season with the Orioles in 1989, Ripken struck a balance between his 1987 rookie triumph and his 1988 sophomore slump. Unlike his brother, Cal, Billy's greatest value to the team will not show up in batting averages; fielding is his forte. His quickness in turning double plays, his sure hands, and his defensive aggressiveness are appreciated by the O's. Offensively, Ripken seems like he hasn't learned to keep his eye on the ball—or, as card collectors noted in 1989, on his bat, either. Ripken gained notoriety for his 1989 Fleer card, which displayed an obscenity written on his bat knob. The card, quickly withdrawn from circulation, is now valued at more than $25.

　His 1990 cards shouldn't have any profanities and will sell for 3 cents or less. Based on Ripken's hitting, his cards are poor investments. Our pick for his best 1990 card is Score.

CAL RIPKEN

	BA	G	AB	R	H	2B	3B	HR	RBI	SB
1989	.257	162	646	80	166	30	0	21	93	3
Life	.277	1315	5055	5848	1402	266	24	204	744	19

Position: Shortstop
Team: Baltimore Orioles
Born: August 24, 1960
　　　　Havre de Grace, MD
Height: 6'4" **Weight:** 225 lbs.
Bats: Right **Throws:** Right
Acquired: Second-round pick in 6/78
　　　　free-agent draft

While Lou Gehrig was nicknamed "The Iron Horse," Ripken could be called "The Iron Oriole." In 1989, he continued his consecutive-game streak and climbed to third place on the all-time list. Ripken was a full-time player for the Orioles, helping the team make its run for the A.L. East pennant. He has notched at least 80 RBI for his eighth straight season in 1989, and he started his sixth All-Star Game in 1989. In 1982, he won the A.L. Rookie of the Year Award. In 1983, Ripken was the A.L. MVP. At 6'4", he is the tallest regular shortstop in history.

　Buy his 1990 cards at a quarter or less. If he breaks Lou Gehrig's consecutive game record, investors will see healthy long-term rewards. Our pick for his best 1990 card is Score.

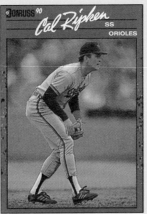

KEVIN RITZ

	W	L	ERA	G	CG	IP	H	ER	BB	SO
89 AAA	7	8	3.16	16	1	103	95	36	60	74
89 Major	4	6	4.38	12	1	74	45	36	44	56

Position: Pitcher
Team: Detroit Tigers
Born: June 8, 1965 Eatonstown, NJ
Height: 6'4" **Weight:** 195 lbs.
Bats: Right **Throws:** Right
Acquired: Fourth-round pick in secondary
　　　　　 phase of 6/85 free-agent draft

A bright spot for the 1989 Tigers was finding Ritz. He was promoted from Triple-A Toledo in 1989 and went 3-1 (with a complete game) in his first six starts for Detroit. In 1989 at Toledo, he was leading the team in wins, strikeouts, and innings pitched when he was called up. He fine-tuned his starting skills with Double-A Glens Falls in 1987 and 1988. In 1987, Ritz topped the team with eight wins and 152 innings. In 1988, batters hit just .229 against him, as he notched a 3.82 ERA. He collected two two-hitters and a three-hit effort to complement his eight victories. The media refer to him as "Puttin' on the" Ritz.

Ritz may be one of Detroit's starters. He'll get lots of chances to succeed, making his new 1990 cards choice buys at 15 cents or less. Our pick for his best 1990 card is Donruss.

BIP ROBERTS

	BA	G	AB	R	H	2B	3B	HR	RBI	SB
1989	.301	117	329	81	99	15	8	3	25	21
Life	.282	223	579	116	163	20	10	4	37	35

Position: Infield
Team: San Diego Padres
Born: October 27, 1963 Berkeley, CA
Height: 5'7" **Weight:** 160 lbs.
Bats: Both **Throws:** Right
Acquired: Drafted from Pirates, 12/85

Roberts got a second chance with the 1989 San Diego Padres, and he made the most of it. He was handed the team's starting second baseman's job in 1986, but lasted only one year after hitting .253. The team demoted the former Pittsburgh farmhand for two years of seasoning at Triple-A, a level he skipped prior to 1986. He polished his craft and was hitting .353 for Triple-A in 1988 before getting a recall. He spent 1989 as the team's utility infielder. He batted .301 (second on the Padres behind only Tony Gwynn). His frequent pinch-running assignments and his 21 stolen bases encouraged San Diego writers to dub Roberts "The Roadrunner."

Watch for Roberts to contend for a starting third baseman's job. Get his 1990 commons while you can. Our pick for his best 1990 card is Fleer.

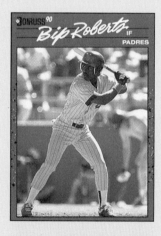

DON ROBINSON

	W	L	ERA	G	CG	IP	H	ER	BB	SO
1989	12	11	3.43	34	5	197	184	75	37	96
Life	92	86	3.62	453	30	1618	1530	651	545	1069

Position: Pitcher
Team: San Francisco Giants
Born: June 8, 1957 Ashland, KY
Height: 6'4" **Weight:** 235 lbs.
Bats: Right **Throws:** Right
Acquired: Traded from Pirates for
    Mackey Sasser and cash, 7/87

Robinson, a starter turned reliever, turned back to starting for the 1989 San Francisco Giants. After 158 consecutive relief appearances from the top of the 1986 season through June of 1988, he drew a starting slot and fared so well that he got only one more relief assignment that season. The result was a career-low 2.45 ERA. In 1989, Robinson ranked first on the Giants in complete games (five) and third in wins. His career high for wins was 15, with the 1982 Pirates. Going into 1989, his .254 lifetime batting average was first among active pitchers. The occasional pinch-hitter was awarded the Silver Slugger in 1982 for his offensive prowess.

Robinson has been riddled with injuries in the past, which has limited his lifetime record. He needs to approach his first 20-win season before collectors will gather his 1990 commons earnestly. Our pick for his best 1990 card is Score.

JEFF ROBINSON

	W	L	ERA	G	SV	IP	H	ER	BB	SO
1989	7	13	4.58	50	4	141	161	72	59	95
Life	39	45	3.80	312	35	677	666	286	246	483

Position: Pitcher
Team: Pittsburgh Pirates
Born: December 13, 1960 Santa Ana, CA
Height: 6'4" **Weight:** 200 lbs.
Bats: Right **Throws:** Right
Acquired: Traded from Giants with Scott
    Medvin for Rick Reuschel, 8/87

Robinson suffered through a slump, which plagued many of the 1989 Pirates. After earning a career-high 11 relief wins in 1988 (second highest in the league), he saw his record plummet in 1989. His 1988 season, his first full campaign with the Bucs, he had a six-game winning streak as he led all major league relievers with 124 2/3 innings pitched. He began 1987 as a Giant and won a reliever of the month honor (with a 2-0 mark and four saves). He joined Pittsburgh in August to finish with a combined career-high of 14 saves in 81 appearances. One of his career highlights was a home run in '87 off Lee Smith.

Robinson's relief job doesn't allow him much room for fame. In his low-profile position, his 1990 cards are likely to stay valued at 3 cents or less. Our pick for his best 1990 card is Donruss.

JEFF ROBINSON

	W	L	ERA	G	CG	IP	H	ER	BB	SO
1989	4	5	4.73	16	1	78	76	41	46	40
Life	26	17	4.15	69	9	377	329	174	172	252

Position: Pitcher
Team: Detroit Tigers
Born: December 14, 1961   Ventura, CA
Height: 6'6"   **Weight:** 210 lbs.
Bats: Right   **Throws:** Right
Acquired: Third-round pick in 6/83
      free-agent draft

Robinson's 1989 season with the Detroit Tigers was prematurely ended by tendinitis in his right elbow. The ailment limited his season to a career-low 16 appearances. He posted a sophomore record of 13-6 with a team-leading 2.98 ERA in 1988, before he ended his campaign one month early due to a circulatory problem in the index and middle fingers of his pitching hand. He was the first Tiger starter since Mark Fidrych (in 1976) to notch a sub-3.00 ERA. In Robinson's successful 1988 campaign, he authored a two-hitter, a one-hitter, and an 11-strikeout performance. He won nine games in that rookie year.

Robinson's 1990 cards will be 3 cents or less. Check on his health before investing. If he is ready to go, sink a few bucks into his cards. Our pick for his best 1990 card is Topps.

RON ROBINSON

	W	L	ERA	G	SV	IP	H	ER	BB	SO
1989	5	3	3.35	15	0	80	83	31	28	36
Life	33	27	3.60	195	19	580	568	232	185	390

Position: Pitcher
Team: Cincinnati Reds
Born: March 24, 1962   Woodlake, CA
Height: 6'4"   **Weight:** 230 lbs.
Bats: Right   **Throws:** Right
Acquired: First-round pick in 6/80
      free-agent draft

In 1989, Robinson started his sixth season the same way he began his first five seasons: recovering from elbow surgery on his pitching arm. Not surprisingly, his number of appearances has been meager for two years. What is surprising is that his ERA, quite fat (4.12) after his 1987 surgery, was a trim 3.35 in 1989. His stats also show some liabilities that have little to do with his arm ailments. Robinson frequently allows almost a hit per inning, a bad habit for a reliever. The owner of above-average fielding skills and a tough curveball, Robinson needs to regain his health soon to benefit the Cincinnati rebuilding program.

Because his elbow is suspect, Robinson's future is unclear. For those reasons, and for his inadequate lifetime stats, bypass his 1990 commons. Our pick for his best 1990 card is Score.

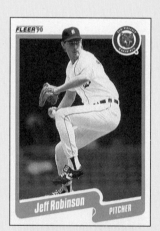
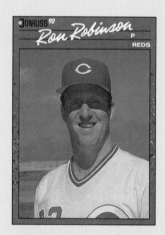

KENNY ROGERS

	W	L	ERA	G	SV	IP	H	ER	BB	SO
88 AA	4	6	4.00	13	0	83	73	37	34	76
89 Major	3	4	2.93	73	2	73	60	24	42	63

Position: Pitcher
Team: Texas Rangers
Born: November 10, 1964 Savannah, GA
Height: 6'1" **Weight:** 200 lbs.
Bats: Left **Throws:** Left
Acquired: 39th-round pick in the 6/82
     free-agent draft

Rogers found a home with the 1989 Rangers. After finishing his little league baseball career, he didn't participate in organized baseball until his senior year of high school. He played exclusively in the outfield, hitting .375. Impressed by his throwing ability, the Rangers signed him to a pro contract. Beginning in 1982 with Sarasota, Rogers embarked on a long minor league journey. He never reached above Double-A through 1988. After off-season elbow surgery in 1987, he made a slow but complete recovery. With the '89 Rangers, he was used more than 70 times in relief. If his arm holds up, Rogers may see more action with Texas in 1990.

Rogers was tireless in 1989. He should continue to get lots of work, and he may start to rack up some saves. Buy his rookie 1990 cards at 15 cents or less. Our pick for his best 1990 card is Fleer.

ROLANDO ROOMES

	BA	G	AB	R	H	2B	3B	HR	RBI	SB
1989	.263	107	315	36	83	18	5	7	34	12
Life	.260	124	331	39	86	18	5	7	34	12

Position: Outfield
Team: Cincinnati Reds
Born: February 15, 1962
     Kingston, Jamaica
Height: 6'3" **Weight:** 180 lbs.
Bats: Right **Throws:** Right
Acquired: Traded from Cubs for
     Lloyd McClendon, 12/88

One reason for the reserve strength of the 1989 Reds was the off-season acquisition of Roomes. After nine professional seasons, he had only 17 games in the majors and batted only .188. Ironically, his first major league hit was against Cincinnati. The Reds had faith in him. He had averaged 16 homers and 20 stolen bases a year in the minors prior to 1989. Roomes was among Reds leaders in stolen bases. At Triple-A Iowa in 1988, he was an American Association All-Star with 16 homers, 76 RBI, and a .301 average. He batted .308 with 21 homers and 95 RBI with Double-A Pittsfield in 1987. Roomes gives Cincinnati power, speed, and defense.

Roomes made a good impression during his first year with Cincinnati. He'll stay busy, a hopeful sign for investors who buy his 1990 cards for 10 cents or less. Our pick for his best 1990 card is Donruss.

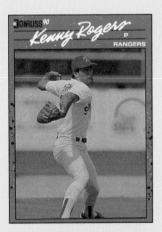

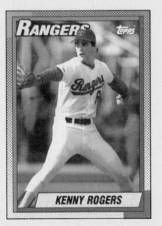

BRUCE RUFFIN

	W	L	ERA	G	CG	IP	H	ER	BB	SO
1989	6	10	4.44	24	1	125	152	69	62	70
Life	32	38	4.04	135	13	621	677	279	259	315

Position: Pitcher
Team: Philadelphia Phillies
Born: October 4, 1963 Lubbock, TX
Height: 6'2" **Weight:** 205 lbs.
Bats: Right **Throws:** Left
Acquired: Second-round pick in 6/85
free-agent draft

For Ruffin, too much too soon has resulted in a slump three years long. The Phillies hurler was an unspectacular 6-10 in 1989, with a 4.44 ERA. This contrasts his meteoric rise to the majors. After beginning his pro career in 1985, Ruffin was a Phillies starter by mid-1986. In 21 starts, he was 9-4 with a career-best 2.46 ERA. The sophomore jinx hit in 1986, when he fell to 11-14 with a bloated 4.35 ERA in 35 starts. His ERA seems to grow every year. So have the number of walks that he gives up per nine innings. Switching to relief in 1988 did little good for him. He allowed 151 hits in 144 frames, and 14.6 baserunners per nine innings. Ruffin returned to the starting rotation in 1989.

He has talent, but until Ruffin has back-to-back winning seasons, steer away from his 1990 commons. Our pick for his best 1990 card is Topps.

JEFF RUSSELL

	W	L	ERA	G	SV	IP	H	ER	BB	SO
1989	6	4	1.98	71	38	72	45	16	24	77
Life	39	48	4.02	250	43	752	740	336	287	460

Position: Pitcher
Team: Texas Rangers
Born: September 2, 1961 Cincinnati, OH
Height: 6'3" **Weight:** 210 lbs.
Bats: Right **Throws:** Right
Acquired: Traded from Reds with Duane
Walker for Buddy Bell, 7/85

Russell spent four of his first five major league seasons bouncing between the minors and the bigs. He managed two winning seasons for Texas in that time span and notched an impressive ratio of strikeouts to walks. The Rangers converted Russell into a starter in 1988. He found quick success as a starter, but began to tire from all the extra innings. He finished the year at 10-9 with a 3.82 ERA. In 1989, the Rangers gave him the sole job of team stopper, asking him to fill the shoes of Mitch Williams. Russell has a fastball that could make him a valued pitcher for years to come.

Russell had his first success in 1989. Avoid his 1990 cards at prices more than a nickel, because he must prove he can be consistent before his cards will flourish. Our pick for his best 1990 card is Fleer.

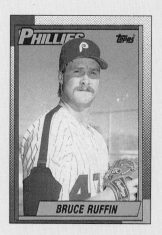

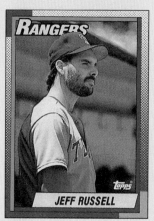

NOLAN RYAN

	W	L	ERA	G	CG	IP	H	ER	BB	SO
1989	16	10	3.20	32	6	239	96	162	98	301
Life	289	263	3.15	710	213	4786	1912	3492	2540	5076

Position: Pitcher
Team: Texas Rangers
Born: January 31, 1947 Refugio, TX
Height: 6'2" **Weight:** 210 lbs.
Bats: Right **Throws:** Right
Acquired: Signed as a free agent, 12/88

Ryan finished his 22nd season as *the* major league power pitcher. In 1989, he led the Rangers in wins and the entire world in strikeouts. The all-time major league strikeout king, he surpassed 5,000 career strikeouts. A master of control (he's walked less than 100 batters per season since 1984), he will surely have to pitch in 1990 to attain the lofty goal of 300 career wins. In 1989, he became the sixth pitcher ever to earn wins against all 26 teams in a career. Ryan now pitches to batters who were born the year he debuted in the majors (1966). In Ryan's one-hit gem against the Brewers, his fastball was clocked at 98 mph.

Try to buy Ryan's 1990 cards at 35 cents or less. Those investments will make consistent gains when he attains 300 wins then reaches the Hall of Fame. Our pick for his best 1990 card is Score.

BRET SABERHAGEN

	W	L	ERA	G	CG	IP	H	ER	BB	SO
1989	23	6	2.16	37	12	262	209	63	43	193
Life	92	61	3.23	204	52	1329	1240	477	258	870

Position: Pitcher
Team: Kansas City Royals
Born: April 11, 1964 Chicago Heights, IL
Height: 6'1" **Weight:** 185 lbs.
Bats: Right **Throws:** Right
Acquired: 19th-round pick in 6/82
free-agent draft

Saberhagen led both leagues with a 23-6 record in 1989, good enough to win a second Cy Young Award in his six-year career. He set career highs in wins, games, ERA, innings pitched, and strikeouts. He became the American League's darling in 1985, when he went 20-6 for the World Champion Royals. He became both the A.L. Cy Young winner and the World Series MVP following two complete-game victories in postseason play. In the Fall Classic, he allowed just one run in 18 innings. Saberhagen, one of the most celebrated pitchers in Royals history, was a 19th-round draft choice in 1982.

The Cy Young Award will jack Saberhagen's 1990 cards up to a quarter. Invest in his cards, but don't expect immediate returns. He has never had back-to-back winning seasons. Our pick for his best 1990 card is Score.

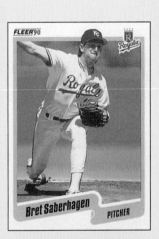

257

CHRIS SABO

	BA	G	AB	R	H	2B	3B	HR	RBI	SB
1989	.260	82	304	40	79	21	1	6	29	14
Life	.267	219	842	114	225	61	3	17	73	60

Position: Third base
Team: Cincinnati Reds
Born: January 19, 1962   Detroit, MI
Height: 6'   **Weight:** 185 lbs.
Bats: Right   **Throws:** Right
Acquired: Second-round pick in 6/83
free-agent draft

The 1988 N.L. Rookie of the Year, Sabo didn't win equal recognition for his sophomore campaign. His rookie acclaim had to do with the way he started his first year. He had ten homers, 28 stolen bases, and a .312 batting average before the All-Star break (he was selected as a reserve). Nick-named "Spuds" for his similarities with the beer company mascot, he finished the season with only one more homer while hitting .271, though his stolen base total climbed to 46 by the end of the year. Nevertheless, the amateur hockey champion burned out sometime during his rookie year, and he hasn't recovered yet.

Sabo is fiery and has talent, but he is injury prone. Don't invest more than a nickel in his 1990 cards; wait to see if he can have a top season. Our pick for his best 1990 card is Score.

LUIS SALAZAR

	BA	G	AB	R	H	2B	3B	HR	RBI	SB
1989	.282	121	326	34	92	12	2	9	34	1
Life	.267	986	3103	340	827	110	27	63	345	113

Position: Infield
Team: Chicago Cubs
Born: May 19, 1956   Barcelona, Venezuela
Height: 5'9"   **Weight:** 180 lbs.
Bats: Right   **Throws:** Right
Acquired: Traded from Padres with
Marvell Wynne for Calvin
Schiraldi, Phil Stephenson, and
Darrin Jackson, 8/89

Salazar joined the Cubs in late 1989, just in time to help the team win a division title. In his tenth major league season, he was used by the Cubs as a backup infielder and pinch-hitter. He started at third base for Chicago in the 1989 National League Championship Series. Salazar was coming off a strong 1988 season with Detroit, in which he tied a career-high with 62 RBI. In 1983, he had a personal best of 14 homers. Switching teams is nothing new for Salazar. He's played with the Padres, White Sox, and Tigers before joining the Cubs. His minor league career, dating back to 1974, includes preliminary stints in the Royals' and Pirates' minor league organizations.

Salazar is a fine utility player, but that won't help make his cards more valuable. Skip over his 1990 commons. Our pick for his best 1990 card is Donruss.

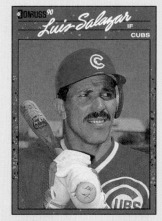

JUAN SAMUEL

	BA	G	AB	R	H	2B	3B	HR	RBI	SB
1989	.235	137	532	69	125	16	2	11	48	42
Life	.260	938	3836	560	997	189	72	103	441	280

Position: Outfield
Team: New York Mets
Born: December 9, 1960   San Pedro
de Macoris, Dominican Republic
Height: 5'11"   **Weight:** 170 lbs.
Bats: Right   **Throws:** Right
Acquired: Traded from Phillies for
Len Dykstra and Roger
McDowell, 7/89

Samuel became the antidote to the Mets center field tribulations in 1989. A Phillies second baseman for the preceding five seasons, he had displayed a throwing arm and range well-suited for the outfield. When his average dropped to .248 with 12 homers, the Phils were willing to trade him. Going to the Mets didn't help him offensively. His average skidded downward to .235. Samuel did maintain his running attack, swiping a team-leading 42 bases. He's been active on base ever since his 1984 rookie season, when he stole a career-high 72 bases. Samuel's lowest total was an impressive 33 swipes, coming in 1988.

Samuel's 1990 cards have great potential since he's a Met. Get them at a nickel apiece, then strike it rich as soon as the Mets win a pennant or Samuel regains his All-Star form. Our pick for his best 1990 card is Score.

RYNE SANDBERG

	BA	G	AB	R	H	2B	3B	HR	RBI	SB
1989	.290	157	606	104	176	25	5	30	76	15
Life	.285	1234	4893	756	1395	226	54	139	549	250

Position: Second base
Team: Chicago Cubs
Born: September 18, 1959   Spokane, WA
Height: 6'2"   **Weight:** 180 lbs.
Bats: Right   **Throws:** Right
Acquired: Traded from Phillies with Larry
Bowa for Ivan DeJesus, 1/82

Sandberg made his fourth starting appearance as the N.L.'s second baseman in the 1989 All-Star Game, an indication of his popularity among baseball fans. "Ryno" has earned this devotion of fans with great fielding and clutch hitting. He maintained a batting average at .290 in 1989 and had a career year in home runs. His presence was valued by the Cubs during their 1989 pennant run, due to Sandberg's past experience as a winner. As a member of the pennant-winning 1984 Cubs, he batted .314 with 19 homers and 84 RBI, winning the N.L. MVP Award. During his first five seasons with the Cubs, Sandberg stole 30-plus bases a year, including a career-high 54 in 1985.

Sandberg's 1990 cards will cost a quarter or less in 1990. Buy them up. He will be a star for years. Our pick for his best 1990 card is Score.

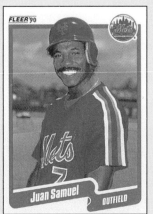

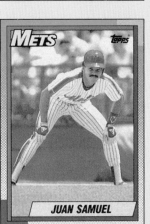

DEION SANDERS

	BA	G	AB	R	H	2B	3B	HR	RBI	SB
89 AA	.286	33	119	28	34	2	2	1	6	17
89 Major	.234	14	47	7	11	2	0	2	7	1

Position: Outfield
Team: New York Yankees
Born: August 9, 1967 Fort Myers, FL
Height: 5'11" **Weight:** 187 lbs.
Bats: Left **Throws:** Left
Acquired: 30th-round pick in 6/88
free-agent draft

Following the example set by two-sport star Bo Jackson, Yankees prospect Sanders plans on playing both major league baseball and NFL football, with the Atlanta Falcons. He was the first player in history to hit a major league home run (during a brief appearance with the 1989 Yankees) and score an NFL touchdown in the same week. A two-time football All-American at Florida State, Sanders has impeccable gridiron credentials. On the baseball diamond, he was ranked in 1989 by Double-A Eastern League managers as the best baserunner and most exciting player in the loop. He is known as "Neon Deion" for his flamboyant personality and exciting athletic ability.

Sanders's 1990 cards will cost 50 cents or more in 1990. If he chooses football full-time, his card values may go up in smoke. Our pick for his best 1990 card is Topps.

SCOTT SANDERSON

	W	L	ERA	G	CG	IP	H	ER	BB	SO
1989	11	9	3.94	37	2	146	155	64	31	86
Life	98	89	3.55	309	32	1620	1567	639	412	1081

Position: Pitcher
Team: Chicago Cubs
Born: July 22, 1956 Dearborn, MI
Height: 6'5" **Weight:** 200 lbs.
Bats: Right **Throws:** Right
Acquired: Traded from Padres for Carmelo
Martinez, Craig Lefferts, and Fritz
Connally, 12/83

Battling back from back surgery in 1988, Sanderson made 1989 count with the third double-digit winning season of his career. His 11 victories marked his highest win total since 1982, when he won 12 games for the Montreal Expos. In 12 major league seasons, he has claimed just five winning seasons. Staying healthy has been the biggest challenge he has faced in the majors. Torn thumb ligaments, back spasms, torn knee ligaments, a sore shoulder, and back surgery have sidelined him throughout his hard-luck career. When he first came up with Montreal in 1978, after less than two years of minor league experience, he had unlimited promise. In 1980, Sanderson won a personal-best of 16 games and stayed with the Expos through 1983.

Sanderson's age and past health problems limit his future. His 1990 commons are unsafe investments. Our pick for his best 1990 card is Score.

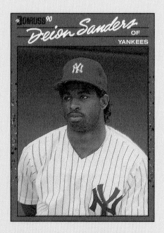

BENITO SANTIAGO

	BA	G	AB	R	H	2B	3B	HR	RBI	SB
1989	.236	129	462	50	109	16	3	16	62	11
Life	.264	431	1562	173	413	73	7	47	193	47

Position: Catcher
Team: San Diego Padres
Born: March 9, 1965   Ponce, Puerto Rico
Height: 6'1"   **Weight:** 185 lbs.
Bats: Right   **Throws:** Right
Acquired: Signed as a free agent, 9/82

After only three seasons in the N.L., Santiago is one of baseball's best catchers. He continued to be a defensive standout, mowing down opposing baserunners with his rifle-like arm. Although he hasn't topped his 1987 rookie season average of .300, he is a good hitter with above-average speed. In 1987, Santiago hit 18 home runs and 79 RBI on his way to unanimous selection as the N.L. Rookie of the Year. His first season ended with a 34-game hitting streak, setting a new record for rookies. He was the first catcher to hit in more than 30 straight games. Santiago hit .297 with 17 homers and 71 RBI at Triple-A Las Vegas in 1986.

Because Santiago's batting average was down, his 1990 cards may cost just a dime. That's a good investment price. He is an excellent catcher. Our pick for his best 1990 card is Score.

NELSON SANTOVENIA

	BA	G	AB	R	H	2B	3B	HR	RBI	SB
1989	.250	97	304	30	76	14	1	5	31	2
Life	.243	191	614	56	149	34	3	13	72	4

Position: Catcher
Team: Montreal Expos
Born: July 27, 1961   Pinar de Rio, Cuba
Height: 6'3"   **Weight:** 215 lbs.
Bats: Right   **Throws:** Right
Acquired: First pick in secondary phase of 6/82 free-agent draft

Santovenia proved in 1989 that his competent 1988 rookie outing for the Expos was no fluke. After trading Gary Carter in 1984, the Expos couldn't find a replacement until 1988 when Santovenia arrived. He adapted to the quirks of his new pitching staff with apparent ease, handling it with the skill of a veteran. Despite being one of Montreal's largest players, Santovenia has deceptive speed for a catcher; he grounds into few double plays and has proven that he can steal a couple bases a year. Slowly, he's raised his batting average, from his rookie season's .236 to a .250 clip in 1989. Santovenia may soon be an All-Star receiver.

Santovenia should have sole ownership of the starting catching chores. His 1990 cards are reasonable investments at 3 cents or less. Our pick for his best 1990 card is Score.

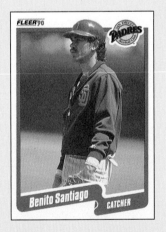
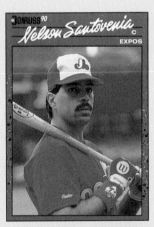
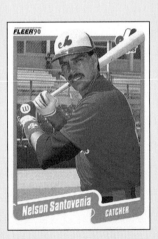

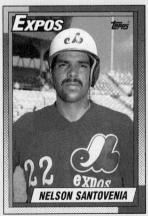

MACKEY SASSER

	BA	G	AB	R	H	2B	3B	HR	RBI	SB
1989	.291	72	182	17	53	14	2	1	22	0
Life	.280	146	332	28	93	24	3	2	41	0

Position: Catcher
Team: New York Mets
Born: August 3, 1962 Ft. Gaines, GA
Height: 6'1" **Weight:** 210 lbs.
Bats: Left **Throws:** Right
Acquired: Traded from Pirates with Tim
 Drummond for Randy Milligan
 and Scott Henioa, 3/88

After his over-the-top 1989 performance, Sasser may be the inside favorite for the catcher's slot with the New York Mets. With Gary Carter getting injured early, Sasser got a chance to prove himself as a starter during his sophomore season. He improved upon his rookie stats that were nothing to sneeze at: 35 hits in 123 at-bats for a .285 batting average. Starting 30 games as a catcher in 1988, he also proved himself a useful substitute in both the infield and outfield. While Sasser's power stats still aren't profuse, he exercises control at bat, racking up few strikeouts.

With Carter out of the picture, Sasser will battle Barry Lyons for the job. If you bet on Sasser to win, pick up his 1990 commons. A year in the spotlight could double his card values. Our pick for his best 1990 card is Fleer.

STEVE SAX

	BA	G	AB	R	H	2B	3B	HR	RBI	SB
1989	.315	158	651	88	205	26	3	5	63	43
Life	.287	1249	4963	662	1423	185	38	35	396	333

Position: Second base
Team: New York Yankees
Born: January 29, 1960 Sacramento, CA
Height: 5'11" **Weight:** 185 lbs.
Bats: Right **Throws:** Right
Acquired: Signed as a free agent, 11/88

After seven years as the Dodgers second baseman, Sax quickly adapted to a new job in a new league in 1989. Signed in November 1988 to a contract by the Yankees, Sax was chosen to bring more offense and speed to the team's keystone position. He did just that, hitting over .300 and topping 40 stolen bases. His success earned him a spot on the A.L. All-Star squad, after three appearances with the N.L. The N.L. Rookie of the Year in 1982, he hit a career-high .332 with the 1986 Dodgers. Sax notched a 25-game hitting streak in 1986, the longest in the majors that year.

Sax was better than ever in his first year with the Yankees. Buy his 1990 cards at 15 cents or less, and wait for quick price increases. Our pick for his best 1990 card is Fleer.

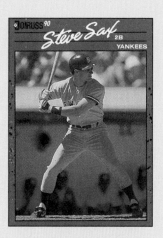

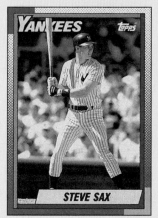

DAN SCHATZEDER

	W	L	ERA	G	SV	IP	H	ER	BB	SO
1989	4	1	4.45	36	1	56	64	28	28	46
Life	68	65	3.80	445	10	1241	1180	524	445	705

Position: Pitcher
Team: Houston Astros
Born: December 1, 1954   Elmhurst, IL
Height: 6'   **Weight:** 195 lbs.
Bats: Left   **Throws:** Left
Acquired: Signed as a free agent, 3/89

Schatzeder beat the odds and made the 1989 Houston Astros pitching staff as a nonroster invitee to spring training. The lefty had been with six teams before joining Houston. After Schatzeder was chosen as a third-round selection in the 1976 free-agent draft, he needed just over one year in the minors before getting his debut with the Montreal Expos in 1977. His best year with the Expos came in 1979, when he was 10-5 with a 2.83 ERA. Traded to the Tigers, Schatzeder had an 11-13 record with nine complete games for the 1980 Bengals, marking his career high for victories.

Schatzeder will close out his career somewhere as a starter and reliever, simply to keep in the majors. This is a noble aim, but it doesn't produce statistics conducive for investments in his common-priced 1990 cards. Our pick for his best 1990 card is Fleer.

CALVIN SCHIRALDI

	W	L	ERA	G	SV	IP	H	ER	BB	SO
1989	6	7	3.51	59	4	100	72	39	63	71
Life	29	30	4.18	190	20	444	412	206	202	396

Position: Pitcher
Team: San Diego Padres
Born: June 16, 1962   Houston, TX
Height: 6'5"   **Weight:** 215 lbs.
Bats: Right   **Throws:** Right
Acquired: Traded from Cubs with Phil Stephenson and Darrin Jackson for Luis Salazar and Marvell Wynne, 8/89

Schiraldi pitched in two pennant races in 1989. He began the year with the Cubs then was traded to San Diego. Although he missed participating in the N.L.C.S. with the Cubs, he was part of the Padres chase. Playing for contenders is nothing new for him. After two brief stints with the Mets in 1984 and '85, he had his rookie season with the 1986 Boston Red Sox. He finished the season by working three ill-fated games in the World Series. At the tender age of 24, he was tagged with two Series losses. The losses marred Schiraldi's fine season, including a 4-2 mark with nine saves, a 1.51 ERA, and 55 strikeouts in 51 innings.

Schiraldi has been unspectacular since 1986. See if the Padres can turn his career around before gambling on his 1990 commons. Our pick for his best 1990 card is Topps.

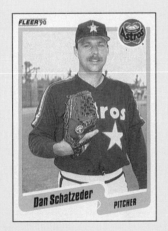
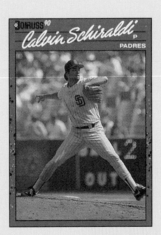

DAVE SCHMIDT

	W	L	ERA	G	CG	IP	H	ER	BB	SO
1989	10	13	5.69	38	2	156	196	99	36	46
Life	51	51	3.77	335	5	846	888	354	219	453

Position: Pitcher
Team: Baltimore Orioles
Born: April 22, 1957 Niles, MI
Height: 6'1" **Weight:** 194 lbs.
Bats: Right **Throws:** Right
Acquired: Signed as a free agent, 1/87

Schmidt had a dismal 1989 season pitching for the Orioles. The O's kept bouncing him from the starting rotation to the bullpen, resulting in his first losing season during his three years in Baltimore. His strikeout-to-innings pitched ratio shrank alarmingly in 1989, while his ERA burgeoned to a career-high 5.69. The Orioles have worked him harder than the Rangers or Cubs ever did: Schmidt has reached a new career-high of innings pitched in each of the last three years. Judging from his stats, the O's would do well to save Schmidt for relief, where he keeps his head and delivers a solid effort.

Schmidt's future rests in getting just one role to pitch in, be it starting or relief. For now, pulling double duty doesn't help his stats. Avoid his 1990 commons. Our pick for his best 1990 card is Donruss.

DICK SCHOFIELD

	BA	G	AB	R	H	2B	3B	HR	RBI	SB
1989	.228	91	302	42	69	11	2	4	26	9
Life	.231	827	2658	315	613	87	23	47	229	87

Position: Shortstop
Team: California Angels
Born: November 21, 1962 Springfield, IL
Height: 5'10" **Weight:** 175 lbs.
Bats: Right **Throws:** Right
Acquired: First-round pick in 6/81 free-agent draft

A fractured left hand limited Schofield to 91 games in 1989, just when it appeared he was having one of his better years offensively. Though he's only 27, he has been in the majors for more than six years. His fielding is what got him to the majors, and it's what kept him there. A frequent league leader in fielding, he makes few errors, considering his occasional assignments to second base. His greatest liability is as a batter. Although he's been successful in about 80 percent of his stolen base attempts, he seems slow going to first base. Schofield still chases some bad pitches. His father, Dick Sr., was a major league shortstop in the 1960s and '70s.

Wait for Schofield to stay healthy for a full season before considering his 1990 commons as investments. Our pick for his best 1990 card is Score.

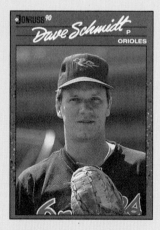

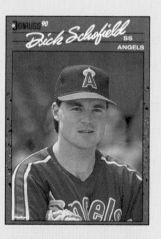

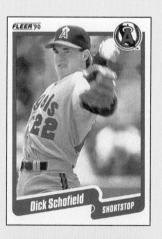

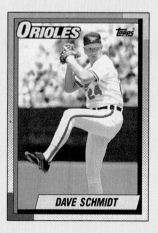

MIKE SCHOOLER

	W	L	ERA	G	SV	IP	H	ER	BB	SO
1989	1	7	2.81	67	33	77	81	24	19	69
Life	6	15	3.24	107	48	125	126	45	43	123

Position: Pitcher
Team: Seattle Mariners
Born: August 10, 1962   Anaheim, CA
Height: 6'3" **Weight:** 220 lbs.
Bats: Right **Throws:** Right
Acquired: Second-round pick in 6/85
free-agent draft

After only two major league seasons, Schooler has started breaking team records for the Seattle Mariners. The sophomore righty earned 33 saves in 1989, seven more than the old M's single-season record from 1983. His saves tied Dennis Eckersley and Dan Plesac for third best in the American League. During his 1988 rookie season, Schooler earned saves in his first seven opportunities. He finished the year with 15 saves and five wins. Already, it seems that he may become the most accomplished reliever in Mariner history. Going into 1990, Schooler needs just five saves to be the team's career leader.

Investing in cards of relievers is quite risky. With Schooler, it's best to see if he has the stamina for a second record-setting year in 1990 before buying his nickel-priced issues. Our pick for his best 1990 card is Donruss.

MIKE SCIOSCIA

	BA	G	AB	R	H	2B	3B	HR	RBI	SB
1989	.250	133	408	40	102	16	0	10	44	0
Life	.261	1070	3245	294	848	151	7	45	316	18

Position: Catcher
Team: Los Angeles Dodgers
Born: November 27, 1958
Upper Darby, PA
Height: 6'2" **Weight:** 223 lbs.
Bats: Left **Throws:** Right
Acquired: First-round pick in 6/76
free-agent draft

Scioscia is a ten-year veteran with the Dodgers, and he got his first All-Star Game berth in 1989. His membership on the N.L. roster was the recognition for his decade of defensive excellence. Scioscia has never been a heavy hitter. He hit a career-high .296 in 1985, although he normally bats 30 to 40 points lower. For years the Dodgers have considered any hitting Scioscia might do to be a bonus. He was an offensive bonus in the 1988 N.L.C.S., hitting .364 with a game-tying homer off Dwight Gooden in the sixth game. Scioscia is considered baseball's best at blocking the plate. His skilled handling of pitchers helps to keep the Dodger staff successful.

Although he's a defensive master, Scioscia's modest hitting doesn't merit investment in his common-priced 1990 cards. Our pick for his best 1990 card is Score.

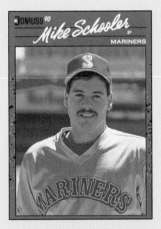
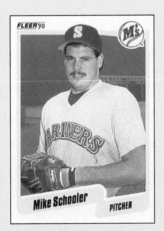

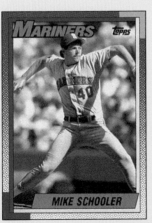

MIKE SCOTT

	W	L	ERA	G	SV	IP	H	ER	BB	SO
1989	20	10	3.10	33	9	229	79	180	62	172
Life	115	93	3.48	313	41	1855	717	1653	557	1345

Position: Pitcher
Team: Houston Astros
Born: April 26, 1955   Santa Monica, CA
Height: 6'3"   **Weight:** 215 lbs.
Bats: Right   **Throws:** Right
Acquired: Traded from Mets for
    Danny Heep, 12/82

All Scott needed for a prosperous 1989 season was a chance to pitch. He won just 14 games in 1988, his lowest total in five seasons. A strained left hamstring kept him on the disabled list for three weeks. In 1989, Scott had surpassed those win totals in July. He led the '89 Astros in wins and strikeouts. He bounced around baseball for nine seasons before he learned the split-fingered fastball. Taught the pitch by Roger Craig, Scott immediately became a big winner. After a 5-11 season in 1984, he won 18 games the following season. In 1986, he pitched the Astros to the pennant with a Cy Young-winning 18-10 year, totaling 306 strikeouts and hurling a pennant-clinching no-hitter that season.

Scott was Cy Young material in 1989. This consistent hurler is a dependable 1990 card investment at 15 cents or less. Our pick for his best 1990 card is Donruss.

SCOTT SCUDDER

	W	L	ERA	G	CG	IP	H	ER	BB	SO
89 AAA	6	2	2.68	12	3	81	54	24	48	64
89 Major	4	9	4.49	23	0	100	91	50	61	66

Position: Pitcher
Team: Cincinnati Reds
Born: February 14, 1968   Paris, TX
Height: 6'2"   **Weight:** 180 lbs.
Bats: Right   **Throws:** Right
Acquired: First-round pick in 6/86
    free-agent draft

Scudder skyrocketed through the Reds' minor league system. He had his major league debut with the Reds in 1989, working both as a starter and reliever. Reaching the major leagues at age 21 might be a shock to some players, but he has tasted success regularly in his baseball career. In 1988 at Class-A Cedar Rapids, Scudder was 7-3 with a 2.02 ERA, including one no-hitter. He fanned 126 in just 102 innings. When he was promoted to Double-A Chattanooga, he had a 7-0 mark in 11 starts, with a 2.96 ERA and 52 strikeouts in 70 innings. Scudder added one victory for his squad in the Southern League playoffs.

The respect Scudder has received in the National League grew during the season. His 1990 cards are tempting investments at a dime or less. Our pick for his best 1990 card is Score.

STEVE SEARCY

	W	L	ERA	G	CG	IP	H	ER	BB	SO
89 AAA	2	3	7.54	9	0	37	41	31	37	26
89 Major	1	1	6.04	8	0	22	27	15	12	11

Position: Pitcher
Team: Detroit Tigers
Born: June 4, 1964 Knoxville, TN
Height: 6'1" **Weight:** 185 lbs.
Bats: Left **Throws:** Left
Acquired: Third-round pick in 6/85
free-agent draft

Searcy got his second shot at the major leagues with the Tigers in 1989, despite an off season in the minors. In 1988, he had been a Triple-A International League pitching sensation, compiling a 13-7 record with Toledo. He logged a league-leading 176 strikeouts in 170 innings to be named the loop's Most Valuable Pitcher. His strikeout totals led the entire Triple-A. His 1987 season at Triple-A Toledo was ended after just ten games, when a batted ball caromed off his kneecap. In 1986, Searcy was 11-6 at Double-A Glens Falls, gaining a spot on the Eastern League All-Star team.

Searcy hasn't been given the chance to prove his worth in the majors yet. Wait until he establishes himself before investing more than 3 cents each in his 1990 cards. Our pick for his best 1990 card is Fleer.

KEVIN SEITZER

	BA	G	AB	R	H	2B	3B	HR	RBI	SB
1989	.281	160	597	78	168	17	2	4	48	17
Life	.304	498	1893	289	576	86	16	26	202	39

Position: Third base
Team: Kansas City Royals
Born: March 26, 1962 Springfield, IL
Height: 5'11" **Weight:** 180 lbs.
Bats: Right **Throws:** Right
Acquired: 11th-round pick in 6/83
free-agent draft

Seitzer took over third base for Kansas City in 1987, and he's been there ever since. The Royals were so pleased by Seitzer's hitting that they moved George Brett to first base. In 1989, Seitzer led the Royals in base hits. He had a first-class rookie season in 1987, batting .323 with 15 homers and 83 RBI. His 207 hits tied Kirby Puckett for the league lead, and it was the first time a rookie topped 200 hits since 1964. Seitzer became the first Royals rookie ever to be named to the A.L. All-Star team. Seitzer played four seasons in the minors and three campaigns at Eastern Illinois.

Seitzer's 1990 cards sell for a quarter each. There will be little profit potential at that price, unless he wins a batting title. Our pick for his best 1990 card is Score.

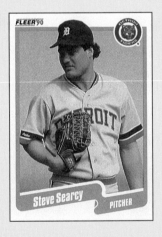

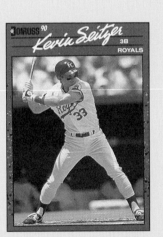

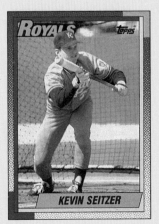

LARRY SHEETS

	BA	G	AB	R	H	2B	3B	HR	RBI	SB
1989	.243	102	304	33	74	12	1	7	33	1
Life	.268	606	1907	233	511	80	3	84	110	5

Position: First base; outfield
Team: Baltimore Orioles
Born: December 6, 1959 Staunton, VA
Height: 6'3" **Weight:** 215 lbs.
Bats: Left **Throws:** Right
Acquired: Second-round pick in 6/78 free-agent draft

After a sensational 1987 season, Sheets had to fight for playing time with the Orioles. The hard-hitting first baseman and outfielder played a reserve role with the 1989 O's, getting into just 102 games. He set career marks with 31 homers, 94 RBI, and a .316 batting average in 1987, becoming one of just five American League players that year to top .300, 30 homers, and 90 RBI. His totals slipped to .230 with ten homers and 47 RBI in 1988. His woes multiplied in 1989, with career lows in round-trippers and RBI. He had socked ten or more homers during his first four seasons with Baltimore. Sheets played in the minors for more than five seasons.

Sheets has long-ball punch, but he'll never fully tap his potential until he keeps a starting job with the O's. For now, don't invest in his 1990 commons. Our pick for his best 1990 card is Fleer.

GARY SHEFFIELD

	BA	G	AB	R	H	2B	3B	HR	RBI	SB
1989	.247	95	368	34	91	18	0	5	32	10
Life	.246	119	448	46	110	19	0	9	44	13

Position: Shortstop; third base
Team: Milwaukee Brewers
Born: November 18, 1968 Tampa, FL
Height: 5'11" **Weight:** 190 lbs.
Bats: Right **Throws:** Right
Acquired: First-round pick in 6/86 free-agent draft

Sheffield suffered a setback in his road to stardom with the 1989 Brewers. He entered the season as the starting shortstop for the Brew Crew but was demoted back to Triple-A Denver in July. It was discovered after Sheffield returned to the minors that he had been playing with a fractured foot since May. Brewers physicians hadn't discovered the injury when he was in the majors. Sheffield first gained national attention in 1988. He batted .314 with 19 homers and 65 RBI at Double-A El Paso in 77 games. When promoted to Triple-A Denver, he hit .344. The Brewers called Sheffield up in September for 24 games, and he had 12 RBI.

Watch for Sheffield as Milwaukee's third baseman. Unlike his 1989 rookie cards, which shot past the $2 mark early, his 1990 issues will be reasonably priced at 50 to 75 cents. Our pick for his best 1990 card is Donruss.

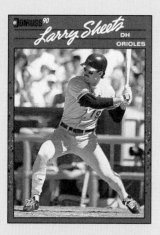
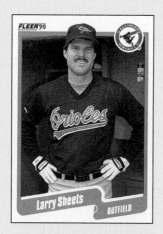
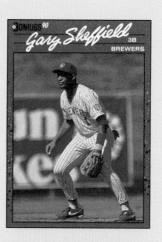

PAT SHERIDAN

	BA	G	AB	R	H	2B	3B	HR	RBI	SB
1989	.205	70	161	20	33	3	4	3	14	4
Life	.256	764	2186	290	559	85	21	44	235	81

Position: Outfield
Team: San Francisco Giants
Born: December 4, 1957 Ann Arbor, MI
Height: 6'3" **Weight:** 195 lbs.
Bats: Left **Throws:** Right
Acquired: Traded from Tigers for
　　　　　Tracy Jones, 5/89

Sheridan's 1989 season of struggles with the Giants came to a painful conclusion in the World Series. In Game Three, the A's took a 2-0 lead when Dave Henderson doubled off the top of the right field fence. Sheridan's leap for the ball was ill-timed, another near miss in a season of near misses. He couldn't hit well enough to win the right field spot full-time. He spent 1986 to 1988 with the Tigers. He hit a career-high 11 homers for the 1988 Bengals. In 1987, his two-run homer gave the Tigers their only A.L.C.S. win over the Twins. Sheridan played college ball at Eastern Michigan.

　Sheridan won't start for the Giants. He'll be a reserve, so don't invest in his 1990 commons. Our pick for his best 1990 card is Topps.

ERIC SHOW

	W	L	ERA	G	CG	IP	H	ER	BB	SO
1989	8	6	4.26	16	1	106	113	50	39	66
Life	94	79	3.43	270	35	1497	1333	571	552	896

Position: Pitcher
Team: San Diego Padres
Born: May 19, 1956 Riverside, CA
Height: 6'1" **Weight:** 190 lbs.
Bats: Right **Throws:** Right
Acquired: 18th-round pick in 6/78
　　　　　free-agent draft

After putting together the best overall season of his eight-year career in 1988, he topped that in 1989 by becoming the winningest pitcher in San Diego history. His eight wins in 1989 gave him 94 career triumphs—all of them for the Padres—besting by two Randy Jones's 1973 to 1980 record. Show's all-time 1988 highs included 16 wins, 13 complete games, and 144 strikeouts. He had twice before won 15 games (in 1983 and '84) and, in 1985, hurled 143 innings pitched and whiffed 141. If he remains healthy, he should have a few more years of such dependability. However, 1989 found Show on the 60-day disabled list with lower back spasms, with marks reflecting his discomfort.

　Show's 1990 cards sell for 3 cents or less, primarily because he's pitched for an also-ran team. Until he lands his first 20-win season, his cards won't climb in value. Our pick for his best 1990 card is Donruss.

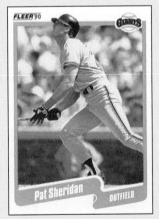

RUBEN SIERRA

	BA	G	AB	R	H	2B	3B	HR	RBI	SB
1989	.306	162	634	101	194	35	14	29	119	8
Life	.273	589	2274	325	620	115	30	98	374	49

Position: Outfield
Team: Texas Rangers
Born: October 6, 1965   Rio Piedras,
Puerto Rico
Height: 6'1" **Weight:** 175 lbs.
Bats: Both **Throws:** Right
Acquired: Signed as a free agent, 11/82

Sierra had 69 home runs before he reached the age of 23. Only 13 other players in history have surpassed him in homers at such an early age (Ted Williams and Joe DiMaggio among them). Still, 1988 was an off year for Sierra, who saw his average, homers, and RBI falter while chalking up some unsightly errors. In 1989, however, he came back with enough force to be among league leaders in slugging percentage, RBI, and total bases, with exemplary marks in runs, hits, triples, and average. A switch-hitter, he continues to improve from the left side. In the 1989 All-Star Game, Sierra had two hits, one RBI, and one run scored.

Sierra is only inches from superstardom. Buying his 1990 cards at 15 cents or less is one of the best investments you can make. Our pick for his best 1990 card is Fleer.

JOHN SMILEY

	W	L	ERA	G	CG	IP	H	ER	BB	SO
1989	12	8	2.81	28	8	205	174	64	49	123
Life	31	24	3.46	137	13	497	432	191	149	319

Position: Pitcher
Team: Pittsburgh Pirates
Born: March 17, 1965   Phoenixville, PA
Height: 6'4" **Weight:** 195 lbs.
Bats: Left **Throws:** Left
Acquired: 12th-round pick in 6/83
free-agent draft

After a notable rookie season in the Pittsburgh bullpen, third-year player Smiley proved his worth as a starter for the 1989 Bucs. He began his major league career in 1987, setting a Pirates rookie record by pitching in 63 games. His four saves and five wins made him the league's top-ranked rookie reliever that year. In 1988, the Pirates made Smiley a starter, wanting a lefthander for the rotation. The move resulted in his gathering a 13-11 record, including a six-game winning streak. Smiley struck out nine Padres in six innings in 1988, and recorded a one-hitter, a two-hitter, and a three-hitter during the year.

Smiley's 1990 cards will sell for a nickel or less. If the Pirates keep him in the starting rotation, he'll make those prices climb quickly. Our pick for his best 1990 card is Score.

BRYN SMITH

	W	L	ERA	G	CG	IP	H	ER	BB	SO
1989	10	11	2.84	33	3	215	177	68	54	129
Life	81	71	3.29	284	20	1400	1310	511	341	838

Position: Pitcher
Team: Montreal Expos
Born: August 11, 1955 Marietta, GA
Height: 6'2" **Weight:** 205 lbs.
Bats: Right **Throws:** Right
Acquired: Traded from Orioles with Rudy
May and Randy Miller for Don
Stanhouse, Joe Kerrigan, and
Gary Roenicke, 12/77

Smith had his sixth season with double-digit wins for the 1989 Expos. The palmball master hasn't approached his career-high 1985 season, when he was 18-5 with a 2.91 ERA. His .783 winning percentage set a Montreal team record. He suffered the next season with bone chips in his right elbow, and underwent surgery in September. After spending a one-month minor league rehabilitation, Smith regained his health and returned to the majors. He was overlooked in the 1974 free-agent draft by all big league teams, but eventually hooked on with the Orioles' organization. Smith toiled in the minors for seven years before getting a chance at the majors.

Smith's 1990 cards will sell for 3 cents or less. They aren't decent investments, because Smith's only remarkable winning season was in 1985. Our pick for his best 1990 card is Fleer.

DAVE SMITH

	W	L	ERA	G	SV	IP	H	ER	BB	SO
1989	3	4	2.64	52	25	58	49	17	19	36
Life	47	41	2.54	514	176	702	601	198	240	479

Position: Pitcher
Team: Houston Astros
Born: January 21, 1955 San Francisco, CA
Height: 6'1" **Weight:** 195 lbs.
Bats: Right **Throws:** Right
Acquired: Sixth-round pick in 6/76
free-agent draft

For the last decade, Smith has been one of baseball's most consistent relievers. He tallied his fifth straight season of 20-plus saves in 1989, the seventh time he's topped double digits. He has appeared in more than 500 games for the Astros in his career, all but one game as a reliever. Possessing a mean forkball, his ERA has climbed above 3.00 only twice in his career. Twice, he's kept his ERA under 2.00—including a career-best 1.65 mark in 1987. He made his first All-Star team in 1986, the year he accumulated a personal best of 33 saves. He doesn't serve gopher balls; Smith compiled a string of 112 innings without yielding a homer, ending in 1988.

Smith has participated in more than 200 victories in just one decade. His common-priced 1990 cards are ripe for long-term price advances. Our pick for his best 1990 card is Fleer.

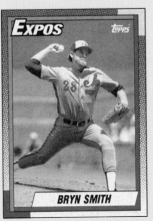

DWIGHT SMITH

	BA	G	AB	R	H	2B	3B	HR	RBI	SB
88 AAA	.293	129	505	76	148	26	3	9	48	25
89 Major	.324	109	343	52	111	19	6	9	52	9

Position: Outfield
Team: Chicago Cubs
Born: November 8, 1963   Tallahassee, FL
Height: 5'11"   **Weight:** 175 lbs.
Bats: Left   **Throws:** Right
Acquired: Third-round pick in 6/84
free-agent draft

Combining with fellow rookie Jerome Walton, Smith helped give the Cubs one of the best one-two first-year punches in the 1989 season. All during the season, Smith kept his average past the coveted .300 mark. He earned his promotion partly due to his fine showing in 1988 at Triple-A Iowa. For the fourth consecutive season, he was among the top ten hitters in his league. He hit .293 with nine homers, 48 RBI, and 25 stolen bases. Smith's best minor league season came in 1987 with Double-A Pittsfield. His 111 runs, 270 total bases, and 60 stolen bases were Eastern League highs, while his .337 average, 18 homers, and 72 RBI were career bests.

Smith's 1990 cards will be going for at least 50 cents. Until he escapes the Cubs platoon system, his cards are an unsafe investment at that price. Our pick for his best 1990 card is Score.

LEE SMITH

	W	L	ERA	G	SV	IP	H	ER	BB	SO
1989	6	1	3.57	64	25	70	53	28	33	96
Life	50	57	2.96	586	234	836	716	275	334	836

Position: Pitcher
Team: Boston Red Sox
Born: December 4, 1957   Jamestown, LA
Height: 6'6"   **Weight:** 250 lbs.
Bats: Right   **Throws:** Right
Acquired: Traded from Cubs for Al Nipper
and Calvin Schiraldi, 12/87

In 1989, Smith earned his lowest save total in seven seasons, but he produced enough to become sixth on baseball's all-time save list. The huge relief ace tallied 25 saves in 1989, which led the Red Sox, but it was his smallest mark since he saved 17 games with the 1982 Cubs. Smith's 234 lifetime saves have come over ten major league seasons. From 1983 (when he led the National League) through 1988, he registered a minimum of 29 saves a season. Smith began his career in the Cubs' system after being selected in the second round of the 1975 draft.

During the 1990 season, Smith will have played a part in more than 300 victories in his career. Pick up his 1990 cards at a nickel or less for some long-term gains. Our pick for his best 1990 card is Donruss.

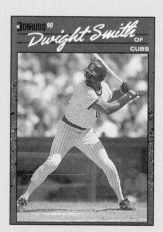
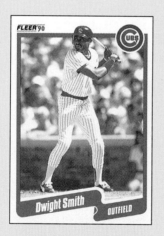

LONNIE SMITH

	BA	G	AB	R	H	2B	3B	HR	RBI	SB
1989	.315	134	482	89	152	34	4	21	79	25
Life	.290	1134	3911	700	1136	210	42	68	385	337

Position: Outfield
Team: Atlanta Braves
Born: December 22, 1955 Chicago, IL
Height: 5'9" **Weight:** 170 lbs.
Bats: Right **Throws:** Right
Acquired: Signed as a free agent, 3/88

The most amazing comeback in 1989 belonged to Smith. He was the only Braves regular to bat above .300 in 1989. He also discovered untapped potential as a home run threat. After never hitting more than eight homers in a season during his prior eight years in the majors, he reached the 20-homer plateau in '89. His best season had been with the '82 Cardinals, when he hit .307, stole 68 bases, and scored a league-high 120 runs. Before his 1989 resurgence, Smith's future looked cloudy. The Royals released him at the end of 1987, and he hit a meager .237 in a 43-game trial with the Braves in 1988.

After his stunning comeback, Smith's 1990 cards will cost as much as 15 cents each. Don't expect long-term gains, but pick up a few to sell quickly if he repeats his success. Our pick for his best 1990 card is Fleer.

OZZIE SMITH

	BA	G	AB	R	H	2B	3B	HR	RBI	SB
1989	.273	155	593	82	162	30	8	2	50	29
Life	.256	1783	6507	849	1668	276	51	18	550	432

Position: Shortstop
Team: St. Louis Cardinals
Born: December 26, 1954 Mobile, AL
Height: 5'10" **Weight:** 155 lbs.
Bats: Both **Throws:** Right
Acquired: Traded from Padres for
  Garry Templeton, 2/82

In his 12th major league season and his eighth as a Cardinal in 1989, Smith received his ninth All-Star bid, seven times being voted as the N.L.'s starting shortstop. He kept his batting average near .280 for most of the season, and maintained his fame as baseball's slickest-fielding shortstop. The perennial Gold Glove winner won his first fielding award in 1980, and had nine consecutive going into 1989. Despite weighing just 155 pounds, Smith is a strong run producer at the plate. In 1987, he drove in 75 runs without one homer. He has more than 400 career stolen bases, third best in St. Louis history. The Cardinals recognize Smith's value to the club.

Smith's 1990 cards are great investments at 15 cents or less. He could provide short-term and long-term profits. Our pick for his best 1990 card is Fleer.

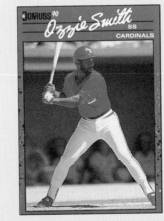

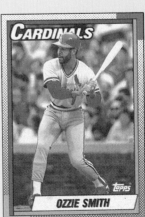

PETE SMITH

	W	L	ERA	G	CG	IP	H	ER	BB	SO
1989	5	14	4.75	28	1	142	144	75	57	115
Life	13	31	4.20	66	6	369	366	172	159	250

Position: Pitcher
Team: Atlanta Braves
Born: February 27, 1966 Abington, MA
Height: 6'2" **Weight:** 183 lbs.
Bats: Right **Throws:** Right
Acquired: Traded from Phillies with
Ozzie Virgil for Steve Bedrosian
and Milt Thompson, 12/85

In two full seasons with the Braves, Smith hasn't been able to fashion a record that truly reflects his finesse. At the end of his 1988 rookie season, he had seven wins, 15 losses, and a 3.69 ERA. Those statistics don't show that he led the Braves with five complete games and three shutouts (the last two back-to-back against the Chicago Cubs). He notched 124 strikeouts, and showed a mastery against left-handed hitters. Although he walked nearly four batters per nine innings in 1989, he posted more than 100 strikeouts for the second straight season, an encouraging sign for the Braves. Smith began his six-year professional career with the Phillies' organization.

Remember that Smith is just 24 years old. With more experience, he should improve. Patient investors who pick up Smith's 1990 commons will see eventual payoffs. Our pick for his best 1990 card is Donruss.

ROY SMITH

	W	L	ERA	G	CG	IP	H	ER	BB	SO
1989	10	6	3.92	32	2	172	180	75	51	92
Life	20	17	4.31	87	3	384	417	184	131	208

Position: Pitcher
Team: Minnesota Twins
Born: September 6, 1961
Mount Vernon, NY
Height: 6'3" **Weight:** 217 lbs.
Bats: Right **Throws:** Right
Acquired: Traded from Indians with Ramon
Romero for Bryan Oelkers and
Ken Schrom, 1/86

Smith proved that patience is one of the keys to his success. Active in pro baseball since 1979, he had stints with the Indians' and Phillies' organizations before starting over with the Twins' farm system in 1987. Prior to 1989, he had spent parts of his first ten campaigns in the minor leagues. He had partial seasons in the majors from 1984 through 1988, with his best effort being a 5-5 record in 1984. In 1989, the Twins gave Smith a full season to win a job. He responded with a career-high 10-6 record, second on the team behind only Allan Anderson. Smith achieved pro highs in both starts and innings pitched.

Smith's minor league days should be behind him. His late start may limit his statistics. Safe investors won't spend more than a nickel on his 1990 issues. Our pick for his best 1990 card is Topps.

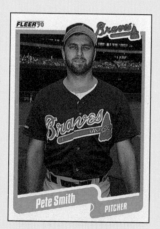

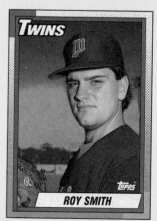

ZANE SMITH

	W	L	ERA	G	CG	IP	H	ER	BB	SO
1989	1	13	3.49	48	0	147	141	57	52	93
Life	39	59	3.93	190	17	901	905	393	385	522

Position: Pitcher
Team: Montreal Expos
Born: December 28, 1960 Madison, WI
Height: 6'2" **Weight:** 195 lbs.
Bats: Left **Throws:** Left
Acquired: Traded from Braves for
    Sergio Valdez, Nate Minchey, and
    Kevin Dean, 7/89

Smith got a new lease on life when he departed Atlanta in a midseason trade in 1989. The move to Montreal was an immediate lift for Smith, who rounded out the season with a 3.49 ERA, his lowest ever. Due to his shocking 1-13 record in 1989, he was allowed only 17 starts. The bullpen work seemed more like a home remedy to restore Smith's ability, instead of a permanent career move. He found his greatest success as a starter in his four seasons with the Braves. He pitched in 42 games for the 1985 club, going 9-10. Smith's best year was in 1987, a 15-10 record with nine complete games and three shutouts.

Let Smith have a complete season with the Expos before investing in his common-priced 1990 cards. For now, they are poor investment choices. Our pick for his best 1990 card is Topps.

MIKE SMITHSON

	W	L	ERA	G	CG	IP	H	ER	BB	SO
1989	7	14	4.95	40	1	143	170	79	35	61
Life	76	86	4.58	240	41	1356	1473	690	383	731

Position: Pitcher
Team: Boston Red Sox
Born: January 21, 1955 Centerville, TN
Height: 6'8" **Weight:** 215 lbs.
Bats: Left **Throws:** Right
Acquired: Signed as a free agent, 1/88

Smithson's 1989 record of seven wins and 14 losses doesn't fully indicate his importance to the Boston Red Sox. Although the tall righty has never suffered such a poor won-lost ratio in his eight-year career, he was the team's fourth-busiest pitcher, both in starts (19 in 40 total games) and innings pitched (143). His 4.95 ERA was undeniably high, but it was smaller than his marks from the past two seasons. Smithson seemed recovered from elbow problems in 1987, and was a willing worker for the 1989 club. The Red Sox value Smithson for his flexibility to work both as a starter or reliever.

Smithson's mediocre lifetime stats and his different job titles with the Red Sox get him little respect from card collectors. His 1990 commons are unlikely to gain value. Our pick for his best 1990 card is Donruss.

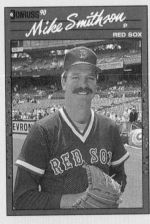

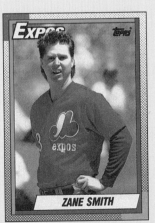

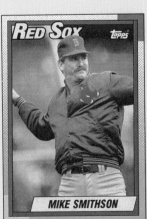

JOHN SMOLTZ

	W	L	ERA	G	CG	IP	H	ER	BB	SO
1989	12	11	2.94	29	5	208	160	68	72	168
Life	14	18	3.54	41	5	272	234	107	105	205

Position: Pitcher
Team: Atlanta Braves
Born: May 15, 1967   Detroit, MI
Height: 6'3"   **Weight:** 185 lbs.
Bats: Right   **Throws:** Right
Acquired: Traded from Tigers for
　　　　　Doyle Alexander, 8/87

In 1989, Smoltz became the ace of the Atlanta staff. The Detroit native spent two seasons in the Tigers' system in hopes of playing for his hometown team. He was traded to the Braves in August 1987, and less than one year later, Smoltz was in the major leagues. With Triple-A Richmond in '88, he was 10-5 with 115 strikeouts. He was ranked as the International League's top prospect. In 1989, Smoltz was named to the N.L. All-Star team. He pitched one inning, suffering the loss. Smoltz won in double digits for the Braves in 1989, keeping his ERA at the 3.00 level.

You may find Smoltz's 1990 cards priced as commons. They're a great buy at a dime or less. If he wins a league strikeout title, his card values will thrive. Our pick for his best 1990 card is Fleer.

CORY SNYDER

	BA	G	AB	R	H	2B	3B	HR	RBI	SB
1989	.215	132	489	49	105	17	0	18	59	6
Life	.247	534	1993	252	493	86	6	101	285	18

Position: Outfield
Team: Cleveland Indians
Born: November 11, 1962   Inglewood, CA
Height: 6'3"   **Weight:** 185 lbs.
Bats: Right   **Throws:** Right
Acquired: First-round pick in 6/84
　　　　　free-agent draft

If anyone's ever had on-the-job training, it's been Snyder. He has logged four years in an Indians uniform. Following his appearance on the 1984 U.S. Olympic baseball team, he was rushed through the Indians' system in less than two seasons. In 1989, Snyder hit only in the .220s. His 1986 debut with the Indians was a memorable one. He batted .272 with 24 homers and 69 RBI in just 103 games. In 1987, his average dipped to .236, but his power output increased to 33 homers and 82 RBI. When Snyder slugged 26 dingers in 1988, it marked only the 11th time an Indian had 20-plus homers for three straight years.

Snyder's 1989 slump will temporarily reduce prices of his 1990 cards. Invest heartily if you find his cards at a nickel or less. He should mount a massive rebound. Our pick for his best 1990 card is Score.

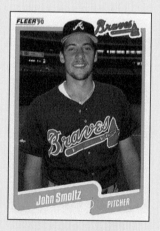

SAMMY SOSA

	BA	G	AB	R	H	2B	3B	HR	RBI	SB
89 AA	.297	66	273	45	81	15	4	7	31	16
89 Major	.257	58	183	27	47	8	0	4	13	7

Position: Outfield
Team: Chicago White Sox
Born: November 10, 1968 San Pedro
  de Macoris, Dominican Republic
Height: 6' **Weight:** 165 lbs.
Bats: Right **Throws:** Right
Acquired: Traded from Rangers with Wilson
  Alvarez and Scott Fletcher for
  Harold Baines and Fred
  Manrique, 7/89

Included in the trade that sent Harold Baines to the Rangers, Sosa paid major dividends to the White Sox. He finished out the 1989 season as a starter, hitting in the .250s and showing good ability in the field. Sosa spent the 1988 season at Class-A Port Charlotte, batting .229 and leading the Florida State League with 12 triples. His speed produced 42 stolen bases, tops on his club. He also popped nine homers, drove in 51 runs, and scored 70 runs in 131 games. In 1987, Sosa racked up a .279 average at Class-A Gastonia, adding 11 homers and 59 RBI. Topping his team in five offensive categories, Sosa was a member of the South Atlantic League All-Star Team that year.

Sosa will be an outfield regular for the ChiSox. At 15 cents, his debut 1990 cards will be healthy investments. Our pick for his best 1990 card is Fleer.

BILL SPIERS

	BA	G	AB	R	H	2B	3B	HR	RBI	SB
88 AA	.280	47	168	22	47	5	2	3	21	4
89 Major	.255	114	345	44	88	9	3	4	33	10

Position: Infield
Team: Milwaukee Brewers
Born: June 5, 1966 Orangeburg, SC
Height: 6'2" **Weight:** 190 lbs.
Bats: Left **Throws:** Right
Acquired: First-round pick in 6/87
  free-agent draft

Everyone was touting Gary Sheffield as the shortstop of the future for the Brewers; after Sheffield received a midseason demotion to the minors, Spiers was quietly vying for Milwaukee's starting shortstop job. Spiers started the '89 season at Triple-A Denver. After he was recalled, his steady defense and speed made him a frequent face in the Brewer lineup. In 1988, Spiers started the season at Class-A Stockton, hitting .269 with five homers and 52 RBI. He stole a career-high 27 bases, and was voted the best defensive shortstop in the California League. After he was promoted to Double-A El Paso on July 8, 1988, Spiers batted .280 in 47 games.

Spiers will probably be Milwaukee's starting shortstop. His rookie 1990 card will be a promising buy at 35 cents or less. Our pick for his best 1990 card is Topps.

MIKE STANTON

	W	L	ERA	G	SV	IP	H	ER	BB	SO
89 AA	4	1	1.58	47	19	51	32	9	31	54
89 Major	0	1	1.50	20	7	24	17	4	8	27

Position: Pitcher
Team: Atlanta Braves
Born: June 2, 1967 Houston, TX
Height: 6'1" **Weight:** 190 lbs.
Bats: Left **Throws:** Left
Acquired: 13th-round pick in 6/87
　　　　　free-agent draft

Switching to relief gave Stanton a head start to the majors in 1989. He joined the Braves on August 24, 1989, in just his second year in pro baseball. In his first ten games in the majors, he registered three saves, four finished games, and a 1.54 ERA. True to his pace of striking out an average of one batter per inning, he recorded 12 Ks in his first 11 $\frac{2}{3}$ frames with the Braves. In 1989, he went 4-1 with 19 saves and a 1.58 ERA in 47 games at Double-A Greenville. He was 2-0 with eight saves and a 0.00 ERA at Triple-A Richmond later that year. In 1988, Stanton was 11-5 at Class-A Burlington, with 160 strikeouts in 154 innings.

　　Stanton looks like the future bullpen ace for the Braves. His rookie 1990 card will be a good buy at a quarter or less. Our pick for his best 1990 card is Topps.

TERRY STEINBACH

	BA	G	AB	R	H	2B	3B	HR	RBI	SB
1989	.273	130	454	37	124	13	1	7	42	1
Life	.275	362	1211	148	333	48	5	34	153	5

Position: Catcher
Team: Oakland Athletics
Born: March 2, 1962 New Ulm, MN
Height: 6'1" **Weight:** 195 lbs.
Bats: Right **Throws:** Right
Acquired: Ninth-round pick in 6/83
　　　　　free-agent draft

Steinbach had a fine season in 1989. Fans got a glimpse of his potential in the 1988 All-Star Game. With a homer and sacrifice fly off Dwight Gooden, Steinbach gave the A.L. all of its runs for the victory and was voted MVP of the event. His 1987 rookie season made him a shoo-in for the 1988 All-Star Game. He finished 1987 with 16 homers, 56 RBI, and a .284 batting average. Trying to match those statistics proved to be a difficult assignment in 1988. Injuries limited him to 104 games, and his totals slipped to .265 with nine homers and 51 RBI. In 1989 he inflated his average to .273, showing more restraint at the plate. With more experience, Steinbach should have many more years on All-Star rosters.

　　Don't be surprised if you find Steinbach's 1990 cards selling as commons. Because he isn't an offensive dynamo, be wary of investing more than a nickel apiece in his cards. Our pick for his best 1990 card is Score.

DAVE STEWART

	W	L	ERA	G	CG	IP	H	ER	BB	SO
1989	21	9	3.32	36	8	257	260	95	69	155
Life	101	74	3.68	357	39	1560	1455	638	594	1036

Position: Pitcher
Team: Oakland Athletics
Born: February 19, 1957   Oakland, CA
Height: 6'2"   **Weight:** 200 lbs.
Bats: Right   **Throws:** Right
Acquired: Signed as a free agent, 5/86

Although Stewart toted a hefty ERA in 1989, he was a master on the mound. He had his third consecutive 20-win season with the A's. The 1989 All-Star Game starter never showed such promise with his first three teams. Small wonder he took time to adjust: Los Angeles drafted him as a catcher in 1975. He was promptly moved to the mound, with dismal results until 1977, when he led his league with 17 wins. After that, Stewart bounced around until 1986, when the A's discovered him. The addition of a forkball made a new pitcher out of him. After nine major league seasons, it seems that the best is yet to come for Stewart.

Stewart's age deters his 1990 card investment potential. Be cautious if paying more than a dime a card. Our pick for his best 1990 card is Topps.

DAVE STIEB

	W	L	ERA	G	CG	IP	H	ER	BB	SO
1989	17	8	3.35	33	3	206	164	77	76	101
Life	148	117	3.37	357	99	2458	2158	921	873	1432

Position: Pitcher
Team: Toronto Blue Jays
Born: July 22, 1957   Santa Ana, CA
Height: 6'1"   **Weight:** 195 lbs.
Bats: Right   **Throws:** Right
Acquired: Fifth-round pick in 6/78
free-agent draft

Every time Stieb pitched in 1989, he increased his hold on many Blue Jays records, including career wins, strikeouts, innings pitched, shutouts, and complete games. In 11 major league seasons, he has appeared in seven All-Star games, starting two of the contests. That places him in seventh on the all-time list, tied with Whitey Ford and Bob Gibson. While Stieb has never won 20 games in a season, he has claimed double-digit win totals in all but one of his seasons in the majors. Stieb lost no-hit bids with two outs in the ninth inning during two starts in 1988 and once again in 1989.

Pay a nickel or less for Stieb's 1990 cards. With the national attention heaped upon Toronto, the perennial All-Star's card values can't stay that low forever. Our pick for his best 1990 card is Score.

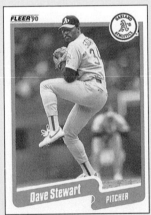

KURT STILLWELL

	BA	G	AB	R	H	2B	3B	HR	RBI	SB
1989	.261	130	463	52	121	20	7	7	54	9
Life	.252	493	1596	200	402	74	20	21	166	25

Position: Shortstop
Team: Kansas City Royals
Born: June 4, 1965   Glendale, CA
Height: 5'11"   **Weight:** 175 lbs.
Bats: Both   **Throws:** Right
Acquired: Traded from Reds with Ted
Power for Danny Jackson and
Angel Salazar, 11/87

Stillwell set new career highs in batting average and RBI with the 1989 Royals. He played in his fourth major league season (and second American League campaign) in 1989. He showed that he could produce runs, scoring 52 and driving in 54. He was coming off a notable 1988 season, one that gained him his first All-Star appearance. Stillwell's ten homers were a single-season best which nearly topped the 11 homers he had hit during the five years of his pro career combined. His 1988 season ended on September 6, due to a stomach ailment. He is continuing a family tradition with his current profession. His father, Ron, was an infielder with the Senators in 1961 and '62.

Kurt is young and experienced. He'll have a long, prosperous career in Kansas City. His 1990 commons are solid buys. Our pick for his best 1990 card is Donruss.

TODD STOTTLEMYRE

	W	L	ERA	G	CG	IP	H	ER	BB	SO
1989	7	7	3.88	27	0	128	137	55	44	63
Life	11	15	4.68	55	0	226	246	117	90	130

Position: Pitcher
Team: Toronto Blue Jays
Born: May 20, 1965   Sunnyside, WA
Height: 6'3"   **Weight:** 190 lbs. .
Bats: Left   **Throws:** Right
Acquired: First-round pick in secondary
phase in 6/85 free-agent draft

While his father and brother are members of different teams, Stottlemyre and his kin may give the Ripkens competition as baseball's first family. Todd was staking out a reputation as a promising starter with the Blue Jays in 1989, while younger brother Mel remained a pitching hopeful for the Kansas City organization. Father Mel Sr., himself a Yankee hurler in the 1960s, is the pitching coach for the Mets. Todd seems the best hope to carry on the family name in the majors. He won a career-high seven games in 1989 in 27 appearances (18 as a starter). He has an overpowering fastball. Starting his third season with Toronto in 1990, Stottlemyre has a bright future.

Stottlemyre's 1990 commons could be good investments. He could be on the verge of his first major success. Our pick for his best 1990 card is Topps.

DOUG STRANGE

	BA	G	AB	R	H	2B	3B	HR	RBI	SB
89 AAA	.247	89	304	38	75	15	2	8	42	8
89 Major	.214	64	196	16	42	4	1	1	14	3

Position: Third base
Team: Detroit Tigers
Born: April 13, 1964 Greenville, SC
Height: 6'2" **Weight:** 170 lbs.
Bats: Both **Throws:** Right
Acquired: Seventh-round pick in 6/85
free-agent draft

After Keith Moreland and Chris Brown proved unable to fill the third base slot for the 1989 Tigers, Strange was summoned from the minors. He was leading Triple-A Toledo in homers and RBI at the time. Sharing the job with Rick Shu, Strange remained with the Tigers through the season. A product of North Carolina State University, he began his pro career in the Tigers' organization in 1985. At Double-A Glens Falls in 1987, Strange was named the Eastern League's All-Star third baseman. His 115-game season included 13 homers, 70 RBI, and a .305 batting average. After a batting slump with Toledo in 1988, Strange returned to Glens Falls to tune up his offense.

Strange has a chance at Detroit's starting third base job. Nonetheless, his paltry average makes his 15-cent rookie 1990 cards unsuitable buys. Our pick for his best 1990 card is Topps.

DARRYL STRAWBERRY

	BA	G	AB	R	H	2B	3B	HR	RBI	SB
1989	.225	134	476	69	107	26	1	29	77	11
Life	.260	957	3361	570	875	169	29	215	625	176

Position: Outfield
Team: New York Mets
Born: March 12, 1962 Los Angeles, CA
Height: 6'6" **Weight:** 195 lbs.
Bats: Left **Throws:** Left
Acquired: First-round pick in 6/80
free-agent draft

Strawberry, despite prolonged batting slumps, made some substantial additions to his lifetime statistics with the 1989 Mets. In 1989, he topped 200 career home runs and 600 RBI, even though he hit .225. In 1988, he became the Mets all-time home run leader in a season that produced 39 homers (for the second consecutive year) and 101 RBI. Prior to 1989, he and Kirk Gibson were the only players to have 20-plus home runs and stolen bases for the past five consecutive seasons. Strawberry has been voted by fans as a starting N.L. outfielder in five All-Star games. He began his career by winning the N.L. Rookie of the Year Award in 1983.

Strawberry's 1990 cards may reflect his slump and sell for as little as 35 cents. Invest now, and you'll see striking price gains within a year. Our pick for his best 1990 card is Score.

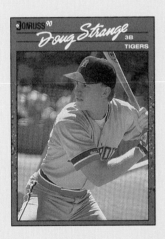

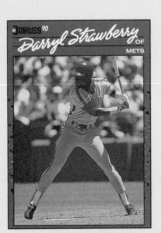

FRANKLIN STUBBS

	BA	G	AB	R	H	2B	3B	HR	RBI	SB
1989	.291	69	103	11	30	6	0	4	15	3
Life	.227	542	1377	166	313	48	7	59	178	31

Position: First base
Team: Los Angeles Dodgers
Born: October 21, 1960 Laurinburg, NC
Height: 6'2" **Weight:** 209 lbs.
Bats: Left **Throws:** Left
Acquired: First-round pick in 6/81
free-agent draft

An injured left knee landed Stubbs on the 60-day disabled list, marring his best-ever batting average. He saw his playing time reduced when the Dodgers acquired first baseman Eddie Murray in 1989. Stubbs shared the first base job in 1988, hitting .223 with eight homers and 34 RBI in part-time duty. In the 1988 World Series, he had five hits for a .294 average. He started at first base for the 1987 Dodgers, batting a previous high of .233 with 16 homers and 52 RBI. His 23 homers and 58 RBI in 1986 are his career bests as a power hitter. Stubbs hit 32 homers and 93 RBI at Triple-A Albuquerque in 1985 and was in the majors to stay.

Stubbs has an awful lifetime average and a penchant for injuries. His erratic play makes his 1990 commons unreasonable investments. Our pick for his best 1990 card is Score.

B.J. SURHOFF

	BA	G	AB	R	H	2B	3B	HR	RBI	SB
1989	.248	126	436	42	108	17	4	5	55	14
Life	.262	380	1324	139	347	60	7	17	161	46

Position: Catcher
Team: Milwaukee Brewers
Born: August 4, 1964 Bronx, NY
Height: 6'1" **Weight:** 190 lbs.
Bats: Left **Throws:** Right
Acquired: First-round pick in 6/85
free-agent draft

Surhoff logged his third season with the Milwaukee Brewers in 1989, handling the club's primary catching duties. He batted a respectable .248, but he failed to recapture the stroke that brought him a career-high average of .299 in his 1987 rookie season. In 1987, he belted seven homers and 68 RBI. He approached those marks with five dingers and 55 ribbies in 1989. He was a 1984 U.S. Olympic baseball player. Although Surhoff is an excellent defensive catcher, he's made occasional appearances as a backup third baseman. One of the speedier catchers in the American League, Surhoff has posted double-digit stolen base totals for his first three seasons (including a career-high 21 in 1988).

Surhoff's 1990 cards will sell for less than a nickel. Because his power stats are minimal, consider waiting for him to mature before investing. Our pick for his best 1990 card is Score.

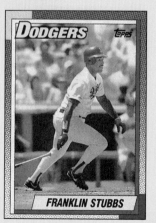

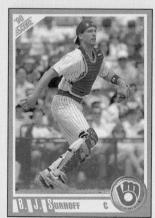

RICK SUTCLIFFE

	W	L	ERA	G	CG	IP	H	ER	BB	SO
1989	16	11	3.66	35	5	229	202	93	69	153
Life	133	103	3.81	352	64	2109	1985	892	844	1405

Position: Pitcher
Team: Chicago Cubs
Born: June 21, 1956 Independence, MO
Height: 6'7" **Weight:** 215 lbs.
Bats: Left **Throws:** Right
Acquired: Traded from Indians with Ron
　　　　　Hassey and George Frazier for
　　　　　Joe Carter, Mel Hall, Don
　　　　　Schulze, and Darryl Banks, 6/84

Sutcliffe notched his third consecutive double-digit winning season for the 1989 Cubs. It is the first time in 11 major league seasons he's put together such a string. His 16 wins in 1989 were only third on the Cubs. By contrast, his 18 wins in 1987 led the league. His 153 strikeouts were best on the 1989 club. Sutcliffe was an immediate hit in the majors, when he collected 17 wins as a rookie with the 1979 Dodgers. His 1984 debut with the Cubs was even stronger. His 16 Chicago wins and his four preceding victories with Cleveland gave him his only 20-win season. Sutcliffe earned the Cy Young for his efforts.

Sutcliffe's 1990 cards will be a nickel or less. Buying his cards could double your investment, if you sell when he's nearing 20 victories. Our pick for his best 1990 card is Score.

BILL SWIFT

	W	L	ERA	G	CG	IP	H	ER	BB	SO
1989	7	3	4.43	37	0	130	140	64	38	45
Life	23	24	4.78	127	7	540	618	287	206	202

Position: Pitcher
Team: Seattle Mariners
Born: October 27, 1961
　　　　South Portland, ME
Height: 6' **Weight:** 180 lbs.
Bats: Right **Throws:** Right
Acquired: First-round pick in 6/84
　　　　　free-agent draft

Swift's 1989 season was filled with firsts. Never before had he played an entire year in the major leagues. He had never worked out of the bullpen so much (21 appearances) and had never posted a winning record in the majors. He has failed to live up to the high expectations placed upon him when the M's made him the second player chosen overall in the 1984 draft. The former U.S. Olympian spent just seven games in the minors before he was rushed up in early 1985. His 6-10 mark fell to 2-9 in 1986, as he was sent to Triple-A Calgary for seasoning. Swift pitched just five games in 1987 due to an elbow injury.

Swift hasn't distinguished himself with the Mariners either as a starter or reliever. Don't invest in his 1990 commons until he finds his niche. Our pick for his best 1990 card is Fleer.

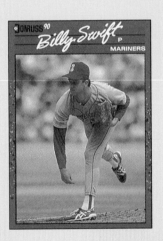

GREG SWINDELL

	W	L	ERA	G	CG	IP	H	ER	BB	SO
1989	13	6	3.37	28	5	184	170	69	51	129
Life	39	30	3.69	86	22	590	573	242	148	452

Position: Pitcher
Team: Cleveland Indians
Born: January 2, 1965 Fort Worth, TX
Height: 6'3" **Weight:** 225 lbs.
Bats: Right **Throws:** Left
Acquired: First-round pick in 6/86
            ·   free-agent draft

Even after just three years of major league experience, Swindell is viewed by many as the dean of the Indians pitching staff. The big lefthander had a stellar 1989 campaign and attempted to become the first Indians pitcher in 20 years to lead the A.L. in winning percentage. In 1988, it looked like Swindell might win 20 games. He began the year with ten wins in 11 decisions, but lost six straight and ended the year at 18-14. Swindell had a distinguished college career at the University of Texas, winning 43 games and All-American honors three times. Swindell pitched only three minor league games at the Class-A level in 1986 before being promoted to Cleveland.

If the Indians score runs, Swindell can win regularly. His 1990 cards are choice investments at a dime or less. Our pick for his best 1990 card is Donruss.

PAT TABLER

	BA	G	AB	R	H	2B	3B	HR	RBI	SB
1989	.259	123	390	36	101	11	1	2	42	0
Life	.287	979	3353	405	962	165	23	44	446	16

Position: Designated hitter; first base
Team: Kansas City Royals
Born: February 2, 1958 Hamilton, OH
Height: 6'2" **Weight:** 200 lbs.
Bats: Right **Throws:** Right
Acquired: Traded from Indians for Bud
            Black, 6/88

Tabler remained a top reserve with the Royals in 1989. The utility player has served the Royals at many positions: the outfield, first base, third base, and designated hitter. Most importantly, he's a prized pinch-hitter. Going into 1989, he had an incredible .579 average (with two homers and 88 RBI) batting with the bases loaded. His finest major league season came with the 1987 Indians, the year of his only All-Star appearance. He hit 11 homers and 86 RBI, batting .307. He has played with five major league organizations in his 14 professional seasons. Tabler began in the Yankees' farm system in 1976 and made his major league debut with the 1981 Cubs.

Tabler is a talented platoon player, but without a full-time position and any home run power, he remains mostly unknown. Bypass his 1990 commons. Our pick for his best 1990 card is Fleer.

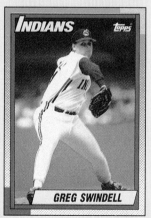

FRANK TANANA

	W	L	ERA	G	CG	IP	H	ER	BB	SO
1989	10	14	3.58	33	6	223	227	89	74	147
Life	198	192	3.49	507	136	3403	3252	1320	966	2345

Position: Pitcher
Team: Detroit Tigers
Born: July 3, 1953 Detroit, MI
Height: 6'3" **Weight:** 195 lbs.
Bats: Left **Throws:** Left
Acquired: Traded from Rangers for
　　　　　Duane James, 6/85

Even though Tanana did not have a winning 1989, he was the most successful of the Detroit Tigers starters. His ten wins were tops for the starting staff. His labor for the last-place club included 33 games, 223 innings pitched, and 147 strikeouts. Losing isn't commonplace for him. The Detroit native hadn't been below .500 since 1983, and has seen losing seasons just four times in his 15 years. By contrast, 1989 was Tanana's sixth consecutive season of double-digit wins. His long career began back in 1972. By age 20, Tanana was in the majors. In his sophomore season (with the Angels), he won 16 and chalked up a league-leading 269 strikeouts in 257 innings.

　　Tanana's 1990 cards will be a nickel or less. In just two wins, he'll reach the elusive 200-win mark, which might spur temporary interest in his cards. Our pick for his best 1990 card is Score.

KEVIN TAPANI

	W	L	ERA	G	CG	IP	H	ER	BB	SO
89 AAA	11	7	3.12	23	3	150	151	52	37	93
89 Major	2	2	3.86	5	0	32	34	14	8	21

Position: Pitcher
Team: Minnesota Twins
Born: February 18, 1964 Des Moines, IA
Height: 6' **Weight:** 180 lbs.
Bats: Right **Throws:** Right
Acquired: Traded from Mets with David
　　　　　West, Rick Aguilera, and Tim
　　　　　Drummond for Frank Viola, 8/89

The Twins discovered that Tapani may have been one of the pleasant surprises of the 1989 Mets trade. When the Twins gave up their former Cy Young winner, they were getting a veteran in Aguilera and a highly touted rookie in West. Tapani was a lesser-known commodity who was 7-5 at Triple-A Tidewater when traded. He had played three years of minor league ball, with his best season being a 10-7 record in Class-A. After a stint at Triple-A Portland, the Twins gave him a chance, allowing him five starts in 1989. He averaged more than six innings per start. Tapani should spend a full season in Minnesota in 1990.

　　Tapani's rookie season may be memorable. Although his rookie 1990 cards will be 15 cents or more, they'll go up quickly if he wins his first few decisions. Our pick for his best 1990 card is Donruss.

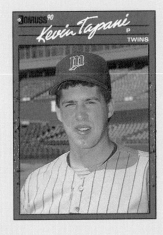

DANNY TARTABULL

	BA	G	AB	R	H	2B	3B	HR	RBI	SB
1989	.268	133	441	54	118	22	0	18	62	4
Life	.283	603	2122	316	601	120	13	106	375	26

Position: Outfield
Team: Kansas City Royals
Born: October 30, 1962   San Juan, Puerto
Rico
Height: 6'1"   **Weight:** 205 lbs.
Bats: Right   **Throws:** Right
Acquired: Traded from Mariners with Rick
Luecken for Scott Bankhead,
Steve Shields, and Mike Kingery,
12/86

Tartabull has racked up double-digit homer totals in his first four major league seasons. In 1989, he was among the Kansas City leaders in several offensive categories. He joined the Royals in 1987, and batted .309 with 34 homers and 101 RBI. After slugging 26 homers and 102 RBI in 1988, Tartabull was rewarded with a $1 million-plus contract. Debuting with the Mariners in 1986, he finished fifth in the Rookie of the Year balloting after hitting .270 with 25 home runs and 96 RBI. Originally a 1980 third-round pick, Tartabull spent three years in the Reds' farm system before Seattle drafted him. Many Kansas City fans remember the Tartabull name: Danny's father, Jose, played for the Kansas City Athletics from 1962 to 1966.

If Tartabull leaves Kansas City as rumored, his 1990 card values will fall. For now, avoid investing here. Our pick for his best 1990 card is Fleer.

GARRY TEMPLETON

	BA	G	AB	R	H	2B	3B	HR	RBI	SB
1989	.255	142	506	43	129	26	3	6	40	1
Life	.275	1823	6940	823	1910	294	101	58	643	238

Position: Shortstop
Team: San Diego Padres
Born: March 24, 1956   Lockey, TX
Height: 6'   **Weight:** 193 lbs.
Bats: Both   **Throws:** Right
Acquired: Traded from the Cardinals for
Ozzie Smith, 2/82

Templeton finished his 14th major league season with his best batting average in four years. The veteran shortstop hasn't hit close to .300 since leaving his six-season post with the Cardinals in 1981, which scouts attribute to the lively artificial turf at Busch Stadium, rather than in any decline of his talent. The only marked decline evident in his performance is in his shrinking stolen base totals, due to knee ailments that grow more problematic each year. Templeton has left a lasting mark on the game, however. In 1979, he became the first switch-hitter in history to collect 100 hits from each side of the plate in a single season (111 lefthanded and 100 righthanded).

Health problems have quieted Templeton's once-stunning accomplishments. His 1990 commons are questionable investments with little short-term hope. Our pick for his best 1990 card is Donruss.

WALT TERRELL

	W	L	ERA	G	CG	IP	H	ER	BB	SO
89 AL	6	5	5.20	13	1	83	102	48	24	30
Life	79	76	4.01	202	43	1350	1352	602	538	661

Position: Pitcher
Team: New York Yankees
Born: May 11, 1958 Jeffersonville, IN
Height: 6'2" **Weight:** 205 lbs.
Bats: Left **Throws:** Right
Acquired: Traded from Padres for Mike
Pagliarulo, 7/89

Terrell's move to the National League was a short one; after the Tigers sent him to San Diego before the '89 season for Keith Moreland and Chris Brown (both third basemen), Terrell had a dismal 5-13 record. The Padres then traded him to the Yankees for third baseman Mike Pagliarulo. Terrell's record was a respectable 6-5 with New York, but his ERA was a huge 5.20. He achieved his greatest success with Detroit from 1985 to 1987. The Tigers gave up third baseman Howard Johnson to obtain Terrell, who won 15 games in 1985 and 1986, and a career-high 17 in 1987. He began his pro career in 1980 in the Texas organization.

Terrell is young enough to have a few more productive seasons. Nonetheless, his marginal lifetime marks should deter investors from pursuing his 1990 commons. Our pick for his best 1990 card is Score.

SCOTT TERRY

	W	L	ERA	G	CG	IP	H	ER	BB	SO
1989	8	10	3.57	31	1	148	142	59	43	69
Life	18	18	3.73	121	2	347	340	144	117	175

Position: Pitcher
Team: St. Louis Cardinals
Born: November 21, 1959 Hobbs, NM
Height: 5'11" **Weight:** 195 lbs.
Bats: Right **Throws:** Right
Acquired: Traded from Reds for Pat
Perry, 8/87

Terry had a losing record in 1989, but he helped the Cardinals both as a starter and reliever. He made 24 starts and seven relief appearances in 1989. In relief, he finished five games and earned two saves. In 1988, his first full season with the Cardinals, he had a 9-6 record, second best on the club. It's no wonder that he is the best-hitting and finest-fielding pitcher on the club; he began his pro career in the Cincinnati organization in 1980 as an outfielder, his position for his first three seasons. Terry socked 21 homers and 142 RBI before taking his strong arm to the mound.

If Terry spends a full year in the starting rotation, he may be a double-digit winner. Wait a year before deciding on the investment potential of his common-priced 1990 cards. Our pick for his best 1990 card is Fleer.

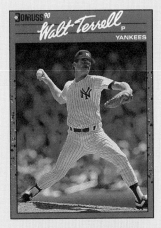

MICKEY TETTLETON

	BA	G	AB	R	H	2B	3B	HR	RBI	SB
1989	.258	117	411	72	106	21	2	26	65	3
Life	.240	486	1403	181	337	58	4	59	183	13

Position: Catcher
Team: Baltimore Orioles
Born: September 16, 1960
    Oklahoma City, OK
Height: 6'2" **Weight:** 214 lbs.
Bats: Both **Throws:** Right
Acquired: Signed as a free agent, 4/88

Tettleton didn't expect former third baseman Terry Stein-bach to usurp him as the A's "catcher of tomorrow" in 1987. Tettleton played with Oakland since 1984 yet was released in the spring of 1988. Snapped up by the Orioles, in 1988, his first year with the O's, he finished third in balloting for team MVP. Part of Tettleton's woes with the A's came from his frequent and prolonged stays on the disabled list. This propensity haunted the O's in his stellar 1989 season as well when—after Tettleton was among the league's leaders in runs, home runs, and slugging percentage—a torn knee cartilage took him out of commission.

Tettleton's 1989 was admirable, but it's dangerous to pay big prices for cards of a one-year wonder. Don't pay more than a nickel for his 1990 cards. Our pick for his best 1990 card is Fleer.

TIM TEUFEL

	BA	G	AB	R	H	2B	3B	HR	RBI	SB
1989	.256	83	219	27	56	7	2	2	15	1
Life	.264	679	2150	297	567	137	10	51	255	10

Position: Infield
Team: New York Mets
Born: July 8, 1958 Greenwich, CT
Height: 6' **Weight:** 175 lbs.
Bats: Right **Throws:** Right
Acquired: Traded from Twins with Pat
    Crosby for Billy Beane, Bill
    Latham, and Joe Klink, 1/86

When Gregg Jefferies became the Mets second baseman in 1989, Teufel's playing time withered. He was limited to the role of utility infielder, seeing action in just 83 games. It's likely that the decline in his power stats has more to do with his infrequent use than with a decline in skills. As recently as 1987, with only 14 more games, he acquired 92 hits, 29 doubles, and 14 homers as well as a career-high .308 batting average. He only hit .234 in 1988. His value as a substitute can be measured by his .444 batting average in three 1986 World Series games. Teufel lights up under pressure, making him an ideal reserve infielder.

Teufel is slated for second-string duty with the Mets. This does not bode well for investors who speculate on his 1990 commons. Our pick for his best 1990 card is Topps.

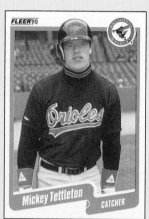

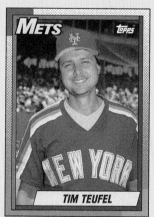

BOBBY THIGPEN

	W	L	ERA	G	SV	IP	H	ER	BB	SO
1989	2	6	3.76	61	34	79	62	33	40	47
Life	16	19	3.07	200	91	293	270	100	109	281

Position: Pitcher
Team: Chicago White Sox
Born: July 17, 1963 Tallahassee, FL
Height: 6'3" **Weight:** 195 lbs.
Bats: Right **Throws:** Right
Acquired: Fourth-round pick in 6/85
free-agent draft

Thigpen moved into second place on the White Sox's all-time saves list in 1989. He's on a pace to top Hoyt Wilhelm's team record 98 saves in 1990. Thigpen became only the fourth pitcher in history to top the 50-save plateau by his 26th birthday. In 1988, he set a single-season team record with 34 saves. He won or saved 39 of the ChiSox's 71 victories, giving him the top percentage in baseball. Thigpen earned 16 saves and seven victories in his first full season in 1987. The White Sox tried to convert Thigpen into a starter in late 1987, sending him to the minors. But after nine starts, the idea was abandoned.

Thigpen's 1990 cards will be shockingly affordable, priced at a nickel or less. Grab his cards now. They'll be big sellers if he plays with a contender. Our pick for his best 1990 card is Topps.

ANDRES THOMAS

	BA	G	AB	R	H	2B	3B	HR	RBI	SB
1989	.213	141	554	41	118	18	0	13	57	3
Life	.237	493	1825	156	432	68	4	37	198	20

Position: Shortstop
Team: Atlanta Braves
Born: November 10, 1963 Boca Chica,
Dominican Republic
Height: 6'1" **Weight:** 185 lbs.
Bats: Right **Throws:** Right
Acquired: Signed as a free agent, 12/81

Thomas continued to live up to his "good hit-no field" reputation at shortstop in 1989. His 13 homers and 57 RBI were among the best power stats for any National League shortstop. But his average was a shocking .213, his lowest in eight professional seasons. His 29 errors were the second-highest in the National League. Only former Braves shortstop Rafael Ramirez, with 30, had more. Thomas matched the 13 homers he hit in 1988, the year he knocked in a lifetime best of 68 runs. He was an undrafted free agent in 1982 when the Braves signed him. He took four minor league seasons to reach the majors.

Until Thomas cleans up his fielding and lifts his average, his job won't be secure. This is a bad time to invest in his 1990 cards, which will sell for 3 cents or less. Our pick for his best 1990 card is Donruss.

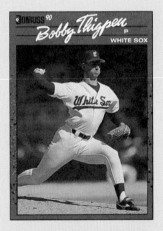

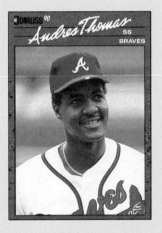
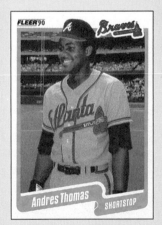

MILT THOMPSON

	BA	G	AB	R	H	2B	3B	HR	RBI	SB
1989	.290	155	545	60	158	28	8	4	68	27
Life	.289	621	2030	270	586	85	22	21	177	132

Position: Outfield
Team: St. Louis Cardinals
Born: January 5, 1959   Washington, DC
Height: 5'11"   **Weight:** 170 lbs.
Bats: Left   **Throws:** Right
Acquired: Traded from Phillies for Curt Ford
and Steve Lake, 12/88

Thompson startled the baseball world after he joined the 1989 Cardinals. The trade that obtained him from the Phillies looked simple: two reserve players for Thompson, another substitute. However, he quickly won the team's starting center field job away from Willie McGee. Thompson set career highs in games played, doubles, and RBI. His 27 stolen bases were third on the Redbirds, but didn't match his personal best of 46 swipes, with the 1987 Phillies. His baserunning and outfield mobility was especially remarkable, considering that he had undergone knee surgery in September 1988.

Thompson is a bit too old to start amassing great career statistics. Regardless, he could be a Cardinals fixture for several years. Buy his 1990 commons and sell for short-term gains when he has a second banner season. Our pick for his best 1990 card is Topps.

ROBBY THOMPSON

	BA	G	AB	R	H	2B	3B	HR	RBI	SB
1989	.241	148	547	91	132	26	11	13	50	12
Life	.259	567	1993	292	517	103	25	37	189	54

Position: Second base
Team: San Francisco Giants
Born: May 10, 1962   West Palm Beach, FL
Height: 5'11"   **Weight:** 170 lbs.
Bats: Right   **Throws:** Right
Acquired: First-round pick in 6/83
free-agent draft

One of Thompson's achievements in 1989 was staying healthy. Recovered from back ailments, he surpassed his prior high of ten homers, which he set in 1987. In 1986, *The Sporting News* named Thompson N.L. Rookie of the Year. In 149 games, he hit .271 with seven homers and 47 RBI. He set a team record with 18 sacrifice bunts (including six suicide squeezes). He topped the team in runs (73) and hits (149). His first-ever hit came against Houston's Nolan Ryan. Thompson made the bigs after spending the 1985 season in Double-A. He handles the double-play pivot well, as evidenced by the club-record 183 double plays executed in 1987 (which also led the major leagues).

Based on his postseason play, Thompson's 1990 cards will sell well. If you see them at a nickel or less, invest heartily. Our pick for his best 1990 card is Score.

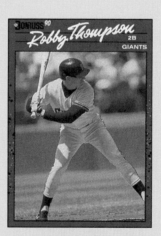

DICKIE THON

	BA	G	AB	R	H	2B	3B	HR	RBI	SB
1989	.271	136	435	45	118	18	4	15	60	6
Life	.270	912	2838	345	765	130	30	49	273	126

Position: Shortstop
Team: Philadelphia Phillies
Born: June 20, 1958   South Bend, IN
Height: 5'11" **Weight:** 175 lbs.
Bats: Right **Throws:** Right
Acquired: Purchased from Padres, 1/88

Thon was acquired by the Phillies prior to 1989. The Phillies' management was unhappy with the play of resident shortstop Steve Jeltz, and wanted to give him some competition for his job. Not only did Thon land the starting job, he wound up being second on the Phils in homers and third in RBI. It's remarkable that he continued playing at all, due to a beaning he received during the first week of the 1984 season. Recurring vision problems ensued, and he missed the rest of 1984. He played 84 games in 1985 and 106 games in '86, but he wasn't himself. Thon's career seemed nearly over before he made his triumphant comeback with San Diego.

Thon's hitting was top-notch in 1989. But he doesn't have the lifetime stats to excite investors. His 1990 commons are subpar investments. Our pick for his best 1990 card is Fleer.

MARK THURMOND

	W	L	ERA	G	SV	IP	H	ER	BB	SO
1989	2	4	3.90	49	4	90	102	39	17	34
Life	38	43	3.71	271	17	781	837	322	244	296

Position: Pitcher
Team: Baltimore Orioles
Born: September 12, 1956   Houston, TX
Height: 6' **Weight:** 193 lbs.
Bats: Left **Throws:** Left
Acquired: Traded from Detroit for
   Ray Knight, 2/88

Thurmond pitched in a career-high 49 games in 1989, his seventh in the major leagues. The veteran lefthander started just two games all season for the Orioles, working mostly in middle relief. His best totals as a reliever came with the 1987 Tigers. He appeared in 48 games, saving five of them. His initial success in the majors came as a starter with San Diego. He first came up with the Padres 1983, after four minor league seasons. The fifth-round selection in the 1979 draft was 7-3 in his rookie season. Thurmond beat Fernando Valenzuela and the Dodgers on a seven-hitter in his first major league start.

Thurmond is a utility pitcher for Baltimore, handling any chore available. This thankless job won't help the value of his 1990 cards, currently priced at 3 cents or less. Our pick for his best 1990 card is Fleer.

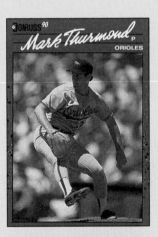

291

JAY TIBBS

	W	L	ERA	G	CG	IP	H	ER	BB	SO
1989	5	0	2.82	10	1	54	62	17	20	30
Life	36	47	4.13	143	13	805	825	369	303	421

Position: Pitcher
Team: Baltimore Orioles
Born: January 4, 1962 Birmingham, AL
Height: 6'1" **Weight:** 175 lbs.
Bats: Right **Throws:** Right
Acquired: Traded from Expos with Alfredo
    Cardwood for Doug Cinnella,
    Rick Carriger, and John
    Hoover, 12/87

Just when it looked like Tibbs could avenge his horrendous 1988 season with the Orioles, a strained shoulder curtailed his progress. Before going on the disabled list in 1989, he was one of Baltimore's toughest pitchers, with a record so good it seems unrelated to the bulk of his career. Tibbs enjoyed a triumphant 14-game debut with the 1984 Reds, when he notched six wins, three complete games, and just 2.86 runners per game. Then he became the victim of expanding ERAs (peaking at 5.39 in 1988). His 4-15 record in 1988 was a career low. Only once, in 1986, in the past six seasons did Tibbs last a whole year in the majors.

 Tibbs may regain his 1989 form if he remains healthy. Even if he does, though, he'll need a miracle to inspire confidence in his common-priced 1990 cards. Our pick for his best 1990 card is Fleer.

ALAN TRAMMELL

	BA	G	AB	R	H	2B	3B	HR	RBI	SB
1989	.243	121	449	54	109	20	3	5	43	10
Life	.286	1689	6143	938	1759	292	49	138	721	187

Position: Shortstop
Team: Detroit Tigers
Born: February 21, 1958
    Garden Grove, CA
Height: 6' **Weight:** 175 lbs.
Bats: Right **Throws:** Right
Acquired: Second-round pick in 6/76
    free-agent draft

Hobbled by injuries for the second straight season, Trammell was only a ghost of his former self in 1989. He continued to be a respectable every-day player, but he couldn't come close to his dream season of 1987. That year, he batted .343 with 28 homers and 105 RBI, all career highs. The five-time All-Star had a 21-game hitting streak and finished the year second in Most Valuable Player balloting. His 1987 season put him in the Tiger record book, making him the first player to have 200 hits and 100 RBI in one year since Al Kaline in 1955. Trammell starred in the 1984 World Series, hitting .450 with nine hits, two homers, and six RBI.

 Injuries limited Trammell's card values. His 1990 cards will sell for 15 cents. Check on his health before buying at prices that high. Our pick for his best 1990 card is Fleer.

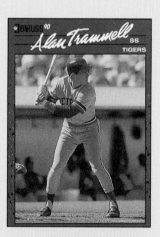

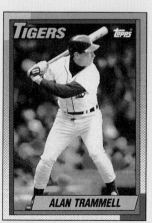

JEFF TREADWAY

	BA	G	AB	R	H	2B	3B	HR	RBI	SB
1989	.277	134	473	58	131	18	3	8	40	3
Life	.274	260	858	97	235	41	7	12	67	6

Position: Second base
Team: Atlanta Braves
Born: January 22, 1963 Columbus, GA
Height: 5'10" **Weight:** 170 lbs.
Bats: Left **Throws:** Right
Acquired: Purchased from Reds, 3/89

Upon joining the 1989 Atlanta Braves, Treadway won the starting second baseman's job away from Ron Gant. Treadway had just one season's worth of major league experience (with the 1988 Cincinnati Reds) before moving to Atlanta. He debuted with Cincinnati in 1987, earning a 23-game trial in the majors. He batted .333 with Cincinnati, batting safely in 17 of his 21 starts. He platooned at second base with Ron Oester in 1988. Treadway started 80 games, but his season ended in late August when he separated his shoulder in a home plate collision. In 1989, he captured several offensive highs with Atlanta. His batting average ranked third among Atlanta regulars. Treadway grew up in Georgia and attended the University of Georgia.

Treadway may hit up a storm in a homer haven like Atlanta. His 1990 commons could bring surprise dividends. Our pick for his best 1990 card is Score.

JOSE URIBE

	BA	G	AB	R	H	2B	3B	HR	RBI	SB
1989	.221	151	453	34	100	12	6	1	30	6
Life	.241	699	2203	221	532	73	23	15	167	63

Position: Shortstop
Team: San Francisco Giants
Born: January 21, 1960 San Cristobal,
   Dominican Republic
Height: 5'10" **Weight:** 165 lbs.
Bats: Both **Throws:** Right
Acquired: Traded from Cardinals with Dave
   LaPoint, Gary Rajsich, and David
   Green for Jack Clark, 2/85

Uribe slipped in 1989, his fifth season as the Giants shortstop. His .221 average was his lowest since he joined the Giants in 1985, and his worst in nine pro seasons. He has been a deceptively powerful hitter in the past, racking up career highs of 43 RBI in 1986 and five homers in 1987. He had a lifetime best average of .291 with the 1987 Giants, but played in just 95 games due to a pulled hamstring. He spent two weeks on the disabled list for emotional stress in 1988. Uribe had to cope with the death of his wife. When he returned to the lineup, he reached new major league-bests in at-bats (493), hits (127), and runs (47).

Baseball is filled with good defensive players. This talent alone doesn't assure stardom. Uribe's lackluster offense doesn't help the value of his 1990 commons. Our pick for his best 1990 card is Topps.

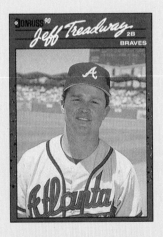

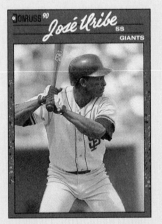

FERNANDO VALENZUELA

	W	L	ERA	G	CG	IP	H	ER	BB	SO
1989	10	13	3.43	31	3	196	185	75	98	116
Life	128	103	3.19	298	102	2144	1876	760	838	1644

Position: Pitcher
Team: Los Angeles Dodgers
Born: November 1, 1960 Navajoa, Mexico
Height: 5'11" **Weight:** 202 lbs.
Bats: Left **Throws:** Left
Acquired: Purchased from Yucatan
    of the Mexican League, 7/79

Valenzuela went through a year of transition while pitching for the 1989 Dodgers. He spent more than a month on the disabled list in 1988 with shoulder problems (for the first time after making 255 consecutive starts). When he recovered, it remained clear that his once-famous fastball had disappeared. He wound up 1988 at 5-8, marking the first time in eight seasons he hadn't topped double digits in wins. In 1989, Valenzuela started offering up a variety of breaking pitches to offset his speed loss. While he may never match his league-leading 21-11 record from 1986, or his 1981 debut when he won both the Rookie of the Year and Cy Young awards, Valenzuela has survived.

His 1990 issues will be 15 cents each. See if the "new" Valenzuela can post a solid winning season before investing in his cards. Our pick for his best 1990 card is Donruss.

DAVE VALLE

	BA	G	AB	R	H	2B	3B	HR	RBI	SB
1989	.237	94	316	32	75	10	3	7	34	0
Life	.243	348	1080	117	262	46	8	35	160	2

Position: Catcher
Team: Seattle Mariners
Born: October 30, 1960 Bayside, NY
Height: 6'2" **Weight:** 200 lbs.
Bats: Right **Throws:** Right
Acquired: Second-round pick in 6/78
    free-agent draft

Valle was billed as "All-Star material" by Mariners manager Jim Lefebvre when 1989 started. That was before the usual rash of injuries limited Valle's playing time again. The sporadic playing time has hindered his offense, but he's still displayed polished defensive skills when he's in the lineup. A veteran of a dozen pro seasons, his injuries have come from grueling work behind the plate. He's played in more than 100 games just twice (in the minors) in his pro career. If he might last an entire season, he might put on an awesome defensive display. Both in 1987 and 1988, Valle topped ten homers and 50 RBI for the M's.

Valle has waited too long to mount great career stats, but he could indeed become a perennial All-Star. His 1990 commons are reasonable buys. Our pick for his best 1990 card is Fleer.

ANDY VAN SLYKE

	BA	G	AB	R	H	2B	3B	HR	RBI	SB
1989	.237	130	476	64	113	18	9	9	53	16
Life	.267	962	3139	463	839	156	57	96	439	184

Position: Outfield
Team: Pittsburgh Pirates
Born: December 21, 1960 Utica, NY
Height: 6'2" **Weight:** 192 lbs.
Bats: Left **Throws:** Right
Acquired: Traded from Cardinals with
    Mike LaValliere and Mike Dunne
    for Tony Pena, 4/87

Van Slyke and the Pirates both had a disastrous season in 1989, after Van Slyke sat out for a month on the disabled list. In 1988, he aided Pittsburgh's second-place finish with career highs in virtually all offensive categories. He was named N.L. Player of the Year by *The Sporting News* and won his first Gold Glove. Van Slyke made his debut with the Cardinals in mid-1983. The Cardinals couldn't find a full-time slot for him, so he played five positions. When he was acquired by the Pirates, they stuck Van Slyke in center field, and he seems to have a long-term home in Pittsburgh.

When healthy, Van Slyke has unlimited abilities. An injury-free season could help him return to top form. Buy his 1990 cards at 10 cents or less. Our pick for his best 1990 card is Donruss.

GREG VAUGHN

	BA	G	AB	R	H	2B	3B	HR	RBI	SB
89 AAA	.276	110	387	74	107	17	5	26	92	20
89 Major	.265	38	113	18	30	3	0	5	23	4

Position: Outfield
Team: Milwaukee Brewers
Born: July 3, 1965 Sacramento, CA
Height: 6' **Weight:** 193 lbs.
Bats: Right **Throws:** Right
Acquired: Fourth-round pick in 6/86
    free-agent draft

Vaughn got a mid-1989 call-up to the Brewers and wound up with three hits and three RBI in his first five plate appearances. In 1988, he batted .301 with 28 home runs and 105 RBI at Double-A El Paso, winning membership on the Texas League All-Star Team. In 1987, he shared the Class-A Midwest League MVP Award with Todd Zeile. Vaughn had 33 homers and 105 RBI while batting .305 that year. He topped the league in homers, runs, and total bases. In 1986 at Class-A Helena, he hit .291 with 16 homers and 54 RBI in only 66 games. Vaughn is a former All-American at the University of Miami.

With a full season in Milwaukee, Vaughn could be one of the Brewers best hitters. If you can find them, buy his rookie 1990 cards at 25 cents. Our pick for his best 1990 card is Topps.

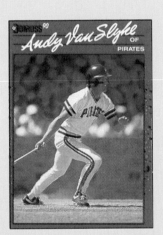

RANDY VELARDE

	BA	G	AB	R	H	2B	3B	HR	RBI	SB
1989	.340	33	100	12	34	4	2	2	11	0
Life	.245	89	237	31	58	10	2	7	24	1

Position: Infield
Team: New York Yankees
Born: November 24, 1962 Midland, TX
Height: 6' **Weight:** 185 lbs.
Bats: Right **Throws:** Right
Acquired: Traded from White Sox with
        Pete Filson for Mike Soper and
        Scott Nielsen, 1/87

Velarde has done a lot of traveling in the past three seasons, most of it between New York and the minor leagues. He spent his third partial season with the Yankees in the last three years. New York hasn't been able to find a starting position for him. He usually spends his time in the majors as a reserve infielder. In 1989, he looked like a hitter, with a .340 batting average. During his 1988 stay with the Yanks, Velarde popped five homers in just 115 at-bats. A shortstop by choice, he has been active in pro ball since 1985, when he began in the White Sox' organization.

Velarde's best chance with the Yankees is in a part-time infield role. His common-priced 1990 cards aren't sound investments until he wins a starting job. Our pick for his best 1990 card is Topps.

ROBIN VENTURA

	BA	G	AB	R	H	2B	3B	HR	RBI	SB
89 AA	.278	129	454	75	126	25	2	3	67	9
89 Major	.178	16	45	5	8	2	0	0	7	0

Position: Third base
Team: Chicago White Sox
Born: July 14, 1967 Santa Maria, CA
Height: 6'1" **Weight:** 185 lbs.
Bats: Both **Throws:** Right
Acquired: First-round pick in 6/88
        free-agent draft

One of the stars of the 1988 U.S. Olympic team, Ventura is the White Sox third baseman of the future. He batted .409 for the gold medal-winning Team USA. He played baseball at Oklahoma State for three years, finishing up with a junior season of 26 home runs, 96 RBI, and a .391 batting average. Ventura's college career was highlighted by a 58-game hitting streak in 1987, which ended in the College World Series. The three-time All-American won the 1988 Golden Spikes Award as the best college player. During his first pro season in 1989 with Double-A Birmingham, he hit in the .270s. Southern League managers ranked Ventura as the circuit's finest defensive third baseman.

Ventura should be Chicago's starting third baseman soon. Get his rookie 1990 cards at a quarter. Prices will climb quickly. Our pick for his best 1990 card is Topps.

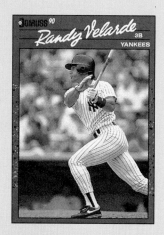

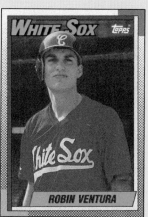

FRANK VIOLA

	W	L	ERA	G	CG	IP	H	ER	BB	SO
89 NL	5	5	3.38	12	2	85	75	32	27	73
Life	109	86	3.84	248	49	1682	1679	718	501	1149

Position: Pitcher
Team: New York Mets
Born: April 19, 1960 Hempstead, NY
Height: 6'4" **Weight:** 209 lbs.
Bats: Left **Throws:** Left
Acquired: Traded from Twins for Rick
          Aguilera, David West,
          Kevin Tapani, and Tim
          Drummond, 8/89

A Cy Young Award winner doesn't usually get traded the next season. But such was the case with Viola, the former Twins ace who was sent to the Mets to fill in for Dwight Gooden. The Twins had lost faith in Viola when he slumped through the first half of 1989. After he posted a 24-7 record in 1988, he sank to an 8-12 mark with a 3.79 ERA before being traded. The New York native was delighted to join a team near his home. The Mets will get considerable mileage out of Viola: from 1983 to 1988, he topped the majors with 214 starts.

   Because of the deal, Viola became an even bigger name. Buy his 1990 cards at a dime or less. New Yorkers will treasure these cards because they'll be the first showing Viola as a Met. Our pick for his best 1990 card is Score.

OMAR VIZQUEL

	BA	G	AB	R	H	2B	3B	HR	RBI	SB
89 AAA	.214	7	28	3	6	2	0	0	3	0
89 Major	.220	143	387	45	85	7	3	1	20	1

Position: Shortstop
Team: Seattle Mariners
Born: May 15, 1967 Caracas, Venezuela
Height: 5'9" **Weight:** 155 lbs.
Bats: Both **Throws:** Right
Acquired: Signed as a free agent, 1984

When the Mariners traded Rey Quinones to the Pirates in April, the M's handed the starting shortstop job to Vizquel. He had five years of minor league experience starting in 1984. Not only has he been more even-tempered and dependable than Quinones, Vizquel has filled in well defensively. He has notable speed, as evidenced by his 30 stolen bases at Double-A Vermont in 1988, second highest on the team. His .959 fielding percentage led all Eastern League shortstops. For his efforts, Vizquel was named to the league All-Star Team. His average has never been outstanding, but he is a fine contact hitter who rarely strikes out. Vizquel's fielding may be one solution to the Mariners defensive problems.

   Vizquel's weak batting average kills any investment hopes for his cards. Overlook his 1990 commons. Our pick for his best 1990 card is Score.

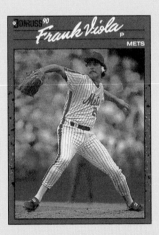

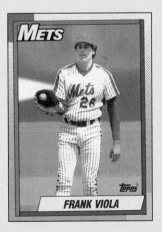

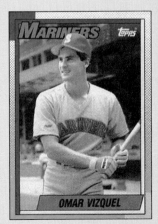

BOB WALK

	W	L	ERA	G	CG	IP	H	ER	BB	SO
1989	13	10	4.41	33	2	196	208	96	65	83
Life	66	54	3.93	231	11	1099	1085	480	422	568

Position: Pitcher
Team: Pittsburgh Pirates
Born: November 26, 1956 Van Nuys, CA
Height: 6'4" **Weight:** 217 lbs.
Bats: Right **Throws:** Right
Acquired: Signed as a free agent, 4/84

Walk won a career-high 13 games with the 1989 Pirates, his best total in more than seven major league seasons. The pitcher seems to improve with age. His prior best for wins came in 1988, when he was 12-10. He has been with the Pirates since 1984, when he was acquired after his release from Atlanta. He played with the Braves from 1981 to '83. Although he won 11 games with the 1982 team, he spent 1983 at Triple-A Richmond and was subsequently released. He began his career as a third-round draft choice by the Phillies in 1976. He made his major league debut in 1980, winning 11 games (including the first game of the World Series).

Walk's seesaw career has kept his card values at a minimum. Don't expect any value climbs out of his 1990 commons unless he wins 20 games. Our pick for his best 1990 card is Fleer.

GREG WALKER

	BA	G	AB	R	H	2B	3B	HR	RBI	SB
1989	.210	77	233	25	49	14	0	5	26	0
Life	.262	749	2825	366	740	164	19	113	442	18

Position: First base
Team: Chicago White Sox
Born: October 6, 1959 Douglas, GA
Height: 6'3" **Weight:** 210 lbs.
Bats: Left **Throws:** Right
Acquired: Drafted from Phillies, 12/79

Walker seemed in fine shape in 1989, a year after a frightening seizure due to a brain infection. On July 30, 1988, he collapsed during batting practice, and then he had another seizure the next morning. His medication caused him to miss the rest of the season. Before his attack, he had hit .247 with eight homers and 42 RBI in his first 99 games. When he returned to the ChiSox in 1989, he had trouble getting back into the lineup. Walker has been one of Chicago's most lethal long-ball threats in the past. In 1987, he led the team with a career high of 27 homers and 94 RBI, besting two 24-homer seasons from 1984 and 1985.

Walker's 1990 commons are long-shot investments that could pay off in short-term gains if he regains his swing. Our pick for his best 1990 card is Fleer.

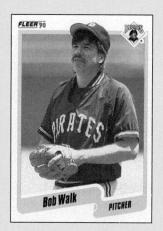

LARRY WALKER

	BA	G	AB	R	H	2B	3B	HR	RBI	SB
89 AAA	.270	114	385	68	104	18	2	12	59	36
89 Major	.170	20	47	4	8	0	0	0	4	1

Position: Outfield
Team: Montreal Expos
Born: December 1, 1966 Maple Ridge,
   British Columbia
Height: 6'2" **Weight:** 205 lbs.
Bats: Left **Throws:** Right
Acquired: Signed as a free agent, 6/85

Walker bounced back from a season-long injury in 1988 to post a good season at Triple-A Indianapolis in 1989. He hit .270 with 12 homers, 59 RBI, and 36 stolen bases. American Association managers ranked him as the third-best prospect in the league. Injured while playing winter ball in Mexico in 1987, Walker had a big season at Double-A Jacksonville that year. He hit .287 with 26 home runs, 83 RBI, and 24 stolen bases. A native Canadian, he started 1986 at Burlington, where he hit .289 with 29 homers and 89 RBI. Walker also hit .283 with four home runs and 16 RBI at West Palm Beach that year.

  Walker has a good shot at the Montreal roster. Combining speed and power, he could fit in well with the Expos. Pay up to 15 cents for his 1990 cards. Our pick for his best 1990 card is Donruss.

TIM WALLACH

	BA	G	AB	R	H	2B	3B	HR	RBI	SB
1989	.277	154	573	76	159	42	0	13	77	3
Life	.263	1305	4789	555	1259	272	24	161	675	40

Position: Third base
Team: Montreal Expos
Born: September 14, 1957 Huntington
   Park, CA
Height: 6'3" **Weight:** 200 lbs.
Bats: Right **Throws:** Right
Acquired: First-round pick in 6/79
   free-agent draft

Wallach showed promising signs of breaking out of a prolonged slump with an improved outing with the 1989 Montreal Expos. After a stellar 1987 campaign (with career highs of a .298 batting average and 123 RBI), he hit a downturn in 1988. His average dropped 41 points, and he had just 12 homers and 69 RBI. His 1989 comeback raised his average to .277 with 13 round-trippers and 77 RBI. This put him back in the All-Star game for the fourth time in his nine-year major league career. Every year Wallach has surpassed double figures in homers, but he's never topped the 28 homers he hit during his 1982 rookie season.

  Wallach's 1990 cards will sell for less than a nickel. Stock up. He could find his home run swing again and set the baseball world abuzz. Our pick for his best 1990 card is Score.

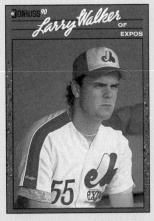
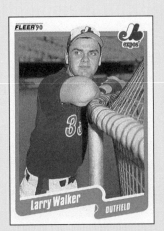

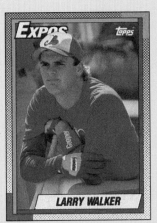

JEROME WALTON

	BA	G	AB	R	H	2B	3B	HR	RBI	SB
88 AA	.331	120	414	64	137	26	2	3	49	42
89 Major	.293	116	475	64	139	23	3	5	46	7

Position: Outfield
Team: Chicago Cubs
Born: July 8, 1965   Newnan, GA
Height: 6'1"   **Weight:** 175 lbs.
Bats: Right   **Throws:** Right
Acquired: Second-round pick in 6/86
free-agent draft

After three minor league seasons, Walton had a .324 career batting average and 112 stolen bases. The 1989 Cubs promoted their star rookie directly from Double-A Pittsfield in 1988, where he won the Eastern League batting title with a .331 performance. Additionally, he notched three homers, 49 RBI, and 42 stolen bases that season. His .993 fielding percentage topped the loop's outfielders. He threw out three opposing baserunners in one night in 1988. With the 1989 Cubs, Walton won the N.L. Rookie of the Year Award. His 30-game hitting streak became the top story in baseball. He set numerous career highs in 1987 at Class-A Peoria, notably a .335 average and 49 stolen bases.

Walton's 1990 cards are hot. They will sell as high as 75 cents by the start of the season. The price may double by the end of 1990. Our pick for his best 1990 card is Topps.

DUANE WARD

	W	L	ERA	G	SV	IP	H	ER	BB	SO
1989	4	10	3.77	66	15	114	94	48	58	122
Life	14	15	4.00	154	30	256	234	114	142	232

Position: Pitcher
Team: Toronto Blue Jays
Born: May 28, 1964   Parkview, NM
Height: 6'4"   **Weight:** 205 lbs.
Bats: Right   **Throws:** Right
Acquired: Traded from Braves for
Doyle Alexander, 7/86

Ward gave the 1989 Blue Jays lots of relief, appearing in a team-leading 66 games. For the first time in his eight-year career, he claimed more strikeouts than innings pitched, while doubling his number of career saves. The first 15 saves were acquired in 1988, his first full season with the Blue Jays. His to-date low ERA of 3.30 came that season, and he claimed a career-best 9-3 record. Though he's walked an unseemly five batters per nine innings in the past, he held opponents scoreless in more than 50 percent of his outings. With Tom Henke, Ward forms one of baseball's deadliest relief duos.

Ward's 1990 commons are risky investments. He works often and can blow out his arm at any time, and he needs to prove that he can handle the strain. Our pick for his best 1990 card is Donruss.

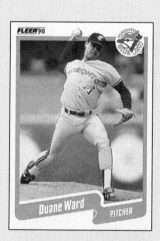

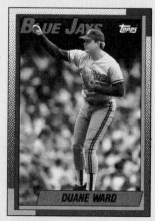

GARY WARD

	BA	G	AB	R	H	2B	3B	HR	RBI	SB
1989	.253	113	292	27	74	11	2	9	30	1
Life	.277	1181	4170	562	1157	185	39	121	142	81

Position: Outfield; designated hitter
Team: Detroit Tigers
Born: December 6, 1953 Los Angeles, CA
Height: 6'2" **Weight:** 202 lbs.
Bats: Right **Throws:** Right
Acquired: Signed as a free agent, 5/89

After his release from the Yankees in early 1989, Ward had no trouble finding a new employer. Detroit snapped him up as a part-time outfielder, designated hitter, and pinch-hitter. While he didn't come close to matching his stats compiled with the Twins, he aided the Tigers with nine homers (fourth highest on the team). Ward spent his first eight seasons in the Twins' organization before he got his first shot with Minnesota in 1981 (after cups of coffee the previous two seasons). *Baseball Digest* named him the A.L. Rookie of the Year for his first-season play. In 1982, Ward had 28 homers and 91 RBI for the Twins, both career highs.

Ward will end his career as a part-timer. His career has been too brief to consider his 1990 commons as investments. Our pick for his best 1990 card is Donruss.

CLAUDELL WASHINGTON

	BA	G	AB	R	H	2B	3B	HR	RBI	SB
1989	.273	110	418	53	114	18	4	13	42	13
Life	.279	1867	6673	919	1865	332	68	163	815	308

Position: Outfield
Team: California Angels
Born: August 31, 1954 Los Angeles, CA
Height: 6'2" **Weight:** 193 lbs.
Bats: Left **Throws:** Left
Acquired: Signed as a free agent, 1/89

Washington played with his seventh major league team in 1989. He had a respectable season for the 1989 Angels, homering in double-digits for the eighth time. Although he has never acquired the superstar status predicted for him at the start of his career in 1974, he has maintained a high-quality, reliable performance at the plate. He first joined the Oakland A's at age 19, after two-and-a-half minor league seasons. Washington hadn't even played high school baseball, only track. His career-high batting average was .308, both in his first full season (1975) and in 1988 with the Yankees. Other teams Washington has performed with include the Rangers, White Sox, Mets, and Braves.

Washington's 1990 cards are 3 cents or less. He's always been good, but never great. His cards are subpar investments. Our pick for his best 1990 card is Fleer.

301

GARY WAYNE

	W	L	ERA	G	SV	IP	H	ER	BB	SO
88 AAA	0	0	6.14	8	1	7	9	5	3	6
89 Major	3	4	3.30	60	1	71	55	26	36	41

Position: Pitcher
Team: Minnesota Twins
Born: November 30, 1962 Dearborn, MI
Height: 6'3" **Weight:** 185 lbs.
Bats: Left **Throws:** Left
Acquired: Drafted from Expos, 12/88

After five seasons in the Expos' organization, Wayne earned his long-awaited chance at success with the 1989 Twins. He was an important part of the Minnesota bullpen, working in more than 50 games. His success in 1989 is admirable considering that he fractured his left foot three times from October 1987 to April 1988. During the 1987 season, Wayne was 5-1 with ten saves and a 2.35 ERA with Double-A Jacksonville. With Class-A West Palm Beach in 1986, he collected 25 saves and notched a 1.61 ERA. As a baseball star in the University of Michigan, Wayne helped his team to NCAA World Series appearances in 1981, 1983, and 1984.

Wayne's active season signals the start of a long, prosperous career. Based on many appearances and his spiffy ERA, his rookie 1990 cards are reasonable buys at 15 cents or less. Our pick for his best 1990 card is Donruss.

MITCH WEBSTER

	BA	G	AB	R	H	2B	3B	HR	RBI	SB
1989	.257	98	272	40	70	12	4	3	19	14
Life	.273	671	2205	342	603	99	36	43	204	120

Position: Outfield
Team: Cleveland Indians
Born: May 16, 1959 Larned, KS
Height: 6'1" **Weight:** 185 lbs.
Bats: Both **Throws:** Left
Acquired: Traded from Cubs for
Dave Clark, 11/89

Webster has a chance to find a starting role with the Indians. In 1989, he saw his playing time with the Cubs curtailed when rookie outfielders Jerome Walton and Dwight Smith arrived. This was quite a switch from the starting duty Webster had enjoyed from 1986 to 1988. He was a midseason pickup from the 1988 Expos, and he went to work immediately for Chicago. The veteran speedster had 21 infield hits in 1988, including ten bunt singles. His .265 average with the Cubs was a notch below his career best of .290, achieved with the 1986 Expos. In his first full season in the majors, he stole a high of 36 bases. Webster's 13 triples set a Montreal record and led the N.L.

Webster may be a starter for the Tribe. But his lifetime stats don't merit investment in his 1990 cards. Our pick for his best 1990 card is Topps.

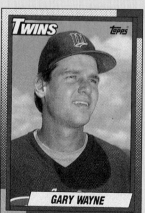

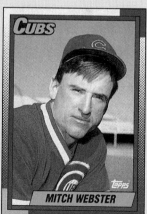

WALT WEISS

	BA	G	AB	R	H	2B	3B	HR	RBI	SB
1989	.233	84	236	30	55	11	0	3	21	6
Life	.252	247	714	77	180	32	3	6	61	11

Position: Shortstop
Team: Oakland Athletics
Born: November 28, 1963   Tuxedo, NY
Height: 6'   **Weight:** 175 lbs.
Bats: Both   **Throws:** Right
Acquired: First-round pick in 6/85
free-agent draft

In 1988, Weiss became the third consecutive Athletic to win the league Rookie of the Year, the first time an A.L. team had accomplished this feat. While he brought the A's distinction in 1988, he had much less success in an injury-plagued 1989. A sprained right knee limited him to just 84 games. In 1988, Weiss played in 147 games, and he hit .250 with three homers and 39 RBI. He won the award primarily through his sterling defensive play, which included participation in 151 double plays and an errorless streak of 58 consecutive games. Weiss's strong arm and good range make him one of the A.L.'s top fielders.

Because of his injury, the prices of Weiss's 1990 cards will drop to 15 cents. It's best to wait on investing at those prices. Our pick for his best 1990 card is Score.

BOB WELCH

	W	L	ERA	G	CG	IP	H	ER	BB	SO
1989	17	8	3.00	33	1	209	191	70	78	137
Life	149	103	3.18	361	52	2273	2059	804	724	1587

Position: Pitcher
Team: Oakland Athletics
Born: November 3, 1956   Detroit, MI
Height: 6'3"   **Weight:** 193 lbs.
Bats: Right   **Throws:** Right
Acquired: Traded from Dodgers with
Charlie Spikes and Jack Savage
for Jesse Orosco, Alfredo Griffin,
and Jay Howell, 12/87

Welch repeated his best-ever 17 wins of 1988 the following year with the Athletics. In 1989, he lowered his ERA from 3.64 to 3.00. He pitched for the Dodgers from 1978 to '87, winning 13 or more games for the club six times. While he was a major contributor to the A's in their World Championship drive, his season ended on a bittersweet note. He was scheduled to pitch the third game of the World Series in San Francisco, but the game was interrupted by an earthquake. When the game was rescheduled nearly two weeks later, Oakland manager Tony LaRussa started Dave Stewart instead of Welch.

Welch's 1990 cards could be less than a nickel if you buy early. All of the A's cards will be popular. Welch's card values could triple if he comes close to 20 wins. Our pick for his best 1990 card is Score.

DAVID WELLS

	W	L	ERA	G	SV	IP	H	ER	BB	SO
1989	7	4	2.40	52	2	86	66	23	28	78
Life	14	12	3.45	111	7	180	168	69	71	166

Position: Pitcher
Team: Toronto Blue Jays
Born: May 20, 1963   Torrance, CA
Height: 6'4"   **Weight:** 225 lbs.
Bats: Left   **Throws:** Left
Acquired: Second-round pick in 6/82
free-agent draft

Wells pitched in a career-high 52 games for the 1989 Blue Jays. The big lefty worked as a middle reliever for Toronto, hurling in his most innings in his past three seasons. Furthermore, his total of seven wins was the most he had ever collected in the majors or minors. In 1988, he pitched in 41 games, winning three and saving four. He endured a long journey to the majors, in a career that started in 1982. His career was in jeopardy after just three years, when he was forced to undergo elbow surgery. Although he missed the entire 1985 season, Wells was back the next year. He divided 1987 and 1988 between Toronto and Triple-A Syracuse.

Wells has an ordinary bullpen job that inhibits his statistics and his potential stardom. Steer clear of his 1990 commons. Our pick for his best 1990 card is Donruss.

DAVE WEST

	W	L	ERA	G	CG	IP	H	ER	BB	SO
89 AAA	7	4	2.37	12	5	87	60	23	29	69
89 AL	3	2	6.41	10	0	39	48	28	19	31

Position: Pitcher
Team: Minnesota Twins
Born: September 1, 1964   Memphis, TN
Height: 6'6"   **Weight:** 220 lbs.
Bats: Left   **Throws:** Left
Acquired: Traded from Mets with Tim
Drummond, Kevin Tapani, and
Rick Aguilera for Frank Viola,
8/89

In the trade that sent Cy Young winner Frank Viola to New York, West was the key to the transaction. A hard-throwing southpaw who just needed a chance to pitch in the majors, West won 54 games after six seasons in the Mets' minor league system. At Triple-A Tidewater in 1988, he was 12-4 with a 1.80 ERA and 143 strikeouts in 160 innings. *Baseball America* ranked him as the International League's third-best prospect that season. West was disappointing with the Twins. But once West adjusts to a new strike zone and a new league full of hitters, he could be a vital force on the Twins staff for the next decade.

West has real potential and could be dominating. But wait for some real progress before investing any more than 25 cents in his 1990 issues. Our pick for his best 1990 card is Donruss.

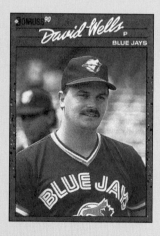
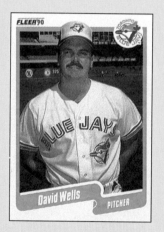

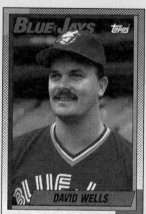

JEFF WETHERBY

	BA	G	AB	R	H	2B	3B	HR	RBI	SB
89 AAA	.268	50	157	19	42	9	0	1	16	5
89 Major	.208	52	48	5	10	2	1	1	7	1

Position: Outfield
Team: Atlanta Braves
Born: October 18, 1963 Granada Hills, CA
Height: 6'2" **Weight:** 195 lbs.
Bats: Left **Throws:** Left
Acquired: 20th-round pick in 6/85
free-agent draft

After clubbing his way through the Braves' farm system for four seasons, Wetherby stuck with Atlanta in 1989. He has a penchant for power hitting, which makes him attractive to the Braves. He was working as Richmond's designated hitter before getting a mid-1989 call-up to the majors. His finest offensive output came in 1987 at Double-A Greenville, hitting .303 with 12 homers and 78 RBI. He won the Hank Aaron award as the top offensive player in the Braves' organization that year. In 1981, Wetherby was named the high school MVP for the city of Los Angeles, and in 1984, he was named California State Community College Player of the Year.

The Braves gave Wetherby a substantial shot at a major league job, but he responded with modest stats. His rookie 1990 cards seem like risky ventures. Our pick for his best 1990 card is Topps.

JOHN WETTELAND

	W	L	ERA	G	CG	IP	H	ER	BB	SO
89 AAA	5	3	3.65	10	1	69	61	28	20	73
89 Major	5	8	3.77	31	0	103	81	43	34	96

Position: Pitcher
Team: Los Angeles Dodgers
Born: August 22, 1966 San Mateo, CA
Height: 6'2" **Weight:** 195 lbs.
Bats: Right **Throws:** Right
Acquired: Second-round pick in 1/85
free-agent draft

After four seasons in the Dodger minor league system, Wetteland vaulted from Double-A to the 1989 major league roster. He worked both as a reliever and spot starter in his first major league season. In 1988, he labored at Double-A San Antonio. In 25 starts, he earned ten wins and 140 strikeouts in 162 innings. Wetteland was 12-7 with seven complete games at Class-A Vero Beach in 1987. He gained a personal best of 144 strikeouts in 175 innings. The Tigers drafted him from Los Angeles in 1987. However, when he missed the final cut for the Detroit roster, the Dodgers reacquired him. As Wetteland improves, that transaction appears to be a great move for the Dodgers.

Unless Wetteland works exclusively as a starter, he isn't likely to assemble the stats needed to make his 15-cent 1990 cards worthwhile. Our pick for his best 1990 card is Score.

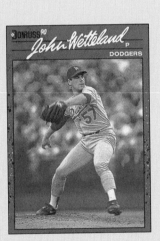

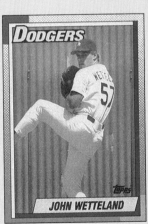

LOU WHITAKER

	BA	G	AB	R	H	2B	3B	HR	RBI	SB
1989	.251	148	509	77	128	21	1	28	85	6
Life	.276	1695	6221	965	1719	279	58	149	721	116

Position: Second base
Team: Detroit Tigers
Born: May 12, 1957 Brooklyn, NY
Height: 5'11" **Weight:** 160 lbs.
Bats: Left **Throws:** Right
Acquired: Fifth-round pick in 6/75
     free-agent draft

In a sour season for the 1989 Tigers, "Sweet Lou" was a rare exception. Even while Detroit was floundering, Whitaker was playing like a champion. By early August, he was notching dingers like never before. He surpassed his former high of 21 homers (from 1985) and topped his club in RBI as well. Such clutch play is nothing new for Whitaker, who won the A.L. Rookie of the Year when he broke in with Detroit in 1978. The four-time All-Star played beside double-play partner Alan Trammell for a record 12th season in 1989. Whitaker is one of the few remaining members of the 1984 World Championship team.

Whitaker has been one of the best second baseman in the last decade and a half. His 1990 cards are solid buys at 20 cents. Our pick for his best 1990 card is Score.

DEVON WHITE

	BA	G	AB	R	H	2B	3B	HR	RBI	SB
1989	.245	156	636	86	156	18	13	12	56	44
Life	.254	487	1788	280	455	74	21	48	197	102

Position: Outfield
Team: California Angels
Born: December 29, 1962 Kingston,
     Jamaica
Height: 6'2" **Weight:** 178 lbs.
Bats: Both **Throws:** Right
Acquired: Sixth-round pick in 6/81
     free-agent draft

In 1989, White was busy helping the Angels in the pennant race. Specializing in the three-base hit, he spent considerable time on the basepaths in 1989. He was among league leaders in stolen bases, surpassing his former high of 32 steals from his 1987 rookie season. Although plagued with injuries in 1988, including bad ribs and knee surgery, the sophomore snagged his first Gold Glove. "Devo" has a strong arm and confidence to match, and shows excellent baserunning skills when leaving the box. Baseball has been White's love from a tender age; White was a four-year varsity letterman at his New York high school.

White hasn't reached the level of stardom predicted for him. His 1990 cards may be a nickel or less in some areas and are still a bargain for prices less than a dime. Our pick for his best 1990 card is Donruss.

FRANK WHITE

	BA	G	AB	R	H	2B	3B	HR	RBI	SB
1989	.256	135	418	34	107	22	1	2	36	3
Life	.256	2242	7618	892	1954	393	57	158	865	177

Position: Second base
Team: Kansas City Royals
Born: September 4, 1950   Greenville, MS
Height: 5'11"   **Weight:** 190 lbs.
Bats: Right   **Throws:** Right
Acquired: Signed as a free agent, 7/70

Perhaps it shouldn't be surprising that White has more Gold Gloves than any American League second baseman ever. He's been at the job a number of years longer than most scouts ever expected him to be. But, even after reaching age 39 at the end of the 1989 season, he continued to produce offense for the Royals and praise for his work. He was at his best from 1984 through 1987, when he had a total of 78 homers and 287 RBI. White's .256 batting average in 1989 was closer to his norm and a step up from his .235 mark in 1988.

Because White has an outside shot at the Hall of Fame, his 1990 commons could be unsung investments. His longevity and consistency will assure him of a lasting place in baseball history. Our pick for his best 1990 card is Donruss.

ED WHITED

	BA	G	AB	R	H	2B	3B	HR	RBI	SB
89 AAA	.245	89	298	41	73	15	1	6	32	8
89 Major	.162	36	74	5	12	3	0	1	4	1

Position: Third base
Team: Atlanta Braves
Born: February 9, 1964   Bristol, PA
Height: 6'3"   **Weight:** 195 lbs.
Bats: Right   **Throws:** Right
Acquired: Traded from Astros with Mike Stoker for Rafael Ramirez, 12/87

Whited was one of many contenders for the starting third baseman's job with Atlanta in 1989. The Braves summoned him from Triple-A Richmond in August for a second time that season. He had a 16-game audition with the Braves in July, but had hit just .190. He batted a sizzling .428 in the two weeks before his recall. He was a Southern League All-Star in 1988. With Double-A Greenville, Whited clubbed 16 homers and 62 RBI, hitting .252. His biggest year came in 1987 at Class-A Asheville, batting .323 with 28 homers and 126 RBI. Whited earned South Atlantic League MVP and All-Star honors that year.

Whited faltered in a substantial tryout with the 1989 Braves. He has little chance at the team's third base job. Don't buy his 15-cent rookie 1990 cards at this point. Our pick for his best 1990 card is Score.

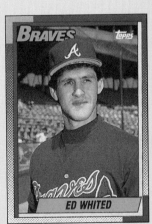

ED WHITSON

	W	L	ERA	G	CG	IP	H	ER	BB	SO
1989	16	11	2.66	33	5	227	198	67	48	117
Life	108	108	3.88	407	27	1933	1932	834	634	1099

Position: Pitcher
Team: San Diego Padres
Born: May 19, 1955   Johnson City, TN
Height: 6'3"   **Weight:** 195 lbs.
Bats: Right   **Throws:** Right
Acquired: Traded from Yankees for
Tim Stoddard, 7/86

When everyone discussed how the Padres could be pennant contenders in 1989, talk focused on newly acquired pitchers Walt Terrell and Bruce Hurst. But Whitson emerged as the Padres pitching ace. No one could be more surprised with Whitson's success than Whitson himself. In a career that has spanned 12 years (beginning with the 1978 Pirates), his best year was with the 1984 Padres. In 1984, he went 14-8 as the team won the N.L. pennant. The Yankees signed him as a free agent after the '84 season, but he never won more than ten games in New York. Reacquired in 1986, Whitson is savoring his second life with the Padres.

Keep any of Whitson's 1990 cards you get in wax packs, but don't invest in his commons. Be prepared to sell when he has another winning season. Our pick for his best 1990 card is Score.

ERNIE WHITT

	BA	G	AB	R	H	2B	3B	HR	RBI	SB
1989	.262	129	385	42	101	24	1	11	53	5
Life	.253	1226	3532	428	892	166	15	132	521	22

Position: Catcher
Team: Toronto Blue Jays
Born: June 13, 1952   Detroit, MI
Height: 6'2"   **Weight:** 205 lbs.
Bats: Left   **Throws:** Right
Acquired: Selected from Red Sox in
11/76 expansion draft

Whitt is the only original Blue Jay left. He was a rookie in 1977, and so was the Toronto team (which joined the American League that season). Their fates have been linked through seasons of feast and famine, including a pennant bid in 1985, when Whitt hit a career-high 19 home runs and enjoyed his only invitation to the All-Star game. He sparked the Blue Jays again in 1989, anchoring the catching chores. Last season, he matched his 1987 career high of 24 doubles. For the last eight seasons, he spurred the team with double-digit homer totals. Although his defensive skills are adequate at best, the Blue Jays love Whitt for his hitting.

Whitt's 1990 cards are priced at 3 cents or less. Outside of Toronto, he remains mostly unknown, making his cards futile investments. Our pick for his best 1990 card is Score.

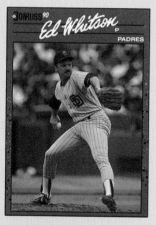

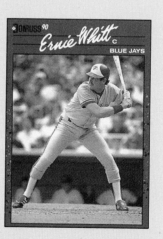

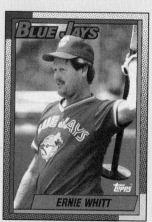

CURTIS WILKERSON

	BA	G	AB	R	H	2B	3B	HR	RBI	SB
1989	.244	77	160	18	39	4	2	1	10	4
Life	.254	687	1751	203	445	54	20	4	116	57

Position: Infield
Team: Chicago Cubs
Born: April 26, 1961 Petersburg, VA
Height: 5'9" **Weight:** 173 lbs.
Bats: Both **Throws:** Right
Acquired: Traded from Rangers with
　　　　Mitch Williams, Paul Kilgus,
　　　　Steve Wilson, Luis Benitez, and
　　　　Pablo Delgado for Rafael
　　　　Palmeiro, Drew Hall, and
　　　　Jamie Moyer, 12/88

Wilkerson did a little bit of everything during his first year in the National League, as a member of the 1989 Chicago Cubs. One of five former Texas Rangers to move to Chicago, he marked his seventh year in the majors in 1989. His offensive marks were typical for a backup infielder, far from the stats he compiled as a starting shortstop and second baseman with the Rangers. He was voted the team's Rookie of the Year in 1984, when he played in a career-high 153 games. In that first season, he batted .248 with a personal best of 30 stolen bases. Wilkerson played in at least 110 games for the Rangers each year, except for 1987, when he was a utility infielder.

As a utility player, Wilkerson's cards have little investment future. Don't purchase his 1990 commons. Our pick for his best 1990 card is Topps.

DEAN WILKINS

	W	L	ERA	G	SV	IP	H	ER	BB	SO
89 AAA	8	11	4.24	38	3	138	149	65	58	82
89 Major	1	0	4.60	11	0	15	13	8	9	14

Position: Pitcher
Team: Chicago Cubs
Born: August 24, 1966 Blue Island, IL
Height: 6'1" **Weight:** 170 lbs.
Bats: Right **Throws:** Right
Acquired: Traded from Yankees with Bob
　　　　Tewksbury and Rich Scheid for
　　　　Steve Trout, 7/87

Wilkins inched closer to a spot on the Cubs pitching staff with a fine showing at Triple-A Iowa in 1989. He worked both as a starter and reliever at Iowa, pitching in 38 games (16 as a starter). He was 8-11 with three saves and a 4.24 ERA. After Chicago obtained him from the Yankees' organization in 1987, they started experimenting with converting him to a reliever. He had spent 28 of his first 32 career appearances as a starting pitcher. In 1988, his third pro season, he made the successful jump to reliever. With Double-A Pittsfield that year, Wilkins set an Eastern League record with 26 saves. He notched five wins and a 1.63 ERA in 59 games.

Wait on investing in Wilkins's 15- to 20-cent 1990 cards. Skip them if he lands in Chicago's bullpen as a middle reliever. Our pick for his best 1990 card is Fleer.

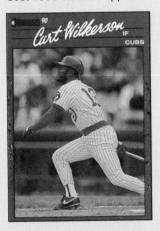

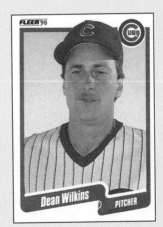

MATT WILLIAMS

	BA	G	AB	R	H	2B	3B	HR	RBI	SB
1989	.202	84	292	31	59	18	1	18	50	1
Life	.198	220	693	76	137	33	4	34	90	5

Position: Third base
Team: San Francisco Giants
Born: November 28, 1965 Bishop, CA
Height: 6'2" **Weight:** 205 lbs.
Bats: Right **Throws:** Right
Acquired: First-round pick in 6/86
free-agent draft

When the Giants demoted Williams to Triple-A Phoenix at the start of the 1989 season, they never imagined the talent the young third baseman would unveil. He stayed at Phoenix for 76 games, hitting .320 with 26 homers and 71 RBI. He learned to hit breaking pitches, which made him a tougher hitter later in the season. When he returned to the majors, Williams was presented the starting third baseman's job. He thanked the team by hitting 18 homers and 50 RBI in 84 games, including 12 homers in his first six weeks back. Williams does more than hit homers: he's a soft-handed infielder with great reflexes and an explosive throwing arm.

Williams's 1990 cards may cost up to a quarter apiece. While this price may seem risky, it could triple by season's end if he reaches his homer potential. Our pick for his best 1990 card is Donruss.

MITCH WILLIAMS

	W	L	ERA	G	SV	IP	H	ER	BB	SO
1989	4	4	2.76	76	36	81	71	25	52	67
Life	22	23	3.49	308	68	356	251	138	272	347

Position: Pitcher
Team: Chicago Cubs
Born: November 17, 1964 Santa Ana, CA
Height: 6'4" **Weight:** 200 lbs.
Bats: Left **Throws:** Left
Acquired: Traded from Rangers with Paul
Kilgus, Steve Wilson, Curtis
Wilkerson, Luis Benitez, and Pablo
Delgado for Rafael Palmeiro,
Drew Hall, and Jamie Moyer,
12/88

Williams was one of the reasons the Cubs emerged in the N.L. East. Acquired in a nine-player deal with the Rangers, he was the stopper the Cubs wanted to replace Lee Smith. Williams wasn't the most experienced hurler available, logging only 32 saves in his first three years. What the Cubs saw in Williams was durability. In his first season in 1986, he led the A.L. with 80 appearances, a major league rookie record. In 1987, he set a Rangers' record with 85 games pitched. Williams proved his competitiveness in 1989 when, after he was hit on the ear by a line drive, he unsuccessfully tried to convince Cubs manager Don Zimmer that he could continue.

Despite Williams's 1989 success, he has mediocre lifetime stats. His 1990 cards should only be purchased at prices under a dime. Our pick for his best 1990 card is Fleer.

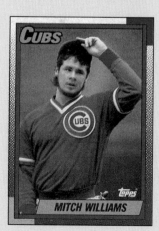

MARK WILLIAMSON

	W	L	ERA	G	SV	IP	H	ER	BB	SO
1989	10	5	2.93	65	9	107	105	35	30	55
Life	23	22	3.99	163	14	350	352	155	111	197

Position: Pitcher
Team: Baltimore Orioles
Born: July 21, 1959 Corpus Christi, TX
Height: 6' **Weight:** 171 lbs.
Bats: Right **Throws:** Right
Acquired: Traded from Padres with Terry
      Kennedy for Storm Davis, 10/86

Williamson earned the status of the Orioles number-two reliever in 1989. He led the 1989 Birds with a career-high 65 appearances, while his ten wins were third on the club. He spent his first full season in the majors in 1989, after dividing his time between Baltimore and Triple-A Rochester during the two prior seasons. He was an important addition in the trade that brought catcher Terry Kennedy from San Diego in 1986. Williamson had three ten-win seasons in the Padres' minor league system from 1984 to '86. While playing college ball at San Diego State, one of Williamson's teammates was Padre star Tony Gwynn.

Williamson's lifetime stats are shaping up, but he's still burdened with middle relief. For now, avoid his 1990 commons. They aren't likely to make any short-term price gains. Our pick for his best 1990 card is Topps.

GLENN WILSON

	BA	G	AB	R	H	2B	3B	HR	RBI	SB
1989	.266	128	432	50	115	26	4	11	64	1
Life	.267	1073	3769	409	1006	195	26	88	466	27

Position: Outfield
Team: Houston Astros
Born: December 22, 1958 Baytown, TX
Height: 6'1" **Weight:** 190 lbs.
Bats: Right **Throws:** Right
Acquired: Traded from Pirates for
      Billy Hatcher, 7/89

When Wilson was swapped to Houston in mid-1989, it marked his fifth team in seven seasons. Don't think that he is a no-account player. He's hit ten-plus homers for five of his eight big-league campaigns. His batting average has never dipped below .240, and he's always been an excellent outfielder with a cannonlike arm. He led N.L. outfielders in assists for three straight seasons. His finest production came in his 1985 All-Star season with the Phillies. He drove in 102 runs while homering 14 times and batting .275. The following season with Philadelphia, Wilson had a career-high 15 homers.

Wilson has been an off-and-on player. His lifetime stats show those gaps. His common-priced 1990 cards are marginal investments that could only pay off if he has a big season. Our pick for his best 1990 card is Fleer.

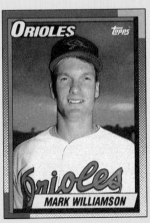

MOOKIE WILSON

	BA	G	AB	R	H	2B	3B	HR	RBI	SB
89 AL	.298	54	238	32	71	9	1	2	17	12
Life	.277	1170	4265	624	1183	179	63	62	359	293

Position: Outfield
Team: Toronto Blue Jays
Born: February 9, 1956 Bamberg, SC
Height: 5'10" **Weight:** 174 lbs.
Bats: Both **Throws:** Right
Acquired: Traded from Mets for
　　　　　Jeff Mussleman, 8/89

After nine seasons with the Mets, Wilson got his first taste of the A.L. in 1989. The first move of his career proved lucky, as it landed him with the division-winning Blue Jays. He didn't miss a beat in the transition, placing second in batting average for the Jays with a .298 mark. The Mets seemed willing to trade their senior member after he hit just .205 in his first 80 games of 1989. Wilson was New York's second selection in the 1977 draft. After four minor league seasons, he got his major league debut in 1980. Wilson is remembered most for his stolen bases with New York, including a personal-best 58 in 1982.

　Wilson's 1990 cards will cost a nickel or less. Because his future remains uncertain, refrain from buying until he establishes himself with the Blue Jays. Our pick for his best 1990 card is Topps.

STEVE WILSON

	W	L	ERA	G	SV	IP	H	ER	BB	SO
1989	6	4	4.20	53	2	85	83	40	31	65
Life	6	4	4.35	56	2	93	90	45	35	66

Position: Pitcher
Team: Chicago Cubs
Born: December 13, 1964 Victoria,
　　　　　British Columbia
Height: 6'4" **Weight:** 195 lbs.
Bats: Left **Throws:** Left
Acquired: Traded from Rangers with
　　　　　Mitch Williams, Paul Kilgus, Curt
　　　　　Wilkerson, Luis Benitez, and
　　　　　Pablo Delgado for Jamie Moyer,
　　　　　Drew Hall, and Rafael Palmeiro,
　　　　　12/88

In the trade between Texas and the Cubs before the 1989 season, probably the player with the least-recognizable name was Wilson. He changed all that when he won a spot on the 1989 Cubs. In his first 40 games with Chicago, he was 5-2 with two saves. He became the lefthanded set-up man for stopper Mitch Williams. Wilson got his major league debut on September 16, 1988, with Texas. He made three relief appearances, posting a 5.87 ERA in eight innings. His four seasons of minor league work consisted mostly of starting pitching. His best year was in 1988 with Double-A Tulsa, when Wilson went 15-7 with five complete games and three shutouts.

　Wilson's middle relief role is a thankless job that limits his exposure. Bypass his 1990 cards unless he moves to the starting rotation. Our pick for his best 1990 card is Fleer.

TREVOR WILSON

	W	L	ERA	G	CG	IP	H	ER	BB	SO
89 AAA	7	7	3.12	23	2	115	109	40	76	77
89 Major	2	3	4.35	14	0	39	28	19	24	22

Position: Pitcher
Team: San Francisco Giants
Born: June 7, 1966 Torrance, CA
Height: 6' **Weight:** 175 lbs.
Bats: Left **Throws:** Left
Acquired: Eighth-round pick in 6/85
free-agent draft

Wilson continued his march to the majors with a strong season at Triple-A Phoenix in 1989. He was 7-7 with a 3.12 ERA and two complete games. With the 1989 Giants, he notched a 2-3 record and a 4.35 ERA. He was called up first in 1988, his fourth pro season. Despite an 0-2 record, Wilson had 15 strikeouts in 22 innings. He earned six strikeouts against the Dodgers on September 24, 1988. He started that season with Double-A Shreveport. In 12 games (11 as a starter), he was 5-4 with a 1.86 ERA. His 1987 season was spent at Class-A Clinton, where he was 10-6 with a 2.01 ERA in 1986. Capable of starting or relieving, Wilson could be a notable hurler.

The Giants should keep Wilson for an entire year in 1990. He's a touted rookie whose 1990 cards are good investments at a dime or less. Our pick for his best 1990 card is Donruss.

WILLIE WILSON

	BA	G	AB	R	H	2B	3B	HR	RBI	SB
1989	.253	112	383	58	97	17	7	3	43	24
Life	.289	1672	6492	1011	1879	228	130	38	467	588

Position: Outfield
Team: Kansas City Royals
Born: July 9, 1955 Montgomery, AL
Height: 6'3" **Weight:** 195 lbs.
Bats: Both **Throws:** Right
Acquired: First-round pick in 6/74
free-agent draft

A chapter in Kansas City baseball history closed when the Royals announced that Wilson wouldn't be offered a contract after the 1989 season. The veteran outfielder did "slump" to .253 with three homers, 43 RBI, and 24 stolen bases last season. Nonetheless, he's been one of baseball's most exciting players for a decade. Part of the problem, scouts say, is that he never found true discipline at the plate. His strikeouts always have been high and his walks low, unlike the ideal contact-hitter mold needed for a leadoff man. He hit his career-high .332 in 1982, and hasn't come close since his 1984 mark of .301. After 16 years in pro baseball, Wilson's future seems uncertain.

Don't speculate on Wilson's nickel-priced 1990 cards until his job plans for the coming season are announced. Invest if he doesn't retire. Our pick for his best 1990 card is Fleer.

DAVE WINFIELD

	BA	G	AB	R	H	2B	3B	HR	RBI	SB
1989				Did not play						
Life	.287	2269	8421	1314	2421	412	74	357	1438	209

Position: Outfield
Team: New York Yankees
Born: October 3, 1951 St. Paul, MN
Height: 6'6" **Weight:** 220 lbs.
Bats: Right **Throws:** Right
Acquired: Signed as a free agent, 12/80

Winfield was sidelined for the entire 1989 season due to back surgery to remove a herniated disk. But it didn't lessen his legend. In 1988, he had one of his best seasons. Winfield batted .322 with 25 homers and 107 RBI. It was the seventh time in his career he had driven in 100-plus runs. He has never hit less than 13 home runs in 15 full seasons. He's won seven Gold Gloves. He began his pro career with the Padres in 1974, with no minor league experience. Hopefully, Winfield will be healthy enough to return in 1990 to put the finishing touches on a Hall of Fame career.

Because of his injury, Winfield's 1990 cards may be down to a quarter. Although your purchases may not see any short-term dividends, they're sure to be hot sellers once Cooperstown comes calling. Our pick for his best 1990 card is Donruss.

HERM WINNINGHAM

	BA	G	AB	R	H	2B	3B	HR	RBI	SB
1989	.251	115	251	40	63	11	3	3	13	14
Life	.240	581	1325	148	318	47	19	14	112	89

Position: Outfield
Team: Cincinnati Reds
Born: December 1, 1961 Orangeburg, SC
Height: 5'11" **Weight:** 175 lbs.
Bats: Left **Throws:** Right
Acquired: Traded from Expos with Jeff Reed and Randy St. Claire for Tracy Jones and Pat Pacillo, 7/88

Winningham saw more action than most starters with the 1989 Reds. He made the most of his opportunities on the injury-plagued team by hitting a major league best of .251. Speed remained the obvious asset of the nine-year professional. He swiped 14 bases in 1989, marking his fifth straight season of double-digit swipes. Winningham stole a career-high 29 bases with the 1987 Expos. Although he hit just .239 as an Expos starter that year, he achieved career bests of four homers and 41 RBI. Winningham was highly pursued from the time he left high school in 1979. Pittsburgh, Milwaukee, and Montreal tried to draft him before he signed with the 1981 Mets.

Winningham won't be a starter in 1990. Due to his part-time status, he'll never get the press needed to make his common-priced 1990 cards worthy investments. Our pick for his best 1990 card is Topps.

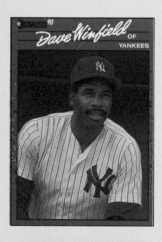

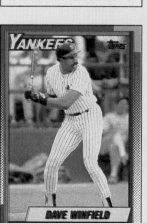

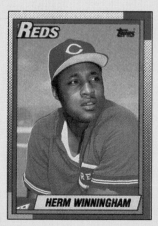

MATT WINTERS

	BA	G	AB	R	H	2B	3B	HR	RBI	SB
89 AAA	.224	74	268	33	60	6	3	13	54	0
89 Major	.234	42	107	14	25	6	0	2	9	0

Position: Outfield
Team: Kansas City Royals
Born: March 18, 1960 Buffalo, NY
Height: 6'3" **Weight:** 215 lbs.
Bats: Left **Throws:** Right
Acquired: Signed as a free agent, 2/87

One of the most inspiring tales of 1989 belongs to Winters. After amassing 176 home runs and 781 RBI in 11 minor league seasons, he finally got his big league debut with the Royals in 1989. Before joining the Kansas City organization in 1987, he labored in the Yankees' farm system ever since going as a first-round pick in 1978. He batted above .290 or better during seven of his many farm stops. Winters has hit better than 20 homers five times in the minors and has driven in 90 or more runs on four occasions. He's landed five All-Star nominations during his stint in pro baseball. In 1988, Winters was named South Atlantic League MVP for his 25 homers and 91 RBI.

Winters should find a spot in Kansas City. His rookie 1990 cards are good investments at a dime or less. Our pick for his best 1990 card is Fleer.

BOBBY WITT

	W	L	ERA	G	CG	IP	H	ER	BB	SO
1989	12	13	5.14	31	5	194	182	111	114	166
Life	39	42	4.86	110	19	669	560	361	498	648

Position: Pitcher
Team: Texas Rangers
Born: May 11, 1964 Arlington, VA
Height: 6'2" **Weight:** 205 lbs.
Bats: Right **Throws:** Right
Acquired: First-round pick in 6/85
　　　　　　 free-agent draft

A veteran of four major league seasons, Witt continued his Jekyll-and-Hyde existence in 1989. Although he suffered a losing season, his 12 wins and 194 innings pitched represent personal bests. His 1986 rookie campaign remains a tough act to follow: 11-9 with 174 strikeouts. Conversely, Witt's ERA that year was an unsightly 5.48, which he almost equaled in 1989. In 1986, he also established a two-year precedent of walking close to a batter an inning, a bad habit he finally seemed to break in 1989. He's also developed a pickoff move as explosive as his fastball. Witt has a bundle of talent and is one of the fastest pitchers in baseball.

Because Witt hasn't neared his full potential yet, his cards haven't gained much interest of value. Now's the time to get in on his 1990 commons. Our pick for his best 1990 card is Donruss.

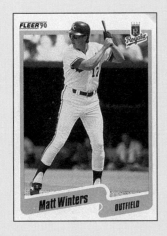

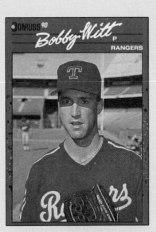

MIKE WITT

	W	L	ERA	G	CG	IP	H	ER	BB	SO
1989	9	15	4.54	33	5	220	252	111	48	123
Life	109	104	3.78	304	70	1945	1913	816	643	1269

Position: Pitcher
Team: California Angels
Born: July 20, 1960 Fullerton, CA
Height: 6'7" **Weight:** 198 lbs.
Bats: Right **Throws:** Right
Acquired: Fourth-round pick in 6/78
    free-agent draft

After five consecutive seasons as California's leading winner (the only Angels pitcher to achieve such a feat), Witt relinquished his title in 1989. After four seasons of 240-plus innings and 220 innings in 1989, with as many as 12 complete games in a given season (and many trips into the seventh innings), he may get burned out before his 30th birthday. His ERA has gained weight over the past three years (going from 4.01 in 1987 to 4.15 in 1988) with two consecutive losing seasons after a string of successes from 1984 to 1987. Still, his 48 walks is his lowest mark since he walked 47 in his rookie and sophomore years, in considerably fewer innings.

Witt has struggled with a two-year slump. Until he learns to win again, his 1990 commons are questionable purchases. Our pick for his best 1990 card is Fleer.

TODD WORRELL

	W	L	ERA	G	SV	IP	H	ER	BB	SO
1989	3	5	2.96	47	20	51	42	17	26	41
Life	28	30	2.64	281	126	361	300	106	142	301

Position: Pitcher
Team: St. Louis Cardinals
Born: September 28, 1959 Arcadia, CA
Height: 6'5" **Weight:** 210 lbs.
Bats: Right **Throws:** Right
Acquired: First-round pick in 6/82
    free-agent draft

The 1989 St. Louis Cardinals didn't overtake the Chicago Cubs because of Worrell's absence. The Cardinals lost him on September 4 with an elbow injury. Without him, St. Louis didn't have the pitching staff to climb out of second place. He has been the Redbirds' bullpen mainstay since 1986, when he led the National League with 36 saves to become the N.L. Rookie of the Year. The following season, Worrell recorded 33 saves to become the first pitcher in history with 30-plus saves in each of his first two seasons. He had 32 saves with a 3.00 ERA in 1988. In 1985, Worrell debuted with St. Louis, after spending four mediocre minor league seasons as starter.

Even though Worrell's 1990 cards will be a nickel or less, don't invest until he proves that his shoulder is recovered. Our pick for his best 1990 card is Donruss.

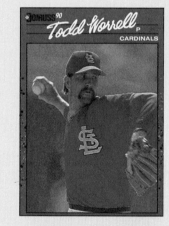

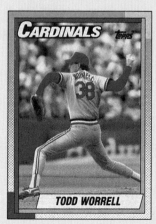

CRAIG WORTHINGTON

	BA	G	AB	R	H	2B	3B	HR	RBI	SB
1989	.247	145	497	57	123	23	0	15	70	1
Life	.239	171	578	62	138	25	0	17	74	2

Position: Third base
Team: Baltimore Orioles
Born: April 17, 1965   Los Angeles, CA
Height: 6'   **Weight:** 190 lbs.
Bats: Right   **Throws:** Right
Acquired: First-round pick in 6/85
free-agent draft

Worthington has given the Orioles their first dependable third baseman since Doug DeCinces. Worthington was among the top homer and RBI men for Baltimore in 1989. The success comes on the heels of his 1988 International League MVP season at Triple-A Rochester. His 16 homers and 73 RBI were second best in the loop, while his total chances and putouts topped the circuit's third basemen for a second straight season. When he had a brief major league debut in April 1988, his first hit was a memorable one—a homer off Bert Blyleven. Worthington has a reputation for offense. With Class-A Hagerstown in 1986, he had 15 homers, a league-leading 105 RBI, and a .300 batting average.

Worthington had a noted rookie season, and could be even better in 1990. Buy up his 1990 cards at 15 cents or less. Our pick for his best 1990 card is Fleer.

RICK WRONA

	BA	G	AB	R	H	2B	3B	HR	RBI	SB
89 AAA	.217	52	189	15	41	8	3	2	13	1
89 Major	.283	38	92	11	26	2	1	2	14	0

Position: Catcher
Team: Chicago Cubs
Born: December 10, 1963   Tulsa, OK
Height: 6'1"   **Weight:** 185 lbs.
Bats: Right   **Throws:** Right
Acquired: Fifth-round pick in 6/85
free-agent draft

When Damon Berryhill went on the disabled list in 1989, Wrona handled much of the catching load. After spending the majority of 1989 with Triple-A Iowa, he rejoined the Cubs August 25. He arrived in time to single and score in the 12th inning to give Chicago a 4-3 win over the Braves, breaking a six-game losing streak. Wrona appeared in just four games for the Cubs in 1988, going hitless. He earned his major league debut on the strength of his 1988 season at Iowa. He batted a career-high .264. Behind the plate, he threw out 26 of 53 baserunners, second best in Triple-A. Expect Wrona to battle for a roster spot in 1990.

Despite his 1989 success, Wrona is likely to serve as a backup for catcher. That means that his 15-cent rookie 1990 cards are futile buys. Our pick for his best 1990 card is Score.

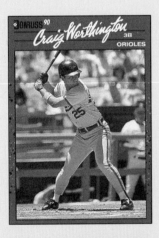

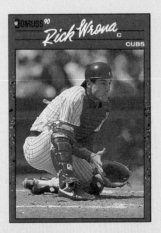

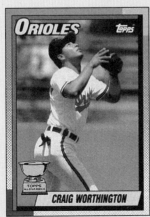

MARVELL WYNNE

	BA	G	AB	R	H	2B	3B	HR	RBI	SB
1989	.243	125	342	27	83	13	2	7	39	6
Life	.250	848	2507	279	626	99	26	36	225	77

Position: Outfield
Team: Chicago Cubs
Born: December 17, 1959 Chicago, IL
Height: 5'11" **Weight:** 185 lbs.
Bats: Left **Throws:** Left
Acquired: Traded from Padres with Luis Salazar for Phil Stephenson, Darrin Jackson, and Calvin Schiraldi, 8/89

When the Padres traded Wynne in 1989, they sent a native Chicagoan home. It marked his fourth trade in just 11 professional seasons, the last three in the National League. As a reserve splitting his time between the Padres and Cubs, he hit a modest .243. His most productive season came with San Diego in 1988, when he amassed 11 homers and 42 RBI in just 128 games. Wynne's storybook career began in 1979, when he was the only player out of 200 applicants signed in a Royals tryout camp in 1978. In 1981, he was traded to the Mets' organization. He finally got his major league debut on June 15, 1983, as a Pirate. Wynne will serve the 1990 Cubs well as a pinch-hitter, defensive replacement and spot starter.

Because he isn't a starter, Wynne's 1990 commons have limited appeal. Such an investment isn't recommended. Our pick for his best 1990 card is Score.

ERIC YELDING

	BA	G	AB	R	H	2B	3B	HR	RBI	SB
88 AAA	.250	138	556	69	139	15	2	1	38	59
89 Major	.233	70	90	19	21	2	0	0	9	11

Position: Infield
Team: Houston Astros
Born: February 22, 1965 Montrose, AL
Height: 6'3" **Weight:** 180 lbs.
Bats: Right **Throws:** Right
Acquired: Signed as a free agent, 4/89

Yelding played a variety of positions as a part-time player for the 1989 Astros, giving his team vital doses of speed and defense. Speed has been his trademark: During each of his five minor league seasons, Yelding had a total of 276 stolen bases in 598 games. He won two stolen base titles during his years in the Toronto farm system. In 1988 with Triple-A Syracuse, Yelding was the International League's top base thief with 59 swipes. He tied for league leads in games played (138) and runs (69). With Kinston in 1985, he had 62 steals to pace the Class-A Carolina League. Yelding won spots on both the midseason and postseason All-Star teams that year.

Yelding is unlikely to start for the Astros. Unless he wins a position, his 1990 cards are so-so investments. Our pick for his best 1990 card is Donruss.

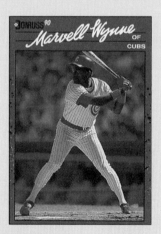

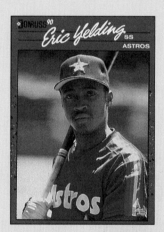

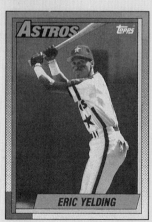

RICH YETT

	W	L	ERA	G	CG	IP	H	ER	BB	SO
1989	5	6	5.00	32	1	99	111	55	47	47
Life	22	24	4.98	132	4	410	438	227	190	227

Position: Pitcher
Team: Cleveland Indians
Born: October 6, 1962 Pomona, CA
Height: 6'2" **Weight:** 187 lbs.
Bats: Right **Throws:** Right
Acquired: Traded from Twins with Jay Bell,
        Curt Wardle, and Jim Weaver for
        Bert Blyleven, 8/85

After three partial seasons in the majors, Yett spent all of 1989 at Cleveland. The stability of a full season in one place had little effect on him. His ERA remained at the 5.00 or above for the third season. He continued to strikeout too few and walk too many in 1989. His problems are augment-ed by an awkward release that often keeps him from fielding well if a hitter does make contact. Even so, streaks of three or more wins (he had a three-game winning streak in 1988) or seven-strikeout games (May 11, 1988, against California) leave management confused: Is he already past his peak, or hasn't Yett reached it yet?

Yett has been given sufficient chances to prove his worth. But his career and the future of his 1990 commons are futile. Our pick for his best 1990 card is Donruss.

GERALD YOUNG

	BA	G	AB	R	H	2B	3B	HR	RBI	SB
1989	.233	146	533	71	124	17	3	0	38	34
Life	.260	366	1383	194	360	47	14	1	90	125

Position: Outfield
Team: Houston Astros
Born: October 22, 1964 Tele, Honduras
Height: 6'2" **Weight:** 185 lbs.
Bats: Both **Throws:** Right
Acquired: Traded from Mets with Mitch
        Cook and Manny Lee for
        Ray Knight, 8/84

National League pitchers caught up to Young during his third major league campaign in 1989. After hurlers were tagged by Young for a .321 batting average in 1987 (for 71 games) and 26 stolen bases, pitchers have been throwing him a steady diet of hard stuff. This has caused his batting average to drop annually. He has compensated by drawing an increased number of walks each season (74 in 1989, up from 66 the year before). He takes more advantage once on base as well, swiping 65 bases in 1988 and 34 in 1989. He is still thrown out a good deal, but he's gaining experience. Young is a polished flyhawker who needs to catch up offen-sively.

Young's 1990 cards will cost a nickel or less. They are a potentially good investment that will pay off if he develops a .300 stroke. Our pick for his best 1990 card is Donruss.

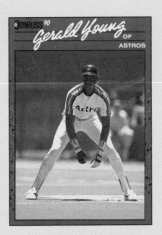

ROBIN YOUNT

	BA	G	AB	R	H	2B	3B	HR	RBI	SB
1989	.318	160	614	101	195	38	9	21	103	19
Life	.292	2291	8907	1335	2602	481	111	208	1084	226

Position: Outfield
Team: Milwaukee Brewers
Born: September 16, 1955 Danville, IL
Height: 6' **Weight:** 180 lbs.
Bats: Right **Throws:** Right
Acquired: First-round pick in 6/73
 free-agent draft

Yount had another great season in 1989, batting .318 with 21 homers and 103 RBI as he won his second A.L. MVP Award. He was also the league's MVP in 1982. Turning 30 seemed to help his game. A hard-hitting star since his splashy major league debut at age 18, "Rockin' Robin" had only two years of .300-plus batting until 1986. Since then, it's been .306 and up, and 1989 was one of his best years yet. Always a league leader in extra-base hits, his recent increase in output coincides with his assignment to the out-field following shoulder surgery in 1984 and 1985. Yount debuted at shortstop with the Brewers after a year of minor league ball.

You'll find Yount in the Hall of Fame in a decade or so. Buy his 1990 cards at a quarter for large long-term profits. Our pick for his best 1990 card is Score.

TODD ZEILE

	BA	G	AB	R	H	2B	3B	HR	RBI	SB
89 AAA	.289	118	453	71	131	26	3	19	85	0
89 Major	.256	28	82	7	21	3	1	1	8	0

Position: Catcher
Team: St. Louis Cardinals
Born: September 9, 1965 Van Nuys, CA
Height: 6'1" **Weight:** 190 lbs.
Bats: Right **Throws:** Right
Acquired: Third-round pick in 6/86
 free-agent draft

Even when he was still in the minors, Zeile was the talk of St. Louis in 1989. In his four-year minor league career, he has made annual jumps from Class-A to Triple-A. In 1989 at Triple-A, he paced Louisville in batting average, homers, and RBI. The American Association managers ranked him as the league's top defensive catcher and best batting prospect in 1989. Going into 1989, Zeile had been a yearly All-Star in three different leagues. In 1987, Zeile shared the Midwest League MVP award for being first in the circuit with 106 RBI and second with 25 homers.

Zeile is *the* rookie 1990 card. His 1989 Upper Deck card soared past the $5 mark. His 1990 cards will sell for about $1 each. That price could double if he has even modest success in his first full season. Our pick for his best 1990 card is Fleer.

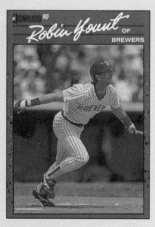   

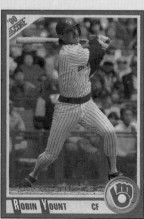